IDEAL MINDS

IDEAL MINDS

RAISING CONSCIOUSNESS IN THE
ANTISOCIAL SEVENTIES

MICHAEL TRASK

CORNELL UNIVERSITY PRESS
Ithaca and London

Copyright © 2020 by Cornell University

All rights reserved. Except for brief quotations in a review, this book, or parts thereof, must not be reproduced in any form without permission in writing from the publisher. For information, address Cornell University Press, Sage House, 512 East State Street, Ithaca, New York 14850. Visit our website at cornellpress.cornell.edu.

First published 2020 by Cornell University Press

Library of Congress Cataloging-in-Publication Data

Names: Trask, Michael, 1967– author.
Title: Ideal minds : raising consciousness in the antisocial seventies / Michael Trask.
Description: Ithaca [New York] : Cornell University Press, 2020. | Includes bibliographical references and index.
Identifiers: LCCN 2020005737 (print) | LCCN 2020005738 (ebook) | ISBN 9781501752438 (hardcover) | ISBN 9781501752452 (pdf) | ISBN 9781501752445 (epub)
Subjects: LCSH: Literature—Philosophy—1971– | Nineteen Seventies—Philosophy. | Neoliberalism in popular culture. | Libertarianism in literature. | Social values—1971– | Self-consciousness (Awareness)—Philosophy—1971– | Autonomy (Philosophy)—History—1971–
Classification: LCC PN51 .T665 2020 (print) | LCC PN51 (ebook) | DDC 809/.047—dc23
LC record available at https://lccn.loc.gov/2020005737
LC ebook record available at https://lccn.loc.gov/2020005738

Excerpts from "Mirabell: Books of Number," copyright © 1978 by James Merrill; "The Book of Ephraim," "Scripts for the Pageant," and "Coda: The Higher Keys" from *The Changing Light at Sandover: A Poem* by James Merrill, copyright © 1980, 1982 by James Merrill, are used by permission of Alfred A. Knopf, an imprint of the Knopf Doubleday Publishing Group, a division of Penguin Random House LLC. All rights reserved.

Excerpts from "Lost in Translation," "The Broken Home," "A Tenancy," "The Doodler," and "The Will" from *Collected Poems* by James Merrill, copyright © 2001 by the Literary Estate of James Merrill at Washington University, are used by permission of Alfred A. Knopf, an imprint of the Knopf Doubleday Publishing Group, a division of Penguin Random House LLC. All rights reserved.

For Stephen
Meet you at the statue in an hour

Contents

	Acknowledgments	ix
	Introduction: From Consciousness-Raising to Neo-idealism	1
1.	Artificial Intelligence and the Rise of the Meritocracy	31
2.	Radical Ecology's Mindfulness	67
3.	That Seventies Cult	100
4.	Millennial America and the World to Come	136
	Afterword: The Marketization of Everything	172
	Notes	191
	Index	235

Acknowledgments

Stefan Bird-Pollan, Peter Kalliney, and A. O. Scott have been indispensable respondents for the ideas in this book. Audiences at Notre Dame, Stanford, and Berkeley have helped me think through some of its claims. I want to thank Nan Z. Da, Mark Goble, Kate Marshall, and Eric Naiman in particular for giving me the opportunity to hone certain ideas at an important early stage of writing. Mahinder Kingra is the gold standard of editors, as engaged and careful a shepherd for this book as an author could dream of having. I'm grateful for superb colleagues at the University of Kentucky, especially Jeff Clymer and Hannah Pittard. And I'm equally grateful for the long and sustaining friendship of scholars elsewhere: Nancy Armstrong, Jared Gardner, Mark Greif, Beth Hewitt, and Jonathan Kramnick.

IDEAL MINDS

Introduction
From Consciousness-Raising to Neo-idealism

This is a compact book—four chapters on the 1970s—with a large revisionist argument. Departing from the prevailing critical wisdom of the last generation, I argue that the late twentieth century ushered in not the death of the subject but the revival of subjectivity in postmodern society. To support this claim, I look to a field with which literary criticism has had only casual contact: moral and political philosophy in the analytic tradition. In exploring this disciplinary intersection, I aim less to join the ethical turn in criticism than to historicize it.[1] Sixties consciousness-raising, I argue, spun out an array of seventies intellectual projects far beyond movement politics. "The rediscovery of the mind," to borrow the title of a 1992 book by John Searle, preoccupied ethicists pursuing contractual theories of justice, radical ecologists interested in the paleolithic brain, members of cults (the decade's signature moral panic), and the devout of both evangelical and New Age persuasions. I make the case for seeing each of these groups as components of a formation I call "neo-idealism," which I define as the effort to retool features of the Kantian tradition as weapons in the struggle against a behaviorism discredited by post-sixties thinkers because it appeared to underwrite the failed policies of the Great Society.

The book's cultural history combines ideas from a mix of disciplines: cognitive science, philosophy of mind, moral philosophy, deep ecology, political theory, neoclassical economics, the sociology of religion. It also delves into more esoteric branches of learning, like Scientology, anarchist theory, rapture prophesies, psychic channeling, and the once ubiquitous study of entropy. My basic premise is that a dramatic inflation in the value of consciousness and autonomy in the seventies accompanied a recognition of the state's refusal to safeguard such values. And this premise's central implication is that figures from different schools and literary traditions—the philosopher John Rawls, the deep ecologist Arne Naess, the anarchist Murray Bookchin, the rapture doomsayer Hal Lindsey, the science fiction writer Philip Dick, the eco-warrior Edward Abbey, the avant-garde novelist William Burroughs, and the formalist poet James Merrill—found alternatives to statism in conditions that, while not reducible to neoliberalism's free market ideal, would lend support to that ideal's consolidation. To put the point this way is to keep in view the distance between neo-idealism (the embrace of subjectivity) and neoliberalism (the embrace of the market). The space between these terms contracts and dilates depending on the positions staked out by neo-idealists. Neo-idealism, I suggest, affords more than an ideology for neoliberalism and less than a stark alternative to it.

The pages ahead explore the frequency with which the idealization of personal autonomy in seventies thought was shadowed by a glorification of hierarchy. If the crucial intellectual developments of the decade appear caught up in a spiral of autonomous and undemocratic impulses, as I shall presently show, it is because a central concern of the decade, from its highest summits in the academy to the louche outskirts of its profuse subcultures, was what Rawls called the "appropriate precedence" of freedom over equality.[2] The immemorial conflict in the history of liberalism between equality and freedom seemed for Rawls and a host of his contemporaries to have been decided in favor of the latter. And that verdict would have important consequences for the emergence in the decade of a disavowal of customary social groupings like citizens or publics. None of the groups I study in this book could be described as popular, in the sense of either populist or representative. But that is partly my point. They are typical in their marginality. It is odd to speak of libertarians as popular for the same reason we would have trouble defining cultists or anarchists as popular. Members of these movements belong to an elect, either permanently outside the lifeworld of their fellows or a vanguard that might blaze a path for at best a handful of them. Radical ecologists who seek an end to farming and a return to the hunting life assume that they will be alone in their pursuit, the world having been nearly purged of human megafauna. Evangelicals who believe in rapture have long since made peace with the realization that all but the faithful will perish before the Last Judgment.

This book explores the productive, problematic, unintended, or simply repugnant implications that followed from the rejection of people en masse. Perhaps scholars have been averse to scrutinizing the seventies because its residents had little interest in spending time there either. They certainly did not care much for the company they kept. For new-school hunters and rapture-ready evangelicals, a saving singularity derived from a brutal eliminationism: either a Malthusian winnowing of the human surplus (in radical ecology) or a divine culling (in evangelicalism). For the collectives in question, smaller was better at every scale. And nothing bested individualism, whose claims on us, in the view of many seventies thinkers, must supersede our most venerable or at least entrenched institutions. Founded by the race car driver Claude Vorilhon ("Raël") in 1973 after his encounter with a UFO, the International Raëlian Movement promotes "selective democracy" by making voting and election to office contingent on scoring a high minimum on an IQ test.[3] In *Geniocracy: Government of the People, For the People, By the Geniuses* (1977), Raël writes: "Only those whose intelligence is 10% above average would be given the right to vote and only those 50% above the average (geniuses) would be eligible to govern."[4] Such views are both bizarre and to be expected of the inferences an assortment of seventies people were willing to draw from the primacy of individualism. This book explains such primacy by looking at the period's "fringe" discourses, a modifier I put in quotes because my goal is to question the term's usefulness when it comes to the seventies.

Chapter 1 considers how IQ reappeared in the era as a proper measure of personhood, and not merely among Raëlians. Numerous figures looked to psychometrics as confirming the objective existence of separate subjectivities. Examining the promise and defeat of artificial intelligence in philosophy of mind and New Wave science fiction, this chapter shows that a suspicion of Great Society welfarism took hold among writers with little in common except their commitment to the idea that human minds could neither be replicated by machines nor reconfigured by state institutions without injury to personhood. If there is something weird about reviving not just classical IQ science but also classical liberalism, at least we can trace the motivation for such retrievals to the widespread seventies attitude that the present itself had little to offer by way of solutions to social problems. Many forward-thinking or progressive figures in the decade preferred to look to the past, a habit of mind that hastened the collapse of the present. Chapter 2 details a dramatic example of this period tendency in the enthusiasm of many ecologists for what I call the "paleo-republic." For such thinkers, the future of civilization was not merely the preindustrial but the preagricultural past, an era before malignant overpopulation and bureaucratic inertia steered our species off its evolutionary path. Chapter 3 considers the unlikely mutuality of two very different seventies formations: the mind-control cult and the libertarian movement that arose out of a longer and more conflicted tradition of anarchism. I show that the cult's principles converge with those of libertarianism in ways we have not recognized, particularly with respect to the prestige both cultists and libertarians assigned to expanded consciousness. Finally, chapter 4 looks at another pair of seeming opposites—New Age spirituality and Christian evangelicalism—in order to reveal their shared embrace of the spiritual possibilities on offer in the free market.

These four chapters generate a framework for recovering the seventies as an overlooked watershed. Rather than a murky vale tucked between the flashy peaks on either side—the revolutionary sixties and the counterrevolutionary eighties—the decade marks an inflection point in contemporary culture, a claim that makes sense once we observe how its vintage fads have converged to buttress a consistent if not precisely lucid worldview in certain quarters of the twenty-first century. The pervasive retailing of "mindfulness" as a smartphone app, not to mention its pride of place on the menu of corporate retreats, can be traced to the seventies boom in monetizing consciousness.[5] Paleo-libertarianism, the quest for immortality, and apocalyptic survivalism are rampant in Silicon Valley, a stronghold of free-market zealotry and meritocracy.[6] It would be a mistake to see the lifestyles of tech millionaires as exemplary of twenty-first-century America were it not that this elite's refusal of the contemporary in favor of the (remote) past and the (equally remote) future *is* in fact prevalent throughout the culture of the present—a culture that repudiates the present.[7] The decade's energetic antisocialism is the enduring legacy of the seventies.[8]

So pervasive was the acquiescence to society's pending dissolution that Jimmy Carter diagnosed the culture of the seventies as "centrifugal," composed of "forces in our society and in our political system . . . testing the resiliency of American pluralism and of our ability to govern."[9] Even at the decade's start, keen observers noticed the specter of exodus looming on the horizon. In *Exit, Voice, and Loyalty* (1970), the economist A. O. Hirschman surveyed the chief "responses" consumers or citizens take toward perceived "decline" in (as his subtitle puts it) "firms, organizations, and states." For Hirschman, unhappiness with an economic transaction occasions withdrawal or defection ("the *exit option*"), whereas unhappiness with a political state of affairs occasions efforts to express the cause of unhappiness ("the *voice option*").[10] The reason for this "fundamental schism" (15) is that market competition allows customers to take their business elsewhere, whereas the nation-state's monopolistic hold on its citizens makes exit (say through expatriation) so costly that most citizens will have no other choice than to voice their grievances in order to pressure the state into redress. "Voice" Hirschman thus defines as "any attempt at all to change, rather than escape from, an objectionable state of affairs" (30), particularly since "exit" is often *criminal*," "labeled desertion, defection, and treason" (17) by the nation-state.

Hirschman's purview is chiefly the economic realm, where "exit" predominates. But his book could not have predicted the degree to which the rhetoric if not precisely the practice of withdrawal from the political order would come to transfix many thinkers in the course of the following decade. While he makes reference to the tendency of economists like Milton Friedman to treat the state's monopolies on institutions like education as surmountable in economic terms (via Friedman's once scandalous yet now widely practiced voucher proposal, for example), Hirschman treats this as a fringe concern, an idea whose time would never really come. Concerned to increase the prestige of "voice" in a culture that "has accorded a privileged position" to "exit" (106), since "to develop 'voice' within an organization is synonymous with the history of democratic control" (55), Hirschman overlooked how sexy the "exit" strategy would seem to a generation enamored of the sorts of categorical withdrawal exercised by dissatisfied customers in a market society.[11] Modeling statist institutions as so many substandard firms, the antisocial seventies opted for flight from their failed promises. This is not news, of course. The seventies' most recognizable cliché is the rise of "alternative lifestyles." Yet we have not appreciated the degree to which the conscientious disloyalty of those who dwelled on the decade's margins—joiners of communes, say—also shaped the outlook of establishment stalwarts like Friedman and his Chicago School colleagues, whose academic scrutiny of competitive markets shaded readily into a political embrace of the virtues of decentralization.[12]

This book takes seriously the "breakdown" of the seventies without the rebuke that term usually connotes.[13] Indeed, when we substitute words like "decentralization" and "centrifugal" for "breakdown," we gain a sense of how seventies thinkers could see in the decade's morass not merely a society in its terminal state but a means to retrieve from the moribund social body new hopes for pluralism and localism, not to say the unwinding of hegemonic categories (anthropo-, Euro-, and ethnocentric) that forms a hallmark of left politics in our own time. To say that seventies culture was centrifugal is to observe that institutions at the culture's center (from Nixon's silent majority to the mass media to academe and government) were drawn inexorably to action on the culture's margins. But it is also to argue, with Peter Carroll, that such attraction followed from "a virtual revolution in popular attitudes about the traditional institutions of American society," namely a wide-scale "separation of Americans from the major traditions of society," a "removal" accompanied by what Carroll calls "an alternative native consciousness."[14]

The motor powering the decade's centrifuge was consciousness itself, as if the prevalence of out-of-body experiences and astral projections suddenly made travel to the culture's outer limits too convenient to pass up. "One need only survey any well-stocked bookshop to appreciate the spectacular variety of exotic experience that has flooded the cultural mainstream in recent days," Theodore Roszak writes in *Unfinished Animal* (1975).[15] "The occult and mystic (often liberally laced with science fiction and comic book fantasy) have become special vehicles of popular culture" (2). All these "sources high and low" (6) point in the direction of Roszak's chief subject: the "consciousness circuit" (3). Consciousness occupied a central role in his influential 1969 book *The Making of a Counter Culture*, which identified "*consciousness* consciousness [*sic*]" (rather than class consciousness) as the "generative principle" of its titular formation.[16] *Unfinished Animal* airs the suspicion that sixties consciousness-raising has become less generative than degenerate, giving way among cultists and UFOlogists to "gullibility" and a "compliant habit of mind" (3). Despite this worry, Roszak takes the "banalities . . . at the extremes" of the consciousness circuit as but a "popular reflection" of "a shift . . . fully as epoch-making as the appearance of speech or of the tool-making talents" (3). "We stand in witness to a planet-wide mutation of mind," he writes with a certain breathlessness, "which promises to liberate energies of will and resources of vision long maturing in the depths of our identity" (4).

In keeping with the prestige accorded to decentering in the period, Roszak construed the mainstreaming of consciousness-raising as a kind of fission rather than cooption (hence its "liberate[d] energies"). It is a mistake to see "the psychospiritual fascinations of the day" as "a sort of mystic chic" rather than "an effort to free the transcendent powers of the personality from the dead hand of the culture's . . . orthodoxies" (6).[17] The reference of course is to "radical chic," the notorious coinage of Tom Wolfe, whose thoughts about the counterculture were much less Pollyannaish than Roszak's. Whereas *Unfinished Animal* situates the period's full-court press of individualism within the framework of "a qualitative great leap forward of our species" (6), Wolfe's "The 'Me' Decade and the Third Great Awakening" (1976) understands the diverse travelers along the consciousness circuit as a "noosphere of souls" connected at root by an "unceasing" "analysis of the self" and a revival of the "great religious wave[s] in American history."[18] Yet in this, "the greatest age of individualism" (293), the "ecumenical spirit" of past awakenings has given way to "a spirit of schism" (291). Like a number of commentators in the seventies, Wolfe saw the "psychic frenzy" (290) of the consciousness circuit belying a serious malaise: the death of cohesive community and its preservative virtues. In *The Culture of Narcissism* (1979), Christopher Lasch construed the mania for self-awareness as the last gasp of "competitive individualism, which in its decadence has carried the logic of individualism to the extreme of a war of all against all."[19]

Chapter 2 surveys the Hobbesian despair pervading the culture of the seventies and the appeal to "community" that a number of thinkers, from political scientists to radical ecologists, invoked as a means to restore social and ecological balance. If a single word defines the period, as that chapter demonstrates, it would have to be "entropy," the shorting of the world's homeostasis and the dissolution of its orderliness. Writing at the decade's start, Alvin Toffler concluded in *Future Shock* (1970) that "the acceleration of change in our time is, itself, an elemental force" with "personal and psychological, as well as sociological, consequences."[20] Not least of these for Toffler is the threat of "a massive adaptational breakdown" (2), the evil twin of Roszak's "quantum leap forward." *Future Shock* shares *Unfinished Animal*'s fixation on what Toffler calls the "subcult explosion" (285): "subcults multiply at an ever accelerating rate, and in turn die off to make room for still more and newer subcults" (286). Yet Toffler's attitude toward "throwaway culture" (38) is relatively sanguine. Its lack of sustainability is compensated for by "the fantastic opportunities for individuality" (156) that "fragmentation . . . brings" (157).

Wolfe, Lasch, and Toffler see the centrifuge of seventies culture as a perpetual motion machine likely to spin civilization into the ether. If consciousness supplies its motor, consumer capitalism affords something of a limit to the machine's range. In "Within the Context of No-Context" (1980), George Trow concludes that "the marketplace itself" stands in for an expanding "vastness" that supersedes our customary social anchors. "The middle distance" has fallen away and only "two grids remained," "the grid of two hundred million and the grid of intimacy."[21] "Whereas Toffler lauds "market segmentation" (145) because it "makes for greater individual choice" (148), Trow finds little "comfort" in the new order (47). The waning of "the important forces . . . that fell outside the new scale of national life" (47) has left us suspended in a void of meretricious freedom with only "the permission given by television . . . to make tiny choices, within the context of total permission infected with a sense of no permission at all" (51).

Trow's absurdist critique of the market and its favorite tool (TV) as purveyors of only the most qualified "modes of choice" (47) places him at odds with the broad swath of thinkers I take up in the pages ahead. Figures as diverse as Milton Friedman and John Rawls tend to side with Toffler in his praise of "the plenitude and complexity of our choices" (164) over the "choiceless life ways" (156) besetting social orders throughout history. From the vantage that this book explores, in fact, Trow's essay is somewhat belated. Its equation of the TV program and the programming of persons relies on an account of culture that assumes that transmissions move unidirectionally from the technology of mass media to the human receiver. By the early seventies, this Skinnerian paradigm had begun to unravel among scientific disciplines in the process of repealing the tenets of operant conditioning. From psychology to philosophy, the holders of vastly discordant views sought to turn the tide of an academic culture that, as Robert Ornstein put it in his 1972 textbook *The Psychology of Consciousness*, had "not been sufficiently concerned with consciousness."[22] Despite the chasm between economists like Friedman and philosophers like Rawls or between New Age seekers and Christian fundamentalists, the seventies presented a united front when it came to the centrality of mind.

My aim in the following pages is to demonstrate this and other underlying commonalities in the sectarian movements that gathered followers in what has often been seen as a hopelessly splintered era. Claims like Lasch's or Wolfe's that consciousness-raising is a debased pursuit masking cultural malignancies scarcely make sense in the context I seek to develop. Roszak was right to point to the "puerile follies" (3) of the consciousness circuit as but one domain on a spectrum that encompassed a good deal more serious thinking on the topic, even if he was wrong about the imminent conquest of the "Aquarian frontier" (5). I argue that the chief consequence of the decade's focus on consciousness turns out to be the period's impatience with models of personhood that work from the outside in, whether the Marxist's historical necessity shaping both individuals and classes or the government planner's commitment to social initiatives that inevitably ricochet on their would-be beneficiaries.

Some readers will surely be relieved to hear that this book's four chapters pay attention to few self-consciously libertarian texts.[23] But I am keenly interested in both the normalization of libertarian beliefs after the sixties and the degree to which a striking number of intellectuals, including literary figures, contributed to such acceptance. I recreate the background conditions in which libertarian appeals to reason, private life, and the market assume a prominent role in the thinking of many people at the end of the twentieth century. But my principal terms will not be "libertarianism" and "neoliberalism." As I have implied, they will be "consciousness" and "subjectivity," categories whose revival I discuss under the rubric of neo-idealism. Neo-idealism develops in reaction to the externalist and objectivist accounts of morality and mind that held dominion in the twentieth century, from physicalism to logical positivism. Neo-idealism is characterized by the view that crucial facts about the human world are what John Searle calls "observer dependent," what Thomas Nagel calls "agent relative."[24] These descriptions attest to the reassertion of subjectivity against the materialism to which much of the last century's philosophy had been pledged. For Searle, the problem with almost all inquiries into consciousness is that they "stud[y] only objectively observable phenomena, thus ignoring the essential features of the mind."[25]

In *Age of Fracture* (2011), Daniel Rodgers observes of the seventies that "conceptions of human nature that in the post–World War II era had been thick with context, social circumstance, institutions, and history gave way to conceptions of human nature that stressed choice, agency, performance, and desire."[26] Rodgers surveys "the intellectual construction of reality" that "took on new breadth and intensity in the last quarter of the 20th century" by way of "think tanks," "media," and "university settings."[27] Yet ironically, his analysis of the decade's "acts of mind" does not consider whether the driving force of such acts was a reclamation of the mind's power to build out the world.[28] Neo-idealism captures the sense that the retrieval of consciousness, which Searle calls "intrinsic and ineliminable," was not only an enthusiasm of Aquarian faddists but a vigorous undertaking across the culture of the seventies, even among philosophers (like Searle) with a pronounced distaste for the counterculture.[29]

We typically trace the resurgence of idealism in US intellectual circles to poststructuralist imports like Jacques Derrida. There is also a homegrown variety associated with the neo-pragmatism of Richard Rorty. Such thinkers have been criticized for doubting an external reality independent of representation, as reflected in the slogans now affixed to their work: "there is no outside the text"[30] (Derrida); "Truth cannot be out there—cannot exist independently of the human mind—because sentences cannot so exist, or be out there"[31] (Rorty); "reality in a world, like realism in a picture, is largely a matter of habit"[32] (Nelson Goodman); "science knows no 'bare facts' at all. . . . [T]he 'facts' that enter our knowledge are . . . essentially ideational"[33] (Paul Feyerabend). One way of marking out the seventies enthusiasm for doubting the objective world is to see it as part of a larger pattern in the history of modern thought, which has been marked by ebbs and flows of idealism since the Enlightenment. In the American context, idealist waves (such as transcendentalism and pragmatism) have followed periods of strongly empiricist and materialist orientations in the broader culture, as if in reaction to Lockean empiricism and the Scottish School of Common Sense (for Ralph Waldo Emerson) or to the Darwinian and Spencerian naturalism of the late nineteenth century (for William James).[34]

One might be tempted to see intellectual currents as cycling over time between materialist and idealist dispensations if this generalization did not risk flattening the contours of historical periods and limiting our sense of how change happens between them. Then, too, materialist and idealist attitudes are often hard enough to separate from one another, much less separate into discrete and observable ideologies. Marxism exemplifies the confounding of materialist and idealist outlooks in the same theory, to say nothing of the difficulty of fixing any epistemic stance to a discernible politics. Nineteenth-century social Darwinism, which underwrote a powerful conservative defense of laissez-faire, shows that there is nothing inevitable about the correlation of materialism or environmentalism with the progressive social programs that spanned US politics from the New Deal to the Great Society. When it comes to refining the context with which this book deals, we immediately see the challenge of assimilating the work of Derrida (hostile to the very idea of subjectivity) to neo-idealism, which takes the view that consciousness and subjectivity are *objective* facts of human identity. It is more accurate to see Derrida and Rorty as antirealists whose idealism takes such a dim view of objective reality that they all but deny the independent existence of subjectivity or reason itself. For antirealists, just as there is no world outside its construction, so there is nothing that cannot be decomposed into smaller parts (turtles all the way down).

By contrast, neo-idealism takes to heart Kant's claim that "the subjective I cannot be divided or distributed, and this I we presuppose in all thinking."[35] Or to quote Nagel: "The subjectivity of consciousness is an irreducible feature of reality."[36] As befits its "neo"-ness, however, neo-idealism is not just a repossession but a revision of the Kantian tradition. It often takes the "reality" of subjectivity to places into which few academic philosophers would dare venture. Where Kant understood consciousness as a *process* experienced through practice (the activity of understanding, in other words) rather than a *thing* available to empirical study, the neo-idealists of the late twentieth century consider neither the mind nor really any aspect of the noumenal realm off limits to perception.[37] Neo-idealists see consciousness not merely as the means by which we acquire knowledge of the world around us (as it was for Kant) but as their preferred object of knowledge. In the most extreme cases of seventies neo-idealism, as in the work of the "psychophysicist" John C. Lilly, consciousness is shorn of the mysterianism that some philosophers of mind attribute to it.[38] A staunch empiricist, Lilly saw mental experience as traversable in the manner of a New World exploration. His goal was to devise "maps . . . for the successful navigation in the inner spaces" of the mind.[39] Summing up the era's passion for consciousness, Lilly writes in his 1978 memoir *The Scientist*: "Over six million landlubbers paddled off from the little private islands of their own minds into the uncharted tropical-arctic realms of the brain. Each was blown by the winds . . . to a different continent and returned with a singular report."[40] The passage exemplifies neo-idealism's dual belief that consciousness and subjectivity are observable facts and that in taking their measure we must all go it alone.

It may appear odd to claim that a commitment to subjectivity has fixated the culture since the late twentieth century. What, after all, is more passé than the subject? Far from ushering in a dissolution of the Enlightenment project, I argue, the seventies spawned a prolific assortment of claimants to what Roszak calls "the deep mind." "We must believe that there exists, at the core of the mind," he writes in a Kantian mood, "a shaft of subjectivity so deep that it can lead us clean through all that is perishably personal and culturally contingent to the universal ground beneath" (17). For the thinkers I am grouping under the rubric of neo-idealism, accessing the "shaft of subjectivity" mandated a rejection of externalist, behaviorist, and environmentalist models of the social, now understood as instruments of statist control. Lilly, for instance, juxtaposed "the deep self" to what he disparagingly calls "the politics of the human consensus reality" (107).[41] The embrace of that self was a strike against a system that sought to mold the plastic human form into a tool suitable for use by capitalism and its political subsidiary, American empire. This argument is a vintage sixties view of political change, to be sure. Yet while neo-idealism often understood itself as political, it did not assume the sixties view, in part because that view was by and large rooted in collective action, in movements. The aggressive individualism of the seventies by contrast construed groupings larger than the Pleistocene band or the evangelical congregation as traps to lure the unwitting into subjection.

As I have indicated with reference to their pitiless reckoning of the human surplus, these different collectives hewed to an apocalyptic calculus that did not scruple to sacrifice the many for the one. And their views occupied a less marginal place in seventies culture than we might expect. "Overpopulation" was a period byword as pervasive as "stagflation" or "malaise." More significantly, even thinkers opposed to the catastrophic sorting mechanisms favored by some radical ecologists and Christian fundamentalists nonetheless welcomed the *inverse* calculus to which their musings on human excess led. Seventies discourses of consciousness, in other words, not only proclaimed that the crowd would not prevail over the singleton but also rejected the sacrifice of the one for the many. This is the infamous calculus of utilitarianism, the philosophical doctrine that "has been," as Amartya Sen points out in the 2017 reedition of *Collective Choice and Social Welfare* (1970), "the 'official' theory of traditional welfare economics" for the last century, and continues "to serve as the 'default program' in mainstream welfare economic analysis."[42] Utilitarianism's axiom—the greatest good for the greatest number—has found many detractors, who fault both the theory's account of the good (the satisfaction of desire) and its seeming indifference to *whose* desires are satisfied (since such satisfaction can entail dubious sacrifices of persons and their rights).

Chapter 1 chronicles the rise of a forceful antiutilitarian critique in the wake of the sixties. "The utilitarian habit of mind," as the Oxford philosopher Stuart Hampshire put it in his 1972 lecture "Morality and Pessimism," "has brought with it a new abstract cruelty in politics," and its "large-scale computations . . . bring with them a coarseness and grossness of moral feeling" especially repellent "to the young in America."[43] That utilitarianism bears a heavy symbolic load in the period sounds more plausible once we recognize that, for a large cross-section of intellectuals, this ethical system came to stand in for the "system" that was a frequent target of the New Social Movements. In *The New Utopians*, his 1965 study of "the "social engineers of our time," Robert Boguslaw contrasts the "esteem" in which some systems are held ("space systems," "computer systems," "management systems") and the disfavor attached to others ("philosophical systems," "social systems," and "economic systems").[44] The "same word" for "the latest in technical fashion and good taste" among scientists, he writes, "is likely to connote loss of individual freedom" among humanists. Boguslaw's book not only discerned this "semantic anomaly" (29) but served as a first pass at closing the gap between these divergent descriptions, at getting readers to see that fields like informatics, committed to "utilitarian efficiency," "do *not* stem from a perspective that views human beings as human beings" (3). By the seventies, Boguslaw's job seemed complete. As chapter 1 demonstrates, computer systems (notably those involving artificial intelligence) and social systems (notably those aiming to curb inequality) became mutual metaphors for the failure of systems thinking to get what Boguslaw calls "our sense of values" (197) in view.

The pivotal antiutilitarian text is Rawls's *A Theory of Justice*. "Before Rawls wrote, utilitarianism was the dominant view in Anglo-American moral and political philosophy," Michael Sandel points out. "Since *A Theory of Justice*, rights-oriented liberalism has come to predominate."[45] For Rawls no less than Boguslaw, systems thinking occasions what Rawls calls "a weakening of our sense of . . . value" (180), in particular the value of subjectivity. "Each person possesses an inviolability founded on justice" (3), he writes, "not subject to . . . the calculus of social interests" (4). If "a utilitarian society" makes it "more difficult" for "men . . . to be confident of their own worth" (181), it is because "utilitarianism does not take seriously the distinction between persons" (27).

Antiutilitarian thought treats this debatable claim as the basis of its critique of the welfare state.[46] "Since 1970," Lincoln Allison notes, "there has been a considerable revival in anti-consequentialist theory," whose "most often quoted theorists" base "their theories on the separateness and individuality of human beings rather than on their part in an aggregate."[47] Echoing Rawls's judgment that utilitarianism is guilty of "conflating all persons into one" (27), his student Thomas Nagel writes in *The Possibility of Altruism* (1970) that the utilitarian "ignores the distinction between persons" and so would have few qualms about the need "to sacrifice one individual life for another."[48]

Critics of utilitarianism see an obvious link between the theory's disdain for the "competing claims" of individuals and its partisans' craven yielding to the will of the crowd.[49] In 1958, the year Rawls published the program essay "Justice as Fairness," Elizabeth Anscombe launched the opening salvo in the contemporary assault on utilitarianism in "Modern Moral Philosophy," which accuses utilitarians of holding a "shallow philosophy" that allows for no means "to revolt against the conventional standards" of society.[50] In *The Forms and Limits of Utilitarianism* (1965), Rawls's student David Lyons concluded that all versions of utilitarianism are reducible, as Anscombe earlier claimed, to an apologia for conformism. "No pure utilitarian theory can account for some of our strongest moral convictions," Lyons writes, because all utilitarians make the "mistake" of "assimilating many kinds of reasons and considerations in morality to one kind."[51] The fact that it doesn't care about the distinctness of persons means that utilitarianism has no use for whatever different views such persons might have. Bernard Williams found "much modern utilitarian theory . . . surprisingly conformist" for the related reason that it doesn't even have much use for its own views: "Modern utilitarian theorists tend to spend more effort in reconciling utilitarianism with existing moral beliefs than in rejecting those beliefs on the strength of utilitarianism."[52]

The positioning of utilitarianism as an unlikely hegemon that secured its advantage through a policy of blanket conformity helps explain some of the impact of *A Theory of Justice*, which could appear revolutionary not merely in Sandel's sense but even in, say, Tom Hayden's or Huey Newton's. The task of Rawls's massive book is to present the case for liberalism as a normative theory superior to any ethics on offer, and chiefly to a utilitarianism that Rawls and others accuse of *illiberalism*. That recovery seems at odds with the strong critique of liberalism afloat in the era ("Politically bankrupt," Lasch writes, "liberalism is intellectually bankrupt as well").[53] Yet the notoriety Rawls's book enjoys outside its home discipline owes much to the receptiveness of readers across (and even beyond) the university to its vision of a society that values the dignity of persons as social if not quite economic equals. Sharing the New

Left's spirited rejection of instrumental selfhood and impersonal systems, Rawls presents contractual liberalism with the vigor of an antiestablishment crusade. Like the New Left radical intent on exposing the false consciousness enforced by a system built on bad faith, Rawls sees utilitarianism as overruling "our convictions about justice" through its willingness "to account for them as a socially useful illusion" (28).

Rawls's neo-idealism was the academic counterpart to what might be described as the period's pop Kantianism, exemplified by Roszak's "shaft of subjectivity." In *The Scientist*, Lilly describes the formative impact his encounter with Kant's *Critique of Pure Reason* had on him as a Caltech undergraduate: "I studied it and studied it" (48). Roszak correlates the Aquarian Age's "mutation of mind" with the Kantian effort "to extend . . . the full dignities of personhood across the entire human spectrum" (4). Pop Kantianism's boldest expression is found in Charles Reich's best-selling book *The Greening of America* (1970). "Of all the qualities of human beings that are injured, narrowed, or repressed in the Corporate State," Reich argues, "consciousness . . . suffers most" (274). Readers of *The Greening of America* will be familiar with the primacy the book accords to consciousness, given its understanding of history as a succession of mental states. The book's Hegelian framework was hardly idiosyncratic. William Appleman Williams, the influential historian of American foreign policy who trained a generation of New Left–inspired students at the University of Wisconsin, argued in the lead essay in *A New History of Leviathan* (1972), "it will no longer do to write history as if the men who made the decisions did not use their minds."[54] For Williams, a methodological "return to the issue of consciousness," to a practice that foregrounds how "men have directly expanded the scope and power of their minds," is the precondition for a liberatory politics, since only "consciousness, if married to morality, can save us" from the "hell" of a "corporate system" that "otherwise . . . will systematize us all."[55]

The editors of *A New History of Leviathan*, the libertarian Murray Rothbard and the (then) New Left activist Ronald Radosh, ranked Reich alongside Herbert Marcuse as pioneers in the use of "radical consciousness" as a defense against the "corporate state."[56] The "greening" of Reich's title is not an ecological flowering but a ripening of what he calls "Consciousness III," the mindset of the new generation of students who wandered past Reich's office window, which looked out on the Yale campus in the late sixties. Given its author's willingness to deduce an epochal shift in consciousness from glimpses of former varsity jocks in bell-bottoms on the quad ("Bell bottoms . . . express the body," Reich writes, "but they say so much more" [255]), *The Greening of America* has long been derided for its starry-eyed idealism. Less noticed is

Reich's brief for idealism in the philosophical sense, his insistence that "the individual, not society, is the reality" (247). Of course, what Reich calls the power to "make a world" (293) requires more heavy lifting for the intellectually cautious Rawls than Reich is willing to ask of his stoners and surfers. Whereas Rawls holds that only the exercise of a rational will nurtured early on in our development can help us construct a "well ordered society" (56), Reich "believes it is essential to get free of what is now accepted as rational thought" (278).

Yet the carelessness and extremity of viewpoint that make Reich a pop Kantian are precisely what makes him instructive in examining the rise of neo-idealism. Proceeding by way of axiomatic pronouncements, *The Greening of America* conveys the extent to which a Kantian sensibility would infuse the seventies zeitgeist. Reich's "Use no other person as a means" (244) is simply Kant's categorical imperative, the recognition of every individual's autonomy, which Reich calls the "single value" (304). Rawls's "principle of equal liberty" is by his account "based upon Kant's notion of autonomy" (221). As a notoriously amorphous concept in Kant, autonomy seems tailor-made for the litany of platitudes with which *The Greening of America* teems. "Consciousness III," Reich asserts, "postulates the absolute worth of every human being—every self" (241). By contrast, Rawls's aim is to make autonomy substantive, to work out what it might look like in practice: "The principles of justice are . . . categorical imperatives in Kant's sense" (223). Yet when Reich writes that "to start from the self . . . means to start from premises based on human life and the rest of nature" in order to "find genuine values in a world whose official values are false" (242), we might as well be in the "original position" (6), Rawls's version of the social contract, in which parties come together to agree on binding rules for a society.

It is worth rehearsing the basics of Rawls's well-known thought experiment. In his account, rational parties behind a "veil of ignorance" that deprives them of any "information" (19) of where they will end up in the social order, yet mindful (by virtue of their reason) that everyone deserves "conditions that enable him to frame a mode of life that expresses his nature as a free and equal rational being" (561), will arrive at two principles of justice. The first is the liberty principle, according to which "each person is to have an equal right to the most extensive total system of equal basic liberties compatible with a similar system of liberty for all" (250). The second is the difference principle, which allows for "economic inequalities" only if they are "to the greatest benefit of the least advantaged" and "attached to offices and positions open to all under conditions of fair equality of opportunity" (83). While the first principle takes priority over the second (no program of economic betterment can override any individual's rights), together these principles sustain the "circumstances" in which "each individual" can pursue "a rational plan of life" (93). The centrality of rational choice is continuous between the original position and the society it envisions into being. Indeed, Rawls treats it as the basis on which "the unity of the person is manifest." Rawls employs a rigorous tautology here. "To formulate and follow a plan of life" means that a person is free to make choices that "fashion his own unity" (561).

Notwithstanding his critique of rationalism, Reich similarly praises "the decision making process" essential to Consciousness III because it prevents the paternalistic state from interfering with the individual's "desire to be an independent being" (247). Paternalism is among the many vices charged to utilitarianism and the welfare state for which it stands in neo-idealist thought. In "utilitarian politics," Williams writes, "benevolence gets credentials from sympathy and passes them on to paternalism."[57] Rawls cautions that because it threatens "to license assaults on one's conviction and character," "paternalistic intervention" is a measure of last resort, only "justified by the evident failure or absence of reason and will" (250). The danger for Rawls and other antiutilitarians is that the caretaker state *induces* such failure, indeed that it cannot help getting between people and "the integrity of their person" (250). Since, as Toffler claims, "welfare programs today often cripple rather than help their clients" (227), the future requires "a new ethos . . . in which other goals," from "social responsibility" to "individualism," "supplant those of economic welfare" (230). Roszak sees the welfare state as an adjunct of a capitalist system that replaces "our need . . . to find both moral dignity and personal meaning" with "forms of economic security which infantilize us" (37). The claim that the Great Society robs us of our agency follows from the passivity utilitarianism is understood to saddle persons with—its "tendency," as Robert Paul Wolff puts it, "to view human beings as nothing more than pleasure-containers, to be filled or emptied like so many water jugs."[58] Echoing this verdict, Robert Nozick argued in his National Book Award–winning *Anarchy, State, and Utopia* (1974) that because it privileges "recipient justice"—that is, a person's right to get things from the state—a utilitarian society appoints a "paternalistic supervisory board" that never adjourns.[59]

Extended to its logical conclusion, according to its opponents, utilitarianism would forbid free rational persons from pursuing their "plan of life" on the view that the utilitarian engineer, deciding in advance what counts as the measure of a decent life, excludes what Reich calls "a non-material set of values" (300). Utilitarianism tends toward a drab uniformity of opinion along with the assumption that no one's life plans are importantly different from anyone else's. Neo-idealism by contrast imagines a pluralistic universe as the ground for the exercise of choice. "The attempt to increase liberty, to lead a full and rewarding life," Paul Feyerabend writes, "and the corresponding attempt to discover the secrets of nature and of man, entails . . . the rejection of all universal standards" (12). Feyerabend's claim that anyone should be free to pick out the "traditions most advantageous to the individual" (265) bears some resemblance to Rawls's insistence that a just society allows all individuals to elect their own "conception of the good" (14). Yet where Feyerabend identifies as an "anarchist . . . who plays the game of Reason" (23), Rawls is neither a relativist nor an anarchist. He believes not only in the universality of reason but also in the idea that reason puts constraints on our choices: "the good is the satisfaction of rational desire" (30). Deriving the original position from the models of bargaining theory, Rawls makes the "free market system" (66) rather than the state the salient basis for a "well ordered society." A "significant advantage of a market system is that, given the requisite background institutions, it is consistent with equal liberties and fair equality of opportunity," Rawls writes. "Citizens have a free choice of careers and occupations" (272).

Because of such judgments, Rawls looks to some readers uncomfortably close in spirit to market cheerleaders like Toffler or Milton Friedman.[60] But it would be a mistake to describe Rawls as an apologist for capitalism. Rawls's principle of liberty explicitly omits property rights from the fundamental rights of equal persons. Yet the frequent charge that *A Theory of Justice* is an apologia for an expansive welfare state is equally misconceived.[61] Rawls's original position rests on the idea, after all, that rational parties can arrive at the right social order without the state's external pressures. It is thus less the case that Rawls "has no theory of the *state*," as Wolff complains, than that Rawls has no immediate use for it (18). The institutions that develop in the "well ordered society" are expressions of what rational parties will into being rather than impositions on subjects who might otherwise choose differently. In Rawls, the rules for a just social order are not programmed into us; we design them ourselves. And this rejection of programming from without clarifies Rawls's impatience with the state understood as anything but an objective manifestation of our considered choices. Distinguishing between a just society and a just government, Rawls sees the latter as insufficient for a "well ordered society" because a government may carry out "just" programs (an income tax that equalized everyone's wealth, say) to whose fairness not everyone (or even anyone) would assent. Far from a robust defense of the state, *A Theory of Justice* insists on the "unanimity" (251) of each decision-making subject in arriving at the principles of justice, which derive only from our cooperative deliberations. Nonnegotiable consent—not state power—legitimizes the social rules, even if a state apparatus maintains them. For Rawls, public authority reduces to the mutual accord of private choices.

R. M. Hare thus concludes that Rawls's procedure amounts to "advocating a kind of subjectivism, in the narrowest and most old-fashioned sense."[62] The force of Hare's criticism is somewhat muted by the fact that Rawls candidly presents his work as subjectivist. Only from the vantage of the utilitarian tradition to which Hare belongs could "subjectivism" amount to a dirty word. For Rawls, what "justifies a conception of justice is not its being true to an order antecedent to and given to us, but its congruence with our deeper understanding of ourselves and our aspirations."[63] Rawls and other contemporary Kantians share the postmodern theorist's denial of objective standards or rules.[64] "There are no moral facts," as Rawls puts it in "Kantian Constructivism in Moral Theory" (1980).[65] Yet such constructivism takes the creation of social norms, no less than personal identity, as chiefly an *internal* affair. "Your identity," the Kantian ethicist (and Rawls student) Christine Korsgaard writes, "is in a quite literal way constituted by your choices and actions."[66] Elsewhere in the humanities, of course, construction works from the outside in. It is hard to imagine Judith Butler endorsing Korsgaard's claim that "human actions are for the most part chosen, not merely impelled."[67] For queer theory stresses the exterior conditions that pressure us into categories and deprecates our agency in withstanding them.[68] A crude but not inaccurate way of marking the advent of neo-idealism is to see it as a shift from externalism to internalism, a reorientation chapter 1 spells out in detail. Hence the premium placed on self-authorization and immanence by Rawls and Korsgaard, for whom human agency is indwelling. More outré versions of internalism include the fetishizing of interiority by figures like Lilly, who claims to have colonized his "inner domains" (180) through self-experimentation with the aid of copious psychedelics.

There is certainly a good deal of intellectual distance between Lilly and Rawls. But that very divide—of reputation, reasoning, and seriousness of inquiry, among other things—suggests how startling Rawls's commitment to the self-possession overacted by Lilly turns out to be. Given that Rawls predicates his theory of justice on a certain voluntarism derived from Kantian autonomy and manifesting as rational choice, it is striking that few critiques of his work have come from the literary humanities, where such premises are widely arraigned as mystifications. This is not to deny the volume of critiques of *A Theory of Justice*. Indeed, the fact that Rawls has been criticized from both left and right highlights his symptomatic role in neo-idealism. I am less interested in the charge (from those to his left) that he is too liberal or (from those to his right) that he is too egalitarian than in the fact that critics of whatever political stripe find common ground in attacking Rawls's endorsement of subjectivity for not being *strong enough*. Hence Nozick considers Rawls's "unexalted picture of human beings" at odds with "a theory that otherwise wishes to buttress the dignity and self-respect of autonomous beings."[69] Arguing from the left end of the political dial, Wolff considers Rawls's "model of rationality . . . appropriate to a firm rather than to an individual human being" (54). And G. A. Cohen faults Rawls for treating parties in the original position as "acquisitive maximizers in daily life," a designation Cohen finds incompatible with the "realization of their natures as moral persons."[70] Even as they claim that he does not deliver on it, these writers concede Rawls's view that the promise of our political ideals lies in what he calls "an ideal conception of the person" (262).

Cohen and Wolff are skeptical that market society can enable the "full realization" of persons because they remain partly committed to a Marxist viewpoint that sees the market as a dehumanizing force. Despite the lip service capitalism's apologists pay to the sanctity of individuality, the market in Marxist thinking does not foster so much as eradicate the individual. Neo-idealism by contrast encourages us to see the market as pivotal to the flourishing of individuals at every step on the social ladder. The Raëlian version of individualism entails an outrageous hierarchy of human specialness based on psychometric test scores. Yet no less perverse, and far more pervasive, is the market-driven defeat of statism that proceeds by treating ordinary people as possessed of a specialness that only free enterprise can ensure. As with other period sentiments, this understanding makes for strange bedfellows. Like Rawls and other antiutilitarian thinkers, the neoclassical economist Friedman and the anarchist philosopher Feyerabend both fault the regnant social order for its indifference to the particularity of persons. "Not live human beings, but abstract models are consulted," Feyerabend complains of the scientific method's technocratic flunkies, who presume that "the producers of the models . . . have a better grasp of the reality of humans than these humans themselves" (263).

In *Free to Choose* (1980), which is both a popular guide to the market economy and an impeachment of the "overgoverned society," Milton and Rose Friedman take the problem of abstraction from another direction.[71] Their grievance is as much with the superimposition of models on persons as with the fact that persons are limited in their own choices by the monoliths that outsize models present. "When you enter the voting booth once a year, you almost always vote for a package rather than specific items," the Friedmans write. "Generally, you end up with something different from what you voted for." And while this looks like the old democratic ill of the tyranny of the majority, for the Friedmans the problem is much deeper, since even those in the majority "will at best get the items [they] favored and the ones [they] opposed" (65).

"The ballot box produces" what the Friedmans see as a no-win situation: "conformity without unanimity." By contrast, "the marketplace" fosters "unanimity without conformity" (66). *Free to Choose* treats the political system symmetrically with the economic system," the Friedmans write in the book's preface. When "both are regarded as markets" (xiv), the "free private market" is the clear winner from the perspective of the "ordinary man" precisely because the political market tends toward "concentrated government power," which is to say, toward safeguarding the state's interests over those of the individual (4).

Free to Choose appeared simultaneously as a book and a PBS documentary series starring Milton Friedman as the celebrity face of competitive capitalism. The show was by public television standards (to be sure, an ironic venue for the Friedmans' message) a huge success. Each of its ten episodes found its soft-spoken host, a Mister Rogers for laissez-faire, visiting various neighborhoods in the modern economic universe, from Hong Kong (with "one of the highest standards of living in all of Asia" and "no tariffs or other restraints on international trade" [34]) to the home of the "tool and die maker" Bob Crawford and his "average American family" victimized by inflation (which the Friedmans call "taxation without representation" [279]), to a sweatshop in lower Manhattan that Friedman praises for enabling immigrants like his mother to better their lives (or at least their children's). In the case of both the "speck of land" (33) next door to the communist behemoth and the nonunionized shop where laborers toil in misery today in order to reap the shared fruits of a dynamic capitalism tomorrow, Friedman frames the free market as a David who will vanquish the statist Goliath as long as the state does not rig the battle with regulations or price controls. The popularity of the PBS series was arguably a tribute not merely to its host's folksy survey of capitalism in action but to his unfailing belief in the market's own populism, its ability to unshackle "ordinary citizens" from "political fetters" and return to them the "power to control their own destiny" (55).[72]

The appeal to the rights of common people against the state's interests is a crucial feature of the decade that roughly begins with *A Theory of Justice* (with its commitment to the dignity of the "least advantaged") and ends with *Free to Choose* (with its commitment to the idea that "the great achievements of Western capitalism have redounded primarily to the benefit of the ordinary person" [147]).[73] And while Rawls's version of this appeal is hardly identical to the Friedmans', nor is it wholly distinct. "Our society is what we make it," the Friedmans write in the spirit of the Kantian constructivism underwriting Rawls's original position. "We can shape our institutions" (37). Like Rawls, the Friedmans conceive of a world *in potentia*, activated by our reason. Just as Rawls denies that our republic counts as "well ordered," the Friedmans balk at the idea that what passes for the free market in American life is truly free.[74] They also endorse a close facsimile of Rawls's "liberty principle." "Personal equality is important precisely because people are not identical," they write. "Their different values . . . and different capacities will lead them to want to lead very different lives" (129). It is just such respect for difference that Rawls has in mind when he rejects utilitarianism's "teleological theory" (25), its view that there is *one outcome* that fits society as a whole regardless of the diversity of people's expectations.

What I have been suggesting here, and what the pages ahead spell out in greater detail, is that Rawls's theory of justice develops out of a neo-idealism that affords a powerful ethical defense of claims that have been easier to dismiss when voiced by free-market zealots like Friedman. From the vantage I am pursuing, the subtitle of the Friedmans' book—"A Personal Statement"—is as important as its title, grounding what looks like a propagandistic argument for laissez-faire in the sanctity of personhood. Like Rawls and the pop Kantians, the Friedmans reject the "paternal state" because it deprives its would-be "beneficiaries" of the "capacity . . . for making their own decisions" (119). Among the entitlements it dispenses, the welfare state makes no room for the idea that, as Reich puts it, "Everyone is entitled to pride in himself" (243). Likewise "*Free to Choose* is a less abstract and more concrete book" (xiii) than their earlier *Capitalism and Freedom* (1962), the Friedmans write, because it embraces the normative ideal that every person's experience is at once ordinary and special. The self-evident dignity of subjectivity authenticates the self-evident virtues of the market. Thus the importance of distinguishing neo-idealism from neoliberalism. Neoliberalism posits what kind of society we should have: deregulated, privatized, shorn of state-sponsored entitlements to everything from health care to social security to public schools.[75] It has seemed easy for many people to disagree with this vision, even if such disagreement has not yielded a powerful countertrend in practice. Neo-idealism by contrast promotes what kind of persons we should be: self-determined, autonomous, our identities recognized and our subjectivity affirmed. It is very hard to imagine right-minded people, of whatever political disposition, disagreeing with this vision.

But disagreement there will be. One way of understanding the subtle hegemony of neo-idealism is through the vigorous critique of its brief for individualism and consciousness in certain high-energy academic circles. The neo-idealist turn has had the interesting effect of making the sort of behaviorist or functionalist arguments of mid-twentieth-century culture look contrarian and even avant-garde in some contemporary schools of thought. Quite independent of its actual and varied research programs, what we might call *strong materialism* is presented (at least by some posthumanist advocates) as a knowing advance over a gullible subjectivism that refuses to give up the ghost. Strong materialism weds a sense of beleaguered minoritarianism to a peculiar optimism: once we dismiss the claims of personhood from the intellectual scene, the essential work can begin. Going Marie Kondo on our conceptual lumber room, strong materialism seeks to declutter it of those démodé Enlightenment holdovers, like *persons* and *reason*, that fail to spark our joy to the extent that they serve as drags on our awareness.

Though some of its proponents would surely balk at the characterization, strong materialism among humanists has much in common with the scientism found in the work of Daniel Dennett (whose materialist account of mind I discuss in chapter 1). Both projects are eliminative. Drawing on Wilfred Sellars's distinction between the "ontology of everyday life" and the "ontology of science," Dennett treats consciousness as what Sellars calls a "manifest image," the sort of experience of the world that arises from our naive perceptions and behind which physicists and biologists have generated a "scientific image" of the world's real action, which transpires on the subatomic plane or at the level of the chromosome.[76] The sacrosanct irreducibility of first-person point of view is an illusion generated by synaptic connections (for Dennett) or by ideologies like possessive individualism and Enlightenment universalism (for strong materialists).[77] Yet where Dennett's chief goal is descriptive (an empirical theory that reduces the "manifest" mind to "scientific" laws), the strong materialist's chief goal is normative (the replacement of a politics based on the "fantasy of human exceptionalism," to cite Donna Haraway, with a "materially entangled ethics and politics" based on "agential realism").[78]

The story I tell in this book suggests how far afield posthuman accounts turn out to be from the most influential ideas in the last generation.[79] This distance is, however, a function not of the devastating sharpness of strong materialism's cutting edge (as some practitioners would no doubt like to imagine) but of its belated commitment to an essentially derelict determinism. This book takes note of the drifting apart and convergence of neoliberalism and neo-idealism to reveal a landscape of the present intractable to the sort of critique we find in the regnant accounts of neoliberalism.[80] When a Bush aide in 2004 distinguished "the reality-based community" from "history's actors" who "create [their] own reality," he (probably Karl Rove, who denies the attribution) spelled out the self-creative implications of a neo-idealism that has been going strong since the seventies. And he could as easily have been citing John Rawls as the Maharishi Mahesh Yogi.[81] When strong materialism dismisses the power of the person in favor of a range of nonhuman actants and networks of force, it ignores the real effects exercised by that power, however fictive it might seem.

It so happens that fiction afforded seventies thinkers a robust pathway for the modeling of neo-idealist concepts. Consider Paddy Chayefsky's *Altered States* (1978), a curio from the tail end of the decade that exemplifies the era's confounding of popular and fringe pursuits. Despite or perhaps because of its far-fetched plot, *Altered States* rather precisely sums up crucial aspects of the seventies fixation on consciousness, as if it were a documentary rather than a somewhat expendable exercise in science fiction. The source material for Chayefsky's novel, which was never intended as more than a rough draft for the 1980 film of the same name, was the career of John C. Lilly, who began experimenting on sensory deprivation tanks at the end of the fifties. In *The Scientist*, Lilly calls the "isolation tank" an "essential tool for . . . respite from external reality" (3), and maintained a lifelong commitment to the view that "from the tank came a new appreciation of the depth within the human mind unfathomed by previous methods of research" (107). Lilly conceived his isolation tank as a scientific experiment in—or more precisely, a control environment for—perfect individuation, a kind of clean room for the discrete human psyche: "a person isolated from his own society was likely to know the same freedom . . . from the usual experiences of the consensus reality that the scientist had found in the tank" (104).

Chayefsky's Ed Jessup, a psychologist intent on "looking at his own brain" and "moving into the grayish masses of thundering neurons," spends long hours in an isolation tank to prove the Lilly-like hypothesis that "depriving a man of external stimuli simply triggered a whole new set of internal stimuli."[82] Positioning himself in "reaction against the establishment psychology of the times" (11), whose proponents "study the behavior of men" rather than "the mind" (19), Jessup thus treats the isolation tank as proof that behavior and other practical, material, or environmental overlays on the human subject are red herrings throwing us off from the recognition of "consciousness as a cosmic, perhaps *the* cosmic force" (147). "Matter, energy, our whole universe, are not absolutes," Jessup concludes. "They are all fictions of human consciousness" (176), "postulates of the conscious mind" (107). It follows for Jessup that in a world where "consciousness" is "the principal force" (170), synonymous with "creation" (151), "manipulation of consciousness" leads inevitably to "the alteration of matter" (101).

Chayefsky's novel is as full-throated a defense of the primacy of consciousness as one is likely to find in the annals of the neo-idealist seventies. It is worth outlining some features of that defense as they touch upon central concerns of the book in front of you. Perhaps the novel's most curious conceit is its conferring of academic prestige on its protagonist. Unlike his real-world pattern John Lilly, who abandoned the university for various self-funded experimental ventures in the slackly regulated Virgin Islands, Ed Jessup is a tenured professor at Harvard. And unlike the poseurs "weekending at est or meditating for forty minutes a day or squatting on floors in a communal OM or locking arms in quasi-Sufi dances or stripping off the deceptions of civilized life and jumping naked into a swimming pool filled with other naked searchers for self" (44), Jessup's resolutely scientific method takes the search *seriously*. His quest for "a quantifiable methodology for studying interior experiences" (8) is backed by generous grants from the National Science Foundation and carried out under the auspices of the world's richest university. At the apex of the prestige system, his eyes squarely on a Nobel Prize, and hailed as "absolutely brilliant" (8) by everyone around him, Jessup embodies the Raëlians' geniocratic ideal. Meanwhile, he insists on his steadfast maintenance of "rational awareness" (4) in the face of increasingly bizarre or simply nonsensical claims on consciousness (such as his vaguely panpsychist attempt to "localize . . . consciousness in one tissue, in one cell even" [135]). Despite his professed zeal for laboratory rigor, Jessup's account of consciousness is *all over the place*, mimicking the "liberate[d] energies" that Roszak ascribes to mind in *Unfinished Animal*.

Considering the circumstances in which Jessup finds himself, a Hirschman-style "exit" is scarcely possible. The isolation tank affords the next best thing—a "structure" for "solitariness" (93), a "moment of total centeredness" (13) that simulates the desired gap between his individuality and an institutional world from whose rewards he can scarcely demur. Jessup's inner journey—what Lilly calls "brain-voyaging" (3)—finds him, in the novel's most outlandish twist, reverting to a proto-hominin after using the tank to unlock the "millions and millions of years stored away in that computer bank we call our minds" (108). Even as it recalls the storylines of naturalist novels like *Vandover and the Brute* (1914), Jessup's atavism would have been familiar to any seventies observer acquainted with the reappraisal of primeval lifestyles in, say, Marshall Sahlins's *Stone Age Economics* (1972). Chapter 2 demonstrates that Chayefsky had ample precedent for grounding Jessup's access to his "first self" (44) in the prehistoric record. If, as Jessup claims, "consciousness was not a noumenal or a spiritual process" but "phenomenologically available" (143), its knowability began with a reconstruction of the Stone Age mind. It is no accident that Jessup's wife studies "the comparative cranial capacities of hominids and primates" (20). Yet as we shall have occasion to observe in the next chapter, Jessup's shape-shifting also captures the most paradoxical feature of seventies neo-idealism, in which the insistence on the mind as a place that can be explored with the tools of physical science is matched by a fantasy of disembodiment. Lilly, who identifies human beings as "biocomputers" (130), typifies the dualism that Searle attributes to the computational theory of mind. "Disconnecting him from his body" and "isolating him within his cortex," the isolation tank permits Lilly "to compute and to generate any inner reality he chooses" (130).

It is arguable that the most salient aspect of Chayefsky's novel has less to do with anything in its plot than with its status as an artifact of a time that entertained somewhat extravagant expectations about the mass marketing of consciousness-raising. While neither the novel nor the film that followed was a commercial success, the project was treated by its corporate shepherds as a potential successor to blockbusters like *Close Encounters of the Third Kind* (1976) and *Star Wars* (1977). In what seems in retrospect a rather optimistic gamble on its bankability, the head of Columbia Pictures met Chayefsky's million-dollar fee for the script.[83] But the movie turned out to be a box office (as well as critical) disaster, enduring more as a cautionary tale of Hollywood sausage-making and creative egos gone awry than as a work of cinematic art. After falling out with its director Ken Russell, Chayefsky would end up removing his name from the film.[84] Even Lilly was disappointed. A manufacturer with which he had partnered nursed dashed hopes for a retail boom in isolation tanks on the strength of the film's impending notoriety. The spirit of opportunism hovered all around the "property," as Hollywood types call screenplays. Chayefsky himself—who scorned fiction as a lesser genre than drama—wrote the novel merely to bump up his payday on the film version.[85] We can nonetheless draw a helpful lesson from Chayefsky's bid for quick success by noting what, from our vantage, might seem its rather implausible route: a would-be blockbuster about a Harvard professor who spends a third of the movie in a sensory deprivation tank. That such a path would even occur to a writer of commercial entertainment reminds us of the caveat I raised earlier about the difficulty of assigning some seventies concerns to a fringe and others to a mainstream role in the culture of the decade, a time after all when entrepreneurs imagined that "relaxation tanks" might become as ubiquitous in American homes as microwaves.[86]

Taking a cue from *Altered States*, with its blithe mixing of high theory and low genre, the following chapters shuttle between academic discourses and works of the imagination without attending overmuch to fine discriminations of form or paying heed to obvious distinctions in analytic and literary protocols. While such indifference is a staple of New Historicist technique, it continues to sit poorly with a number of critics, who have long argued that the technique earns its diagnostic power at the cost of literary specificity. New

Historicism finds it hard to make room for literary autonomy when it conceives of literary texts as (at best) subordinate or (at worst) incidental to historical contexts. Even if it has become a cliché, this charge against New Historicism is no less forceful now than it was twenty or thirty years ago.[87] When they have defended against it, the technique's practitioners have fallen back on justifications that reproduce the method's implicit commitment to thematic criticism. Ideas in a culture apply to literary texts, which in turn articulate those ideas in either subtle or unsubtle, direct or indirect ways.

New Historicism, the accusation goes, treats literature as history's parasite. Is it any wonder that two of the most important New Historicists of the first generation have seemed anxious in their more recent work to distance themselves from the hazards of thematization through a return to form and style? The latter is the primary subject of D. A. Miller's *Jane Austen, or The Secret of Style* (2005), which affords both a master class in what Frances Ferguson calls "too-close reading"[88] and a polemic aimed at the very critics Miller himself has schooled in "the *esprit de géométrie*, more familiarly known as theory," and for whom "the paradigm" is "the only object of their peremptory, poverty-stricken desire."[89] Then, too, in *The Beauty of a Social Problem* (2015), Walter Benn Michaels attends to a set of artists whose "new commitment to form and meaning as technologies of autonomy" is very hard to separate from his own late-in-life conversion to a method that plumbs the formal intricacies of artworks with an eye to how their aesthetics might yield "political meaning."[90]

The approach I take differs from these models even as it cares deeply about categories like "formal autonomy," which no scholar of pop Kantianism or neo-idealism could overlook. Yet let us first observe that however forceful the critique of New Historicism has been, its effect in the profession has been to obscure the degree to which that method has never really abandoned form for context.[91] (Indeed, the critical power of Miller's and Michaels's work has always ensued from a rigorous if heretofore implicit attention to form.) In this book, I scarcely ignore the fact that discrete discourses are often with good reason fenced off from one another. Awareness of such boundaries is the enabling condition of the interpretations that follow. We can't know how philosophy of mind and moral philosophy are alike in their concerns, for example, unless we begin with the acknowledgment that these are highly distinct registers in the discipline of philosophy. And we certainly cannot find it interesting that political philosophy has something in common with science fiction, or that rational choice economics has affinities with postmodern poetry, if we do not start with a strong sense of their separateness.

So too with various literary brow levels, although here stable discriminations are less easy to discern. While I tend to mingle genres throughout this book in a way that appears to deflect recognition of cultural hierarchies, I do so (as I have noted) to question our assumptions about categories like the subcultural or fringe. Science fiction is often understood as a "popular" genre, for example, but this is something of a misnomer (a conclusion we might observe by simply looking at the failure of Chayevsky's "popular" text, whether as novel or film, to achieve popularity). In the case of Philip Dick, "popular" tends to signify *nonliterary*, to announce that the handful of people who read Dick's novels in his lifetime did so for pleasure of a vaguely debased sort, at least compared to the edifications of the literary seminar. But Dick never made the best seller list. In fact I discuss a number of best sellers in the following pages, like *The World According to Garp* (1978) and *The Clan of the Cave Bear* (1980). That these books are scarcely read today, and certainly not by critics, while Dick is as much a fixture on the contemporary literature syllabus as Toni Morrison, makes it hard to squeeze much meaning out of the term "popular." While it is not an explicit argument of this book, it is safe to say that a novel like *Do Androids Dream of Electric Sheep?* (1968) finds its way into college classrooms, just as Dick's work in general has been the subject of countless adaptations, because he himself brilliantly voices a set of neo-idealist positions that resonate into our present.

Considering that I canvass a good deal of territory beyond the literary, it is best to be as clear as possible about how I understand the fit of imaginative literature to the history of ideas developed in this book. In some instances, that fit is fairly straightforward. The compatibility of the libertarian imagination with science fiction is a given of libertarian thought. "Seeking an art form to express the horror potential of the State and extrapolate the many possibilities of liberty," Samuel Konkin writes in *New Libertarian Manifesto* (1980), "libertarianism found Science Fiction already in the field."[92] And much environmental literature of the seventies is self-consciously *"engazhay,"* to use Nabokov's delicious word for those "document[s]" prized "In English Lit" for having the correct politics.[93] Which is only to say that novels like Ernest Callenbach's *Ecotopia* (1975) and Edward Abbey's *The Monkey Wrench Gang* (1975) aimed to bring about in at least some of their readers a passion for ecological activism—an aim at which both succeeded. In these cases, the fit between the discourses feels quite snug. Abbey was not only a radical ecologist but the author of ecological fiction.

Most of the cases I detail in this book's dual literary and intellectual history cannot be justified by serendipities of biography. And such cases oblige us to understand the interplay of literary and nonliterary discourses by means of a different justification—one implicit in the instances of science fiction and ecological fiction, which do their performative work by consciousness-raising, world-building, and utopian imagining. Many nonliterary thinkers in the period analogized literature's creative powers to the neo-idealist potential for self-creation, to the possibilities latent in what Rawls calls "constructivism." Some of the period's most memorable philosophical arguments derive from thought experiments with science-fictional premises, as chapter 1 makes plain. Nozick, who authored one of the most influential of these experiments, explicitly correlates fiction and philosophical reflection when he asks his reader to "compare the thinness of the social scientists' description of man to that of the novelists," as though literature alone provided an account of personhood rich enough for philosophical interest.[94]

In *Literary Interest* (1993), a critique of context-driven literary analysis, Steven Knapp defines his titular subject as what "offers an unusually precise and concentrated analogue of what it is like to be an agent in general," "an unusually pure experience of what liberal agency, for better or worse, is like."[95] Literary texts, for philosophers like Nozick and philosophically minded critics like Knapp, make us human, or rather make us feel what being human "is like." My tactic is not to situate literature as the secretly privileged discourse of philosophy or any other discipline, however, but to trace the symbiosis between modes of thought that all take a heightened interest in mindedness in the period. As chapter 3 argues, writers who embrace the cause of the seventies cult are drawn to the parallel between the religious and the novelistic imagination as sites of consciousness expansion. Even if William S. Burroughs produces a very different response to that parallel from Don DeLillo's, both novelists see the cult as harboring certain possibilities for "liberation" that the anticult panic of the seventies by and large obscured, with the consequence that we miss something important in the history of the present not only by getting the cult wrong but also by failing to take account of how novels like Burroughs's *Cities of the Red Night* (1980) and DeLillo's *The Names* (1982) get the cult "right."

Many of the period's philosophers and social and political thinkers appealed to literature's allegedly special relation to the representation of consciousness as a way of asserting the latter's primacy. Yet more intriguing is the fact that literature itself, understood as the production of imaginary worlds, came to stand in a special relation to consciousness as such. Literature on this view both represents and enacts mindedness.[96] This is how we might account for the presence in this book of James Merrill. As a poet studiously engaged in distancing himself from a profane worldliness, Merrill turns out in surprising ways to *embody* that worldliness, if we understand that term to mean—as I argue it does in the framework of the seventies—a commitment to subjectivity as a kind of sovereignty. Merrill's otherworldly epic, *The Changing Light at Sandover* (1982), which purports to transcribe a cosmology (and eschatology) of the human race based on conversations with the spirits in Merrill's head, is in its imaginative reach (no less than in its profoundly antisocial impulses) a poem whose composition makes the clearest sense in the context of seventies neo-idealism, with its vigorous bid for internalism and its dream of abstracting the individual from the social manifold.

To frame Merrill's poem in this way is to rouse the specter of another problematic feature of the New Historicism: its claustrophobia-inducing penchant for folding the most seemingly autonomous literary work in the suffocating embrace of its historical moment, for subsuming all postures of transcendence under what Miller calls "the paradigm." The sorriest implication of this gesture is its nullification of the political value of literary texts. In the proverbial formula, every aspirant to subversion will end by being contained. Some moments in the following pages might lead a reader to fault my analysis for just such a pessimistic outlook. So it is again best to be clear about what I take to be at stake in this book's often corrosive scrutiny of ideas like justice as fairness and movements like radical ecology. It would be a great failing were a reader to deduce from my analysis of the strain of seventies ecology I take up that we should abandon the project of environmentalism. And it would be just as unfortunate were a reader to mistake my critique of Rawls for an effort to repudiate the project of economic equality. Neither conclusion is meant to follow from what I argue.

Indeed, my critical genealogies of radical ecology and antiutilitarianism are occasioned by my sense that environmental action and economic justice are the most pressing causes on the globe. By drawing attention in chapter 2 to their highly selective brand of communitarianism and their virtually nihilistic individualism, I show how advocates of the paleo-republic fall short of the ecological ideal, and thus hope to introduce to ecocriticism a wariness toward a seventies Malthusianism that still influences many environmental thinkers. By the same token, I seek to show how the forswearing of "system," "environment," and "context" by Rawls and other antiutilitarians in the period runs counter to the goal of economic equality, particularly when ameliorative social programs collapse as a result of the rejection of "teleological" principles that antiutilitarians treat as coercive or paternalistic.[97] The Rawlsian version of liberal ethics, with its insistence on personal dignity, helps furnish the veneer behind which antistatists have sought to camouflage their own less savory commitment to rolling back the meager but precious advances of Great Society welfarism. If Rawls charges utilitarianism with an impermissible willingness to sacrifice the one for the many, conservative think-tankers and policymakers do not scruple to sacrifice whole socioeconomic classes to the preferences of elite singletons.

It is important again to be as clear as possible. My aim is not to impeach Rawls in particular or antiutilitarianism in general for having provided aid and comfort to the enemy. It was scarcely Rawls's intent that a Kantian contractualism designed to serve the cause of justice has also become amenable to a neoliberalism that fetishizes contract. Rather, it is precisely because I am impressed by the strength of the philosophical case for subjectivity that I pursue its repercussions through the end of the American century. But to grasp those repercussions obliges us to borrow yet one more stratagem from the New Historicist arsenal, which is that method's attitude toward the vagaries of history, its conviction that interpretive interest lies in the counterintuitive. My method here is to pursue the unanticipated consequences, cunning ellipticals, and untoward misappropriations to which influential ideas and prevailing ideologies are liable. I return to these matters in more detail in the book's conclusion. There, I examine the afterlife of neo-idealism and clarify my own stance on questions of social justice, utilitarian ethics, and the nearly universal repudiation of statism in our time. But before we can reach those considerations, we must first trace the sinuous routes of neo-idealism.

Chapter 1

Artificial Intelligence and the Rise of the Meritocracy

Test Subjects

The most famous set piece in *Anarchy, State, and Utopia* is the "experience machine" Robert Nozick devises to contest utilitarianism's disregard for "sovereign individuals."[1] While promising "to give you any experience you desired," the machine deprives you of what no system, however benevolent, can deliver: the ability "to be a certain sort of person" and to have "actual contact with . . . deeper reality" (43). "We learn that something matters to us in addition to experience," according to Nozick, "by imagining an experience machine and then realizing that we would not use it" (44). That "something" is "the fact of our separate existences" (33), which Nozick sees as irreducible "to a world no deeper or more important than that which people can construct" (43). Nozick takes issue not with the construction but with the hypostatizing of society. If the "process" whereby "worlds are created, people leave them, create new worlds, and so on" (299) is crucial to "utopian experimentation" (306), the utilitarian version of the world thwarts this capacity for human flourishing with its "disturbing" interest in the "living of our lives for us" (44). Utilitarians who "talk of an overall social good," ignoring the fact that "there are only individual people" (33), would thus not hesitate to automate the good life even if it means reducing the person to "an indeterminate blob" "floating in a tank" (43).

Nozick's mainstreaming of late twentieth-century libertarianism gained a valuable assist from his conclusion that no one would buy the product the utilitarian is selling. "Plugging into the machine," he concludes, "is a kind of suicide" (43). But the terms of his critique already enjoyed a certain notoriety by the time his celebrated book appeared.[2] A precursor to the experience machine can be found in the 1970 essay "The Self and the Future," in which Bernard Williams reasons that "if . . . being attached to a machine would provide one for the rest of one's existence with an unending sequence of delicious and varied experiences, one might very well reject the option" because these serial delights would come at the cost of self-identity.[3] Then, too, Ursula Le Guin's *The Lathe of Heaven* (1971) imagines something like a reverse experience machine meant to yield the same outcome as Nozick's—a refutation of the value hierarchy that places society ahead of individuals. Because George Orr's dreams can change reality, his psychiatrist Dr. Haber (the head of "Human Utility") hooks him up to an "Augmentor" that programs Orr's dreams to deliver his preferred outcomes.[4] Joining an upbeat utilitarianism to an overconfident behaviorism, Haber sees "the reduction of human misery" (147) as "purely a matter of the right conditioning" (163). Orr plugs into the machine not to take in gratifying experiences but to transmit Haber's ideal visions to the world at large. Yet the programmed changes are disastrous. Plague ends overpopulation; world peace leads to alien invasion. Haber blames these fiascoes on Orr's normalcy; a "battery of tests" proves him "so sane as to be an anomaly" (137). Such banal sanity prevails over the mad scientist's ruinous interventions.

Though *The Lathe of Heaven* ends with the world nearly restored to its former imperfections, Orr's dreamwork leaves one especially telling remainder. Heather, the African-American attorney with whom Orr has fallen in love in a prior reality, appears in the book's last world as a "legal secretary" (182). Reversion to the status quo entails a marked demotion for the black female lawyer down the meritocratic ladder. And lest it seem merely contrarian to couple the feminist science fiction writer with the libertarian theorist, we need only consider her 1974 masterpiece, *The Dispossessed*, to see that Le Guin could take an even harder line than Nozick in defending the inviolateness of persons from "the most vile kind of . . . utilitarianism."[5] *The Dispossessed* charts the physicist Shevek's plan to recover the planet Anarres's "libertarian tradition" (342). Despite Anarres's settlement by followers of the anarchist philosopher Odo, who made them "aware that . . . centralization was a lasting threat" (96), "the social conscience" so "dominates the individual conscience" (330) that Odonians no longer believe in the "idea of freedom" (345) but instead in the idea, central to utilitarianism descending from Jeremy Bentham, that it is "right to count people like you count numbers" (312). "If we must all agree," Shevek notes in pitting Odonian anarchism against submersion in groupthink, "we're no better than a machine" (359). "Freedom" means "recognition of each person's solitude" (106).⁶

Pairing Le Guin's dystopian vision of utilitarianism run amok with Nozick's utopian defense of the libertarianism that will defeat it allows us to see the reach of the antiutilitarian turn around 1970. We can also register one of that turn's most important features: its embrace of an intrinsic subjectivity that relied on assumptions about individual distinctness that mental testing appeared to confirm and that behaviorism appeared to deny. That Le Guin and Nozick exalt human singularity by calling on the number-crunching science of psychometrics seems paradoxical, but the move has a clear logic in both writers. *The Lathe of Heaven* treats Orr's statistical averageness as the measure of his world-preserving uniqueness, making his status as "the man in the middle of the graph" (138) a mark of distinction. Embodying the "sovereign[ty]" Nozick prizes, Orr's perch atop the bell curve amounts to a kind of throne: "He was the strongest person she had ever known," according to Heather, "because he could not be moved away from the center" (91). Orr's obdurate mind undoes Haber's equation of "the properly trained brain" (145) and socially beneficial advances. Nozick meanwhile enlists mental testing to indict those "principles of distributive justice" that "institute (partial) ownership by others of people and their actions" (172). It helps to recall that *Anarchy, State, and Utopia*'s chief target was John Rawls's *A Theory of Justice* (1971), which itself targeted what Rawls saw as "the dominant utilitarianism of the tradition."⁷ Nozick chides Rawls for "attributing *everything* noteworthy about the person completely to certain sorts of 'external' factors" (214). On Nozick's view, Rawls looks more like a behaviorist than a Kantian. Citing "Richard Herrnstein's discussion of the genetic factors in a society's pattern of class stratification" (20), Nozick argues that Rawls's defense of "human dignity" (214) has no traction absent a defense of "people's abilities" even if such "natural assets" (228) lead to inequality.

Herrnstein's *IQ in the Meritocracy* (1973) claimed that the Great Society's answers to social ills were powerless to thwart the birthright of different class and racial groups. Herrnstein himself insisted on the surprisingly direct route from behavioral psychology to the world of Head Start programs and black female lawyers.⁸ "Mental testing," he writes, "has not waxed and waned with the prevailing dogma" of "unrestrained environmentalism."⁹ That "dogma" was identified with Herrnstein's (and Nozick's) Harvard colleague, B. F. Skinner, who routinely derived political precepts from behaviorist ones.¹⁰ "The test score itself" (8) helps Herrnstein unravel the "egalitarian orthodoxy" (11) behaviorism cherishes: "the belief," as Arthur Jensen put it in "How Much Can

We Boost IQ and Scholastic Achievement?" (1969), "in the almost infinite plasticity of intellect."[11] These scientists replaced the behaviorist's "plasticity" with a fatalism more congenial to conservativism. "The connection between social position and genetic inheritance," Herrnstein hastens to point out, "cannot be legislated out of existence by any extant, or even any plausible, social reform" (14). This view would later receive a far more famous defense in *The Bell Curve*, the 1994 book Herrnstein coauthored with Charles Murray.

Yet however revanchist their politics, Herrnstein and Jensen were in the vanguard of psychology's shift from behaviorism to its embrace of what Jensen calls "biological reality" in the closing decades of the twentieth century.[12] The repeal of behaviorism began in the fifties through the influential example of Noam Chomsky, whose defense of "inborn structures" helped launch the cognitive revolution.[13] This swing paralleled the rejection of behaviorist theory by a significant contingent of the period's philosophers, particularly those who critiqued the materialist account of mind because it omitted what John Searle calls "first-person ontology" from its explanations.[14] For these thinkers, philosophy of mind had been overtaken by various materialisms that explained away subjectivity by relegating it to neurophysical reduction or treating it as an epiphenomenal spin-off of the brain's operating system. The reassertion of subjectivity among some philosophers of mind bore directly on the antiutilitarian turn not least because critics of materialism were frequently opponents of utilitarian ethics—a theory that also appeared to eliminate the fact of subjectivity from its calculations.

Although the rejection of behaviorism is well attested among recent philosophers, less recognized is the degree to which this rejection often accompanies a denial of utilitarian reasoning.[15] In the sixties, Charles Taylor—a prime mover in the neo-idealist revival—embarked on an influential critique of behaviorist psychology, whose quest for physical laws he construed as an instance of "the ideology of scientism."[16] Later, in *Sources of the Self* (1992), he would include utilitarianism alongside the "reductive views" of a "naturalist philosophy" that purges "qualitative distinctions" from the "ontology of the human."[17] The common failing of discourses of "scientism" is their misguided effort to "prescind . . . anthropocentric properties" (69) from endeavors like psychology or ethics. For Taylor, the fact that it takes "our motives as homogeneous" (83) reveals how "threatening the utilitarian outlook is" (340). Its singleminded "search for happiness," he writes, "can lead to appalling destruction in a society's way of life"; everything from "the Poor Law Act of 1834 to the catastrophe at Chernobyl" can be attributed to its "refusal to define any goods other than the official one of instrumental efficacy" (340).[18]

Such claims point to the links I'm interested in developing across domains of thought with seemingly little in common. As my coupling of Le Guin and Nozick suggests, I argue that philosophers and New Wave science fiction writers in particular converged on the view that utilitarianism repeatedly played out the hazards of "appalling destruction" Taylor discovers in policies of statist overreach. Both camps filtered that judgment through the critique of what was until recently cognitive science's regnant account of mind: the computational theory, or what John Searle dubbed "Strong AI" (artificial intelligence) in the 1980 essay "Minds, Brains, and Programs."[19] My aim is not to identify philosophers with science fiction writers but to reveal their mutual interest in an account of subjectivity with many adherents in the post-sixties milieu. And in any event, from one angle there is nothing strange about these bedfellows. Though sci-fi writers hardly trouble themselves over Kantian constructivism or the debate between act- and rule-utilitarians, it is undeniable that science fiction invents worlds in which Strong AI is *true*.

Originating in Alan Turing's 1950 essay "Computing Machinery and Intelligence," Strong AI holds that human minds are computer programs lodged in the hardware of the brain and thus that, by the transitive property, "computers given the right programs," as Searle puts it, "can be literally said to understand and have other cognitive states" ("MBP," 417). For Turing, any proof of such cognition was to be gleaned from his eponymous test, which he called "the imitation game."[20] Through a teletype device, a human examiner quizzes a human and machine (both hidden from view) to detect which is the real person, and the machine's score is the percentage of tests in which it fools the questioner. Searle's essay aims to show the impossibility of Strong AI by placing its author in the role of a Turing machine. His premise is that even a perfect score on the test would not evince intelligence. Searle imagines himself "locked in a room and given a large batch of Chinese writing" ("MBP," 417) along with English instructions. Though the ideograms are "meaningless squiggles" to him, the instructions allow him to pair different "squiggles" ("MBP," 418) and thus to send from the room those that provide correct answers to questions while having no idea what the questions or answers are. Likening his task to a computer sorting symbols, Searle concludes that the computer has no more understanding of what is asked of it than he has of Chinese, despite passing a Turing test in the language. This is because the program has "syntax" but no "semantics" ("MBP," 420), the actual content of thought. Proponents of the "systems reply" ("the standard argument against the Chinese Room"[21]) by contrast claim that "while a person doesn't understand Chinese, somehow the *conjunction* of that person and bits of paper might understand Chinese." This is a view only those "in the grip of an ideology," Searle writes, "would find . . . plausible" ("MBP," 419).

Searle's name for that ideology is "behaviorism" ("MBP," 423), and his impeachment of Strong AI reveals much about behaviorism's staying power as a shame word well beyond the moment the method itself fell into disrepair. Like the IQ innatists, Searle is frequently on the lookout for signs of a lingering behaviorism. Even a professedly nativist account like the computational theory of mind can thus appear to backslide into behaviorist dogma based on its allegiance to the surface trappings of *system*, synonymous with the IQ innatists' "environment." What Searle's assault on Strong AI shares with the IQ innatists' assault on public policy is the claim that no program will increase the mental prowess of persons or machines whose capacities are fixed by physical laws. For IQ innatists, the social engineer's leveling fantasy bespeaks a quest for artificial intelligence as doomed as the one Searle finds in cognitive science. Pointing to the failure of "compensatory efforts" to bridge the postwar schoolroom's class divides, Nixon adviser Edward Banfield concluded in *The Unheavenly City* (1970) that "even the most comprehensive programs have yielded little or no measurable benefit" with regard to "IQ score."[22] Compare Banfield's verdict to that of Hubert Dreyfus's *What Computers Can't Do* (1972), which chronicled the "failure" of AI researchers to make "any predicted progress" in machine intelligence despite their own well-funded programs.[23] Unlike Nozick's experience machine, which no one is apparently gullible enough to purchase, by the seventies "intelligent" machines filled Strong AI's institutional investors with buyer's remorse.[24]

Both Dreyfus and Searle see Strong AI as pledged to what Dreyfus calls "the general swing from behaviorism to mentalism in psychology" (76) while secretly keeping faith with precepts that are "unashamedly . . . behavioristic" ("MBP," 423). That at least is how Searle describes Alan Turing's 1950 essay. Like those behaviorists condemned by Herrnstein and Jensen for proceeding as if society were a laboratory that could synthesize native endowments, Turing aimed to dislocate intelligence from the cogito to the world at large. Between teletype device, examiner, and subjects, or so the Turing test hopes to convince us, intelligence manifests as an atmospheric effect across a range of linked entities irreducible to the human mind. When pressed "to give a definition of thinking" in a 1952 roundtable, Turing confessed himself "unable to say anything more about it than that it was a sort of buzzing that went on inside my head" (*ET*, 494). Turing asks not "What is consciousness?" but "Where is it?"

No philosopher has more fully leaned in to Strong AI's context-driven account of mind than Daniel Dennett. In "Where Am I?" (1978), his fable about having a "spare brain," Dennett's answer to the Turing-style title question is that consciousness is a kind of phantom limb within a "functional structure" whose parts are "prosthetic[s]" completing one another.[25] Dennett has also proved a tireless defender of Strong AI's systems reply. In *Content and Consciousness* (1969), he calls mind an "intentional system";[26] in *Consciousness Explained* (1991), he calls mind a set of "control functions" in a "connectionist system."[27] The "content" of consciousness is the "multitude of switching elements" (*CC*, 59) in the brain itself, rather than what "identity theorists" like D. M. Armstrong believe: "mental states are purely physical states of the central nervous system."[28] Identity theory is "wrong" (*CC*, 6), says Dennett, because it posits the mind as an organ whose phenomenal contents (wishes, beliefs) need to be reconciled with biological facts. For Dennett, there is no "ontic bulge" (*CC*, 5) to fear because "there is no respectable motivation for believing" (*CE*, 406) in phenomenal consciousness to begin with. "We are . . . composed of robots," he writes, "and all the intentionality we enjoy is derived from the more fundamental intentionality of these billions of crude intentional systems."[29]

Dennett argues contra Searle that because our minds are already systems of robots, the systems reply must be valid. In Samuel Delany's *Babel-17* (1966), the novel that made his reputation, we find a similar effort to dispense with Searlean objections to Strong AI in terms that prefigure Dennett's dismissal of the "anthropocentric prejudice" (*CE*, 448) he finds in the philosophical insistence on "first-person point of view" (*CE*, 336). Delany's novel sanctions the Turing test by flipping its terms. Whereas Turing thought the challenge was to show how a processor could simulate human mental states with the right inputs, Delany's novel (like Dennett's concept of mind) takes for granted that the computer is the template for cognition. Because humans start off as thinking computers, Babel-17, a linguistic weapon in a galactic war, is less language than software, "a flexible matrix of analytical possibilities" not acquired by users so much as implemented in them.[30] Babel-17 allows its makers to "get one mind into another head" (198), to "program a . . . personality into the mind of whoever learns it" (220).

In Delany as in Dennett, thinking consists of interactions affording the mirage of depth.[31] Like Dennett, Delany treats mental life as a fiction we tell ourselves: "thought is information" (23) from out there that we mistake for reflection in what Dennett calls "the inner Cartesian theater."[32] "The self," Dennett writes, is just "the Center of Narrative Gravity" (*CE*, 431), the "product" rather than "source" of "a narrative-spinning human body" telling "tales" of the person as a "unified agent" (*CE*, 418). *Babel-17* dispenses with this illusion. "*There were no words in your mind*" (184) because there is no "inner" identity: "What self? There was no 'I'" (181). Delany's novel owes its account of language to the Sapir-Whorf hypothesis. This now discredited theory holds that, as Steven Pinker puts it, "the language people speak controls how they think."[33] Or to cite Delany's protagonist, the poet-linguist Rydra Wong: "Most textbooks say language is a mechanism for expressing thought. But language *is* thought" (23). And befitting its source in the "unashamedly behavioristic" Sapir-Whorf hypothesis, which deletes subjectivity from the mind's determinations, Babel-17 too has "no word for 'I'" (139).

Its omission of first-person pronouns nonetheless gives Babel-17 an inherent advantage over the "clums[iness]" of "any other tongue" (221). Clearing away the mistake of first-person point of view is key to Babel-17's "amazing... form," a supremely efficient "grammar and vocabulary" ("the most analytically exact imaginable" [221]) that answers, by annulling, Searle's charge that the computer program has no semantic understanding absent a point of view. "Since everything ... in the language is 'right'" (221), understanding is automatic—or irrelevant. Even if "the brain wants [I] to exist" (167), Babel-17 treats that desire as an obstacle to true open-mindedness as well as to the political inclusiveness that would become a signature theme of Delany's later work. Along with "discorporates" (dead people whose "thinking ability can be tapped if anyone wants it" [48]), the novel features an ecumenical cast of posthuman polymorphs. Unlike its Old Testament namesake, Babel-17 engenders "compatibility" among "species of galaxy-hopping life forms, each as widespread as our own, each as technically intelligent" (165). Real communication becomes possible once first-person ontology is not.

Babel-17's disavowal of subjectivity puts the novel in dialogue with an array of efforts to politicize Strong AI on behalf of a more commodious view of personhood, a view rooted in Turing's sense of the possibilities of machine intelligence. As we'll see, one such account comes from Dennett, who has long decried "the introspective trap" (*CC*, 149) that began to snare some of his colleagues around 1970, when philosophy took a renewed interest in subjectivity in both moral theory and philosophy of mind.[34] Utilitarianism's critics in particular pitted Kantian ethics against what they understood as a materialism even more vulgar than Dennett's. Thus Rawls assails the utilitarian's belief "that a just and good society must wait upon a high material standard of life" (290). Together with its view of persons not as "separate" but as "fused" into "one coherent system of desire," utilitarianism's commitment to functional results makes it a sort of systems reply for ethical life. Since "individuals are thought of as so many different lines along which rights and duties are to be assigned," Rawls argues, the only "correct decision" the utilitarian feels compelled to make "is essentially a question of efficient administration" (24). In "Morality and Pessimism" (1972), Stuart Hampshire treats utilitarianism's "computational morality" as a species of operant conditioning, "a kind of psychical engineering" designed "to induce desired or valued states of mind": "men might be trained . . . with a view to their experiencing the kinds of feeling that alone lend value to their morally neutral surroundings."[35] Hence while "utilitarian philosophy was until quite recently a constant support for progressive social policies," Hampshire concludes, "it is now an obstruction."[36]

Taking up the charge that it shares behaviorism's contempt for introspection, other critics fault utilitarianism for paying too little attention to moral merit. "To base moral judgments or public-policy decisions on utility," writes Thomas Schwartz, "is to attach undue weight to the preferences of those who are mercurial, lustful, greedy, bigoted, earnest, meddlesome, and the like, bringing about unjust allocations of social benefits."[37] Insufficiently attentive to questions of character and overinvested in the mitigation of material wants, utilitarianism can never really attend in Schwartz's view to "the *health* of the intellect."[38] Like Schwartz, Williams indicts utilitarianism for its refusal to acknowledge that "each person has a character," since it prioritizes structures over subjectivity: "As a Utilitarian agent, I am just the representative of the satisfaction system who happens to be near certain causal levers at a certain time."[39] Utilitarians deny that our "reasons for action" are "internal reasons."[40] In "A Critique of Utilitarianism" (1973), Williams mingles his contempt for its externalism with a political condemnation by arguing that utilitarianism values only "states of affairs" that it voids of meaningful agents: "it makes no . . . difference who produces them."[41] Whereas the average person construes "projects" as "central to his life . . . at the deepest level," the utilitarian seeks "to make him a channel between the input of everyone's projects . . . and an output of optimific decision" (116). As a result of such "very different" approaches to "social reality," Williams concludes, "it must surely be that government" by a "utilitarian elite" (139) "is very importantly manipulative" (138).[42] Relatedly, John Elster indicts utilitarianism for construing personal preferences and individual rights as nothing more than useful fictions. "From the rulers' point of view" in a utilitarian society, according to Elster, "the inner states of the subjects . . . *are essentially byproducts.*"[43]

These critics present utilitarianism as if it were as indifferent to first-person ontology in the moral realm as Dennett's account of consciousness is in the philosophy of mind. It is thus notable that Williams's "A Critique of Utilitarianism" appeared in *Utilitarianism: For and Against* (1973) alongside an essay by J.J.C. Smart, who not only stood *for* utilitarianism (in "An Outline of a System of Utilitarian Ethics") but elsewhere defended psychophysical reduction. In a 1971 essay endorsing the identity theory, Smart skirted the issue of subjectivity by arguing that "behavior is epistemologically prior to inner experience."[44]

This is the sort of claim Williams's "Critique" has in view when chiding utilitarianism's "simple-mindedness," its "having too few thoughts . . . to match the world as it really is" (149). Utilitarians like Smart appear to treat moral reasoning as a version of what the AI pioneers Herbert Simon and Allen Newell call "heuristic search," in which cognition is "determined by the demands of [a] task environment."[45] Because they reduce "fairness, gratitude, and fidelity" to "conventions and codes" instead of seeing them as "the basic . . . operations of morality itself," according to David Lyons, utilitarians equate ethical decisions with "performing moves in a game" as opposed to doing the right thing.[46] Aligning such "moves" with the dicta of behaviorism ("the point of . . . rules is to channel behavior so as to promote human welfare most effectively"), Lyons explains the utilitarian's attraction to Skinnerian techniques by noting the frequent slippage in behaviorism from *studying* behavior to *changing* it—a slippage to which Skinner was openly committed.[47]

In utilitarianism and Strong AI, the object of analysis (morality, mentality) appears out of focus because it shrinks from view (reductionism) even as it expands to cover the whole (environmentalism). The absent term in both is subjectivity. Thomas Nagel famously defended "the subjective character of experience" as what cannot be "captured" by materialist arguments of mind in "What Is It Like to Be a Bat?" (1974).[48] "The effort to substitute an objective concept of mind for the real thing," he argues, collapses once "we acknowledge that a physical theory of mind must account for the subjective character of experience" and "that no presently available conception gives us a clue how this could be done" (MQ, 166). Nagel had no less vigorously defended the claims of subjectivity from a *moral* point of view in "War and Massacre" (1972), which pitted an "absolutist" ethic against "the abyss of utilitarian apologetics" that rationalized the US policy of "large-scale murder" in Vietnam (MQ, 57). "Using the easiest available path to some desired goal," according to Nagel, the utilitarian favors "a purely bureaucratic operation" indifferent to "addressing the victim at all" (MQ, 67). The "absolutist" by contrast insists that "whatever one does to another person intentionally must be aimed at him as a subject" (MQ, 66). While utilitarians aspire to become "instruments for the realization of . . . the impersonal standpoint," Nagel writes in *Equality and Partiality* (1991), "the personal standpoint must be taken into account directly in the justification of any ethical system."[49]

For Hubert Dreyfus, a similar omission of "the personal standpoint" hampers AI research. *What Computers Can't Do* takes that field to task for imagining "that the brain or mind performs some sequence of discrete operations" (78) in isolation from the "human form of life from within" (133). Dreyfus likens Simon and Newell's "guided search" (12) model of thinking to the running of a Skinnerian "maze" (24). Since our intelligence consists in being able "to exclude most . . . possibilities without explicit consideration" (21), we are less intent on "trying all possible combinations" (24) through the maze than on skipping it altogether. Calling out its "covertly empirical character" (98), Dreyfus argues that notwithstanding its penchant for *"rules in the mind"* (90), the computational theory is forced back on the "appeal to context" (128). Dreyfus homes in on the externalist fix that has beset Strong AI since Turing, whose view of mind was a busy swirl of formalizing and contextualizing rationales.[50] The belief that "intellectual activity consists mainly of various kinds of search" (*ET*, 431), as Turing concluded in "Intelligent Machinery" (1948), follows from the account of intelligence we have seen in effect in the Turing test. Far from governed by intrinsic laws, thinking must be *verified*, and its proof assumes the form of successful "searches carried out by brains" (*ET*, 431).

Given his view that thinking can never be taken for granted, it is fitting that Turing sought to distill intelligence to the rather specific behavior of *passing a test*. He concluded his 1947 lecture to the London Mathematical Society with a "plea for 'fair play for the machines' when testing their IQ" (*ET*, 394). In a BBC radio lecture five years later, he proposed "a viva-voce examination" to assess whether machines "might be programmed to behave like brains" (*ET*, 484). If Turing presumes that the brain behaves by answering exam questions, it is partly because the circles he moved in after 1945 involved "much talk about IQ tests," according to his biographer Andrew Hodges.[51] The same zeal marked the origin of psychometry in the late nineteenth century, a moment of high enthusiasm for rendering intangible things tangible, whether minds or souls. Indeed, as espoused by the spiritualist Joseph Buchanan in his *Manual of Psychometry* (1885), the titular subject meant the art of divination by touching objects.

Apart from their name, modern psychometrics has little to do with Buchanan's "soul-measuring."[52] Yet while not exactly mystical, psychometrics functions as something of a superstitious faith to which not only Richard Herrnstein and Arthur Jensen but most of us, if only unwittingly, are pledged. It is after all the house specialty of the Educational Testing Service (ETS), the meritocracy's inescapable gatekeeper, whose wares shape millions of destinies while the organization itself remains largely unaccountable.[53] Though some account of merit has accompanied liberal ideology since Locke, only since the mid-twentieth century has the meritocratic appeal, helped greatly by the rise of standardized testing, come into its own as the means employed by rich Western democracies to justify their inequalities. The British Labour stalwart Michael Young's *The Rise of the Meritocracy* (1958) predated by a generation the argument of Herrnstein and Murray, who prophesy in *The Bell Curve* that "the heritability of success is only going to increase" as long as we retain "the ideal of letting every youngster have equal access."[54] In contrast, Young argued that the genetic lottery obliged a just society not to abandon but to fortify egalitarian ideals. His imagined future threatens to reduce subjectivity to quantum: "there was no obligation on anyone to put anything more than his current IQ in his *Who's Who* entry."[55]

Turing, on the other hand, had few misgivings about the power of numbers to confer identity. He finds it safe to "assume" that "half a million digits . . . is equivalent to half a million nerve cells" (*ET*, 500). Such orders of magnitude have long entranced computational theorists.[56] But Turing's faith in the prestige of numbers did not incline him to view them as measures of *social* prestige, and Strong AI's proponents have followed him in inferring from machine intelligence the promise of an enlarged radius of subjectivity. In a 1964 essay on whether robots rate "civil rights," Hilary Putnam advises "extend[ing] our concept so that robots are conscious—for 'discrimination' based on the 'softness' or 'hardness' of the body parts of a synthetic 'organism' seems as silly as discriminatory treatment of humans on the basis of skin color."[57] Worried that "prejudices of a traditional anthropocentric and mentalistic kind would all too likely develop into conservative political attitudes," Putnam forges an unusually strong link (for a philosopher at least) between epistemology and politics. The multiple realizability of mental states yields a "pro-civil-libertarian" vision.[58] This link reappears in Dennett's plea for forsaking "the person" as "the subject of experience" (*B*, 154) on the view that the "concept" is "inescapably normative" (*B*, 285). "Human beings or other entities can only aspire to being approximations of the ideal," he argues, "and there can be no way to set a 'passing grade' that is not arbitrary" (*B*, 285). Like intelligence for Turing, "personhood" for Dennett must be attested, and the "conditions" of its proof are never innocent (*B*, 285).

Magic Numbers

Dennett's reference to "a 'passing grade'" pays tribute to the fact that tests for measuring human rather than artificial intelligence have long functioned as tools of social-Darwinist policies like those found in Young's meritocracy, where "every selection of one is a rejection of many."[59] The mental testing that IQ innatists construed as a defense against environmentalist ideology had, unsurprisingly, a less positive reception in the counterculture (a fact confirmed by Herrnstein's account of his conflict with student radicals, as we shall see). Whereas Herrnstein and Jensen complained that liberals did not take the results of mental testing seriously enough to repeal their social engineering initiatives, radicals targeted psychometrics for affixing mental distinctions in the official record. What is notable about the latter attack is that in certain quarters of the counterculture, the critique of psychometrics takes aim at its serving the interests of a statism, and indeed a welfarism, found no less wanting by science fiction writers like Philip K. Dick and Thomas Disch than by Herrnstein and Jensen.

Dick's *Do Androids Dream of Electric Sheep?* (1968) and *Ubik* (1969) both feature an examiner tasked with running a test to determine the capacities of his respective subjects. In *Androids*, the relevant test helps Rick Deckard tell a person from a robot on the basis of empathic response. In *Ubik*, it is a means to distinguish the psychically gifted from the average Joe (like the tester himself, Joe Chip). And while neither of these is a canonical Turing test, since neither tests for "intelligence" as such, both tests gauge personhood by assigning value and disvalue to those with more or less empathy, more or less ESP. *Ubik*'s test also nods to Turing's interest in the "overwhelming" "evidence . . . for telepathy" (*ET*, 458). The "Argument from Extra-Sensory Perception . . . is to my mind," Turing writes with a conviction we associate with the likes of Joseph Buchanan, "quite a strong one" (*ET*, 453). *Ubik* imagines a world in which Turing's hunch proves correct. Joe Chip's test measures "psionic capabilities" because some people indeed have them.[60] That world is built in fact to the specifications of the systems reply. The sentient appliances and doors in Joe's apartment presuppose the validity of "distributed cognition," the idea that, as Katherine Hayles puts it, "decision-making is distributed between human and nonhuman agents."[61] Rick Deckard's empathy test meanwhile is administered in a world where "intelligence tests hadn't trapped an andy in years."[62] For Dick, there is no question that human beings lack a monopoly on consciousness. Hence the appeal to "empathic response" (119) as the site of the human. Androids can grasp "hollow, formal, intellectual definitions" of things but have no "feeling-sense" for *"actual meaning."* They lack not Searle's "semantics" exactly but something like "emotional awareness" (190).

While the fact that machines really can think makes testing for them difficult in *Androids*, the human-machine split is not the only or even crucial axis along which the novel's society divides. The Terran government employs a "minimum mental faculties test" (18) that serves as a cutoff for human worth. Even the outcast androids scorn "chickenheads" like John Isidore, who has "failed" his "IQ test" (72), as a result of which he is sterilized on behalf of a eugenic maximization of the good. (Note that Dick presents the test itself as pass-fail.) The government also sponsors a state religion, "Mercerism," whose followers worship by plugging into an "empathy box" (21) that blends their feelings with all the other Mercerists who happen to be "fused" (173) at the same moment. Just as "mood organ[s]" (5) allow citizens to dial in their preferred feelings with an ease of use reminiscent of Nozick's experience machine, so Mercerism evolves a hive mind in which, to borrow Rawls's version of utilitarian social modeling, "many persons are fused into one" (24). "The basic condition of life," Mercer tells Rick, is "to violate your own identity" (177). Like Nozick with his "indeterminate blob" in a tank, Dick sees the state as accelerating "entropic ruin" (20) through policies that reduce all "social situations" to "a number" (48). Calculation in *Androids* even puts narrative itself at risk. *Androids* uses its author's notoriously threadbare exposition to cinch the point that numbers are the enemy of story. The precise values assigned to each feeling by the mood organ ("888" equals "Desire to watch TV, no matter what's on") reflect the fictive world's denial of narrative, as if the certitude attached to numbers, negating the element of surprise, also annulled "awareness of the manifold possibilities open . . . in the future" (6). The story every Mercerist shares on infinite playback is of their prophet climbing a Sisyphean hill only to lapse into the "tomb world" (31).

The homology between utilitarianism, behaviorism, and AI is rampant in Dick's work, which consistently treats mental testing as the emblem for a social order that seeks to reduce persons to "android mentality" by submitting their humanity to a series of fixed questions.[63] In "The Short, Happy Life of a Science Fiction Writer" (1976), Dick recounts a hallucination in which "Mr. Death walked into [his] bedroom" with "some simple puzzles, the sort you give grammar school children," which Dick "failed to pass"; as a result he is spirited to the underworld (*SR*, 31). In chapter 4, I take up Dick's late-in-life conversion to something like gnosticism, but here it is worth noting that according to the "cosmology" he develops in his infamous *Exegesis*, the world as we know it is "a projection by . . . a computerlike teaching machine that . . . generally controls us as we act" (*SR*, 281). This "ruthlessly deterministic" (*SR*, 283) feedback loop inverts the Turing test. The "teaching machine" presents us "during our lifetimes" with "puzzles" designed to measure human value in terms of the problem-solving Dreyfus critiques in AI research. "If we solve the puzzle we go on to the next step," Dick writes, "but if we do not, then we remain where we are . . . enslaved by the teaching machine" (*SR*, 291).

Dick's novels routinely highlight the complicity of state power and standardized tests in ratifying an invidious biopolitics of merit. In *The Simulacra* (1964), the totalitarian global government forces its citizens to take periodic tests that determine everything from their social class to their occupations and residences. To fail them is to "revert to a despised and ancient status."[64] Just as *Androids* treats a "passing" score on IQ tests as the grounds for fertility and emigration rights, so *We Can Build You* (1972) features a world in which the "McHeston Act" dictates that citizens must pass the "Benjamin Proverb Test," the *"sine qua non* for establishing the norm,"* before they can enter society.[65] In a nod to *Androids*, in fact, *We Can Build You* includes a character, Pris (the name of an android in the earlier novel), whose "level of integration" is limited by her "phrenic" mind, a condition that the authorities "picked up . . . on their test" (29). Having been in "a Federal Mental Health Clinic" (where "one person out of every four has served time" [31]), Pris is "on loan to the outside world" (22). *We Can Build You*'s Pris is human rather than robot, but the novel, in a callback to the earlier book's testing protocols, suggests another reason Rick Deckard cannot "trap an andy": testing itself turns people into androids. The Benjamin Proverb test, after all, measures a person's aptitude for reproducing a culture's axiomatic beliefs. A normalcy defined by replicating the automated reasoning contained in proverbs would seem to efface in advance the distinction between self-originating subjectivity and machine consciousness.

This is only to say that, for Dick, the threat posed by AI is not the ascent of machine consciousness but the becoming "android" of the human subject, a process he considers well underway. *We Can Build You*'s narrator Louis Rosen describes the 'phrenic mind thus: "it was as if the brain part . . . had been lopped off and then skillfully replaced with some servo-system or some feedback circuit of selenoids and relays, all of which was operated from a distance off" (28). Testing by "teaching machine" is Dick's standard trope for this transition. In the early story "Progeny" (1954), robots have taken over the rearing of human children, an upbringing that is (unsurprisingly) weighted toward tests for ability and fit and that (also unsurprisingly) enables what, in the 1972 essay "The Android and the Human," Dick calls "the wholesale production of the android life form" (*SR*, 191). Everywhere he looks in that essay, Dick finds an epidemic of "pseudo-human behavior exhibited by what were once living men—creatures who have . . . become instruments, means, rather than ends" (*SR*, 187). Just as Nozick concludes that beneficiaries of "recipient justice" (168) are deprived of agency when acted upon by the state, so Dick imagines that "government and such-like agencies," however "'good' in the abstract sense," turn everyone into an inmate of the experience machine, "inanimate" and reduced to "reflex behavior" (*SR*, 187). Even at its most benign, government renders persons able only to "receive signals from others" and unable to "generate any of [their] own" (*SR*, 201).

Notwithstanding his self-identification as a child of Berkeley who "inherited from it the social consciousness that spread out over this country in the sixties" (*SR*, 86), Dick turns out to be something of a classical liberal in the Nozickian mold. In a 1980 interview he proudly recalls "a piece" he wrote in 1952, the year he sold his first short story, "on the superiority of the American governmental system of checks and balances," an essay that he managed to get to "the then governor of California, Earl Warren," who praised it in a fulsome reply (SR, 47). A fan of "limited government," Dick shares the antiutilitarians' view of benevolence as a slippery slope that leads the utility theorist from seeing persons as recipients of the state's largesse to seeing them as "creatures . . . of sheer utility," "objects" in themselves (SR, 107). In Dick, such objectification paves the way for totalitarianism, manifest in "a secret police apparatus that had worked since the forties, completely invisible in terms of its lawless acts against Americans," and against which "we are *helpless*" (SR, 33). In Dick's view (though not his alone), the state cannot avoid reducing persons to helplessness. In *We Can Build You*, welfarism is thus tantamount to captivity. "When I consider all the people I know who've been victims of mental illness, it's amazing" (32), Louis Rosen observes before reciting a litany of friends involuntarily committed to the Federal Mental Health Clinics swamping the landscape. These are minds made ill or atrophied in the first place by a too-indulgent state.

Even the most redistributionist state cannot alleviate suffering, in Dick's view, because as a suprahuman abstraction it cannot put itself in anyone's shoes. Like the android, "who does not care about the fate which his fellow living creatures fall victim to," the state lacks "proper empathy" (SR, 211). *Androids*' empathy machine turns out to be a contradiction in terms. Because only a person can see another person as what Nagel calls "a subject," welfarism might provide a stopgap against physical suffering, but its unidirectional treatment of the human object denies mutuality, denies what Dick calls, in the 1981 "Headnote" for his early story "Beyond Lies the Wub" (1951), the "crucial ingredient" of his life's work: "empathy, or what in earlier times was called *caritas* or *agape*" (SR, 106). If this standard of what we owe each other sounds familiar, it is because charity has long been the default virtue for exponents of laissez-faire. Dick's innovation is to tie the interpersonal dynamic of voluntary giving to a spontaneous humanity antagonized by the rote mechanisms of cost-benefit analysis that government favors. The consequence of the latter is a demotion of empathy no less tragic than the reduction of persons to the answers they give on standardized tests.

Dick's paranoia might seem to account for his suspicion of mental testing as yet another instance of how a hegemonic state can retool anything to its cause. Yet he is scarcely unique in connecting psychometrics and utilitarian social modeling. In the 1974 novel *334*, Thomas Disch gives us a world in which mental testing is as prevalent though not nearly so Manichean as in Dick's novels. Like *Androids'* Terran government, the "Regents system" in *334* administers a universal test for reproductive fitness, but as Birdie Ludd learns from his guidance counselor after he has been "reclassified," "a low score didn't . . . disbar him from any of his civil rights."[66] Sharing Dick's distrust of mental testing, Disch arrives at a somewhat different conclusion about the regime it underwrites. Birdie's score is weighted according to various factors outside the test proper. His father's diabetes and employment history have taken five points off, but the "Revised Genetics Testing Act," a piece of affirmative action legislation, compensates him for "being a Negro" (12). Designed to "measure potentiality," the Regents test serves as "a source of motivation," not as the end of one's story but its beginning. That story is called *"By Their Bootstraps"* (20), the title of a book by "the architect of the Regents system" (21). Urged to see his "reclassification as a setback rather than a permanent defeat" (15), Birdie enrolls in college, writes an essay on "creativeness" (25), and joins the army in an effort to boost his grade. In *334*, the system allows—indeed requires—one's score to change.

In that respect, Disch's novel describes a more insidious dystopia than Dick's: not a police state but a "welfare state" (174) in which numbers, adjustable through interventionist policies, steer the citizenry toward the "plasticity" of *bildung* that Arthur Jensen condemns. In *334*, where all living is assisted, no one's life is exempt from rearrangement. Though Disch spent most of the sixties abroad among British New Wave writers, he was no stranger to the American counterculture's loathing for the institutions of late modernity. This is how we might read the novel's politics, such as they can be gleaned. From one angle, *334*'s society is less dysfunctional than ideal. Time unfolds not as a cataclysmic break with the past but with "a benign predictability" (78); there are plenty of "caseworkers" (86) to go around; diversity is the norm; nonproductive sex is encouraged; gays can marry; women can become priests; formerly "useless degrees in the humanities" (94) are now society's most precious credentials. Like Dick, Disch appears to take the Nozickian view that even the most desirable social goods can't compensate a populace automated into redundancy by "the great machineries of the welfare service" (97).

Just as he shares Dick's account of mental testing as a means for the state to plan our lives under the guise of a specious meritocracy, so Disch follows Dick in combining a suspicion of governmentality with a critique of cybernetics. Consider his 1969 novelization of *The Prisoner*, the cult British TV show that aired in 1968. Later reprinted as *I Am Not a Number!* (which might be the antiutilitarian's cri de coeur), Disch's novel trades in the antiestablishment clichés beloved of its source material. These include the "brainwashing" of the protagonist (Number 6) by a psychologist (Number 14) who uses a "cybernetic eidolon" to enter her patients' dreams.⁶⁷ "Like the computers we've fashioned in our image, we operate on a binary code of pleasure and pain," Number 14 explains. "Everything can be reduced to one or the other" (211). *The Prisoner* merges the calculus of utilitarian ethics (a perpetual reckoning of "pleasure and pain") with the computational theory that pictures the mind as suspended not in an "impregnable . . . ego structure" (41) but in a conjunctive system. Drawing out the analogy between the computational theory of mind and what Taylor calls the utilitarian's habit of "eschewing subject-related properties," Disch suggests that a society organized on utilitarian precepts is one in which no one would prefer to live.⁶⁸ For the very notion of a preference—allegedly utilitarianism's most privileged desideratum—is negated by the theory's subsuming of qualitative experience into algorithmic code. Their commitment to the "commensurability of value," Williams argues, obliges utilitarians to inhabit a world ultimately free of "content."⁶⁹

In the spirit of such vacuity, Disch's novel insists on all the earmarks of a police state—"one seldom knows," Number 6 notes, "which are the prisoners and which are the guards" (114)—while withholding any clue about the cause to which that state might be pledged. The Village is overseen by a "dictator" (Number 1) whose motives never obtrude on the story line (209). Heteronomy in *The Prisoner* serves no political doctrine. The only dogma in the Village is a "faith in mere *measurements*" (207). Untethered from ideology, the Village thus realizes "the purpose of *any* organization," according to Number 1: "to grow as much as we can" (232). And as with those "utility monsters who," in Nozick's view, "require that we all be sacrificed . . . in order to increase total utility" (41), in *The Prisoner* the goal is simply surfeit. "There is pleasure in the exercise of power," observes Number 2, the Village's second in command, "and more pleasure in the exercise of more power. I can hope not only to perfect my prison . . . but also to fill it with more and more and more prisoners" (104). Yet to give *The Prisoner* this dreary Foucaultian spin, as if the utilitarianism descending from Bentham were just window dressing for his infamous panopticon, risks misreading a novel that finally cannot be said take its dystopian conceit seriously. Attuned to the mass appeal of countercultural critiques of officialdom, the novel panders to a fan base for whom angst over "the autonomy of the individual" (57) is a genre convention. That Disch sees this formula as past its prime is clear from his casting the elderly "Grandmother Bug" (149) in the role of Number 1, who turns out to be a cyborg. The novel's deus ex machina is a passé Turing machine, "a mechanical person, like in *The Tales of Hoffmann*." *The Prisoner* ends by mocking Strong AI's pretensions. "Reduced to the condition of a machine," the Village's mastermind is in the terminal stage of "senility" (141).

Standard Deviations

In 1968, Disch published a book that takes the topic of manufactured consciousness rather more seriously than his novelization of *The Prisoner*. As its title implies, *Camp Concentration* shares with *The Prisoner* a somewhat campy view of authoritarianism. Its protagonist even writes a play called "Auschwitz: A Comedy."[70] Yet *Camp Concentration* is interested less in a *Producers*-style farce than in the moral absurdism that Hannah Arendt, reporting on Adolf Eichmann's trial, termed the "banality of evil."[71] Disch seems to have Arendt in mind when he glosses the lesson of *Camp Concentration* thus: "the way to survive is to accept being in complicity with a social structure that is evil."[72] The novel's emblematic "social structure" is Camp Archimedes, a military prison whose name evokes the totalizing perspective that state power no less than utilitarian theory seeks to embody—"the point of view of the universe," as the great nineteenth-century utilitarian Henry Sidgwick put it.[73] The novel comes to us as a journal written by Louis Sacchetti, a poet detained as a conscientious objector. The "typewriter" his jailers give him to record his thoughts is "part of a master-slave hookup that automatically produces, in another room . . . impressions of everything I type" (17).

The novel's take on the Turing test does not put Sacchetti's humanness in question so much as his willingness to submit to proofs of it through the exposure of his mental life. In keeping with the "Hegelian" (155) dialectic it is meant to evoke, the "master-slave hookup" compels Sacchetti into unwelcome bouts of self-recognition. His jailers want Sacchetti's views on the "new educational techniques" the camp's scientists are "exploring." Their goal is, as the prison psychologist Dr. Aimee Busk puts it, "to maximize intelligence without vitiating its social utility" (25). Government doctors inject prisoners with "Pallidine" (55), a derivative of the syphilis bacterium that augments their minds but gives them a fatal disease. The novel takes place in a near-future where Robert McNamara is president. The US is clearly though not "officially at war" (23) in a conflict similar to the one for which McNamara served as architect. Guided by the domino theory, with its consequentialist assumption that a nation's surrender to communism triggered its neighbors to fall in turn, Kennedy's (then Johnson's) defense secretary escalated the conflict in Vietnam to prevent "vitiating [the] social utility" of capitalist society.[74]

Vietnam begat "the abyss of utilitarian apologetics" that Nagel attacks in "War and Massacre," which sees ethical arguments for "indiscriminate destructiveness" (*MQ*, 57) as "really justifications to the world at large" (*MQ*, 68). Nowhere does the "regress" of "utilitarian rationality" appear more "hopeless," Williams writes in "A Critique," than in its having "something to say even on the difference between massacring seven million, and massacring seven million and one" (93). "Persecutions, massacres, and wars have been coolly justified by calculations of long-range benefit to mankind," according to Stuart Hampshire, "and political pragmatists in the advanced countries, using cost-benefit analyses prepared for them by gifted professors, continue to burn and destroy."[75] To the extent that it confirmed these philosophers' view of it as an alibi-generating mise en abyme, Vietnam gave utilitarianism a very bad name. Disch trades on the mystification with which McNamara's war had become synonymous by 1968. In *Camp Concentration*, the nation's war footing is ambiguous; while it may be unauthorized, the war is not exactly secret. Sacchetti has been imprisoned for resisting the draft, and *Time* reports that McNamara has green-lighted the use of "'tactical' nuclear weapons" (11) in Indochina. McNamara's cronies, Disch writes, "perpetuate this incredible war" with a "sincerity . . . that in doing so they perform a moral action" (7). And as if taking cues from Williams's scheming "utilitarian elite," convinced of the justice of their cause but not enough to lay it out for public inspection, the president "and his like" treat the "electorate" as "simply practiced upon" with any number of "neo-Machiavellian" (7) maneuvers.

After a stint in a federal prison, Sacchetti ends up in Camp Archimedes as an "observer" of its "experimental program" (23) through the intrigues of Mordecai Washington, the "ringleader" (27) among the camp's "guinea pigs" (44). Mordecai and Sacchetti were high school classmates, though Sacchetti appeared to the underperforming, African-American Mordecai ("a dumb son of a bitch") as an intellectual superman with his "hundred and sixty IQ" (34), a number at which the now mentally superior Mordecai continues to marvel. Noting that "those tests are gimmicked," Sacchetti demurs with the self-assurance of the high scorer: "Measuring intelligence isn't as simple as taking a blood sample" (34). Insisting otherwise, Mordecai appears predisposed to the camp's mind-expansion program by virtue of his belief that consciousness manifests in the system at large. He wonders if "curtains interfere with your brain waves" (33) and recalls the teenage Sacchetti's "octopus intellect" as a "brain in a glass tank" (30). Drawn to the external tokens of mind, Mordecai shares with his wardens the view that consciousness is an open access platform. The camp's chief administrator, General Haast, construes intelligence as gavage: the prisoners are "geese" into whose "gullets Haast and Busk are stuffing Western Culture" (33). In Camp Archimedes, the mind is engineered through group effort to soak up knowledge long past the point of saturation. The "Inner Space" of the mind, Haast claims in a statement that would do Dennett proud, involves *"teamwork"* (90).

The camp's view of mental life assumes its indefinite plasticity, which explains why Haast, on the hunt for "an elixir of long life" (74), encourages Mordecai's pursuit of alchemy, the "hermetic science" (46) of transmutation.[76] In the novel's climax, Haast and Mordecai are hooked up to "a battery of dials and winkers and spinning reels of tape, homage to the cult of Cybernetick" (92), which will deliver the life-prolonging elixir into their veins. But while Haast feels rejuvenated, Mordecai dies. Not until the novel's last pages do we learn that Mordecai and Haast have switched bodies, and that it is only by "a happy accident" that "Haast's mind, finding itself suddenly in Mordecai's exhausted frame, should panic so hectically as to produce an embolism" (183). The "'alchymic' twaddle" was "code" for the prisoners' real research: "brain-wave duplication and storage" (182). Mordecai's "philosophical egg" (74) hatches a "mind reciprocator" that enables "recording and playback" (182) of consciousness. By this means, the dying prisoners "infiltrate the staff" and download into "their 'replacement bodies'" (183).

In matters of mind, *Camp Concentration* combines a strong physicalism (in which mental states are strictly caused by bodily processes, on the order of digestion) with a version of Strong AI (in which mental states are independent of the bodies that host them). The novel thus appears to confirm the verdict by some critics that, in either its computational or reductionist guise, the materialist philosophy of mind will finally alight on the dualism it sets out to abolish. It is worth recalling (from the introduction) how easily John Lilly moves from seeing the mind as a "biocomputer" to shrugging off his bodily form. As if giving proof to this charge, the identity theorist Armstrong faults "any theory of mind . . . unable to admit the logical possibility of disembodied existence."[77] Searle, the computational theory's foremost detractor, finds the "disembodied" mind not just allowed but entailed by Strong AI despite its "frequent fulminations against 'dualism'" ("MBP," 424). "If you accept [Strong AI's] weird mixture of dualism and behaviorism," he observes, "it will seem perfectly natural to think that the mind is not a substantive physical process, but is rather something formal and abstract."[78] Computational theorists deny "that actual human mental phenomena might be dependent on actual physical/chemical properties of actual human brains" ("MBP," 423).

A scorn for antirealism pervades Searle's work, which has long defended "direct realism."[79] Searle sees himself providing a reality check for a field that prefers the mistaken claims of (biological or digital) system over first-person ontology. That tactic applies no less to *The Campus War* (1971), his postmortem on Berkeley in the sixties. Searle finds the book's titular clash puzzling because each side of the conflict—student radicals and their administrative overlords—harbors the same "epistemological skepticism."[80] Their failure to communicate results not from a lack of shared terms but from the failure of their shared terms to say anything coherent. Offspring of the "computerized era" (*CW*, 3), students and officials alike are "used to" the same "explanatory categories—functionalism, behaviorism . . . , technological determinism" (*CW*, 68), all of which assert the primacy of context. The students' grievance is not with the system, as nearly every pamphlet of the SDS (Students for a Democratic Society) had it, but with the college's failure to deliver them over to system: "the student today wants the university to help him . . . invent an identity" (*CW*, 161).

The breakdown of campus governance for Searle thus results from a breakdown *internal* to systems thinking, a "built-in irresponsibility" to which the students' immersion in groupthink disposes them (*CW*, 139). "The most striking" thing about contemporary students, he observes, is "how groupy they are" (*CW*, 162). His autopsy of Berkeley's "epistemological skepticism" resonates with Herrnstein's critique of environmentalism in *IQ in the Meritocracy*. Also given to settling scores with the student left, Herrnstein writes that "an assortment of SDS members" (15), soi-disant champions of "the egalitarian-environmental outlook" (45), mounted a "fall offensive" (19) against him after his essay "IQ" appeared in *The Atlantic* in summer 1971. Herrnstein attributes the radicals' "repellent . . . tactics" (36) to their "doctrinaire" (19) unreason. Searle likewise sees the student movement as replacing rationality with "states of consciousness of all kinds" (*CW*, 47) and with "adolescent sexuality carried to a pitch of frenzy" (*CW*, 45).

Though his critique of Strong AI omits the orgies and LSD, Searle's dim view of the student radicals' investment in "academic structure" as "something to fill the vacuum of their own identity" (*CW*, 162) predicts his critique of the systems reply, which he also indicts for its emptiness and its presumption to spawn alternative "states of consciousness." In *Camp Concentration*, on the other hand, the computational theory does in fact precipitate the hedonistic "anomie" (88) that Searle sees as the upshot of a culture committed to system. For though the novel proclaims the mind's portability, the Pallidine drug's other "breakthrough" (166) comes about not by transcending the body but by sinking into it. Like the "social disease" (59) from whose spirochete it is derived, Pallidine spreads by sexual transmission. Mind in the novel is not just "fluid and capable of re-formation" (58) but what sex education instructors call a *bodily fluid*. Even as the drug is "fermenting" his "brainjelly" (66), Mordecai has been "bugger[ing]" (165) Dr. Busk, whose flight from Camp Archimedes turns her into patient zero for the "epidemic" of "soaring genius" (161) about to befall the "entire country" (160). Sodomy is pivotal to the Pallidine disease's etiology. Despite her dalliance with Mordecai, Busk is almost "certainly a Lesbian" (164), a detail that seems to have figured into his calculations. He has "outflanked" her "from the rear" (165), as though her lesbianism entailed a (hard to credit) penchant for anal sex.

The novel's point seems to be that queers of any stripe are vulnerable to penetration from all angles. "The fact that promiscuity . . . is more common among homosexuals," Sacchetti observes, "would . . . tend to accelerate the process" of "rapid dissemination" (166). This aspect of Disch's novel invites us to make an argument about the queer underside of the systems-theoretical account of mind, a move rendered irresistible by the gayness of both Turing and Disch. Such an argument might praise the subversive intent of a brainworker (mathematician, novelist) keen to disrupt institutions of domination (intelligence service, military prison) by appropriating the tools of power (informatics, germ warfare) in the service of a deeper commitment to the free play of desire. In that argument, various dualisms—mind and body, self and society, freedom and necessity—"would melt . . . into their opposites," as Mordecai puts it, in a "Hegelian" sublation through which these opposed "values" (155) emancipate each other.

But *Camp Concentration* is hard to read as a subversive text in these terms. For the novel has little interest in the anarchic potential of "promiscuity." Its conclusion instead presents us with the society utilitarians are assumed to want, a society in which—since everyone is made special as the genius bug infects the population—no one's specialness counts. As Bentham put it in a dictate virtually unmodified through two centuries of utilitarian thought: "Everybody to count for one, nobody for more than one."[81] This is the dire scenario Rawls evokes when he chastises utilitarians for not "tak[ing] seriously the distinction between persons" (24), or for making the "bare person" the object of moral concern.[82] Such bareness in turn evokes the utilitarianism analyzed by Frances Ferguson in *Pornography, the Theory* (2004), which links the classical utilitarian's indifference to "individual character" with an indifference to erotic specialness, to how desire feels from the inside.[83] Ferguson ranks pornography among those late eighteenth-century "technologies" engendered by utilitarianism for bringing "latent values" forward by "framing action" as more definitive of persons than their mental states.[84]

Disch's effort to express a "latent" category like consciousness—through "mind reciprocators" (184), "performances on various psychometric tests" (122), or casual sex—looks continuous with those utilitarian "social structures" that make it possible, Ferguson writes, to "literally see the effects of one's actions in a system."[85] In keeping with *Camp Concentration*'s own devotion to system (rather than its undoing), Mordecai's intrigues must be seen as less

"Faustian" (127) than compensatory. Mordecai distills the "abomination" (69) of the Nazi camps to the "fundamental . . . principle" that "there be no relation between the prisoners' behavior and their rewards or punishment" (77). To the extent that Camp Archimedes practices the same dissociation, it fails the central mission of utilitarianism as Ferguson sees it: the allotment of objective (because performance-driven) deserts. Restoring the entitlements the camp has withheld from him, Mordecai makes his superior gifts bring him out on top.

Yet this is not to suggest that *Camp Concentration* ought to be read as a defense of utilitarianism. We might instead see the book as exemplifying the continuity between utilitarianism and what Nagel calls "the reward schedule of a meritocratic system" (MQ, 99), a continuity that the long association of utilitarianism and welfare-state policies has submerged. For Ferguson, classical utilitarianism's power lies in its ability to make the case for either merit-based or need-based rewards. The only criterion that matters is that such rewards be grounded in the objectification of persons as units in a larger, and largely hierarchical, pattern (a 1400 on the SAT; an income below the Federal Poverty Line). Modern meritocracy, by contrast, cleaves its understanding of persons far enough away from the utilitarian view to make context or system antithetical to subjectivity, even as any individual's meritocratic accomplishment can only make sense in a system. (Hence the longstanding controversy over the SAT's cultural "neutrality.") This cleavage becomes ideologically prominent, I have argued, through the alliance of unexpected bedfellows.

I have been interested in moments from the recent past when philosophers who are usually mindful of what Nagel calls the "absurdity" of treating "ethical theory as . . . public service" (MQ, xii) do not quite manage to fence off "moral argument" from "public policy" (MQ, xiii) or even from arguments elsewhere in their discipline. My strategy has been to show that for some twentieth-century philosophers a set of claims about how society *should* work appears to follow from their account of how the mind *does* work.[86] And I have tried to relocate disciplinary fences like those separating cognitive scientists from ethicists within a larger enclosure: the perpetual struggle, to quote Arjun Appuradai, "between liberal social theory and democratic norms," a struggle that since the late sixties has meant the eclipse of egalitarian ideals.[87] While we can concede that Herrnstein and Jensen's innatism is scarcely of a piece with the internalism of Searle or Nagel, it would be shortsighted not to observe the respects in which such philosophers' arguments resemble those of policy-minded biological determinists. Calling for the day when the college will once again function as "an aristocracy of the intellect" (CW, 224) rather than a "youth city" that "tolerate[s] indolence . . . and organize[s] radicalism" (*CW*, 223), Searle might be ventriloquizing Edward Banfield in his worry that "rampages and forays are to be expected . . . in the inner cities."[88] On the meritocratic campus Searle envisions, "pathological outgrowth" (*CW*, 223) never arises because unqualified students are never admitted.

In the 1973 essay "The Policy of Preference," Nagel claims that "when racial and sexual injustice have been reduced, we shall still be left with the great injustice of the smart and the dumb" (*MQ*, 104). Defending affirmative action "on grounds of social utility"—it "mitigate[s] a grave social evil" (*MQ*, 103)—Nagel nonetheless shares the IQ innatists' view that no policy can address the "socially produced inequalities . . . between the intelligent and the unintelligent . . . without recourse to increased coercion or decreased liberty" (*MQ*, 105). Though they may serve to fight discrimination based on outward physical differences, Nagel suggests, there can be no strong utilitarian arguments against the claims of innate mental differences. The implication in "The Policy of Preference" is that insofar as distinctions between the smart and dumb correspond to inequities between the well-off and struggling, the latter might somehow be *legitimate*—or more legitimate than the "gigantic increase in total social control" (*MQ*, 104) it would take to level the field. By contrast, the utilitarian Peter Singer claims in *Practical Ethics* (1980) that even if "the genetic hypothesis turns out to be correct," IQ would not touch our obligations to equality, since "important human interests . . . are not affected by differences in intelligence."[89]

For the contract theorist, to set aside differences in IQ for the sake of "a more egalitarian result" (27), as Singer puts it, fails to put what Rawls calls "limits on fair terms of social cooperation" (19). Since utilitarian and other redistributive accounts of society envision a "big *social pot* so that it's not clear what's coming from where and what's going where," Nozick concludes, everyone becomes "a *part-owner* of you" (172). Unlike the utilitarian, who apparently has no problem steering the ship of state toward social leveling, the justice theorist sets definitive "limits" on the degree to which my interests could or should be identified with yours. That such limitation is built into the Rawlsian account of subjectivity makes for another striking overlap with IQ innatism, whose defenders are certainly invested in the view that subjectivity is inalienable from one person to another yet prize Rawls's "distinction between persons" to the degree that it is rank ordered. Stephen Jay Gould calls IQ testing a *"theory of limits"* in which hierarchies are affirmed as "inborn" and numbers are no more than "a measure of where [status differentials] should and must be."[90] As we have seen, Nozick claims that Rawls's justice as fairness should be treated as another such theory. For though justice as fairness amounts to a deeply egalitarian view by almost any standard, Rawls's insistence that "equal basic liberties" are "lexically prior" (266) to material equalities occasions Nozick's judgment that his consecration of individual liberty commits Rawls to the meritocracy that, elsewhere in *A Theory of Justice*, he eloquently renounces.[91]

This is why Singer, in a 1975 review of Nozick's book, concludes that "Rawls's theory is a half-way house between utilitarianism and Nozick's own position" and that "in having gone half-way with Rawls we are forced by the logic of our position to go all the way with Nozick."[92] The utilitarian Singer, by contrast, holds "that society should, so far as its resources allow, provide for the most important needs of its members."[93] Utilitarianism appears to its critics as a theory of limitlessness precisely because it does not scruple to program the social world to bring about what it perceives as best outcomes. Notwithstanding Ferguson's claim that utilitarianism objectifies hierarchies of difference, it is just as interested in dislocating them. Its policy of "agglomerative indifference," as Williams calls it, means that individuals are contingent on contexts that can be perpetually reshaped.[94] Like Nozick with his utility monsters, Williams sees utilitarianism's "demands for maximum welfare production" as unnervingly "boundless," allowing for "no limit to what a given person might be doing to improve the world."[95]

Because utilitarianism is understood to wed its quantifications to a contextualism that appears like a continual shifting of goalposts, many of its opponents can't help imagining its ostensibly rational calculus erupting into a numerical sublime. Whereas statistical induction in IQ science means being affirmed in your distinctness, statistical induction in utilitarianism means being bled of your distinctness. Yet in Disch's work, it is not only utilitarianism that partakes of boundlessness. Homosexuality appears in *Camp Concentration* not as a revolt against society but as native to the meritocracy, after all, because the meritocratic ideal amounts to a form of "deviance," to a continual exceeding and destabilizing of norms and limits. Just as the fact that everyone is a genius makes genius valueless, so it makes Mordecai's supremacy temporary. "Behind the mask of Haast/Mordecai's face lurks the dark knowledge of another, further-off future," Sacchetti concludes, "a height beyond the first rosy peaks, of a coldness and strangeness extreme as death" (184). Such anxious musings on the receding baseline are the default for a meritocracy that condemns its would-be beneficiaries to perpetual performances of the sort that we associate with means testing and other indignities of the caretaker state.

Mordecai of course presents a special case for the performance anxieties that meritocracy instills. He not only changes his body but swaps out his race.

In the context of IQ testing's damagingly tenacious account of racial difference, this switch cannot help being charged.[96] In increasing his consciousness, Mordecai effectively *becomes* white—a point that would seem to confirm the authors of *The Bell Curve* in their conclusion that white brains are better than black ones.[97] Yet Mordecai's mind remains "black"; his change is all on the surface. *Camp Concentration* thus gestures more toward the passing narrative, a staple of African-American literature, than toward the innatist conclusions of Murray and Herrnstein. Like James Weldon Johnson's ex-colored man, Camp Archimedes's survivors, whose minds are lodged in "replacement bodies" with prior histories, are now committed to perpetrating a "well-executed imposture" (183) in order to "maintain the mystery" (185) of their quondam identities.

Walter Benn Michaels notes that passing, while "a negligible sociological phenomenon," marks a "significant theoretical advance" in racial logic because it insists that racial identity "requires a relatively autonomous set of practices to complete its constitution."[98] Yet I would say that passing's logic itself poaches on the more prevalent "theoretical advance" of twentieth-century behaviorism. Passing's practices are only "relatively autonomous" because they are yoked to the inevitably superior claims of biology. The fact that Nella Larsen's Clare Kendry can pass as white in *Passing* (1929) arises only because of her "strain of black blood."[99] Severing the biological tether, behaviorism makes the "technology of passing" universal by making trial personhood the norm.[100] Behaviorism maintains that just as there is no practice of subjectivity that cannot be proved through testing, so there is no subjectivity without proof of its practice.

The great drawback of the behaviorist approach is that in making the imitation of characteristics count for their presence, it leaves the door wide open for deceit. It is worth recalling that Turing constructs his test as an "imitation game" in which deception plays a crucial role. Disch took pride in his own mastery of role maintenance, even calling science fiction "the art form best adapted to telling lies."[101] Yet his commitment to the "right to lie"[102] did not stop him from putting his faith in the numerological truth-telling of the meritocracy, if we are to believe this admission in his 2008 memoir *The Word of God*: "I aced the entrance exam for Cooper Union; someone who worked in the admissions office told me I got the highest score ever on their entrance test."[103] Disch did not graduate from Cooper or any college. He took pride in having opted out of that particular system: "shamans don't need a college degree."[104] Yet his withdrawal was not so complete that he could resist letting us know the score. Like Mordecai, he wore the mask of one man while measuring himself against the standards of others.

Being Replaceable

For Disch, meritocracy's "reward schedule" turns out to be no less unsettling for self-identity than the welfarism that antiutilitarians criticize for seeming to deprive us of the power even to identify as selves. The vectors of disruption move in opposite directions. Where meritocracy insists on command performances aimed at ever-increasing opportunities, welfarism fosters an inertia aimed at ever more circumscribed ones. According to novels like *Camp Concentration* and *334*, meritocracy offers no respite from the perpetual surveillance of utilitarian spectators over their wards. It simply replaces the welfare state's supervisions with assessment culture's endless qualifying exams. Disch typifies the countercultural suspicion of the social alternatives on offer, but this is not a niche concern. The conflict between artificial intelligence and human consciousness in New Wave Science Fiction resounds into the common culture of both Disch's time and ours. Examining Daniel Keyes's *Flowers for Algernon* (1966) and Richard Powers's *Galatea 2.2* (1995), I argue that in these texts, written decades apart and for quite different audiences, the tension between the individual and society—that hoariest of literary themes—takes on fresh urgency when refracted through the science of mind and its ambition to reshape our sense of what counts as a person.

Like *Camp Concentration*, *Flowers for Algernon* has as its backdrop psychology's transition from a science of social engineering to a theory of native limits. Its title character is a lab mouse in a Skinnerian maze whose intelligence has been artificially enhanced by chemical treatments and surgeries. And again like *Camp Concentration*, the book presents as the journal of a human subject, Charlie Gordon, whose IQ increases dramatically over the course of the novel through the same procedures. Unlike *Camp Concentration*, whose narrator is a genius even before his infection, Charlie starts off with an IQ of 68. Keyes renders Charlie's advancement orthographically. His diary entries begin in a garbled idiom rife with misspellings, growing into standard English as his IQ increases. And again unlike *Camp Concentration*, in which the changes to intelligence are permanent, the effects of Charlie's "psychosurgery" are temporary (a decline measured by the reversion of his journal entries to illegibility).[105]

Charlie's journal records his memories of a childhood spent in the doctors' offices to which his mother dragged him in a desperate quest to make him "normal," to "grow up like other people" (71). Rose Gordon's desire to change her son through outlandish medical interventions ("encephalo-reconditioning" [140], "psychosubstantiation tests" [138]) originates in shame over having given birth to a defective child. Her private yearning mirrors the institutional desire to replace her son with a better version of himself. "In place of a feeble-minded shell, a burden on the society that must fear his irresponsible behavior," according to Professor Nemur, the doctor who effects that replacement, "we have a man of dignity and sensitivity, ready to take his place as a contributing member of society" (162). As in *Camp Concentration*, raising an individual's IQ does not benefit society quite the way Nemur anticipates. While the "new techniques" used on him may have "created a superior human being" (161), Charlie's superiority renders him an "antisocial bastard" (247), "incapable of making friends or thinking about other people" (253). In Keyes's novel, the social demand for exceptionalness—the requisite demand, in other words, of the meritocracy—turns out to be bad for social order.

"The old Charlie was not really gone," he confides to his journal after a night of drunkenness. "Nothing in our minds is ever really gone. The operation had covered him over with a veneer of education and culture, but emotionally he was there—watching and waiting" (195). In construing "the old Charlie" as a prisoner he is obliged to liberate for the sake of his own sanity (and unity), Charlie embarks on the self-discovery that countless Americans would pursue in the next decade, under circumstances that they would not infrequently describe in the terms he uses. Hence he "resent[s]" not just "the attitude that I am a guinea pig" but "Nemur's constant references to having made me what I am, or *that someday there will be others like me who will become real human beings*" (145). Throughout the New Social Movements, the men and women revolting against the oppressive techniques of social engineering were armed with a powerful sense of their own authenticity, their bedrock existence as *"real human beings."*

The difference is that Charlie is a literal rather than metaphorical experiment. No less than Joseph Weizenbaum's ELIZA or IBM's Deep Blue, Charlie is a test subject in both senses of the term. Forced to take tests that measure his progress, he is also a test run, a beta version, for applications that will supersede him. The novel's frequent references to his becoming "like" others suggest that he can only approximate or simulate "normal people" (200). Like AI programs, in other words, Charlie is *replaceable*. Unlike them, he has an intuitive grasp of his obsolescence. Describing his imminent intellectual decline in terms that might have been drawn from the Port Huron Statement, Charlie writes: "knowing the paths I have followed and the ones left to take will help me understand what I am becoming" (221). His consciousness-raising, however, leads him not to a life conceived as a plurality of options but to the "Warren Home School" (309), a state-run asylum where there is "no talk of rehabilitation, of cure, of someday sending these people out into the world again" (231). Its name speaks to the nexus of paternalism and deindividuation that the utilitarian society cannot help generating in its structures. Charlie is doomed to life in a rabbit hole whose inmates are characterized by multiplicity and animality.

If *Flowers for Algernon* is an immensely *moving* novel, an enduring sentimental classic that spawned an equally beloved 1968 film (*Charly*, which won an Oscar for its leading man, Cliff Robertson), its pathos derives from the gap between Charlie's account of himself and the identity-depriving fate that awaits him in what Erving Goffman calls the "total institution" of the asylum, emblematic of the caretaker state at its most abstract and dehumanizing.[106] We can now see the strategic advantage of the novel's diary format, which has the effect of making Charlie's use of the first-person singular the unwavering feature of his life regardless of his mental capacity. His own "I" remains fixed even when he cannot properly transcribe the letter in other contexts: "I felt good when he said not everbody [sic] with an eye-Q of 68 had that thing like I had it" (9). From the novel's point of view, the sentence "I was a person just like evryone [sic]" (310) is less performative than redundant. To speak as an "I" is already to be a person, a conclusion the novel reaches through Charlie's "voice," whose defects turn into the distinctions of an inimitable signature. "He doesn't realize that I was a person before I came here," Charlie says of Nemur (145). No less than the social worker who warehouses hard cases, the behavioral psychologist who fetishizes externalism can see only a "feebleminded shell" where a "man of dignity" already exists.

In *Practical Ethics*, Singer considers the merits of the "replaceability argument" (120), whose proponents (including Singer) support the permissibility of killing severely disabled newborns on the view that they can be replaced with healthy infants with the chance of a happier life. And while Singer does not include infants born with Down syndrome as candidates for killing (since "their lives, like those of children, can be joyful" [164]), that exemption clearly does not touch upon the real challenge the replaceability argument makes to our intuitions about valuing personhood. Nagel would say that Singer's vantage entirely misses the *subject* when it refers persons to what Singer calls a "moral ledger of debits and credits" (114).[107] Singer rejects the desirability of children born with Down syndrome by tabulating all the things such children cannot do: "We cannot expect a child with Down syndrome to play the guitar, to develop an appreciation of science fiction, to learn a foreign language, to chat with us about the latest Woody Allen movie, or to be a respectable athlete, basketballer or tennis player."[108]

For Singer, the permissibility of aborting fetuses that test positive for Down syndrome follows from the view that a life is no more than a catalog of experiences (the fuller the catalog, the better the life). It is a revealing irony that Singer, whose bioethics are founded on a brief for the quality rather than the sanctity of life, defends that position by recourse to the quantitative. If Nozick gives us reason to reject the view of the person as merely a sum of experiences, Keyes's novel affords what we might see as an affective version of this rejection. The "old Charlie" remains, according to the Charlie who avails himself of interesting experiences, "as a separate and distinct individual still functioning in his consciousness . . . struggling for control of the body" (248). It is a version of the experience machine shot through with pathos, where the "old Charlie" occupies the role of the sovereign individual that a well-meaning but invidious program of social betterment has imprisoned within the cage of an artificially enhanced system. In the view of genius Charlie, he himself is the simulation usurping the rightful place of "old Charlie."

Flowers for Algernon treats its villainous doctor as equal parts Skinner and Herrnstein. Nemur believes both in "artificially induced intelligence" (255) and in the idea that IQ reveals one's place in an inalienable hierarchy, in particular "that someone with an IQ of less than 100 doesn't deserve consideration" (248). Keyes was no countercultural radical, though his book profited from a vague association with the objections raised by the antipsychiatry movement to scientific business as usual.[109] Keyes's novel takes the side of the person by treating psychology as a dehumanizing discipline. By contrast, Powers's *Galatea 2.2* takes an admiring view of cognitive science, a field in which its author also manifests a good deal more expertise than Keyes had in psychology. Powers's subject is no less fantastical than what transpires in *Flowers for Algernon*. The difference is that no reputable neurosurgeon believes that an operation could increase a human IQ, whereas quite a few cognitive scientists—not to mention countless nonscientists—believe that a computer can be programmed with consciousness.[110] Like IQ racialism, Strong AI is always with us.

Powers's novel chronicles a year in the life of a character, Richard ("Rick") Powers, "the token humanist" in the "Center for the Study of Advanced Sciences" at a Midwestern research university known only as "U."[111] Rick is brought on as "liaison with the outside community" (5), tasked with putting the Center's complex "cognitive neuroscience" (181) into lay terms. At the Center he falls in with Philip Lentz, "an old reductionist" (169) who convinces him to take part in a wager among his colleagues to determine whether a computer-based "neural network" (16) is capable of passing a Turing test. The twist is that the test in question will be based on the comprehensive exam of a master's candidate in literature (a test that Rick took at U. fifteen years earlier). After a number of misfires, the experimenters develop a program, "Implementation H," shortened to "Imp H" (171) and then christened "Helen" (179) by Rick. Keeping faith with the computational theorist's view that consciousness is the sum total of information or experience, Rick feeds Helen information both from the MA list and from what he calls "a catalog" of "worldliness" (247) in order to prepare her for the exam. Another twist is that not Helen but Rick turns out to be the actual subject of the cognitive scientists' experiment, the goal of which is to determine whether Rick can be led to see Helen as conscious.

Like *Flowers for Algernon*, *Galatea 2.2* is preoccupied with replaceability. Helen supplants the prior iteration of the program, just as all but the first (Imps B through G) have replaced their predecessors. One of the novel's jokes is that the comps for which Rick is training Helen are based on a "Euro-retro" list that has itself been replaced. His "version of literary reality is a decade out of date," he learns from A., the master's student he signs up to vie with Helen (284). Richard in turn imagines A. herself as an assemblage of replacement parts, "a conflation of every friend who had ever happened to me" (238). If replacement looms large in the book, it is everywhere accompanied by doubts over its suitability as an account of how the world runs. This is true from the opening line: "It was like so, but wasn't," a sentiment whose antecedent seems to be Rick's admission in the next paragraph that he has "lost" his "thirty-fifth year" (3). Just as Keyes makes it a moral question whether Charlie should be replaced by a "normal" version of himself, so Powers simultaneously embraces and challenges the idea that there are adequate substitutes for loss. At the novel's end, in reply to the question of "what love replaces," Rick answers: "nothing" (310). Elsewhere his account of replaceability is more sanguine. Following "Emerson," after all, he concludes that "life was metonymy, or at least stood for it" (55). His commitment to this neatly recursive axiom primes Rick for Lentz's experiment. Where the "operationalist" Lentz exhibits a Dennett-like cynicism about the mind—a "shell game" that "runs Turing tests on its own constructs every time it ratifies a sensation or reifies an idea" (276)—Rick takes the Turing test's performance-driven results for real.[112] This is because Rick, a pure product of the meritocracy, is a true believer in testing as a "metonymy" of identity. "Life meant convincing another that you knew what it meant to be alive," Rick observes at the end of the novel. "The world's Turing test was not yet over" (327).

This epiphany is worth exploring. Let us begin with the obvious point that in prepping Helen for the MA exam, Rick repeats his own studies for that graduate school milestone. He makes a perfect guinea pig for the Center's scientists because he already approaches life as a series of examinations. Powers presents Rick as a savant who can lay claim to any subject: physics, literary theory, computer programming, novel writing, cognitive science. Unlike Keyes's Charlie, whose path describes an ellipsis that takes him to the outer reaches of human intellect before slingshotting back to the resting place of his subnormal IQ, Rick's genius appears to take him ever upward. Yet this appearance is deceiving. Rick is a verificationist who demands constant proofs

ARTIFICIAL INTELLIGENCE AND THE RISE OF THE MERITOCRACY   63

of his value, whether from his English professor ("for whose approval I'd developed my labyrinthine style" [202]), Lentz (whose put-downs of Rick alternate with praise for his star pupil's progress), or his former lover C., the woman at the heart of the book's parallel plot. In an inversion of *One Thousand and One Nights*, Rick plays Scheherazade to C.'s disaffected sultan in order to save her from her own sense of "unworthiness" (277). He takes her life experiences and transforms them into fiction "to amuse" her at night in their small Boston apartment (140), an arrangement that highlights Rick's perpetual need for a validating audience.

His efforts to enliven her end up making the situation worse. When Rick's books reach a larger audience, C. feels diminished: "My success killed her last chance" (278). But this is really the surface through line of the novel's parallel plot, which itself splits into parallel lines, with the human intimacy between Rick and C. gradually replaced by Rick's identification with his own projects. What starts as an elegy for a seemingly irreplaceable romance becomes the biography of Rick's novels, whose vicissitudes so predominate the action that it is hard to tell where Rick leaves off and his books begin: "*Gold Bug* appeared in the States," Rick writes of Powers's third novel, "and won a slice of attention" (277). Rendering the books that came out of the relationship more *present* than the relationship itself, the novel gives "token humanist" another meaning altogether. For Rick's identity manifests in the world through the keepsakes of his well-compensated imagination.

Although Rick claims that he "began to think of [himself] in the virtual third person" (9) while working at the Center, his whole life has consisted in a self-objectification in which his performances attest to—or, to use his term, metonymize—his subjectivity. Hence his "third novel earned [him] the post" at the Center; and he spends the early part of his yearlong residency revising his "fourth," only to see it suffer at hands of a merciless review in the *New York Times* near the residency's end (5). Each of his previous books appears to augment his status even as it corrodes his bond with C.: "People I'd never meet wrote me letters, awarded me prizes" (139). But the failure of his fourth novel to earn acclaim triggers a crisis of confidence that finds Rick threatening to abandon fiction before it abandons him. Just as C. breaks up with him because she believes Rick has replaced her with his novels, so his romance with the meritocracy appears to have succumbed to the fear of supersession. Like Mordecai Washington looking with terror on "heights beyond the first rosy peaks" of his own provisional supremacy, Rick comes to fear he will finally be replaced by the next big thing.

Of course, a pan in the "paper of record" (207) might be the paradigmatic first-world problem. Yet Powers gooses the emotional impact of Rick's plight by tying it to a subplot that amounts to a sentimental "household drama" (134) of the bell curve. Rick befriends Diana Hartrick, a neuropsychologist who "fractionate[s] monkey hippocampi" (303) when not raising her two sons: Peter, who has Down syndrome, and his older brother William, whom Rick calls "the most extraordinary boy I will ever meet" (132). What draws Rick to the older son's brilliance is obviously its familiarity. William is a consummate test-taker. Bedtime reading of the "World Almanac" is thus "more foregone quiz game than story time" (136). Diana is single because her ex-husband "found the drop from Will to Pete a bit steep" (136). The line pointedly implicates Rick, given his distress at Peter's "spatulate face," which brings his "worst-case fears . . . home to roost" (131). As unable as their father to avoid invidiously comparing Diana's sons, Rick "fears" a being whose learning falls outside the protocols and rewards of mental testing.

Thus despite William's boast that Peter is a "genius" by "Down's baby" (131) standards, Rick remains dubious. Like Peter Singer, he is on record in regarding a life like Peter's as a misfortune; much to his shame, Diana has read his "third book," in which "the narrator ties her tubes in fear of bearing a child with birth defects" (183). It is a peculiar form of shame, since what makes Rick self-conscious is his putting into words what *everyone* allegedly feels: the omission of self-consciousness from Peter's makeup compromises his quality of life. (It is due to its recursiveness that Silvan Tomkins defines shame as the "most reflexive of affects": "shame is an experience of the self by the self."[113]) Even after the ostensible broadening of Rick's mind toward the value of disabled children, Peter makes Rick "cringe in anticipation" (288) when the boy is introduced to A. Richard's hope that Helen is conscious mirrors his suspicion that Peter is not. Just as Helen looks to most observers like a "gifted cockatiel" (223) parroting the views of her human teacher, so Peter appears doomed to an autonomic empathy, as when his brother's "red-faced distress made Peter break out in tears and lower his face into his plate" (134). The sons together add up to a version of Rick's "course of . . . training" (300) with Helen. He serves her his version of the world almanac in the hope that she will learn enough to pass the test; he despairs that her learning is real, that theirs is other than a one-way conversation.

Gradually Rick comes to find Peter's empathy authentic precisely through the thing that he first laments: the Down's baby's exemption from the stern expectations of test-taking. A scene late in the novel clarifies this point. No sooner has William "come home" than he "burst into tears, bringing Pete sympathetically along with him." The source of the older boy's anguish is the last day of school: "'First grade,' he choked. 'Done. Perfect. . . . Everything they wanted. Now I'm supposed to do second. There's another one after that, Mom.

I can't. It's never-ending'" (317). The melodrama of the prodigy, wherein the "precocious and brilliant" (141) child's slightest misstep might result in social death, is rendered more heartbreaking by its indefiniteness. Rick knows this dynamic well. "Edging toward humiliation" while trying to demonstrate Helen's progress to the Center's scientists, Rick "needed one good answer to show them what my girl could do" (220). Such answers mean the difference between acclaim and disgrace. The proofs that affirm his self-worth can doom it by their absence. Given Rick's own bouts of performance-driven insecurity, it makes sense that he chooses to see the disabled brother providing the brilliant one with a safe harbor, a respite from his own excellence. Because his mental life seems to Rick incurably limited, Peter escapes the devil's bargain by which "only more lessons could cure the effect of lessons" (259). During their first meeting, Rick tells us, Peter "let loose a chortle of euphoria at nothing." Such aimless joy reveals the silver lining of his beclouded existence: "domestic peace" (134). Although Rick cannot help envisioning what he takes to be the dreary fate awaiting him—"the thought of this child going to school, struggling to speak, finding some employer that would trust him with a broom and dustpan gripped me around the throat" (316)—Peter as permanent child will never face the complement of rigors that await his brother, destined for (or doomed to) the meritocracy.

Peter's counterpart is the novel's other cognitively impaired human being: Lentz's wife Audrey, whose stroke has left her "locked out of her own home" because she is cut off from her memories ("ten years ago, childhood, past life analysis: all sealed off" [167]). Befitting his commitment to the computational theory of mind, Lentz describes her brain damage in the language of Strong AI: "'Her database is still intact. . . . As is the retrieval. It's just meaning that's gone'" (168). Audrey has syntax but no semantics. Rick describes his failure to understand advanced theories of mind with the figure of homelessness he uses for Audrey: "I would be locked out, as consciousness locks us out from our own inner workings" (297). While the figure evokes the bruited mystery of consciousness, Rick's sense of being "locked out" calls back to the domesticity *Galatea 2.2* romanticizes in the bond between Diana and Peter, who appear as a "lovely contrapposto" (181) to the novel's perpetually exiled narrator. Aestheticizing the asymmetrical relationship of gifted mother and unbrilliant son, Rick harmonizes what he understands as the incongruity between Peter's ability and value into a pietà that affords one of the novel's tableaux, the image of the permanent infant being held: "She took Peter from me and hugged him to her" (317). Like Charlie in the Warren Home School, losing the realm of intellect even as he gains the kingdom of subjectivity, Peter represents to Rick an inaccessible state of grace: "Here was the home I would never have" (88).

Whereas the novel imagines Peter's identity with "home" as an innate capacity, its counterpoint is the "training" that characterizes behaviorist specimens like rhesus monkeys and Rick himself.[114] "My life with C. was a long training," he writes toward the end of the novel. The sentence appears to be intended ironically; it begins a paragraph meant to confer hard-earned awareness on Rick's look back at his fateful relationship. But the paragraph points to the rote quality of Rick's learning, what we might call its paradoxically unthinking (because compulsory) aspect: "I learned most of my adult truths with her. I learned how to travel light, how to read aloud. I learned to pay attention to the incomprehensible. I learned that no one ever knows another" (280). In the context of *Galatea 2.2*'s melodrama of meritocratic striving, the anaphoric "I learned" shifts Rick away from first-person ontology toward the "virtual third person"; subjectivity and training nearly converge only to pull apart. It is as though Rick is trying to convince himself of the "Hebbian rule" that "repetition makes things real" (268).[115]

"They were running your training" (318), Diana tells him when she reveals that Lentz and his coconspirators have made Rick their experiment. If Rick can never go home again, it is because the meritocracy, far from overcoming the "plasticity" of being that IQ innatists and antiutilitarians charge to the behaviorist social model, likewise keeps its subjects "running."[116] Rick must keep on the move, but without Audrey Lentz's reprieve. Though barred from her home, she is "locked in the absolution of perpetual forgetting" (251). Not grasping her condition, she presumably does not experience it as misery, a point confirmed by her bouts of lucidity. "In a flood of understanding that percolated up from her undamaged self," she pleads with her husband: "'Take me out of here'" (308). Where Audrey's amnesia is a kind of release, Rick cannot escape the "flood of understanding" and the erosion of peace it brings in its wake. Just as "thought, once mobile, was condemned to carry its confusion out into the dimensioned world" (321), so his "fate," Lentz jokes, "is to be a wanderer" (328). There will never come a time when Rick can imagine himself neither submitting to an "empirical test of meaning" (287) nor "push[ing] regret on to the next unreachable landmark" (312). In the novel's final twist, Helen opts out of the test to determine her existence, refusing the wager's terms through a self-erasure. The machine declines "the world's Turing test" to which Rick still applies himself.

CHAPTER 2

Radical Ecology's Mindfulness

The Entropic Turn

Deep ecology emerges out of a fatigue with what the term's coiner, the Norwegian philosopher Arne Naess, refers to as the "shallow ecology" movement's "central objective: the health and affluence of people in the developed countries." Naess rejects "anthropocentrism" in favor of *"the equal right to live and blossom"* of all "ways and forms of life."[1] Deep ecology (or radical ecology, the term I use to refer to an environmentalism that includes but is not exhausted by deep ecology[2]) might seem to cause trouble for the previous chapter's claim that a neo-idealist revolt against system and embrace of first-person ontology would prove conducive to certain meritocratic tendencies in the late twentieth century. Radical ecology thrives on the systems theory favored by AI theorists, materialist philosophers of mind, and utilitarians. Like those thinkers, ecologists typically have little patience for individuals; in their disciplines, holism and externalism reign supreme. "The total-field model" of deep ecology, as Naess puts it, "dissolves not only the man-in-environment concept, but every compact thing-in-milieu concept" (3). In some cases, such as population restriction and resource consumption, ecologists even advocate the sort of coercive state intervention to which antiutilitarian philosophers object.

Notwithstanding these points, I shall argue that radical ecology—or the influential strain of it that this chapter examines—offers less a rebuke to neo-idealism than a hyperbolic extension of its crucial conceits. We can begin by noting the large number of its practitioners who believe that ecology's task is to raise not merely human awareness of ecosystems but consciousness as such. In the view of these ecologists, the environment, if not quite sentient, confers a heightened sentience on persons. In *Deep Ecology* (1985), George Sessions and Bill Devall see the "interior work" of "cultivating ecological consciousness" as the movement's distinctive feature.[3] Whereas reform ecology focuses on technological fixes and policy positions, deep ecology involves "becoming more aware of the actuality of rocks, wolves, trees, and rivers," "being honest with ourselves and seeking clarity in our intuitions, then acting from clear principles," and drawing on the example of "people seeking local autonomy from centralized state authority."[4]

As we have seen, antiutilitarian thinkers seek to restore first-person ontology as the locus of value in persons. Their account of value is internalist—proceeding, in other words, from what Bernard Williams calls "the inside point of view." "People's dispositions," Williams concludes, "are the ultimate supports of ethical value."[5] Yet despite their commitment to systems over persons, radical ecologists are not exactly externalists when it comes to value. The first principle of deep ecology's eight-point "platform," according to Naess, is the claim that "the well-being and flourishing of human and nonhuman life on Earth have value in themselves (synonyms: intrinsic value, inherent value)."[6] "Each stone, each plant, each grain of sand exists in and for itself with a clarity that is undimmed by any suggestion of a different realm," Edward Abbey declares in *Desert Solitaire* (1968).[7] The question for radical ecologists is how to square "intrinsic value" with the systems-theoretical dictum that process trumps essence. Their answer is to model the ecosystem on the order of a transcendental subject, the mainstay of the idealist tradition. This may sound perverse, since ecology is nothing if not a consequentialist account of the world; for the ecologist, context is all.[8] But the positing of a closed universe of pure context (evidenced in one of the period's pet figures for the planetary system, "spaceship earth") turns that context into an equally pure formal structure. In ecology, context scaled up to cover all actions—human and nonhuman, organic and nonorganic—becomes ontotheology (evidenced in another of the period's favorite figures, Earth as Gaia).

The biologist James Lovelock claims that some early readers of *Gaia* (1979) took issue with his naming the biosphere after a Greek goddess because it appeared to violate science's taboo on personification. Yet even while denying that he sees the planet as "sentient," Lovelock maintains that we must "love and respect the Earth with the same intensity that we give to families and our tribe," since "our contract with Earth is fundamental."[9] The distinction

Lovelock wants to make is between acting as if Earth is a contractual subject and actually believing it. For many radical ecologists, this is a distinction without a difference. An important (if not the dominant) strand of radical ecology reimagines the self-regulating system of the biosphere as a self-*realizing* one, a being whose interest in its own becoming we are obliged to support.[10] Moreover, for this strand of radical ecology, our indifference to that obligation causes the biosphere to exact justice by holding our worst transgressions accountable under the second law of thermodynamics. The law of entropy turns out to be a moral law.

While radical ecology slips with ease between the universe of physical facts and the realm of ethics, its more interesting habit concerns its frequent assignment of a moral compass to the environment itself. In "Animal Liberation: A Triangular Affair" (1980), Baird Callicott claims that neither utilitarian nor Kantian views—"humane ethics"—are adequate to the "land ethic" first developed by Aldo Leopold (one of deep ecology's founders) and now broadly accepted among environmentalists.[11] "The land ethic manifestly does not accord equal worth to each and every member of the biotic community," Callicott writes. "The moral worth of individuals (including, n.b., human individuals) is relative, to be assessed in accordance with the particular relation of each to the collective entity that Leopold called 'land'" (327). Callicott admits that "there can be no value apart from an evaluator" (325), yet the eruption of the passive voice in this passage makes it hard to see who is making the appraisals. Since human beings are scarcely equipped to pass judgments of "moral worth" on the ecosystem, the "collective entity" must assume the task (325). This "autochthonous" being stands in relation to all organisms as a universal arbiter, rendering judgments in line with "natural biological laws, principles, and limitations" (334).

Callicott's argument became notorious for its unapologetic endorsement of the misanthropic implications of the land ethic in particular and of radical ecology in general. "The extent of misanthropy in modern environmentalism," he concludes, "may be taken as a measure of the degree to which it is biocentric" (326). Its infamy also derived from Callicott's startling claim that if the "preciousness of individual deer, as of any other specimen, is inversely proportional to the population of the species," then "environmentalists, however reluctantly and painfully, do not omit to apply the same logic to their own kind" (325). In Callicott's version of the land ethic, individual persons lack value to the extent that their numbers are not merely superfluous but deleterious to the "collective entity" of the ecosystem. "The population of human beings should be roughly twice that of bears," he concludes, "allowing for differences of size" (325). Callicott holds that the quality of persons is driven down by an increase in quantity, as when a market is flooded with excess inventory: "human life . . . is a commodity altogether too common in relation to wildlife and to wild landscapes" (327).

Most radical ecologists are less enthused than Callicott by the prospect of thinning the human herd for the biosphere's benefit. But among such figures, the critique of anthropocentrism shades repeatedly into a defense of the planet's subjectivity at the expense of any specifically human version, along with a certain resignation toward the eliminative steps the planet must take to right itself. Rejecting the premise of Callicott's "collective entity" busily assessing organisms in light of its own "functional system of value" (319), Alan Drengson shares Naess's view that essential to deep ecology is a recognition of the "intrinsic value of all life."[12] The locus of this value is ubiquitous in the biomass at large and centralized in what Drengson calls the "planetary person" (74). Drengson appeals to Kant's argument for reciprocity to defend this ethical ideal over and against "utilitarianism," which he (like most antiutilitarians) sees as a "technocratic paradigm" (86). Of course, the appeal to Kant entails a revision of Kant. Kant's kingdom of ends doesn't allow any but *rational* persons to be accorded our reciprocity. Drengson holds that this "concept of persons is impoverished," with the consequence that "nature" is not "understood" as a "living subject" (84). Along the same lines, Bill Devall concludes that far from "just 'dead matter,'" "Nature . . . is a self-realizing, internally connected cosmos" with a "will-to-live."[13]

If the planet is a person with what Drengson calls a "biography" (95), what kind of person is she? (Environmental discourse—following Lovelock's Gaia thesis, which itself follows a long history of feminizing nature—assumes that the planet's gender is female.) Callicott's land ethic grants sovereignty to the land as self-legislator. But his "collective entity" recalls Rawls's dim view of utilitarianism's "impartial spectator" tasked with doling out social benefits in the service of making *society* better, whether or not this betterment applies to any specific (or specifically needful) individuals. "By reference to a single good," Callicott writes, again in the passive voice, "competing individual claims may be adjudicated and relative values and priorities assigned to the myriad components of the biotic community" (338). The difference is that in ecological discourse, the biomass—like a Hobbesian Leviathan who has lost the plot—dispenses to persons not the paternalistic favors that Rawls condemns but a far rougher justice: their impending extinction, an extreme but necessary measure when, as Callicott points out, "the enormous human population is at present a global disaster . . . for the biotic community" (329).

Callicott's theory of value finds a surprising echo in the work of Ayn Rand, who claims that "it is only the concept of 'Life' that makes the concept of

'Value' possible."[14] The resonance appears unlikely because Rand's Objectivism is premised on an egoism that treats human life as a privileged category above "Life" as such. Yet the libertarian view of human specialness turns out to be more proximate to radical ecologists' understanding than we might expect. Like many of his contemporaries, Callicott grounds environmental ethics on a Malthusian terror.[15] What the cranky environmental activist Paul Ehrlich called "the population bomb" in his best-selling 1968 book of that title licensed the most authoritarian social policies: "We must have population control," Ehrlich writes, "by compulsion if voluntary methods fail."[16] Published the same year as Ehrlich's book, Garrett Hardin's famed essay "The Tragedy of the Commons" argued both for coercive governmental intervention (with a policy of zero population growth) and *against* the welfare state, which he blamed for runaway birth rates. "The Tragedy of the Commons" ends with the dire prediction that the "freedom to breed will bring ruin to all."[17] Like Callicott, Hardin imagines that the value of human personhood declines as the sheer number of human bodies mounts. "Making great and spectacular efforts to save the life of an individual makes sense only when there is a shortage of people," Hardin writes in the "Economics of Wilderness" (1969). "I have not lately heard that there is a shortage of people."[18]

Later in his career, Hardin would take a vocal role in support of Herrnstein and Murray during *The Bell Curve* controversy of the mid-nineties. As this biographical snippet reveals, some radical ecologists relied not only on a "Kantian" appeal to subjectivity but on the claims set forth by IQ innatists in their forecasts of social collapse. Ecological implosion follows a similar arc and for similar reasons to those found in Herrnstein, Jensen, and Banfield. This is to say that Hardin and Ehrlich's is no blanket anti-anthropocentrism. Just as Callicott asserts that the biotic community has higher esteem for "rare . . . species" (326) than common ones, so population doomsayers rate some varieties of *Homo sapiens* more valuable than others. It is easy to see why some critics have taken a dim view of ecologists for what appear to be the latter's unseemly illiberalism.[19] Ehrlich lobbied against aid for famine-struck countries, considering them lost causes.[20] And Hardin's fondness for eugenics might have accounted for his dislike of both non-European immigration and affirmative action.[21] These thinkers just barely stop short of Rand's outrageous division of persons into "rational, productive, independent men" and "moochers, looters, [and] brutes."[22] Their willingness to divide the human population into valuable assets and waste products shows us that, among radical ecologists predisposed to apocalyptic musings, the human species comes to figure not merely as the purveyor of pollution but as an instance of pollution, not merely a cause (and so possible solution) to ecological dysfunction but identical to ecological dysfunction.[23] In this discourse, the world can be purified and its value restored by expelling its toxic human matter.[24]

Drengson, perhaps the most humanistic of deep ecologists, is thus the most revealing in his commitment to the view that "human values" (98) are irreconcilable with the biosphere's, which Drengson refers to as "the values within a natural process, independent of human interests" (91). For Drengson, people are too egoistic, too "purely subjective" (89), to imagine "values in the world apart from our interests" (91), much less the idea that a "river . . . has a value in itself" (92). Hence while conceding the internalist account of value, Drengson takes that account's premise that subjectivity alone is the predicate for value as the basis for a vast expansion of subjectivity's ambit. As a result of our hopeless partiality, it "is not for us to judge," he writes, "what . . . deer and bear want" (93). And in any event, such judgments would be irrelevant, since nature's value ("inherent worth, as it is in the world as a whole" [96]) precedes any view we might take of it. It is merely there to be discovered, like a precious metal that our species—hobbled by "utilitarianism, mechanism, and anthropocentrism" (86)—lacks the conceptual equipment to mine. While resource extraction proceeds at an alarming rate, then, the "intrinsic value of all life" (76) remains thus far unavailable for (and so undepleted by) human use. This is not a casual conceit. Fixating on value as an inaccessible substance indistinct from life itself, radical ecology assimilates the notion of "intrinsic" value to the internalist accounts of value we find in philosophers like Williams and Nagel by reimagining the web of life as a person with a deep subjectivity and a person's robustly proprietary sense of what belongs to her.

The idea that the planet as such feels the sting of trespasses against its possessions, the way that Nozickian individuals feel violated in their property rights by the state's takings, comes into focus at a time when numerous social scientists had become enamored with what we might call the *entropic turn*. This would be the discovery that the world was a closed system whose limits as dictated by the laws of thermodynamics could not be breached by the most ingenious human design. "The degradation of the universe is even more extensive than that envisaged by classical thermodynamics," Nicholas Georgesçu-Roegen writes in *The Entropy Law and Economic Process* (1971). "It covers not only energy but material structures."[25] Based on his unorthodox interpretation of the second law, Georgesçu-Roegen maintained that late industrial civilization triggered not merely a gradual dissipation of energy but a rapid deterioration of the object world, "a continuous transformation of low entropy into high entropy" that converts matter to "*irrevocable* waste" (281). Georgesçu-Roegen became the guru for environmentalists concerned to show that, as he puts it, "any use of natural resources for the satisfaction of nonvital needs means a smaller quantity of life in the future" (21).[26] His most ardent disciple was Jeremy Rifkin, who declared in *Entropy: A New World View* (1980) that "within a few years every academic discipline will be turned inside out by the new entropy conception."[27]

Entropy serves seventies thinkers as an all-purpose metaphor for cultural and natural erosion, a trope recruited to shore up not just predictions of environmental collapse but critiques of phenomena ranging from planned obsolescence (in Georgesçu-Roegen) to the "used-upness of certain forms" of literature (as John Barth puts it in "The Literature of Exhaustion" [1967][28]) to what the sociologist Robert Nisbet calls "a bureaucratized welfare state that prizes uniformity above ... the complexity of real life."[29] If the first law of ecology (as formulated by Barry Commoner) is that "everything is connected to everything else," the second law of thermodynamics supplies the rhetorical adhesive.[30] The process that entropy describes, of structures moving from difference to indifference, from order to randomness, captures the logic through which the fiercest proponents of the entropic turn feel at liberty to override divergences among any conceivable categories, natural or artificial. For radical ecology, entropy not only describes but *licenses* dedifferentiation. "The Entropy Law," Rifkin observes, "is the assassin of the truths of the Modern Age," chiefly "the notion of history as progress" (7).

Even when they demurred from Rifkin's tendency toward overstatement, many thinkers shared his view that "science joins ... ethics" (50) in the entropic turn, whose guiding principle was the arresting of economic growth. For Herman Daly, who coined the term "steady-state economy," the "ethics of human convention must not run counter to those of thermodynamics," which "tells us that ... nature really *does* impose 'an inescapable general scarcity.'"[31] "There is ample evidence that people are beginning to suffer from a sense of claustrophobia," E. J. Mishan writes in *The Costs of Economic Growth* (1967). "Our planetary home, once thought to be immense, now begins to look dwarf-sized."[32] Hence the alarm sounded by the Club of Rome in its influential report, *The Limits Growth* (1972): the "attempt to grow forever in a limited environment" will result in "a disastrous collapse."[33] In the "inevitable" clash between a system built for "the increase in wealth" (118) and "the intractable limits of the natural ... cycle" (122), Commoner points out in *The Closing Circle* (1971), "human activity ... *must* accommodate to the demands of ... the ecosphere" to "survive" (123). For post-sixties thinkers, the global economy is a version of Kenneth Boulding's "entropy trap." "The present period will be seen as a very brief period," Boulding writes, "in which man managed to maintain a high-level society over a part of the earth at the cost of ... rapid exhaustion of his geological capital."[34]

Luckily for the biosphere, nature's own drive toward complexity counteracts our hyperactive society's dissipation of meaningful structures into low-grade waste. "Ecosystems," Drengson points out, "are both entropic and antientropic" (87). The "steady flow of energy" from the sun to the earth, Lewis Thomas observes in *Lives of a Cell* (1974), "is mathematically destined to cause the organization of matter into an increasingly ordered state . . . against entropy, lifting it, so to speak, into a constantly changing condition of rearrangement."[35] Because its perpetual complexity conflicts with the human drive toward monoculture, the planetary person's autonomy is not merely indifferent but increasingly hostile to our own, whether we define the latter as the freedom to "*objectify* . . . nonhuman nature" (82) (in Drengson's view) or the "freedom to breed" (in Hardin's). Both the proliferation of human bodies and the clogging of the world with human artifacts contradict nature's commitment to open places. Hence Gary Snyder praises "the tiny number of persons who come out of the industrial societies . . . and then start to turn back to the land" away from the "great edifice called 'the state.'"[36]

"From the point of view of . . . our welfare state," whose "norms require . . . connection," Naess writes in "Self-Realization" (1987), "the scattered human habitation along the arctic coast of Norway is uneconomic."[37] Naess objects to the state's willingness to sacrifice the arctic people's "personal identity" by "concentrating them in so-called centers of development" (19). While his argument recalls the critique of utilitarian theory's indifference to the individual, Naess believes that nature rather than contract should prevail when it comes to answering the question, "Who am I?" "If people are relocated from a steep, mountainous place to a plain," he writes, "they are not the same as they were" (19). For Nozick and Rawls, the goal of bypassing utilitarian social structures is to reassert the sovereignty and dignity of individual persons. For Naess, that goal proves impossible on the view that personal identity does not stay intact from one environment to another. The welfare state is thus problematic because, esteeming only the "social self" (14), it forces people into situations of purely human mutuality that sever them from the multitude of "living beings" (13) to which their identities need access.

As Naess's argument shows, proponents of the entropic turn's mandate against unlimited growth take aim less at the capitalist marketplace than at the coercions of runaway statism. Despite the "bizarre" "fascination with society" (61) that first arose among urban centers and still dominates our "civilization," according to Snyder, "people's own sense of identity" (31) is "something that could not be learned by continually consulting other human teachers, but could only be learned by venturing outside the borders and going into your own mind-wilderness" (37). The antisocial environmentalist, for whom other people get in the way of our communion with nature, is the oldest chestnut in the history of modern ecological thought. "We go to the woods to escape," Bill McKibben laments in *The End of Nature* (1989). "But now there is nothing except us and there is no escaping other people."[38] Naess and Snyder call less for a Thoreauvian retreat from sociality, however, than for a new (or rather very old) kind of polis. For Snyder, it is the embrace of "'primary' culture" ("the Paleolithic is where it's at" [34]). For Naess, it is a return to "local self-government" ("Shallow" 6), accompanied "by a reduction in the number of links in the hierarchical chains of decision" (7). These are not alternatives but mutually reinforcing ideals. In radical ecology, the "Paleolithic" implies "self-government."

Paleo-Republics

In Paul Shepard's *The Tender Carnivore and the Sacred Game* (1973), the ecology runs unusually deep. We'll find no respite from our "over-dense society and apocalyptic culture" in the bucolic fields of pastoral life, since "the disaster facing us now is a continuation of an earth trauma that began about ten thousand years ago," with the transition to agriculture and its "aim of completely humanizing the earth's surface, replacing wild with domestic."[39] Shepard's book pleads for a return to the "cynegetic" (144) life of hunter-gatherers before the "agrarian mind" (4) perverted our species with the "lust for more children and more production" (244). The "drive for more offspring" (96) also appears to have triggered the birth of false consciousness: "a thousand 'goofy' ideologies have been exploding since agriculture shattered the life ways of the hunting clan" (103). Shepard shares the IQ innatists' view that programs meant to engineer equality override inborn differences at their peril: "It is futile to pronounce, at the end of fifteen million years of hominid evolution, that men and women are alike" (120). But the most insidious ideology—a master category absorbing all the rest—is "the idealizing of social change" (104), which Shepard traces to the "boredom" that is "agriculture's 'beginning point'" (30). At constant risk of inanition, settled peoples have resorted to ever more drastic artifices to fill their "distorted lives" (90) with meaning.

"Human consciousness was reorganized," Shepard claims, "when the cynegetic life was shattered" (7). Whereas agricultural civilization makes for a bovine existence, "cynegetic society" allows the hunter to engage the world with complete awareness ("the hunter is the alert man" [147]), to avoid self-interest ("sharing is built into the life style" [133]), and to radiate a spontaneity of being ("in no other life style is personal experience so ecstatic and authentic" [146]). Let us name Shepard's rhapsodic speculations on the cynegetic life "really deep ecology." Though appearing to skirt the fringes of academic thought in the seventies, Shepard was scarcely alone in his view that domestication launched our species on a fast track to entropic destruction by encumbering us with artificial drives. "Ten thousand years ago we initiated the production of food and people in such quantity that we could never again return to the hunting way," Robert Ardrey writes of our "abnormal" reliance on "plant foods" in *The Hunting Hypothesis* (1976). "And there is only one way back— starvation, decimation, death."[40] From the vantage of "interplanetary archeologists of the future," according to Richard Lee and Irven Devore, "agriculture and thermonuclear destruction will appear as essentially simultaneous."[41]

While his revisionism is certainly less dramatic than Shepard's, the anthropologist Marshall Sahlins shares the latter's commitment to undoing the "Neolithic prejudices" of a historical record penned by the agrarian victors.[42] Sahlins makes the case for hunter-gatherer life as "the original affluent society," as he puts it in his celebrated 1968 essay of that name (1). Only because consumer culture has "erected a shrine to the Unattainable" of *"Infinite Needs"* (39) do we ascribe "poverty" to nonsettled peoples and overlook their "unparalleled material plenty" (2). Innocent of the "double tragedy" of consumerism, where "what begins in inadequacy will end in deprivation" (4), hunter-gatherers choose a "low standard of living" (2) to spare themselves "an acquisitiveness that in reality was never developed" and "desires that were never broached" (13). The "pristine affluence" that "colors their economic arrangements" arises from the right relation to scarcity. "Living well" demands both an "ascetic economy" and "a draconic population policy." Hunter-gatherers are natural "Malthusian[s]," using "practices" of infanticide "cruelly consistent" with the desire to "maintain a certain physical and social stability" (34).

In *Ecology and the Politics of Scarcity* (1977), the political theorist William Ophuls concurs with these thinkers' generally dim view of *Homo domesticus*. But whereas Sahlins sees "scarcity" as an artificial category that "exists only in relation to felt need" (10), Ophuls (like Herman Daly) sees scarcity less as a matter of perception than as part of the "fundamental laws of the universe."[43] "Ever since he acquired technology in the form of fire," Ophuls writes, "man's actions" have resulted in an "anti-evolutionary" (37) squandering of the biomass's "exceedingly precious capital stocks" (112), "the stored wealth of the ages in their plants, animals, and soil" (37). For Ophuls, modernity has hastened this depletion not (as Sahlins sees it) through insatiable consumerism but (as Naess and Snyder see it) through hypertrophied governmentality. The liberal state's pattern of "satisfying rapidly rising expectations while allowing very large expenditures for social welfare" (186) runs afoul of the "thermodynamic economy" (112).

Founded in "an era of abnormal abundance" (8), Ophuls thus concludes, the open society can no longer be sustained. If "liberal democracy as we know it . . . is doomed by ecological scarcity" (3), its successor must be a "steady-state society in which men and their demands are in balance with the environment and its resources" (136), a world "characterized by great frugality" (2). Though he takes the idea of the steady state from Daly, Ophuls insists that reimagining collective life on this footing obliges us to borrow a page from nature itself:

> Design is nature's way. As a consequence of certain basic physical laws (the design criteria), natural systems and cycles operate automatically to produce an integrated, harmonious, self-sustaining whole that evolves in the direction of greater biological richness and order, eventually reaching a climax that is the ultimate expression of the design criteria. . . . The political and social philosopher of the steady state is therefore to devise design criteria that will be just as effective and compelling as those of nature in creating an organic and harmonious climax civilization. (229)

Ophuls's preferred "design" for such a civilization is a "closed polity" (145) resembling "the pre-modern city state in size and spirit," a "minimal polity" that "can place primary reliance on the inherent virtue of the citizen" (241).

Ernest Callenbach's curious 1975 best seller *Ecotopia* suggests what such a polity might look like. The titular country (comprising the West Coast of the US, with the telling exception of Los Angeles) has seceded and reestablished society on a footing of "almost anarchic decentralization" (120). Ecotopians have given "local communities . . . control over all basic life systems" (67) and "try to decentralize and personalize wherever possible" (122). And while Callenbach's narrator insists that "Ecotopians are *not*, contrary to popular belief, headed back toward a Stone Age life," their social order is nonetheless based on the fact that "human beings are tribal animals" (35). Ecotopians live in "constellations of mini-cities" (27), "each one a self-contained community" populated by "groups of between five and 20 people, some of them actually related and some not" (70), while the land between the cities, "where animals are . . . left as wild as possible," makes for good "hunting just outside town" (16). Shepard proposes a similar cynegetic municipal system on a vaster scale; his plan involves turning the flyover states into large game preserves and relocating people to city-states along each coast.

Notwithstanding these "deliberate throwback[s]" (16) to the Paleolithic, Callenbach's Ecotopians imagine themselves as progressive rather than nostalgic. Having "crossed over into the age of biology" out of the "prison" of a "system" that is "still physics-dominated" (126), and rejecting the view that "mankind" was "meant for production," Ecotopians want "humans . . . to take their modest place in a seamless, stable-state web of living organisms, disturbing that web as little as possible" (47). Such minimal impact requires "proper population size," about "the number of Indians who inhabited the territory before the Spaniards and Americans came" (67), as well as a localism that preempts use of high-entropy transportation technologies ("they seldom travel 'on business'" [42]). Callenbach's narrator, an outsider from the US, is initially horrified by what he sees as Ecotopia's "medieval approach to things" (122), though he is (of course) eventually won over. "The risky social experiments undertaken here," he concludes, "have worked on a biological level" (163). Ecotopians have what Ophuls calls "a genuinely post-modern civilization that combines the best of ancient and modern" (232).

Callenbach's ancients, like Shepard's or Sahlins's, belong to the Pleistocene. Ophuls's belong to the Hellenic world. "Those who live in the steady state," he notes, "will have to be genuinely political animals in Aristotle's sense" (228). And "the political thought of Plato" (160) will guide the steady state away from a "politics . . . devoted almost exclusively to the utilitarian satisfaction of desire or appetite" (237). One striking claim in *Ecology and the Politics of Scarcity* is that an adherence to the pattern of nature's causally closed universe will forestall the decline into *ethical* entropy precipitated by the modern bureaucratic state. "The steady-state society," Ophuls concludes, "will undoubtedly be characterized by genuine morality" (231). The second law of thermodynamics proves the bankruptcy of utilitarianism. "Where this seems to lead," Ophuls writes of his effort to derive politics from physical laws, "is toward a decentralized Jeffersonian polity of relatively small, intimate, locally autonomous, and self-governing communities rooted in the land . . . and affiliated at the federal level only for a few clearly defined purposes" (241). Though feigning dissent from the main Enlightenment tradition ("the golden age of individualism, liberty, and democracy is all but over" [145]), Ophuls has more in common with the Lockean Nozick than with ecologists who promote holistic systems over anthropocentric individuals. The salient difference is that Nozick's state of nature (following Locke's) is a frontier of abundance, whereas Ophuls's is a virtual corpse leached of all but a scant remainder of its once-flush resources.

Ophuls's Jeffersonian appeal shows us that some radical ecologists take issue less with the privileging of the human over the natural world— "homocentricity" (20), as Shepard calls it—than with a decline from a once and future individualism to which modern political theory pays lip service. "It has generally been claimed that modern Western religion or political democracy discovered the importance of the individual," Shepard claims, but this is a mistake, "for evolution defined this long ago" (101). For Shepard, as we have seen, the transition from "cynegetic man" (145) to *Homo domesticus* bespeaks not increased self-awareness but "mental fogging" (150). With "blunted minds and coarsened bodies" (15) and a "willingness to drudge" (20), agriculturalists resemble their own "domestic animals" (15) more than their free-ranging Pleistocene predecessors. Whereas farmers have "achieved independence from the demands of style by having no style" (15), hunters, "being small in population—hence a rare species—have highly personalized lives" (144). And like other carnivorous predators, human animals are most "intelligent" when "few in number" (126).

Only by reducing our numbers, according to many radical ecologists, can we recover our primal sense of individualism. If "civilization" is "ego gone to seed and institutionalized in the form of the State," as Snyder puts it in *The Practice of the Wild* (1990), employing a figure of overgrowth that resonates with Shepard's polemic, then a superior individualism must lie beyond the harms that settled life inflicts on subjectivity.[44] The embrace of what we might call the paleo-republic in radical ecology follows from the invidious distinctions entertained by Malthusians like Ehrlich and Hardin, who see excess populations as the lamentable outcome of states that encourage large numbers. "A mass democracy," according to Edward Goldsmith and Robert Allan, authors of *Blueprint for Survival* (1972),

> is, in fact, a contradiction in terms, and as our society becomes ever more massive and ever less organized, i.e. as entropy and randomness increase, so must there be a proportionate increase in the precarious asystemic controls required to maintain a semblance of social order, and a similar reduction in its stability and hence in its capacity to survive.[45]

Blueprint takes no prisoners in its diagnosis of ecological imbalance. Every "social disease" (115) from "alcoholism" to "illegitimacy" (113) to "the black ghettoes of New York" (109) is a symptom of *étatist* modernity's having forgotten "how to live within one's ecological means" (118). Thwarting ecological and social catastrophe requires "a decentralized society." "It is probable," *Blueprint*'s authors conclude, "that only in the small community can a man or woman be an individual" (51).

Such arguments feel as indebted to the platform of radical ecology as to the emergent antiestablishment theory known as "communitarianism," whose proponents were some of the leading lights of the new conservatism in the seventies. According to one of that movement's most respected thinkers,

Robert Nisbet, there was a clear correlation between the decline of community in modern life and a disregard for the environment. "No civilization, no group within a civilization, has ever removed itself as far from nature as we have," he writes in the preface to the 1962 edition of *The Quest for Community* (1953).[46] By the seventies, Nisbet had zeroed in on the true nemesis of communities. "The Western structure of political power has been a process of almost permanent revolution," he writes in *The Twilight of Authority* (1975), "against the social groups and authorities that lay intermediate between individual and state" (205). The state's secret weapon in that ongoing coup is "the ideal of equality," "insatiable in its demands" (202). The "new despotism" of "equalitarianism" sponsors "programs"—"affirmative action, mandatory busing to achieve ethnic quotas, open admissions"—designed to bring about an "equality of condition" (221) that optimizes the state's hold over its subjects.

Nisbet describes this insidious power grab in terms befitting the entropic turn. As "populations have grown hugely" under modern governments, so "local and regional boundaries have eroded away in large measure" (210). As if mimicking the decay from complexity to simplicity in entropic systems, modern societies enact "a transfer to the state alone of powers previously resident in a plurality of associations" (199). And just as he stamps his critique of the state's alleged "passion for leveling" (199) with a thermodynamic veneer, so Nisbet echoes the call for a more authentic individualism found among some radical ecologists. "The Western state," he writes, creates "the illusion of individual freedom in a society grown steadily more centralized . . . and destructive of . . . diversity" (229). Such "manufactured individualism" is the alibi for the "atomization . . . of the social impulse" (278), a divide-and-conquer strategy the state uses to accelerate the "disintegration of old social unities" (210). Nisbet exhorts his readers "to form . . . associations or groups which are distinct from political government" (276), since only in "structures as ingeniously designed as clan, moiety, and tribe" (280) can "the individual" be "rescued from ineffectuality and insecurity" (282). "Contemporary commune[s]," the number of which he puts at about "10,000" (11), are the best hope for reviving the "substantial contexts" that "put the individual at the center of a series of concentric circles" (284).

While many environmentalists shared Nisbet's rejection of "the incessant spread of centralized power" (110), some were explicitly globalist in outlook, like the Club of Rome (with its "world system" model), or intent on using global power to force what *Blueprint for Survival* calls "a conscious drive to restructure society" (57). *Blueprint* originated as a draft platform for the United Nations' 1972 International Conference on the Human Environment. Yet radical ecologists appealed to the strong state not only to forge policies to make the world sustainable but to sustain individualism of a decidedly Enlightenment vintage—"teaching each person," as Rifkin puts it, "to become self-sufficient" (232). *Blueprint* insists that the small communities it favors must afford "an essential source of stimulation and pleasure for the individual" (51). Even as *The Limits to Growth* concludes that "the world system is simply not ample enough nor generous enough to accommodate . . . egocentric . . . behavior by its inhabitants" (195), its authors preserve a ration of hope for the "opportunities for limitless individual and social development" in "a society in a steady state of economic and ecological equilibrium" (196). Limitlessness—which also posed a threat to antiutilitarians like Williams—can be recuperated for a project that shifts attention inward, toward the self, and away from the imperatives of profit and growth.

Nisbet looks to the state as what stands between the individual and any conceivable balance. Many radical ecologists look to the state as a means of securing the individual in an ecologically balanced world. It is thus striking that these two very different outlooks should find common cause in the need for strong *authority* as the guarantor of autonomy. In "The Nemesis of Authority" (1972), Nisbet concludes that "freedom" is "inseparable from a structure of authority . . . which can alone give the stamp of character to the free mind." Strong authority is desirable when not located in the superstate but "built into the very fabric of human association."[47] *Blueprint*'s authors likewise argue that "in communities small enough for the general will to be worked out and expressed by individuals confident of themselves," people will "accept the restraints of the stable society as necessary and desirable and not as some arbitrary restriction imposed by a remote and unsympathetic government" (50). And Ophuls suggests that "coercion is not some evil specter resurrected from an odious past" but "an inextricable part of politics, and the problem is how best to tame it" (150). The "full political awareness" that will prevail in the steady-state society, he concludes, "will dispel its seeming nastiness" (151).

The Stone Age Mind

They might share Nisbet's view that authority is legitimate when it is "intermediate" between the self and large-scale abstractions (including the biosphere), but radical ecologists do not share his view of its origin. For Nisbet, such authority is like the unanimous contract in Rawls's *Theory of Justice*—purely social. For ecologists, such authority derives from nature. Hence Ophuls identifies "community"—"the most important [concept] in ecology" (22), where it names interactions of organisms in a given habitat—as the byword for a legitimate human state. When we agree that "the basic political problem is the survival of the community" (7), none will deny the need for "a truly just civil authority" (143) to take the reins from our "'adhocracy'" (193). "Community" oscillates in radical ecology between scientific description and normative appeal. "The land ethic," Leopold writes, "simply enlarges the boundaries of the community to include soils, waters, plants, and animals, or, collectively, the land."[48] *Blueprint for Survival* grounds its ideal community on the "evolutionary fact" that "it is a basic feature of all bonds that there is a limit to their extendability" (99). Community turns out to be an adaptation.

"It was some form of community living that made humans 'human,'" the radical ecologist Kirkpatrick Sale argues in *Human Scale* (1980).[49] And if the "need and capacity for communality is genetically encoded" (180), then evolution must afford lessons in rightsizing the social order.[50] "The limits of a human scale community . . . beyond which it ought not to grow" (182), Sale claims, is set by "the human brain" at "an optimum size of 500" (184). Sharing his view that the "brain . . . cannot truly comprehend the labyrinthine involutions of any very vast scale" (397), many of Sale's contemporaries see the small group as cultivating, and modern society as imperiling, the mind.[51] In *Small is Beautiful* (1973), E. F. Schumacher calls for a "system of production" that "mobilizes the priceless resources which are possessed by all human beings, their clever brains," to replace a "mass production" that is "stultifying for the human person."[52] Such a system will entail "self-sufficient local communities" where people "are less likely to get involved in large-scale violence than people whose existence depends on world-wide systems of trade" (53).

The worry that the machinery of industrial society begets violence on planet and self, "making . . . brains redundant" (163), as Schumacher puts it, finds a clear articulation in Nisbet, who condemns the modern state for its "penetration of the recesses of culture, of the smaller unions of social life, and then of the mind itself" (226). The history of the state has entailed not merely violent annexation outward (Nisbet, to his credit, objects to America's imperialist wars in the strongest terms) but an equally brutal internal colonization. "Mind and spirit are invaded . . . in however soft a form" (207) by the modern welfare state, which is in turn born from "the relentless increase of military-political power" (182): "the national programs . . . to equalize income, property, education, working conditions, and other aspects of life have been in the first instance adjuncts of the war state and of the war economy" (220).

Nisbet traces the state's extraterritorial incursions (whether in Indochina or into the soul) to bad political theory. His culprits are Plato and Rousseau. Radical ecologists see such colonizing tactics in human affairs not as theoretically flawed but as unnatural. Warfare exists because people are forced against their nature into territorial confines. "In the cynegetic society the kill is always a singular event," Shepard writes, whereas "in modern warfare man behaves like a captive animal" (216). Hunter-gatherers are "mobile" and "nonterritorial" (271), traits that keep populations trim and brains in prime working order. Pegging "the human group size best for mental and physical health" at "about twenty-five" (106), Shepard concludes that "over-dense society" (23) has led to an "overdone head," a "crisis of mental overreaching" in which "the human cerebrum," pushed past "its tolerable limits," has become "unfit."[53] "A brain of razor-sharp keenness useful in a world of human rarity," he writes, "may be too large in a world of billions of people" (124).

Shepard, we have seen, treats the advent of agriculture as the turning point in *Homo sapiens*' catastrophic relation to the environment.[54] In *One Cosmic Instant* (1974), the ornithologist John Livingston goes even further back: "By the time modern man penetrated all the continents during the Pleistocene 20,000 years ago, his 'dominion' over nature was well established."[55] The conflict between the human animal and the biosphere begins with the "astonishingly large brain of a man," an "overspecialization" out of sync with the "moderation" nature makes "not only a virtue but an evolutionary necessity" (80). "The arrogant human brain" (81) has brought about "a breakdown in homeostasis" (64). Signs of the current ecological crisis ("a monoculture of one dominant species of mammal") were already visible in the "Pleistocene overkill," whose "magnitude . . . was appalling" (123). Various ecologists share Livingston's view that the human brain is prone to imbalance. Whereas "the original brain was an efficient receiver of sensation and director of appropriate . . . responses in the rest of the body" (1), René Dubos and Barbara Ward argue in *Only One Earth* (1973), the "enormously larger and more complex" modern brain has resulted in a withering of "instinctive reactions" (2) and a privileging of "man-made surroundings" in lieu of the "natural variety" through which "the first men began to . . . feel their way toward fully conscious and creative humanity" (93). Such takes on the brain's terminal state in industrial culture bring the entropic turn to bear on consciousness. "The practice of meditation is designed to slow down the wasteful expenditure of energy," Rifkin writes (235). For Dubos and Ward, oases of "face-to-face . . . community" (94) forestall the mind's decline into the disorganization wrought by "urban misery" (93).

One thing that makes radical ecology radical is its rejection of the reform ecologist's view that human resourcefulness can repair the environmental damage human beings have wrought. "The so-called optimists believe that . . . continued scientific and technological ingenuity will keep the ecological wolf from the door indefinitely" (2), Ophuls writes in a representative dismissal of "technology's Faustian bargain" (156). Consciousness is both a problem for the environment (leading to overkills or severed instincts or the logistics of agriculture) and something only the environment can fix, as though the biosphere could cleanse the human mind on the model of the water cycle. In *Operating Manual for Spaceship Earth* (1969), Buckminster Fuller cautions against "pollution not only of our air and water but also of the information stored in our brains," as if the dramatic increase in "intellectual specialization[s]" were like chemical runoffs, begetting a kind of mental heat death operating on a time line exponentially faster than that of the universe.[56] Rifkin traces "breakdown and serious mental illness" to "the increasing flow of information" in mass society, since "our nervous systems and brain are only equipped to take in and use a certain amount of information at a time" (171).

Shepard traces the malaises of industrial culture back to *Homo sapiens*' tragic lapse into settlement. Livingston traces them to our species' brain. Shepard claims that the agrarians' relentless incentive to produce is an evolutionary misfire because it leads to "identifying culture as the opposite of instinct" and "putting the idea of culture at the center of a fantasy world" (112), the sort of world where people fail to see men and women as biologically distinct. Livingston argues that the desire to fabricate things, to make a culture hostile to nature, is a strategy of our consciousness, which appears as a parasite to which our bodies play unwitting host. Liberated from the rhythms of nature not by husbandry but by an oversized brain, our early forebear's "mind was free to assimilate whatever touched him, whatever would contribute to the edifice he was building . . . the monument to man's intellect" (165). In Livingston, "reason" verges on a maladaptation, "a liability" (181) that may "no longer have survival value" (182). If our species had "less consciousness" (158), it would stand more of a chance in the evolutionary sweepstakes. Livingston represents the extreme version of a view to which much seventies ecology is committed: the mind's matter is no less subject to thermodynamic decay than minable zinc or natural gas. In fact, modern technologies have accelerated the process. It would be fair to say that radical ecology does not reject the consciousness-raising of the counterculture (which also faulted industrial society for stifling awareness) but redirects its focus. For the sixties generation, mind expansion lay in reading Frantz Fanon or dropping acid. For radical ecology, it lay in a deep dive into the prehistoric. Whereas "we are captives" of a culture that has "fragmented our minds," according to Rifkin, "our ancestors" had an "intuitive grasp of reality" (251).

Published in 1980, Jean Auel's *The Clan of the Cave Bear* gives a narrative shape to the radical ecologists' view of the superior mental life of ancient peoples. The first volume in Auel's wildly successful "Earth's Children" series, the novel follows the Cro-Magnon Ayla from the earthquake that orphans her through her adoption by the titular clan of Neanderthals, her life with her adopted parents (Iza and Creb, the clan's medicine woman and high priest), and finally her exile. The blond and blue-eyed Ayla is an ugly duckling by Neanderthal standards; her "gawkiness" and "flat face" are endlessly played for laughs.[57] But the joke is on the clan. Growing into a leggy Aryan beauty (immortalized on screen by Daryl Hannah), Ayla represents the displacement in Eurasia of Neanderthals by *Homo sapiens*, a master race that Auel names "the Others" (20). Committed nonetheless to establishing the humanity of Neanderthals, Auel's book treats self-consciousness and a high level of culture as humanity's crucial factors. Neanderthals: they're just like us, with a complex system of rituals to mark life stages from birth through menarche (for women) and the first kill (for men) to death and burial.

The problem with this account of Neanderthals is the lack of incontestable traces of "culture"—like symbolic art and ornamentation—in the archeological record.[58] Auel's solution to this absence is partly ingenious, partly demented. Her Neanderthals require no representations because their minds have evolved the means to internalize all their lore and traditions. Iza's knowledge of the healing arts "acquired by her ancestors" is thus "stored in her brain at birth" (37). Departing from Shepard's view of Neanderthals (in whose oversized "craniums" he sees "evidence of accompanying cannibalism and ritual murder" [124]), Auel shares his view that life goes best when we follow the hunter-gatherer's lead and refuse the bad habit of "identifying culture as the opposite of instinct." Indeed, her Neanderthals have one advantage over Shepard's cynegetic humans. Whereas Shepard seizes on the Paleolithic "fascination" with *"objets trouvés"* as evidence of the hunter's interest in "linking the given and the created" (166), the Neanderthal needs no such reminders because that linkage is automatic. Objects never lost need not be found. If "cave art" is a "memory bank" (166) that "binds the group" (167) in Paleolithic society, as Shepard writes, *The Clan of the Cave Bear*'s Neanderthals forgo things like cave paintings and figurines because their culture is genetically wired: "stored in the back of their large brains were not just their own memories but the memories of their forebears" (29).

Genes do double duty in Auel's Neanderthal society, working to express not just the slowly evolved choices of natural selection but also the more rapid uptake of information performed by memes in human culture: "Ways that had once been adaptations for convenience had become genetically set" (25). Yet although their minds are capable of recalling everything their species has thought and even of "join[ing] . . . telepathically" (29), the clan has no ability to "conceive a future any different from the past." "All their knowledge," Auel writes, "was a repetition of something that had been done before" (30). The Neanderthal failure to "think ahead" (30) arises from a "psychic overdevelopment" (430) that Auel treats as a maladaptation. "As more memories built up, crowding and enlarging the storage capacity of their brain . . . there was no more room for new ideas." Incapable of learning because "their heads were already too large, "the Clan lived by unchanging tradition" (30). They thus believe in what Shepard calls "permanence instead of progress" (278), while the Cro-Magnon Ayla's "brain followed different paths," with "forward-thinking frontal lobes" (164).

Auel's view of the mind is a farcical rendition of the sort of militant physicalism satirized by Thomas Disch in *Camp Concentration*. But *The Clan of the Cave Bear* is not a brief for the materialist theory of mind. It is a female bildungsroman, and so best understood as a late entry in the annals of feminist consciousness-raising whose masterpiece is Erica Jong's *Fear of Flying* (1973). Auel turns Ayla into a poster child for constructionism in opposition to the clan's rigid gender hierarchy.[59] It would appear that the knowledge Iza genetically inherits can also be taught; even though "she doesn't have the memories" (120), Ayla thus becomes a distinguished medicine woman in her own right. Crossing the gender barrier "imposed by nature, and only cemented by [Neanderthal] culture" (37), Ayla also trains herself to become a gifted hunter, using her superior *Homo sapiens* rotator cuff to master the sling far beyond the skill of any wielder of this weapon in the clan.

Despite Ayla's triumph, it would be hard to argue that the lesson we are meant to take from the book is that only in *Homo sapiens*, with our superior capacity for abstraction and consequentialist thinking, for thinking beyond nature, lies the hope for progress. For even as it praises its heroine's plucky resourcefulness, *The Clan of the Cave Bear* is equally insistent that its incapacity for "surviving radical change" (430) is not to be held against the clan. Auel treats its extinction indeed as an entropic catastrophe precipitated by the species whose dominance amounts, according to radical ecology, to a continual mistaking of destruction for progress. Late in the novel, the telepathic Creb, the clan's high priest, taps into Ayla's brain and catches a glimpse into the Others' evolutionary future. There he witnesses the extinction of his own kind, of course, but also "a confusing kaleidoscope of landscapes, laid out not with the randomness of nature, but in regular patterns"—in other words, a suburbanized modernity with "boxlike structures reared up from the earth and long ribbons of stone spread out" (433). This rationalization of the natural world contrasts with the primordial harmony of Neanderthal experience. "The earth we leave is beautiful and rich," Creb thinks in reference to the looming dominion of Ayla's kind, "it gave us all we needed for all the generations we have lived" (438).

While Auel identifies the Neanderthals' extinction with their failure to change, the book actually construes this failure as less curse than blessing. The supposed inflexibility of the species arises from a calculated effort to retain as much of the world's richness as possible. It turns out that Creb's "all we needed" includes a veritable cornucopia of expert knowledges. The Neanderthals have not only a vibrant spiritual and cultural life but a preternatural sense of chemistry and the life sciences, from toxicology to anatomy: "The women dissected while preparing dinner and applied the knowledge to themselves" (37). Foods are cooked to bring out not only their nourishing but also their curative and psychotropic properties. In addition to a "bag of mind-altering roots" (429), Iza has contraceptives, sedatives, and stimulants within foraging reach. Auel's Neanderthals are like Callenbach's Ecotopians, who treat "technology" as if it "all sprang . . . from the womb of nature" (51). Ecotopians drive trucks "built of driftwood" (28) and learn "how to carve a pot holder from a branch" (39); they prefer "collaborating with the wood rather than forcing it into the shape of a building" (52). In the clan, "rib bones were stirrers, large flat pelvic bones were plates and platters along with thin sections of logs. Jaw and head bones were ladles, cups, and bowls" (82). Based entirely on recycling, the low-entropy technologies of Ecotopians and Neanderthals brake the conversion of worked energy from usable to unusable. "The clan used nearly every part of the animal," Auel writes. "Little was wasted" (245).

That Neanderthal cognition is "almost totally devoid of abstractions" also proves less a liability than an asset, at least from the environment's point of view. Unable "to synthesize," Auel writes, "they had a name for everything. They knew oak, willow, pine, but they had no generic concept for all of them; they had no word for tree." Because they don't sum up the world—Creb, the clan's brightest member, cannot count past 20—pluralism is their default: "Their language was replete with color and description" (128). Auel suggests, then, that the clan is an evolutionary dead end less because *Homo sapiens* represents a superior species than because of the Neanderthals' inborn refusal to overwrite nature's multiplicity with their own order.[60] Compare the clan's lack of a "word for tree" to Edward Abbey's aspiration in *Desert Solitaire*: "If a man knew enough he could write a whole book about the juniper tree. Not juniper trees in general but that one particular juniper tree which grows from a ledge of naked sandstone near the old entrance to Arches National Monument" (*DS*, xii). For radical ecologists, early *Homo*'s seeming ignorance masks a deep awareness. "The further back we go to communities that lack economic classes and a political State," the anarchist Murray Bookchin writes in *The Ecology of Freedom* (1982), "the greater evidence we find of an outlook toward life that visualized people, things, and relations in terms of their uniqueness."[61]

For Bookchin's early humans, "nature is not merely a habitat" but "a participant that advises the community" (47). He concludes that "private property" doesn't "become a category of consciousness" (50) until the "kinship . . . with nature" is severed (49). Likewise deprived of the power to categorize nature as other than kin, Auel's Neanderthals pattern their relation to the object world on what Bookchin approvingly calls "the practice of *usufruct*" (50). Hence in the clan a man's mate may be his "property," but "any man could take any woman whenever he wished to relieve himself" (134) whether or not she is mated.[62] Ayla on the other hand has what the novel treats as an instinctive sense of private property. "This will be my own place," she determines after finding a cave where the "men never climb up" (163)—a taking possession that mitigates her inability to "know her place" (224) in the clan's hierarchy. But it is not obvious that Auel wants us to see Ayla's self-realization as an unambiguous good. Notwithstanding her Pleistocene feminism, her independence and proprietary sense pull against the communal values that follow from what Bookchin calls the *"consociation"* between "humanity" and "nature" (47).

The novel does in fact present another "feminist" figure in Iza, whose rule-breaking and defiance of the clan repeat the patterns of conformation and optimization that mark the clan's interaction with its environment. Iza continually drugs herself to prevent conception in order to withhold a child from her abusive husband, thus damaging his status. And while "it was impossible for people of the Clan to lie" (66), it is apparently easy for Iza to keep secrets, specifically about her extensive use of birth control potions for herself and other women: "She never mentioned the magic she had learned from her mother, but she had been using it" (66). When Iza conceives the idea to train Ayla in the arts of medicine, her aim is to secure her adopted daughter a dignified status even without a mate. Her very adoption of Ayla gives us our first view of Iza's conciliatory style, a way of conducting oneself that presumes the fixed limits of the physical as well as social world. Playing the part of "imploring woman" (13) in her effort to convince the clan leader, Brun, to allow her to rescue Ayla, Iza exploits his sense that humoring her whims is an act of largesse befitting his role as the clan's alpha. Iza's resistance to patriarchy takes the form of a steady knapping away of the clan's monolithic cosmology that leaves its mineral essence—the maintenance of the clan in its steady state—intact.

Whereas even the clan's most reflective members place community above individuals, Ayla manifests an unclan-like ability to go it alone. For the crime of hunting while female, Ayla is sentenced to a "death curse," "the supreme punishment that was inflicted upon members of the Clan" (132), a ceremonial ostracism that amounts to social death. Even though Ayla's curse is "temporary"—"a whole moon"—the clan assumes that "it might as well be permanent" (271), and no one expects her to survive. Ayla retreats to her mountain hideout to while away her monthlong exile, hunting, stockpiling food and fuel, and generally making a cave of her own. Solitude poses no hardship for her because Ayla originates in a world without clans. The earthquake that sends her fleeing through "a wilderness of grassy steppes and scattered forests" (2) has swallowed "a hide-covered shelter" where she lived alone with her mother. Evolution in Auel's account has designed Ayla not only for flexibility but for egoism. At the end of the book she receives a permanent death curse that launches her on a journey through five sequels.

Iza's demise makes for an instructive contrast. Left behind with the elders who cannot make the journey to the massive tribal gathering far away from the cave, Iza succumbs hours after the clan's return. The summer of relative isolation spells her doom. As if confirming Sale's point about the survival advantage of community, Iza dies of loneliness. Ayla, on the other hand, has learned by the second book in Auel's series, *The Valley of Horses* (1982), that her "survival" no longer "depended on conforming to a way of life foreign to her nature" but rather "on her ability to overcome her childhood conditioning and think for herself."[63] But even its "conforming" ways ultimately afford an adaptive advantage inconsistent with Auel's portrayal of the clan as "hidebound" (164). Despite their supposed extinction within an "inherently changing environment" (31) dominated by *Homo sapiens*, Auel's Neanderthals endure by interbreeding with the Others. Ayla gives birth to a child, "a mixture of her and Clan" (465) who "will carry the Clan on." Ayla "came," Creb concludes, "not to bring us our death, but to give us our one chance for life. It will never be the same, but it is something" (485). That "something" recalls Creb's earlier "all we needed"—a Sahlins-like principle of modest wants rather than what Shepard calls the "innate capacity to increase" (97) characteristic of *Homo sapiens*.

To attribute even this much messaging to Auel's novel, however, feels like a category mistake. The book's politics and literary pretensions are fairly muted. It does the novel no disservice to say that it is escapist fantasy (and exceedingly rewarding on those grounds). Yet partly because of its conventionality, *The Clan of the Cave Bear* inadvertently reveals certain difficulties in sustaining ecologically minded fiction. For the novel to be the kind of novel it is (a coming-of-age story), Auel's protagonist needs to be *emphatically* human as specified by that genre since at least the eighteenth century: yearning for self-realization, bidding for individuation against the backdrop of a social order by turns confining and affirming, her nimble yet errant consciousness developing into a majestic self-consciousness. And while Ayla's viewpoint presides over the novel, the book is rife with equally introspective Neanderthal points of view and interior monologues. However symbiotic the "kinship" between clan and environment, the latter remains an *out there* to the novel's engrossing human interest plots. The laughable parts of Auel's book—the Neanderthals' telepathy, say—nonetheless take place within a human framework. It is easy to imagine that narrating from a mammoth's or a tree's perspective would be just as risible, but it is hard to imagine that it would be *interesting*.[64] Hence the virtually universal tropism in environmental writing toward personifying nature, a device that not even the deepest ecology can avoid.[65] That *The Clan of the Cave Bear* is a firmly anthropocentric novel is thus no strike against it. It may well be that anthropocentrism is simply inescapable for the novel as a genre. Yet this suspicion makes things difficult for any environmentalist literary text that aims to unseat "homocentricity" as the basis of value.

Abbey's Autochthons

I conclude this chapter by turning to a writer whose far more explicit ecological message (not to say literary seriousness) poses as strong a challenge to anthropocentrism as we find in the period. Edward Abbey's *The Monkey Wrench Gang* (1975) is a contender for the title of most influential novel in radical ecology. With its exuberant narration of the titular band of "eco-raiders" battling the forces that would tame the desert landscape, the book has certainly inspired a good deal of activism.[66] Abbey's novel tells the story of four characters, Doc Sarvis, his aide (and girlfriend) Bonnie Abbzug, the "jack Mormon" (29) Seldom Seen Smith, and the Vietnam vet George Washington Hayduke III, who meet on a rafting trip organized by Smith. Bonnie and Doc spend their nights on a "neighborhood beautification project, burning billboards along the highway—U.S. 66, later to be devoured by the superstate's interstate autobahn" (9). Seldom nurses "a healthy hatred" for the damming of desert canyons and the resulting "blue death" of reservoirs these structures have created (31). And Hayduke does not hesitate to identify his government's carpet bombing and denuding of the Asian jungle with its assault on the canyonlands: "The open desert was being scraped bare of all vegetation, all life, by giant D-9 bulldozers reminding him of the Rome plows leveling Vietnam" (15).

All feel "a higher destiny calling" (13) them to convert their environmental discontent into action. Their enemy is "the U.S. Bureau of Reclamation" (31), and their mission is "to slow if not halt the advance of Technocracy, the growth of Growth, the spread of the ideology of the cancer cell" (207). Whereas the "engineer's dream is . . . the planet Earth with all irregularities removed, highways merely painted on a surface smooth as glass" (75), the monkey wrench gang's dream is a "place where not only space but time itself has come unglued. Has lapsed. Elapsed. Relapsed. Prolapsed. And then collapsed" (7). Far from "the clear and classical desert" Hayduke "roamed in dreams" (15), the novel's Southwest is strewn with "all that tragic and abandoned trivia of the American road" (14). The real "filth" in the novel is not litter (the gang actually has a policy of throwing trash out car windows) but the road itself. Ever "more roads, power lines, railways and pipelines" disfigure "what was once semi-virginal wilderness and still is the most spectacular landscape in the forty-eight contiguous bloody states" (49).

Like the neo-Malthusians of the entropic turn, Abbey categorizes virtually any human artifact as pollution: "the evil is in the food, in the noise, in the crowding, in the stress, in the water, in the air" (166). This attitude finds a revealing counterpart in another influential text of the era, Robert Venturi, Denise Scott Brown, and Steven Izenour's *Learning from Las Vegas* (1972), which does not necessarily encourage but certainly does not condemn the prospect of the Southwest as what Doc calls "one big strip city" (50). Among that book's provocations is its authors' breezy insight that "You can like billboards without approving of strip mining in Appalachia."[67] In fact, they claim, "billboards are almost all right" (6). The authors of *Learning from Las Vegas* assume that when people object to billboards, they object to their content, and that the architect's job is to improve on the latter while leaving the aesthetic of "enormous signs" intact: "it does not follow that we architects who learn from their techniques must reproduce the content or the superficiality of their message" (162).

Such sentiments have left *Learning from Las Vegas* open to the charge that its authors endorse what they notoriously (if sardonically) call "silent-white-majority architecture" (154). *Learning from Las Vegas* furnishes an important foil to Doc and Bonnie's contempt for the billboards they have "cut down, burned up, defaced and mutilated" (49). For Venturi and his coauthors, human intention trumps all. They imagine an architectural practice that, working with rather than against the vernaculars of mass society, would bring a "human scale" (as Sale calls it) to an environment overwhelmed with the "dead ducks" (163) of high-modernist monumentality. In *The Monkey Wrench Gang*, on the other hand, human design is unsalvageable. In its place, Abbey devises an animism that counters the built environment. Whereas *Learning from Las Vegas*'s billboards want improvement, Abbey's billboards want to sacrifice themselves, and Doc and Bonnie's beautification project is a kind of mercy killing. "Dehydrated by months, sometimes years of desert winds," Abbey writes, "the pine and paper of the noblest most magnificent of billboards yearned in every molecule for quick combustion, wrapped itself in fire with the mad lust, the rapt intensity, of lovers fecundating" (10).[68]

Teeming with animate matter both natural and manufactured, Abbey's object world is a rejoinder to the anthropocentrism that novels cannot but introduce whenever they focus on character consciousness. A "river" is "puzzled" by the "fat wedge" of the gravity dam that diverts its flow (2); a "juniper" is "anguished-looking" under "the fierce July sun" (4). Drill rigs send "resonant vibrations shudder[ing] through the bone structure of the earth," causing "more mute suffering" (75). "Under the heavy burden of water going nowhere" in Lake Powell, "the old rocks of the river channel waited for the promised resurrection" (112). "No one knows precisely how sentient is a pinyon pine . . . or to what degree such woody organisms can feel pain or fear," Abbey writes, "but this much is clearly established as scientific fact: a living tree, once uprooted, takes many days to wholly die" (74). The novel's panpsychism corresponds to a diminution in human potential. The novel's answer to the question, "What were . . . men worth?" is a familiar Malthusian reckoning: "In a nation of two hundred and ten million bodies . . . mass production lowers the unit cost" (83).

Because the object world is understood to retreat to a kind of dormancy under the thrall of human design ("the world hesitated, waiting for something" [91]), the gang's task is to set natural processes on trajectories that developers have temporarily arrested. "One crack in that dam and nature she'll take care of the rest" (258), Seldom tells Doc about his plan to pilot an explosive-rigged houseboat into the Glen Canyon Dam. Such gestures evoke the earthworks of the artist and critic Robert Smithson, who was closely identified with the entropic turn (as evidenced in his most famous essay, "Entropy and the New Monuments" [1966]). Earthworks enact "an art that takes into account the direct effect of the elements," an "ongoing dialectic" in which the earth tools its own raw material with a catalytic human assist, "gradually wearing down" the slowly churning planetary mass into interesting contours and textures.[69] Earthworks, Smithson claims, thwart the "retreat to scenic beauty" (164) that privileges a manipulation of the natural world on behalf of human standards and at the expense of nature's autonomy. "The best sites for 'earth art,'" he writes, "are sites that have been disrupted by industry, reckless urbanization, or nature's own devastation" (165).

Along the same lines, sabotage in *The Monkey Wrench Gang* amounts to embracing the entropic destiny of technology, as thinkers like Ophuls understand it, in order to bring about a cessation of human encroachment on wild space (as when "fifty-one tons of tractor" morph into "one unified immovable entropic white-hot molecular mass" [224]). The gang's activism consists in turning the machines of industrialism against themselves, but here too the objects require no more than a quickening of their supposed inanimateness. Thus "tractors" and tanker trucks, once powered up, "go on without human hands," in fact "come suddenly alive, wrenched into movement by an unseen force," colliding "as if pulled by invisible bonds . . . as all diminish steadily toward the rim . . . of Armstrong Canyon" (292). While it is hard to see Abbey as other than ironic when he calls the machine slaughter "deicide" (81), the repeated descriptions of "masochistic machinery [and] steel in pain" (206) suggest a pathos at odds with the novel's comic stylings. *The Monkey Wrench Gang*'s considerable length has much to do with the number of pages Abbey devotes to narrating the destruction of the earthmovers that remake the desert into a hub of what Georgesçu-Roegen calls "high entropy" civilization.[70] Flooded with detail, such scenes crowd the book, as if Abbey expects his readers will never tire of the "murder of a machine" (81) on the page, the way his characters "watched with satisfaction" (94) the various slow-motion catastrophes they have started: disintegrating billboards, collapsing bridges, "the thunderous barrage of avalanching iron, uprooted trees, slabs of rock embraced in gravity, falling toward the canyon floor" (292).

One reason for this stylistic quirk may involve the novel's commitment to the idea that, as Rifkin puts it, "entropy . . . destroys the notion of history as progress" (7). Like Smithson, Abbey sees this idea as entailing an aesthetic as well as a moral commitment. In "Entropy and the New Monuments," Smithson "celebrate[s]" (10) works that "bring to mind the Ice Age rather than the Golden Age," that "cause us to forget the future," that are "built not for the ages, but against the ages" (11). Smithson's is an aesthetic of desertification, typified by "a sand box" he photographs in Passaic, "a model desert" that "became a map of infinite disintegration and forgetfulness," suggesting "the sullen dissolution of entire continents, the drying up of oceans . . . a vast deposit of bones and stones pulverized into dust" (74). Abbey also rejects "scenic beauty" (which is why his characters treat littering as a perversely moral act) and also considers desertification an ideal to be sought rather than a fate to be avoided. "Creative destruction" (207) is prerequisite not to the maintenance of capitalism (which is what Joseph Schumpeter meant by it) but to recovering the "pink wasteland" (3) from the "machine-made wastes" of "real-estate development" (15). And just as Smithson maintains that "we have to accept the entropic situation and more or less learn how to reincorporate these things that seem ugly" (307), so Abbey appears to welcome entropy, or at least to see the fear of entropy among his contemporaries as shortsighted.

The reason is that, while entropy might pose problems from a human vantage, from nature's it is simply business as usual. In *Desert Solitaire* (1968), Abbey reports on the body of a dead hiker in terms that might give even the most misanthropic radical ecologist pause: "His departure makes room for the living. Away with the old, in with the new. He is gone—we remain, others come. . . . A ruthless, brutal process—but clean and beautiful" (*DS*, 214). The human terror of entropy—of systems that run down and fail—is the obverse of what Ophuls calls nature's "negentropy" (49), the sweeping away of debris. Abbey considers people problematic when they flout nature's purgative cycles. Looking forward to the time "when the glass-aluminum skyscraper tombs of Phoenix Arizona barely show above the sand dunes" (101), Hayduke welcomes "the kind of land to cause horror and repugnance in the heart of the dirt farmer, stock raiser, land developer" (111):

> he felt he could be let off anytime, anywhere, in the middle of nowhere, with his backpack, a gallon of water, a few relevant topo [sic] maps, three days' food supply, and he'd make it, survive and thrive, on his own, man. (All that fresh beef wandering around on the range; all that venison on the hoof down in the box canyons; all those sweet-water springs under the lucent cottonwoods a convenient day's march one from the next.) [106]

Like Auel's Neanderthals, Hayduke has "the conservative instinct to keep things not as they are but as they should be . . . to keep it like it was" (19), even while such preservation paradoxically requires dramatic collapse.

"When they . . . invented agriculture," Seldom Smith reflects in an echo of Shepard's enthusiasm for the cynegetic life, "the human race took a big step backwards. From hunters . . . down to farmers, that was one hell of a Fall" (332). Unlike Smithson, for whom nature's inexorable decline entails our own inanition ("one's mind and the earth are in a constant state of erosion, mental rivers wear away abstract banks, brain waves undermine cliffs of thought, ideas decompose into stones of unknowing" [100]), Abbey finds apotheosis in uncivilizable nature. On the run in the Utah canyonlands, with "nothing but rock, silent and uninhabited for thirty million years" (349), Smith has "the concentrated intensity of a buck in hunting season," can smell water a thousand feet away, and "feels" the "many big feet" of the gang's pursuers "marching over rock and shuffling through the sand" (337). The ideal "wilderness" may be "roadless" for Abbey, then, but it is hardly "uninhabited" (77). As Hayduke puts it: "The desert world appeared empty of all human life but himself" (142). The novel shares the Malthusians' view that less is more when it comes to human intellect: "One man alone can be pretty dumb sometimes, but for real bona fide stupidity there ain't nothing can beat teamwork" (338).

Abbey's antianthropocentrism appears short-lived, giving way to a radicalization of the precepts of the steady state, the paleo-republic that sanctifies individuals who commit to the "essential": "survival with fucking honor" (314). Though Abbey's characters profess themselves "against all forms of government" (158), they take the communitarian ecologists' respect for authority to its logical extreme. They eschew "even good government" (158) because nature's authority suffices. Whereas Ophuls and Nisbet see the rigors of communal life mitigated by face-to-face encounters among people, *The Monkey Wrench Gang* locates legitimate coercion in the face-to-face encounter with a wilderness—a cliff face, say—that issues the only edicts with which we must comply. Seldom Seen Smith considers himself a "true autochthonic patriot" whose loyalties "phase out toward the borders of the Colorado Plateau" (358). And for Hayduke, "home" doesn't "mean Tucson" but "the canyons" and "the mountains" (330). Nature's coercions are manifest in physical obduracy—like the "totally indifferent wall" (340) of a box canyon. But something like communion with stone is no less real than interpersonal bonds. "With cheek and ear pressed against the canyonland bedrock," Abbey writes of Hayduke scaling an impossibly vertical precipice, "he feels, hears, shares the beating of some massive heart, a heavy murmur buried under mountains, old as Mesozoic time. His own heart" (341).

The novel ends with a contest between Smith and Hayduke in which each vies to outlast the other before surrendering to the posse of state police, FBI agents, park rangers, and vigilante Utahans hunting them through the canyonlands. Abandoning the flight because there "ain't no permanent water" and "hardly no game" (352), Smith is finally apprehended after stealing "two pounds of lean red hamburger" (360) from tourists in a national park. It is as if the novel penalizes him for refusing to earn his meal the hard way. But Hayduke, now revealed as the novel's true hero (as attested by the "Free Hayduke" bumper sticker seen even today in countercultural enclaves), predicts that he can "survive" on "one deer a month" and "be fat and happy" with "one every two weeks." Rather than embark on this cynegetic idyll, Hayduke makes a dramatic last stand in Canyonlands National Park, ostensibly dying in a gunfight that knocks his bullet-riddled body "like a sack of garbage into the foaming gulf of the canyon, vanishing forever from men's eyes" (374). Hayduke has concocted a decoy of himself by dressing his clothes in the various detritus—scrub, branches—along the canyon cliff. Far from a "Jurassic morgue," the "dead city"

(345) of stone abounds in resources for his survival. The sacrifice of Hayduke's "prefabricated man" (327) recalls the various entropic cascades the gang has triggered. Whereas "gobs and gouts of burning slag fall through space" only to "splash with a steaming sizzle into the water" (297), however, Hayduke himself rises from the wreckage of his scarecrow's descent, upcycled for even greater things. His reappearance in the novel's finale on Doc's doorstep is "single and posthumous (out of the earth)" (381).

Thus, while his fellow eco-raiders have been reintegrated into the symbolic order, hiring lawyers and paying for their crimes by doing jail time and agreeing to live law-abiding lives on probation, Hayduke takes himself outside the human realm. In one sense his faked death really does amount to what an onlooker calls "the physical destruction of a human being" (373). Prevented from disappearing into the "ultimate world" of the canyons, "the final world of meat, blood, fire, water, rock," Hayduke manages to "lose himself" and "become pure predator dedicated to nothing but survival" (355), his quarry the fauna of industrial civilization, "the green beasts of Bucyrus, the yellow brutes of Caterpillar" (75). Yet the most telling detail in the scene of Hayduke's resurrection is his companion, a masked man he calls "the Lone Ranger" (225)—an appellation that makes Hayduke Tonto. *The Monkey Wrench Gang* deploys one of the oldest tropes in the national imaginary, the white man going native. Hayduke sees no difference between "Indian country" and "our country" ("the wilderness belongs to *us*" [82]) and imagines himself at home in an Anasazi ruin ("there's where I should live" [361]). Yet while such primitivism typically invokes a sentimental attachment to Indian identity, the novel's Indians play a distinctly *unsentimental* role.[71] Abbey presents Indians as an embodiment of the entropic turn. The gang passes "vacant lots where drunk and abandoned Navajos lay half hidden among the weeds," indistinct from the "shattered wine bottles" and "junked cars" around them (150). In *The Monkey Wrench Gang*, the phrase "genuine nonworking Indians" (154) indexes not merely their unemployed status but the breakdown of thermodynamic work, a dwindling of the energy needed to regroup and organize one's scattered parts.

At one point, the media attribute the gang's misdeeds to a "renegade clan from Shoshone tribe," an error Doc encourages: "We'll blame it on the Indians" (164). And Hayduke takes to signing his crimes "Native Avenger" and "Remember Wounded Knee" (254). This misdirection involves less an effort to frame the native Americans for the gang's crimes than to invoke a normative ideal. If "the real trouble with the goddamned Indians, reflected Hayduke, is that they are no better than . . . white folks" (25), the gang's deception projects a fantasy of the Indian as white folks' superior, an "autochthonic patriot" warring against the machine. Abbey's Indians do nothing but drink themselves into a stupor and cash their government checks in the "pastoral slums of Navajoland" (53), "land of . . . overloaded welfare caseloads" (24). If Indians are no better than the rest of us "now [that] they're domesticated" (164), the gang members in effect become better Indians. While Doc argues that "wearing a headband doesn't make you an Indian" (133), fleeing through the canyons apparently does. Unlike the "Stone Age savages riding around in pickup trucks" (200), Smith "walks like an old-time prewar pre-pickup-truck Indian, with a steady loping stride, the feet pointed straight ahead, perfectly parallel" (319). And Hayduke's identification of Indian country with his own turns out to be premature. Since even the "overdeveloped hypercivilized goddamn fucking Indian country" is not what it used to be, he plans on "going back to the canyons where people like us belong" (249).

The phrase "genuine nonworking Indian" (*DS*, 110) appears earlier in *Desert Solitaire*, but there it has another connotation: "The pre-Columbian Indians of the Southwest, whether hunting, making arrowpoints, going on salt-gathering expeditions or otherwise engaged, clearly enjoyed plenty of leisure time" (*DS*, 101). Whereas their forebears were "unburdened by the necessity of devoting most of their lives to . . . production" (*DS*, 102), enjoying the primordial affluence that Sahlins posits, today's Navajos are merely poor and unemployed. Or rather, as Abbey puts it, "poor and multiplying" (*DS*, 103), like "one big wretched family sequestered in sullen desperation, pawed over by social workers" (*DS*, 104). The problem for Abbey is not that Indians have been dispossessed or subject to genocide but that they *haven't* vanished. *Desert Solitaire*'s Indians retain a faint trace of their cynegetic past. Their "acquisitive instinct is poorly developed" (*DS*, 106), and they dimly recall that "once upon a time . . . they were horsemen, nomads, keepers of flocks" (*DS*, 109). But the writing is on the wall: "the Navajos will probably be forced in self-defense to malform themselves into the shape required by industrial econometrics" (*DS*, 109). Abbey treats the Indian as living proof of the seamlessness of ecological catastrophe and political oppression. Hence while their "uncontrolled population growth" has played havoc with the environment, "transform[ing] the range . . . from a semiarid grassland to an eroded waste" (*DS*, 103), Indians themselves have been the victims of ecological imperialism. Like other "self-sufficient types," Abbey argues in an echo of Naess's sentiments about place and personal identity, "Indians . . . are difficult to manage unless displaced from their natural environment" (*DS*, 110).

If Indians allow Abbey to imagine autonomy on the model of nature, the reverse also holds true. A well-balanced environment follows from local autonomy. But Abbey also departs from the views of radical ecologists who take the state as a kind of necessary evil, or a transitional phase, on the way to good (decentralized) government. Abbey's antistatism is well known. He wrote a master's thesis in philosophy on anarchism as a moral system. But the nature of that antistatism is also revealing. Abbey is uninterested in cultivating the small group sociality that advocates of the paleo-republic desire. In *Ecotopia*, togetherness is both a virtue and necessity. "The bonds that hold the communal groups together" (70) keep Ecotopia from devolving into anomie. Yet for Abbey, wilderness offers the best model for human aggregates. What distinguishes "the pinyon pine-juniper community" (DS, 29) or "the community of the quiet deer" (DS, 127) is "the comparative sparsity of the flora and fauna: life not crowded upon life as in other places but scattered abroad in spareness and simplicity" (DS, 26). The "generous spacing among plants and animals" (DS, 126) found in the desert ecosystem provides the moral and political basis of human habitation. Hence "good neighbors" should "build their houses . . . four miles" apart "if by foot" and "if by motorcar, twenty-four miles" apart (DS, 58).

The radicalness of Abbey's ecological vision even within radical ecology, then, lies in his denial of community as anything but a temporary defense against ecological imbalance or domination by the state. "The Invisible Republic," he concludes, is "based not on power or institutions but on isolated men" (DS, 245). Indians again prove instructive. Speaking of the Anasazi who abandoned their cliff dwellings hundreds of years earlier, Abbey traces their decline to the fateful choice to settle down in "fortlike homes," suggestive of a "manner of life" that "was constricted." Only "pervading fear could keep such a community together" (DS, 178). And while *Desert Solitaire* praises the Mormon settlers' "communitarian approach to the problems of settlement" in terms that Nisbet would approve (their "emphasis on mutual aid" [DS, 236] renders "welfare service[s]" [DS, 237] superfluous), even the Mormon community cannot withstand "the new American mode" of "industrialism, commercialism, urbanism" (DS, 237). "Accelerating . . . urbanization" has come "unto the Land of Moab". (DS, 238). Since "the city . . . can also be made to function as a concentration camp" (DS, 131), "thinly dispersed populations" are the only way to combat "the totalitarian organization of men and institutions" (DS, 130). "The herd is for ungulates," Abbey writes, "not for men and women" (DS, 58).

Whereas "the extreme individuation of desert life-forms" (DS, 26) furnishes Abbey's preferred model for human individuals, the obdurate desert geology furnishes his preferred model for autonomy. One of the onlookers to *The Monkey Wrench Gang*'s climactic standoff perceives Hayduke's body as a "semihuman figure rising to the waist out of what appeared to be . . . a solid mass of stone" (373). In Abbey, the canyonlands can create autochthonic patriots precisely because they cannot be civilized or domesticated. "In this part of Utah there are not many fences," he notes in *Desert Solitaire*, because "there is no ground to dig postholes in—nothing but solid rock" (*DS*, 84). By preemptively making itself unavailable to human utility—"There is something about the desert that the human sensibility cannot assimilate" (*DS*, 242)—the rock bucks the trend toward entropy: "It all seems like a geologic chaos, but there is method at work here, method of a fanatic order and perseverance" (*DS*, 10). So too with the style of human resistance *The Monkey Wrench Gang* embraces. Though he is not quite "genuine[ly] nonworking," Hayduke is imaginarily so at the end of the novel. His shattered effigy, surrogating a social death that the novel treats as a state of pure freedom, has a clear advantage for Abbey over Indians willing to "malform" themselves to survive. And this is how we might take *The Monkey Wrench Gang*'s Smithson-like interest in the implosion of the natural world, its combustion or erosion or breaking down into its elements. These parts once sundered cannot go back together. But more crucially for Abbey, they *should* not.

CHAPTER 3

That Seventies Cult

Beyond Belief

A panorama of American culture in 1980 would show a cult on every outcropping of the collective consciousness. *Time* magazine devoted untold column inches to the cults; scholarly journals teemed with articles; congressional hearings were convened; survival guides were issued in mass-market paperback (*The Cults Are Coming! The Cult Explosion*). This is to say nothing of the cult's foray into prime time. The Jonestown massacre begat a CBS miniseries; the ABC sitcom *Soap* featured a storyline in which the "Sunnies" entrap the scion of the show's wealthy family. One might see the cult's rapid uptake by the decade's media as a logical extension of its affinity for mass: marriages; murders; and, we might add, culture. No move in cultural studies is more familiar, after all, than that of seeing the mass media's attitude toward their captive audience as a variant of the brainwashing in which the cult traffics.

Although it remains a staple of folk psychology, brainwashing has fallen on hard times among social scientists.[1] The issue is whether the methods cults use to strip members of self-worth—confinement, starvation, forced labor—overwrite their mental firmware. The case for such reconditioning is not strong. Courts have ruled that deprogramming violates cult members' civil rights even more than the mind control from which the deprogrammer purports to save them. Yet the notion that a victim's *mind* can be captured—or that such captivity trumps enslavement as a form of abuse—reminds us that the cult and its critics prospered in a decade that paid fresh attention to minds in general. That brainwashing claims found skeptics even among anticult crusaders is instructive for our effort to piece together the neo-idealist seventies. In *Snapping: America's Epidemic of Sudden Personality Change* (1978), Flo Conway and Jim Siegelman admit that, given "the brain's sturdy machinery," brainwashing fails to explain "cult induction."[2] The cult's "unchecked spiritual entrepreneurs" are guilty less of hindering "freedom of thought" than of running "heedless experiments" in "the mind's unlimited creative potential."[3] For *Snapping*'s authors, the problem with cults is not mind control but deregulation.

Actually, diagnosing the cult as symptomatic of a free market run amok is less far-fetched than it sounds. Given its association with hierarchy and coercion, it is easy to overlook what the sociologist Roy Wallis, in a 1977 book on Scientology, calls the "central characteristic" of "cult organization": "epistemological individualism."[4] Recapturing this dimension of cult thinking, I argue that cults were something of a test run for what Murray Rothbard called "the resurgence of libertarianism . . . in the seventies."[5] Some cults benefited from the tax exemption religious groups enjoy, and were likewise shielded from government intervention under the establishment clause (which gives wide latitude to religious freedom). Then, too, some cults centered their doctrine on the spiritual merits of the free market; the Indian guru Bhagwan Shree Rajneesh held fast to the teaching that "capitalism is a state of freedom."[6] But more important than these libertarian-friendly aspects of its brief tenure was the cult's feverish though hardly eccentric appeal to the power of thinking itself, whose virtues were central to seventies libertarianism.[7]

"Man alone can promote his life through thought," the philosopher John Hospers writes in *Libertarianism: A Political Philosophy for Tomorrow* (1971), the manifesto that launched the national Libertarian Party, on the platform of which Hospers ran for president in 1972.[8] Behind the frequent encomia to the mind in libertarianism lies a set of theories derived from the Austrian School, whose subjectivist economics libertarians aggressively proselytize. Originating with Carl Menger in the nineteenth century, though associated in the twentieth with Ludwig von Mises, the "subjective theory of value" holds that "the psychic revenue and the psychic cost" of any transaction, as Rothbard puts it in *Man, Economy, and State* (1962), "are purely subjective to the individual."[9] Like other disciplinary putsches of the era, libertarianism began in an effort to dislodge what it saw as a misguided appeal among economists to the hard sciences and mathematics. The Austrian school's "methodological individualism," F. A. Hayek writes, "condemned the use of statistical aggregates as not belonging to economic theory."[10] The touchstone for the libertarian critique of "scientism" is Hayek's *The Counterrevolution of Science* (1952), which insisted that "neither a 'commodity' nor an 'economic good' . . . can be defined in physical terms but only in terms of views people hold about things."[11] In *Cost and Choice* (1969), James Buchanan, a mainstream economist sympathetic to the Austrian cause, mounted the same argument for the study of commodity exchange that Nagel made for the study of consciousness. Cost, like experience, is so observer-dependent that it cannot be reduced to explicit features of a commodity like physical labor: "utility is a subjective phenomenon, and it is not something that can be externally or objectively measured."[12] Or as Rothbard puts it: "The only 'natural laws' in human action . . . are *qualitative* rather than *quantitative*."[13]

The paradigm shift sought by libertarians has not quite materialized in economics, where math continues to reign supreme. But as we have seen, the period that saw libertarians emerge from the intellectual fringe *did* bring about an explosion in efforts to reclaim the "qualitative" and "subjective" from usurpation by reductive materialisms. In fact, whereas Rothbard claimed that "the only 'natural' course for man to survive . . . is by using his mind," the period's cultists saw the mind as built not merely to help us cope with the world of matter but to usurp it.[14] In 1981, the anthropologist Marvin Harris observed the "extreme forms of mentalism" and "belief in the omnipotence of thought" among cult members, who sought "techniques for mastering the world rather than for retreating from it."[15] Fifteen years earlier, in his landmark *Doomsday Cult* (1966), the sociologist John Lofland noted that San Francisco Moonies believed that "one would be able to create material objects simply by thinking about them."[16] "If there's some dimension that the mind can conquer," Jim Jones, the Prophet of the Peoples Temple, concluded, "I'm all for pursuing it."[17] Adherents of est, founded by used car salesman-turned-large-group-awareness-trainer Werner Erhard (né John Paul Rosenberg), imagined they could end world hunger through a shift in consciousness. The idiocy and disingenuousness of this claim should not prevent us from seeing that est was less opposed to the decade's serious intellectual concerns than a wishful (or bad-faith) instance of neo-idealism. The vogue for mind-altering experiences in New Age circles reflected a less mystical though no less extravagant insistence in philosophical circles on the mind's powers to alter the secular world.

Large group awareness might be seen as a version of Rawls's thought experiment in *A Theory of Justice,* in which agents behind a "veil of ignorance" use nothing but their reason to imagine the conditions of a "well ordered society."[18] It is a debased version of Rawls's experiment because no one pays for an est seminar to make the world a better place. The idea is to better one's place in the world. Yet as seriously as he takes justice, Rawls shares with libertarians no less than cultists the understanding that only through the world-building prowess of ordinary minds can we overcome the statist belief that a good society should be determined by experts rather than mindful citizens. His disdain for "paternalistic interventions" (219), as I have noted, launches Rawls on the path toward the empowering individualism celebrated by Robert Nozick, his canonical rival. And while the liberal Rawls has a far stronger defense of the social contract than the libertarian Nozick, together their work heralds the post-Fordist, opt-in society in which both union and company men have been ousted by the freelancer. Just as the original position requires "unanimity" (122) among the parties in order to get justice going, so in the attention economy it will not do to gather members by Hobbesian force.[19] Participants must choose the invitation for themselves.

Such a shift in social arrangements and attitudes explains why the idea of brainwashing, out of favor in scientific circles, cannot be said these days to be adequate to cultural critique either. However little escape there appears to be from the "totalistic environments" of cults and media alike, epistemic closure has come to depend at least for the latter on making room in their programming for the fickleness of end users continually at risk of tuning out.[20] The subliminal intrigues of hidden persuaders implanting ideas in unwitting subjects have given way to the "good choice architecture" built by "public-spirited" content providers.[21] That at least is the view of Richard Thaler and Cass Sunstein, whose 2008 book *Nudge* advocates "helping people to . . . make better choices on their own" (99). Thaler and Sunstein favor "self-conscious efforts, by institutions in the private sector and also by government, to steer people's choices in directions that will improve their lives," yet also "make it easy for people to go their own way" (5).

They label their "new movement" "libertarian paternalism" (5) and happily confess to the oxymoron, since its aim is to entice people, for their own good, to exercise the rational decision making that Rawls understands as both opposed to and in some cases importantly safeguarded by paternalism. "It is . . . rational," Rawls writes of people in certain instances, "for them to protect themselves against their own irrational inclinations by consenting to a scheme of penalties that may give them a sufficient motive to avoid foolish actions" (249).[22] Thaler and Sunstein argue that good choice architecture should direct people away from their "automatic system" (which is "rapid and . . . instinctive" [19]) toward their "reflective system" (which is "more deliberate and self-conscious" [20]). Like Rawls, *Nudge*'s authors maintain that paternalism is valid for people if it can "increase their ability to contract with each other" (199). *Nudge* exhibits a verity of the neo-idealist age: even our paternalism must be libertarian. "The whole idea of nudging is designed to preserve freedom of choice," Sunstein writes, "and in that sense both autonomy and dignity."[23] While Thaler and Sunstein draw on the insurgent field of behavioral economics, it would be remiss to see that term as entailing the opprobrium that philosophers like Searle attached to "behaviorism." Thaler and Sunstein are not opposed to rational choice economics so much as intent on reconciling it with concepts in evolutionary psychology. As in a gentrifying neighborhood, good choice architecture infills yesterday's dilapidated Skinner boxes with cognitive dwellings built on the open floor plans coveted by twenty-first-century house-hunters.

L. Ron Hubbard bases Scientology on a premise not unlike libertarian paternalism: "What is true is what is true for you. No one has any right to force data on you and command you to believe."[24] And notwithstanding that its votaries sign contracts for a billion years, a detail that might lead us to query their decision-making powers, Scientology's founding principle is that the mind is divided into the same "systems" whose conflation Thaler and Sunstein see as making our "freedom of choice" suboptimal. In *Dianetics* (1950), Hubbard contrasts the "reactive mind," which "seeks to direct the organism solely on a stimulus-response basis," with the "analytic" mind, "a perfect computer" that "cannot err in any way."[25] The analytic mind, Hubbard writes, "is the person" (76). Hubbard embraces the computational theory of mind with a fundamentalist zeal. Yet at the same time, his account of "the person" as divided between reflex and reflection rehearses as ontogeny the phylogenetic shift in the disciplines of mind from a Skinnerian paradigm of observed reactions to a cognitivism that foregrounds mental processes.[26] Like Thaler and Sunstein, Hubbard favors a reason-enabling paternalism to move the person from impulsive behavior to deliberate thought. Unlike Thaler and Sunstein, who turf that paternalism out to the built environment, Hubbard believes that the means of shepherding our "preclear" (151) selves toward clarity reside within us. Accessing these means with an E-meter, the religion's *Jetsons*-era interface, Scientology roots out "engrams" (160), "wave-recordings" that transmit "false data" to the reactive mind's "radio set" (135). "Going clear" refers to zeroing out these kernels of psychic unfreedom (quite literally, since the reference is to the reset button [C] on a calculator). Once the mind is purged of engrams, "self-determinism" (123) can flourish: "rationality and efficiency are enormously heightened, health is greatly increased and the individual computes rationally" (124).

Many cults use telecommunications to amplify their gospel, but in Scientology media are both the means to deliver the Church's message and their McLuhanesque embodiment. For Hubbard, our world is the trace memory of a "space opera" that transpired seventy-five million years ago, when Xenu (the dictator of a galactic confederacy) brought millions of his people to earth, immolated them with hydrogen bombs in volcanoes, and forced their immortal spirits to binge-watch a movie for thirty-six days.[27] Eventually these spirits, or thetans, found their way into our bodies, which have taken on their trauma. To escape from the thetan's intergalactic prison-cum-Cineplex obliges the Scientologist to use the masters' tools against them.[28] Equipped with soundstages to rival a Hollywood backlot, the Church's Golden Era Productions is the most conspicuous emblem of its exaltation of "tech."[29] The Church's inroads into the culture industry are meanwhile unsurpassed. While "many young recruits" believe that Scientology gives them "superhuman powers," according to Lawrence Wright, the most coveted endowment is not the power to levitate or time-travel but the sublunary (if still largely out-of-reach) ability to become famous.[30]

Hubbard's assertion that "absolutism is a fine road to stagnation" (104) places *Dianetics* squarely within the pragmatist tradition that would resurface in the seventies, notably in Richard Rorty's *Philosophy and the Mirror of Nature* (1979), a return to philosophical idealism as influential as Rawls's in its insistence that minds shape rather than merely respond to the world. Rorty's book contested mainstream philosophy's "reflective" epistemology by attacking its central categories ("truth as correspondence and . . . accuracy of representation") as inventions projected by the mind to justify its pursuit of a reality that does not exist apart *from* the mind.[31] "The really important question is not, 'Is it true?' but 'Does it work?'" Hubbard writes in sentences that might be plagiarized from Rorty (or William James). "If it works, we can use it and pretend it's true; if it is true, that's an added bonus" (256). Hubbard's crudely mechanical account of mind coexists with neo-idealist precepts that Scientology takes to a cartoonish extreme. Where Rorty posits that our minds determine the frames in which we present the world to ourselves, Hubbard insists that the human world consists of projections from both our conscious and unconscious lives, past and present. "Engrams," he writes, "are a complete recording, down to the last accurate detail, of every perception present in a moment of partial or full 'unconsciousness'" (74). The scare quotes around "unconsciousness" remind us that Scientology recognizes no such state. Even when comatose or prenatal, the mind is a "bank" (57) in which ideas are permanently deposited, from which no thought can ever really be withdrawn.

Just as Hubbard shows us that cult libertarianism pairs well with the decade's resurgent antifoundationalism, so Scientology's techno-fetishism and celebrity centers remind us that seventies cults, breaking with an earlier generation's despair about mass media's atomizing effects, go all in on the euphoria of togetherness. Moonies practiced love bombing on new recruits; Children of God were encouraged to have sex with them.[32] As with cult consciousness-raising, this swing toward the communal foretells the new connectivity much celebrated in the prospectuses of social media start-ups. This is not Robert Nisbet's communitarianism, which looks to the neighborhoods of yore as models for mutualism. In line with the word of mouth that can make or break the studio blockbuster, cults in their heyday—notwithstanding their notoriety as strongholds of harshly policed esotericism—happily paid lip service to the oversharing that sustains what Claude Lefort calls the *"entre-nous"* of late capitalism's "invisible ideology."[33]

Lefort introduces that phrase in the 1974 essay "Outline of the Genesis of Ideology in Modern Societies," written in response to Louis Althusser's "Ideology and Ideological State Apparatuses" (1970). No longer will it do to speak, with Althusser, of ideology as a top-down "interpellation" of individuals who know their place in a rigid division of labor. Althusser's account may have been an improvement on Karl Marx's "purely negative" theory of ideology; but in Lefort's view, it was equally out of touch with its time.[34] For Althusser, ideology secures "subjects" who "work by themselves," by which he means that ideology is internalized as subjectivity (although he also means that subjects are individuated from one another).[35] Lefort argues by contrast that "invisible ideology" ratifies "the occultation of social division" with a "constant assurance of the social bond."[36] By virtue of the "phantasmagoria of reciprocity" generated by mass media, "ideology completes its task" and "brings about the great closure," "the legitimation ... of the real as such."[37]

Lefort is striving to capture a tightening of the ideological noose in the post-ideological world, the reinstatement of ideology in the guise of its refutation.[38] In this view, communication and transparency are not weapons to dispel ideology but ruses employed by the corporate state to cut off the move beyond ideology's reach.[39] Because Lefort sees this process as an insidious loop for recapturing our hearts and minds, he is convinced that the effect of the invisible ideology will be an upwelling of religious feeling, a return of the repressed whereby the masses in the rich democracies will find the absence of palpable ideological unifiers so intolerable that they will resurrect divinities as a retort to a state that mystifies even as it exerts its policing functions. "Despite all the changes that have occurred," Lefort writes in "On the Permanence of the Theologico-Political" (1981), "the religious survives in the guise of new beliefs and new representations ... and can therefore return to the surface ... when conflicts become so acute as to produce cracks in the edifice of the state."[40] For Lefort, worship manifests our inescapable desire to believe in a transcendent "form," the desire that underpins every "institution of the social" ("OP," 220). On this account, which owes much to Lefort's teacher Maurice Merleau-Ponty, persons are hardwired to imagine objective forms because they must organize their otherwise scattered experiences of the lifeworld into a meaningful framework. That formalizing urge has been hijacked in modernity by powers that have installed the "political" as the only legitimate "domain" ("OP," 216). Yet beneath that system lurks the "primordial reference," the drive to "shape" "forms of society" ("OP," 217). Invisible ideology's "great closure" amounts to the political form's bid to make us forget the capacity for formal invention that is immanent within us and expropriated by a state that divides us while insisting on our togetherness.

In Lefort's analysis, states come and go, but society is permanent. It is the necessary means of preventing our descent into chaotic subjectivism. On first glance, Lefort looks as if he is arguing for a version of the Rawlsian insistence that people have the ability to make a world. Yet that is not quite the case. To recur to terms I have introduced in earlier chapters, Lefort appears committed to an externalist ideal of transcendence, whereas Rawls, like many of the period's influential thinkers, pursued an internalist ideal. Lefort is more skeptical of a unifiable subjectivity than his American counterparts. By "primordial reference," Lefort means that persons can't have coherent existences until they externalize their minds, outsourcing them to an agreed-upon authority as if for safekeeping, lest they descend into "the illusion of pure self-immanence" ("OP," 244). By contrast, what Roy Wallis concludes of the seventies cult—that it recognizes "no clear locus of final authority beyond the individual"—applies to a vast array of the period's thinkers, including Rawls, who concludes that "the prized virtues" of "obedience" and "fidelity to authoritative persons" (465) must have "but a restricted role in fundamental social arrangements" (466) based on "the contract doctrine" (478).[41]

Disobedience to authority is perhaps nowhere so prevalent in sixties culture as among the wide assortment of anarchist movements the decade spawned. Anarchists of course have little patience for Lefort's conviction that society is necessary. The disdain for what Paul Goodman calls the "odd abstraction Society," an abstraction that on Lefort's view we cannot help embracing, connects cultists and anarchists.[42] Repeatedly in the period's anticult literature, a Lefort-style "assurance of the social bond" among the cults coexists with a removal from society. "At war with the rest of the world," Children of God "are exempt from its rules."[43] Thus write the authors of *All God's Children* (1977), who also decry the "antinomian" Hare Krishnas' "scorn for the laws of this nation."[44] The combination of social bonding and antisocial resistance has clear anarchist antecedents. Lefort's charge that the new forms of togetherness merely belie the "occultation of social division" is indeed incoherent from the vantage of the period's anarchists, who see interpersonal ties as a way of announcing their *own* division from the social.

For cultists and anarchists alike, society is synonymous with ideology. The "ideologies of the doctrinaire capitalists or of the doctrinaire Marxists," Richard Sennett writes in *The Uses of Disorder* (1970), "rob men of the chance to care about something small enough to grasp."[45] Compare Sennett's refusal of "servitude" to "coherent ideology" (111) with Jim Jones's prophesy that "ideology . . . shall be removed from the consciousness of mankind . . . when freedom comes."[46] Part II of *The Uses of Disorder*, "A New Anarchism," is a brief for a "more direct" and human-scaled "concept of care" (121). For Sennett, overcoming abstractions like Marxism, capitalism, and society itself allows us to reestablish gemeinschaft as the basis of social life. Seventies cultists likewise presented themselves as crusaders against gigantism and orthodoxy on behalf of tender attentions. The "assholes . . . roboting through life" who enroll in an est seminar, according to Luke Rhinehart, learn over two weekends of "intimate sharing" to undo "the way of life that est itself attempts to explode: namely, the adherence to the mind's belief systems."[47] Sixties anarchists no less than est disciples favored an idealism that prioritized "self-consciousness," to cite Murray Bookchin, over "class-consciousness." "It is we who have to be liberated . . . and not universals like 'History' and 'Society,'" Bookchin writes in *Post-Scarcity Anarchism* (1971). "The self must always be *identifiable* in the revolution."[48]

Bookchin, who made a cameo in the previous chapter, was a farsighted ecologist as well as anarchist. He is also exhibit A in the case against the distinction some academics like to make between good (egalitarian) anarchism and bad (free-market) libertarianism.[49] Bookchin identified as a libertarian at various points in his life. It is not hard to see why. In *For a New Liberty: A Libertarian Manifesto* (1974), Rothbard (who began as a devotee of an anarchism he never fully abandoned) claims that "one of the prime errors in social theory is to treat 'society' as if it were an actually existing entity" (45). Anarchists and libertarians seek to correct this "superstitious compulsion," to use Bookchin's term, through an act of will, as if authority laid claim to us by implanting the sort of false beliefs Hubbard and Erhard see as obstructing self-realization.[50] "Men have become so habituated to thinking of the state as essential to their well-being," writes anarchist philosopher William Reichert, "that they find themselves enslaved by it."[51]

"Being a conscious anarchist is a continuously difficult situation," Nicolas Walter writes in *About Anarchism* (1969). "It is difficult to break through the thought-barrier . . . and to work out a whole new view of the world."[52] If there is a sacred cow common to all cults, it might well be the *personal breakthrough*, when the individual rejects what Kurt Zube, in *The Anarchist Manifesto* (1977), calls "those paths which lead . . . to petrified ways of thinking"[53] and achieves what the Maharishi Mahesh Yogi, the guru of Transcendental Meditation, calls "the level of the transcendental being."[54] Anarchism for Reichert is an "'idea'" that "makes it possible for the individual to transcend the physical restrictions and limitations he finds himself surrounded by."[55] Or as Luke Rhinehart's est trainer describes the process of "ceasing to identify . . . with the machine mind, and experiencing all as 'self'" (192): "Most people passively absorb the imaginary structures and game rules of others. The wise man creates his own" (172).

It may seem perverse to claim that groups like Scientology and est are both post-ideological and anti-authoritarian, much less aligned with anarchism. This is not exactly my claim. While seventies cults were without question predacious swindles of often unhappy people, they nonetheless attached themselves to the antiestablishment rhetoric that movements like anarchism and libertarianism favored. Thus in much of the era's anticult literature, the cult's assault on officialdom is as perilous as its holding members against their will; the assumption was that no one in her right mind would choose radicalization. According to the "deprogrammer" Ted Patrick, author of *Let Our Children Go!* (1976), the Children of God scorn their parents as "Systemites" and gleefully sing of the state's demise: "America's sinking fast in the sand / The system is fucked and it's getting me down."[56] Cults leveraged antiestablishment feeling and consciousness-raising into a lucrative wildcat industry. And like most high-risk ventures, the cult's heyday had a predictable brevity. The Peoples Temple collapsed with the mass murder in Jonestown in 1978. An unavoidable topic in seventies life, est was disbanded in 1981, only to divide into ever more eccentric and less well-attended "seminars." In the era's most dramatic makeover, the Unification Church has sought the sectarian mainstream, looking to replicate Mormonism's trajectory from scourge to near-respectability almost a century ago.

Even more significant than the withering of the cults themselves was the waning of the moral panic they incited. In the aftermath of Reagan's election, it became clear that the Christian fundamentalists who helped him into office not only pioneered the assault on the cults but also embodied a particularly rabid mutation of the neo-idealist turn, a commitment to spirit inextricable from a supremely phobic rejection of the body politics of post-sixties culture.[57] It is fair to say that the bourgeoning evangelical movement went about building its ranks in the shadow cast by the anticult media circus evangelicals largely fomented. "Though . . . the Hare Krishnas and the Unification Church attracted so many column-inches in the newspapers of the seventies," Philip Jenkins observes, "these movements were numerically insignificant when set aside the thriving new protestant sects."[58] Once in power, the moral majority turned to its preferred Kulturkampf: recriminalizing abortion and homosexuality. Deprogramming Moonies gave way to conversion therapy; nightly news segments on cult aberrations were replaced by syndicated televangelists who outperformed anything on network TV. From 1980 on, the cult is reduced from daily disturbance to special event. The spectacle of Waco or Heaven's Gate takes place alongside such catastrophic affairs as a third-world tsunami or a terrorist attack.

In the new millennium, both cults and their antagonists have been relegated to the margins of mainstream life.[59] To speak of the cult nowadays is to refer to something that is not quite popular *enough* (hence the slightly oxymoronic "cult hit").[60] Yet we could also see the cult's shuttling from the fringe to the center and back to the fringe not just as a fad—with its sortie into and speedy retreat from the common culture—but as paradigmatic for a common culture that has, like the Hare Krishnas, lost interest in its *core identity*. Seventies cults prefigure the balkanization of society into fragmented demographics and market niches. "Cults . . . are fragile institutions," Wallis writes. "Collectivities themselves tend to be transient," and because "commitment" is "slight," "members typically move between groups, and between belief systems, adopting components to fit into the body of truth already gleaned."[61] From the vantage Wallis urges, cults were in the vanguard of the subcultural pluralism that Nozick entertains in Part III ("Utopia") of *Anarchy, State, and Utopia*, modern libertarianism's legitimizing text.

Keen to show that the free market was not just compatible with but essential to the lifestyle diversity that the counterculture envisioned, Nozick imagined "many different and divergent communities" that would be able to restrict members' actions without infringing on libertarian precepts.[62] While "people are free to do their own thing" (312) in the "face-to-face communities" (322) that would thrive in what Nozick calls the "minimal state" (17), "the recalcitrant individual . . . has no right that the others cooperate in making his nonconformity feasible" (322), only the right to take his dissent elsewhere.[63] Nozick's argument for manifold, renegotiable social contracts echoes Robert Paul Wolff's claim in *In Defense of Anarchism* (1970) that the small community is the only form of organized life the social contract can justifiably bear. Envisioning a plurality of communities between which one can shift at will, Wolff favors breaking up "our present society," populated by "obedient, authority-respecting masses," into "units of manageable size."[64] Faced with a society that presents itself as too big to fail, "men would have increasing freedom to act autonomously" only by downsizing.[65]

These sentiments resonate into the argument made by ecologists for the paleo-republic. But it is also likely that anarchists conclude that "small is beautiful" (to cite E. F. Schumacher) as a way of making a virtue of the necessarily limited appeal of their movement. It is tempting to say that just as cults all but vanished from the cultural map after 1980, so the vogue for anarchism also precipitously declined. But anarchism has never been a craze. Anarchist thought flourished briefly in certain quarters during the sixties and seventies as one among various approaches to modeling decentralization and raised consciousness. Yet for the project of attracting followers, anarchism is finally a self-defeating enterprise. There will never be a mass anarchism because, to adapt the radical ecologist's formula for human population and quality control, from Shepard to Abbey: the fewer anarchists, the better. And such not-so-secret exclusivity troubles the claim that, as Nicolas Walter puts it, for anarchism "freedom and equality are in practice the same thing."[66]

The tension between a politics of equality and a politics of individualism is the subject of Bookchin's late essay, "Social Anarchism or Lifestyle Anarchism: An Unbridgeable Chasm" (1995). Bookchin's target is the prevalence, since the seventies, of the self-styled anarchist who "interprets anarchism as a philosophy not of social freedom but of personal autonomy."[67] His attempts to distinguish these concepts ("while autonomy is associated with the presumably self-sovereign individual, freedom dialectically interweaves the individual with the collective" [12]) suggest that the titular "chasm" involves a hairsplitting built into the anarchist project, which (like virtually every radical movement) looks to proliferate ever finer discriminations, more rigorous qualifications for membership, and subtler parsings within the group, followed by the latter's inexorable calving into splinter movements.[68] While "Social Anarchism" concludes with the sad realization that "it is already no longer possible . . . to call oneself an anarchist without adding a qualifying adjective" (61), Bookchin himself practiced an almost parodic version of Nozick's utopian venue shopping, oscillating over his lifetime between anarcho-syndicalism, libertarianism, democratic socialism, and communalism before landing on what he called "libertarian municipalism."[69]

Yet Bookchin always remained a diatribe-composing defender of the one true anarchism. "Social Anarchism" is a tour de force hatchet job on the "trendy posturings" (19) of (among others) Robert Paul Wolff, Richard Sennett, Michel Foucault, and other faux anarchists. Anarchists and libertarians share a strong preference for retaining their theories *in potentia*. The latter remain purest when they reside in the imagination, and any effort to implement them in "real world" contexts amounts to a betrayal. Samuel Konkin's *New Libertarian*

Manifesto (1980) emerges out of its author's Bookchin-like disgust with libertarianism's sellouts, from the founders of the Libertarian Party (guilty of "partyarchy," or what Konkin calls the "anti-concept of pursuing libertarian ends through statist means") to the "Kochtopus" whose total capture of the national party by 1980 occurred, in Konkin's view, because "party politics" are the natural prey of "plutocrats."[70] (The reference of course is to the billionaire Koch brothers, Charles and David, whose foundations underwrite much of the contemporary conservative movement.)

Konkin advocates a policy of complete withdrawal, what he calls "countereconomics," a secession from the legal marketplace in favor of extralegal gray and black markets designed to "evade, avoid, and defy the State."[71] Evasion amounts to a kind of ideal in anarchism and libertarianism, just as rupture is each movement's default practice. If it is hard to take seriously his worry that lifestyle anarchism "threatens to render the very word anarchism politically and socially harmless" (26), this is due less to Bookchin's shifting loyalties than to the versatility of "the very word" itself. As John Bucci puts it in a 1971 essay, "anarchism is an elusive term," denoting "a protean philosophy which by its very nature involves constant change and a lack of dogmatism."[72] Bookchin's essay is an anxious response to the tendency to treat anarchism as a catchall, the name for the politics of those whose views—nihilistic, antisocial, or simply mad—we cannot comfortably categorize as progressive but whom we want to claim for radicalism regardless. The next section considers one such figure, William S. Burroughs, who has often defied critics eager to sort his work into the left-hand column of cultural politics. Burroughs has also been labeled a "cult novelist" for the better part of the past seventy-five years. This identification turns out to be more apt than critics may realize, given his dalliance with the cult's "epistemological individualism" throughout his life.

Going Clear with Burroughs

In Burroughs's 1981 novel *The Cities of the Red Night*, the possibility of Wolff- or Nozick-style autonomy requires that there be not just an absence of central authority but also a complete severance from territoriality. In the newly liberated Panama City, each of the liberators rotates into the role of commander for one day, but the book does not take place in that or any other locale. Burroughs's book takes place rather throughout the early Americas, when a band of pirates founded a "colony . . . called Libertatia" with "Articles drawn up by one Captain Mission," who offered "refuge to all people everywhere who suffer under the tyranny of governments."[73] The novel chronicles an alternative history of the age of revolution, detailing how "The Articles" come to infuse the Western Hemisphere with "the possibility of communes" (xv) based on the supreme value of noninterference. The novel's donnée is libertarianism's origin myth. As Rothbard puts it, "America . . . was born in an explicitly libertarian revolution, a revolution against empire" (7), only to be thwarted by forces of reaction that "replace[d] individual liberty and minimal government with absolute rule and Big Government" (11).[74] The outcome of the war between statists and the party of liberty is clear. "There is simply no room left for freedom from the tyranny of government," Burroughs writes in *Cities*. "Your right to live where you want, with companions of your choosing, under laws to which you agree, died in the eighteenth century with Captain Mission. Only a miracle or a disaster could restore it" (xv).

Of course, Burroughs doesn't believe in miracles. More exactly, he doesn't believe that the things we might categorize as miracles, like mind reading or astral projection, are miraculous (or even false). He thinks they are scientific truths. "I know from my own experience," he wrote as early as *Junky*, "that telepathy is a fact."[75] Thus in addition to being an alternative history of the age of revolution, *Cities* offers up a secret history of the Enlightenment, a world in which "body control" (100), "sex magic" (76), and other forms of occult knowledge turn out to be not only real but emancipatory. The motto of the ancient "university city" of Waghdas, "where the arts and sciences reached peaks of attainment that have never been equaled" (153), serves as Burroughs's own: "Complete permission derives from complete understanding" (158). This axiom, not to mention the arcane mental arts taught in Waghdas and into which Burroughs's eighteenth-century pirates and their descendants are initiated (for *Cities* is also a novel of time travel), is close to the prime directive of the Church of Scientology, in whose lessons Burroughs had invested serious time and money during the sixties, rising steadily in the Church's clearness hierarchy before a 1968 feud led to his being put in a condition of treason.

Burroughs collected his rants about Scientology in *Ali's Smile / Naked Scientology* (1973). Though incensed by his discovery that "Scientology is a model control system, a state in fact with its own courts, police, rewards and penalties," Burroughs waxes rhapsodic about the Church's teachings: "Scientology can do more in ten hours than psychoanalysis can do in ten years"; its lessons "support the theory of mind over matter."[76] He is especially impressed by the E-meter, which he sees as an effective tool of "brain wave control," a vital sextant in the navigation of "inner space" (76). Burroughs condemns his erstwhile faith because, like a government agency, Scientology guards its truths as though they were state secrets. "Hubbard says he wants recognition for his discoveries," he writes. "Let him show his material to . . . Marshall McLuhan and Noam Chomsky. Let him show his material to those who have fought for freedom in the streets. . . . Above all, young people have a right to see his materials" (77). This plea for open access is at odds with the sense of election that Burroughs often embraced. In *Cities of the Red Night*, the "sorcerer's revolution" belongs to the young, who travel the Americas founding "a series of settlements" (112) and for whom "decentralization is key" (135). Yet the young in the book are also quite old, since Libertatia's pirates are the reincarnated souls of the ancient Cities of the Red Night, who were divided into "an elite minority known as transmigrants" (able to achieve immortality through mental training) and "a majority known as receptacles" (who surrender their bodies to the transmigrants) (154). Hubbard would call these, respectively, operating thetans and reactive minds.

Like the pirates who are really transmigrants, the Articles are also an instance of metempsychosis, the reconstitution of the esoteric books of the Red Night for application to the contemporary world. Just as the proximity of Burroughs's story to the Dianetic myth is made clear in the novel's view of the world as "a prerecorded universe" (166), so the tactics of the "Libertatian" ascendancy are straight out of the Scientology playbook: "We are migrants who move from settlement to settlement in the vast area now held by the Articulated" (220). Or more precisely: what *should* be the Scientology playbook. To the extent that *Cities of the Red Night* is a reparative novel, it aims less to rejoin the perpetual revolution squandered by bourgeois society than to quicken the fever dream of Scientology. Burroughs's seafaring "adventurers plotting to appropriate a continent and remake it to their taste" (111) are the ancestors of the Scientologists who staffed Hubbard's floating headquarters, a fleet that sailed the North Atlantic throughout the late sixties in defiance of the overreaching grasp of various hostile nations. The Church's 1975 retreat to a landlocked command center (in Florida no less) gives the lie to the "Sea Org" whose name Scientology's inner circle now takes in vain. Libertatia is what Scientology would look like if it owned up to its emancipatory potential, if it opened its secret books to all comers and took everyone on board.

"Constantly under siege," Burroughs writes in *The Place of Dead Roads* (1983), the sequel to *Cities*, "Waghdas changes location often. In houseboats and caravans, burnt-out tenements and ghost towns . . . now you see it, now you don't."[77] Like Captain Mission's pirates, the novel's protagonist, Kim Carsons, is a constant traveler whose yearning for "immortality" requires the ultimate in nomadic ventures: the ability to depart the "planet," "a penal colony" that "nobody is allowed to leave" (202). Carsons builds a worldwide network of spies and assassins in order to liberate the secrets of eternal life from an alien race, not Hubbard's thetans but "Venusians in human bodies" (33), who jealously guard the key to immortality by preventing those they possess from reaching outer space. The plot of *The Place of Dead Roads* is as outré as anything in the Burroughs canon, but its essentials appear drawn (again) from the gospel of L. Ron Hubbard. The Venusians "stand in the way of every increase in awareness" (97), "stunting and degrading the human host" (170) by forcing the "human cattle" (172) to watch "a whole prerecorded and prefilmed universe" (210) on infinite repeat. If "human history" is "a vast film spread out in front of you" (218), Carsons's "unforgivable sin is to tamper with the prerecordings" (218), thus "breaking the immutable rules of the universe" (256).[78] Carsons's war with the aliens takes place on multiple fronts. Since "the church must be seen as a dedicated instrument of alien invasion" (102), his people "encourage . . . cults, devil worship, and rarefied systems like the Ishmaelite and the Manichaean" as means to "force Christianity to compete for the human spirit" (98). They also "uphold States' Rights" against "any further encroachment of Washington bureaucrats" (158).

In *The Place of Dead Roads*, then, the critique of mental enslavement by alien forces converges with the critique of governmentality on behalf of a decentralist and communitarian vision. The aliens stand for "arbitrary and dogmatic authority" (97) in all the institutions they have commandeered. But Kim Carsons is scarcely an egalitarian. While aggrieved that the aliens have sought to "limit . . . immortality" (270) to the wealthiest castes throughout history, Carsons is not exactly committed to democratizing eternal life. For one thing, it is too heady a brew for most people, given that "the slave classes" (262) cling to "anything to keep us from seeing the horror of our origins" (257). "Free from harassment," Carsons asserts, "the human artifact can evolve into an organism suited for space conditions and space travel" (172). But few are willing or able to heed the call. Using the wealth he acquires from the capitalist system ostensibly to defeat it from within, Carsons is a deranged Elon Musk aiming "to rid the spaceship Earth of malefactors who are sabotaging our space program" (167).

Carsons's goal, like that of the Heaven's Gate cultists, is to level up to "the astral or dream body" (41) in order to achieve escape velocity from Earth's confines: "As a prisoner serving a life sentence can think only of escape, so Kim takes for granted that the only purpose of his life is space travel" (40). Burroughs's diary records the "mass cultist suicide" of the Heaven's Gate cult led by "Piper Do [Marshall Applewhite]" in April 1997. "Thirty-nine went peacefully," he writes on April 2, 1997. "They were headed for a higher human condition . . . disencumbered of their earthly raiments."[79] The same entry finds him pondering how William Faulkner's brother Jack (an FBI agent who apparently arrested Burroughs in New Orleans in the fifties) became a "shameless advocate of bureaucratic rule . . . opposed to the states' rights advocates left over from the Civil War" (140). For Burroughs, shrugging off one's "earthly raiments" and seceding from an overbearing nation-state seemingly amount to the same order of revolt. The "basic law" of "a fascist regime," according to *The Place of Dead Roads*, is "never go too far in any direction" (194). Whereas the dream of *Cities of the Red Night* is to recover the "right to live where you want," the dream of *The Place of Dead Roads* is to live forever. These dreams converge in Burroughs's defense of a self-determination under siege in every facet of our existence, from our thoughts to our movements to our words.

Exceeding the worst fears of the most individualist anarchists, Burroughs's vision of total social control is in continuous tension with its opposite number: a fantasy of total self-control. Control for Burroughs is a zero-sum game.[80] In *The Place of Dead Roads*, the repudiation of the social is the only way to access individual power: "Look around you on the street and what do you see, a creature that functions at one-fiftieth of its potential and is only saved from well-deserved extinction by an increasingly creaky social structure" (216). Taking his cue from radical ecology's Malthusians, Burroughs puts his own spin on the entropic turn. In the spirit of Rifkin or Ophuls, he rejects "the Industrial Revolution, with its overpopulation and emphasis on quantity rather than quality," but his reasons have less to do with its fiction of progress than with its having "given" the Venusian colonizers "a vast reservoir of stupid bigoted uncritical human hosts" (97). *The Place of Dead Roads* indicts "the present directive" of "scientific materialism," which holds that "anyone writing about so-called ESP should be publicly horsewhipped and barred from further activity" (172). Whereas Rothbard sees libertarianism as restoring the thwarted promise of the Enlightenment, Burroughs doesn't see the Enlightenment as having promised anything but a rationality that has become weaponized by what his diary calls the "thought police" (178).

It is now commonplace in Burroughs scholarship to trace his politics through stencils cut by Gilles Deleuze and Félix Guattari, whose rhizomatic and nomadic theories his work is taken to enact.[81] Rarely do critics pay more than a squeamish moment of attention to Burroughs's affinity for *auditing* and *going clear*, the privileged gerunds in Scientology's grammar. There are good fringes and bad fringes in academic scholarship, and Scientology is so obviously the latter that the only way to square Burroughs's fifteen-year devotion to Scientology is to ironize it. Yet though he broke with the Church after leaving England (along with his E-meter) in 1974, Burroughs never broke with its teachings. Like Scientologists, he remained convinced that the control society exercised its power by denying us the possibility of physical or mental transcendence. We do a disservice to Burroughs and the full force of his weirdness by failing to respect the seriousness of his belief in astral projection or telepathy. But taking him seriously also obliges us to reconsider the degree to which Burroughs's work can be tailored to a progressive criticism.

Some of his readers have chosen to seize upon his rejection of control society while ignoring the fact that, for Burroughs, that society's original sin is the control it exercises over *him*. "Burroughs wishes to free not only his own consciousness but that of others as well," Kathryn Hume writes, and "to bring alternative social options into existence."[82] For Hume, *The Place of Dead Roads* "considers how utopian alternatives to middle-class society might operate in capitalist America" (123). But Burroughs's "alternatives" are not especially comforting. If "all utopias" have a "flaw" (237), according to the novel, it would be their neglect of inescapable power differentials. "Those who seek happiness for itself seek victory without war" (237), Burroughs writes. Or as he puts in "The Electronic Revolution" (1970): "Mr. Hubbard says that Scientology is a game where everybody wins. There are no games where everybody wins. That's what games are all about, winning and losing."[83] Burroughs's aim might be, as Hume suggests, "to construct a mental picture of the world in which his spirit feels at home" (113). And he may wish to open the secrets of Scientology to all comers. But his is not a politics of inclusiveness. It would be remiss to ignore how thoroughly Burroughs shares the Manichean view of *Place*'s narrator, who observes that "in this universe there is only the pure and the foul" (243).

When Burroughs's politics can be reduced to coherence, as in his brief for states' rights, they appear impossible to salvage, especially given his acknowledgment that "states' rights" have long been code for legalized racism. But incoherence may be the hallmark of many positions Burroughs takes. Like the lifestyle anarchists condemned by Bookchin, Burroughs appears to look upon the world of ideas as an endless intellectual buffet, choosing among eclectic systems of thought and, within those, absorbing what works for him and discarding the rest. That Burroughs took a purely instrumental approach to Scientology has perhaps made it hard to see the depth of his commitment. In his diary, he claims that in pursuing est, Scientology, and the Alexander technique, he was searching not for "the secret" but for "just what I need to know, to do what I can do" (195). Yet it is of the essence of Scientology, as I have presented it, that it embraces this opportunism, turning it into the faith's great virtue. That he was disillusioned by its lack of any real virtues does not really touch Scientology's original attraction for Burroughs: its promise of an instrumentalist consciousness-raising, its insistence that persons can heighten their mentality only by abolishing foundational beliefs. What Burroughs needs to know is what Kim Carsons discovers: how to be "aware at all times of what you are doing" (59), how to engage to its maximum "the subversive practice of *thinking*" (16).

Some critics have sought to explain Burroughs's disorienting style by referring his writing to a lifetime of mental anguish.[84] This is understandable. The most stable thing—the only anchor—in the Burroughs corpus, arguably, is Burroughs himself. Yet even so, critics have been insufficiently mindful of the self-absorption of Burroughs's writing. By "self-absorption" I am referring less to Burroughs's narcissism than to his epistemology.[85] While critics have aligned his cut-up technique with the death of the author and other assaults on intentionality, all roads through his work lead back to Burroughs, the ultimate wellspring of his richly documented and endlessly publicized inner life. Hence the prevalence of the term "alter ego" in analyses of his novels. Burroughs never disappears from the page even as he manically insists on the virtues of an ego-shattering dissolution of identity.[86] His interest in cloning—amply on display in *The Place of Dead Roads*—is less about the defeat of the original by the culture of the copy than about proliferating versions of his own person. Hallucinations, prejudices, superstitions are legitimated, as clues to the unity of Burroughs's fiction, by the fact that they emanate from Burroughs's mind, in which there are no stray or throwaway thoughts.

This is perhaps the clearest instance of the impact Scientology made on Burroughs, since that church teaches that there is no such thing as a forgotten memory, an accidental or random idea, a careless word. Burroughs's appeal to being "aware at all times of what you are doing" can take on urgency only in a world where (like Hubbard's) there are no trivial thoughts. "My attitude is that nothing happens by accident," Burroughs told his biographer Ted Morgan. "The dogma of science is that the will cannot possibly affect external forces, and I think that's just ridiculous. . . . Nothing happens unless someone wills it to happen."[87] Burroughs had an unfailing commitment to the validity of his own self-authorized perspective even or especially when it was at odds with external reality. He was never in doubt about the essential *rightness* of his own beliefs in the face of demonstrable proof of their wrongness. That he maintained this faith while also holding a reductively mechanical account of mind and a behaviorist account of agency may seem inconsistent. But such inconsistency confirms rather than undermines an idealism that could appear indistinct from solipsism. Consider his use of "dogmatic" as a term of contempt. Scientology's fatal flaw is the surrender of its empowering technologies and its "science of communication" to a "dogmatic policy."[88] Any authority looks dogmatic to a subjectivity unwilling to cede ground in the tug-of-war over facts and values.

Domesticating Anarchism

It is difficult to imagine two novelists as unlike as John Irving and William S. Burroughs. Even if they are less hostile to readerly comfort than their precursors in the Burroughs corpus, *Cities* and *Place* remain aggressively opaque. Yet Irving's middlebrow best seller *The World According to Garp* (1978) is arguably the stranger beast genre-wise. *Garp* aspires to fit the tradition of classic realism to the demands of the sixties. Committed to "doing" the counterculture in the manner of a Victorian triple-decker (even its girth recalls a Dickensian doorstopper), Irving populates his novel with a cast of zanies and a series of flat characters (in particular, dead and abused children) designed largely to push our sentimental buttons. Yet to call *Garp* a social novel is slightly inaccurate, given the book's misanthropic take on society. "'Droves' of anything, but especially of people, were not comforting to T. S. Garp," Irving writes.[89] Associating such masses with a "world" that "doesn't respect the rights of an individual" (23), the novel sanctifies "Garp's introversion" as the "way to live" (164).

Irving's novel forwards privatization not just as the personal preference of its novelist-hero but as a rebuff to statist planning. In the wartime world Garp is born into, "privacy was not sacred," "nothing was a secret" (6), and conscription is the rule. His mother, a nurse named Jenny Fields, notes that "everyone was a soldier" (4). Garp's father, a fatally injured ball turret gunner who daydreams of "being alone" and envies his fellow gunner's "private place" (16), is a casualty of the colonization of personal life, to quote Murray Rothbard, "by the nation-state and its war-making machine" (14). That the novel has a dubious view of the political in general is attested by Garp's first novel, "*Procrastination*" (138), which concerns "a young anarchist who has to lie low, after the Anschluss, waiting for just the right blow he can strike against the Nazis" (137) and who is eaten by the animals he tries to free from the Vienna zoo. After his death, the anarchist's mother, hitherto "unconcerned with politics" (137), seeks to carry out the son's act. Garp writes that her "gesture of liberation is well intended" but "completely meaningless" (138).

Garp's book draws on his relationship with his own mother, who accompanies him to Vienna, where each embarks on a writing life. But in Irving's book, Garp is an apolitical recluse, while Jenny's memoir, *A Sexual Suspect*, becomes a catalyst for "the women's movement" (134). Yet to say that Jenny is political is not quite right, since she "never wholly understood how 'political' [her memoir] was—or how it would be used as such a book" (132). She is merely "the right voice at the right time" (132). Thus the veiled analogy at the heart of Garp's first novel is essentially accurate. "Aggressive in the way only someone who believes totally in himself can be aggressive" (221), Garp shares the anarchist's refusal of the world's expectations (hence Irving's title). His mother by contrast is the butt of the novel's central joke. "Adopted by women's politics" (135), she is mistaken for a "decision maker" (134) even as her approach to life is unreflective. Whereas her neglect of her appearance results in her wearing her nurse's uniform for the rest of her life, that sartorial choice is quickly taken up by her "entourage" of "adorers" (134) as if it were a radical act. Jenny is the accidental center of a cult of personality.

Garp's own contempt for politics arises not just from his valorization of privacy but from his having joined the world already liberated. Long in advance of the groundswell occasioned by *The Feminine Mystique* (1963), Garp is a "happy homemaker" (133) raising the kids while his wife, Helen, works toward tenure as an English professor. Marshaling an intriguing post-sixties revisionism, Irving's book retrojects onto the prefeminist culture the sort of equitable domestic contract for which Pat Mainardi argued in "The Politics of Housework" (1969). Having arrived at gender parity without any help from feminism, the Garps find its lessons redundant. Indeed, the novel is ostensibly about sixties upheavals without actually placing its protagonist *in* any sixties upheaval. Born in 1943, Garp forgoes college (and so no Students for a Democratic Society for him); nor is he at risk of getting drafted, since as far as the novel is concerned the Vietnam War never happened.

That *The World According to Garp* prefers to keep the sixties at arm's length may explain why feminism in the novel continually manifests as a fringe phenomenon, on the order of what deprogrammers call a "deviant cult." But the novel turns the deprogrammer's logic inside out. In the cult of Jenny Fields, the leader does not manipulate the followers; the followers manipulate *her*, "trying to make your mother into something she isn't" (272). Jenny's role makes her "a potential victim, exposing herself . . . to all the hatred and cruelty and violence in the world" (164). She is assassinated by a New Hampshire hunter, a proto–men's rights activist outraged by "Group Female Living" (343). The novel's most menacing cult is not the "damn lesbian crowd" (272) around Jenny Fields, however, but the Ellen Jamesians, "a whole *society* of women" (135) who have had their tongues removed in solidarity with an eleven-year-old whose rapists cut hers out. As in the anarchist lexicon, "*society*" here is emphatically a slur. The Ellen Jamesians carry notepads to introduce themselves to strangers and witness for victims of male violence, "like the religious morons who bring those righteous pamphlets about Jesus to one's very door" (249). But Ellen James herself "*hated* being tongueless and hated the Ellen

Jamesians" (386). Far from "true believers" (423), the Ellen Jamesians form a paradoxical cult of apostates. As with Jenny Fields, the leader seems more a pretext for the collective than its end.

The novel's penultimate chapter details the heating up of the "long-time cold war" (387) between Garp and these "devout fanatics who . . . insisted they knew more about Ellen James than Ellen James knew about herself" (397). Garp encourages Ellen to publish an article denouncing the group, which leads the Ellen Jamesians to accuse the "poor child" of being "brainwashed into her antifeminist stance by the male villain, Garp" (397). The charge goes both ways. "They are capable of making mindless decisions," Garp observes, "and they believe they are so *right*" (386). Yet the novel does not make it easy to pinpoint what the Ellen Jamesians feel so right about. Their mission seems less a matter of doctrine than mood. Though "they really resent the entire *society*" (384), this impulse takes the form not of defending but of denying privacy and individuality. As if following the anticult script as written by deprogrammers, the Ellen Jamesians are zombies merely posing as freethinkers. Even if "occasional individuals" (388) might live among them, *"they force you to be like them"* (397). The Ellen Jamesians become Garp's "sworn enemy," then, because he "insisted . . . on the superiority of a *personal* vision" (423) whereas they make Ellen into a "public casualty" and betray her "private trauma" (387). Far from affirming the feminist commitment to self-empowerment, they deny "names . . . of their own making" (420) and surrender to complete absorption by the group.

Irving's novel ends with Garp killed by an Ellen Jamesian, his childhood playmate Pooh Percy. The militant Pooh earlier appears at his mother's funeral wearing "a U.S. Army shirt with sergeant stripes" (367). When she shoots him, she is wearing a nurse's uniform, the ironically labeled "Jenny Fields Original" (411), a fashion trend long past its expiration date. Indeed, everything about Pooh is passé. Her reemergence in the novel's eleventh hour speaks to Irving's verdict on the belatedness of her politics. The site of Garp's murder, the Steering School where he matriculated and now coaches wrestling, has already begun to admit girls. And while Pooh blames Garp's teenage seduction of her older sister Cushie for Cushie's dying in labor, the unapologetically horny Cushie in fact seduced Garp. Like the other women in his life, Cushie is emancipated without benefit or need of "women's lib" (395). Garp's fatal error, according to Helen, is to bait the Ellen Jamesians rather than "ignore them": "although . . . the Ellen Jamesians were fading from fashion, they could not fade fast enough to suit Garp" (386). The wisdom of letting be is the lesson imparted by his unfinished novel, "about an idealistic father" who "keeps establishing little utopias" that turn out to be "dreadful." One "disaster" after another leads him to the Vermont governorship, where he "thinks of himself as a king" (333).

The lesson is that to force utopia is to court absolutism, and a laissez-faire attitude is the best rebuke to "crusades" (390) and "crude causes" (136). For Irving, more patient than Garp, nothing is required to make progress happen beyond an open mind. This Panglossian view is also foundational to seventies libertarianism, which takes it over from the anarchist tradition's "whole new view of the world," as Nicolas Walter puts it. It is worth recalling that, in Garp's first novel, anarchism itself goes awry when it shifts from idea to "meaningless" act. Nozick uses "invisible hand explanations" to show how "some overall pattern or design, which one would have thought had to be produced by a group's successful attempt to realize the pattern, instead was produced and maintained by a process that in no way had the overall pattern or design 'in mind'" (18). For Nozick, the "intentional coordination" (343) of free individuals amounts to an attempt to rig the game in favor of (to use Goodman's term) the "odd abstraction Society." "The complexity of interpersonal institutions and relationships" makes it "enormously unlikely that . . . one ideal pattern for society . . . could be arrived at" without distorting the lives of those who people it (313). Nozick concludes that "novelists" are better at describing the lifeworld's "thickness," its "intertwined and interrelated levels, facets, relationships," than "social scientists" (313).

"One of the things that upset [Garp] about his mother," Irving notes, "was that she was always discussing the *news*" (135). The suggestion is that "*news*" inflates society's events and nonevents alike into public affairs while failing to recognize private life as the scene of its real and meaningful actions. "News" is the Ellen Jamesians' "shallow, wholly political imitation" (538) of experience scaled up to the dimensions of mass culture. The difference between Burroughs and Irving lies less in their attitude toward surmounting authority than in their view of where to locate that revolt. For Burroughs's pirates, utopia has never arrived, and one needs superhuman powers of the sort learned in the magic schools of Waghdas to equip oneself for the struggle to achieve it. Cults in Irving's novel, on the other hand, mutilate rather than enhance their members. Placing "family matter[s]" (418) outside and above politics in the fashion of the most politically suspect nineteenth-century novel, *The World According to Garp* domesticates the powers of mind that arcane cults bestow in *Cities of the Red Night* and *The Place of Dead Roads*. But its thick descriptions of "personal vision" are scarcely retrograde. In Garp's world, utopia is already here, inside us, if we would just let our mind's eye see it—no superpowers required.

World's End in Vidal, World System in DeLillo

I bring this chapter to a close by looking at two novels preoccupied with cults at the turn of the eighties: Gore Vidal's *Kalki* (1978) and Don DeLillo's *The Names* (1982). Like those of Irving and Burroughs, these novels move in illuminatingly different directions. When *Kalki* was published, Vidal was a best seller as famous for his public feuds as for his historical fiction. When *The Names* was published, DeLillo scarcely had name recognition outside New York literary circles. His celebrity would come three years after *The Names* with *White Noise* (1985). In Vidal, the Kalki cult (like Vidal at the time) is a global phenomenon. In DeLillo, the Names cult (like DeLillo at the time) has no reach whatsoever. "In one sense we barely exist," a cultist tells DeLillo's protagonist.[90] Yet both novels understand the cult as intervening in a world of too many people and too much control. Like radical ecologists, Vidal's narrator, the "aviatrix" Teddy Ottinger, fixates on "overpopulation" via the second law of thermodynamics: "entropy was sovereign."[91] DeLillo's narrator, the "risk analyst" (44) James Axton, fixates not on the rundown of the world and the dissolution of its systems but on its capacity to self-organize into ever more ornate structures: the "world" consists of what Axton calls "rapt entanglement" (262). The problem for Vidal is a civilization on the verge of collapse through the fraying of its connections. The problem for DeLillo is a world of not too little but too much connection.

Like Jenny Fields, Theodora "Teddy" Ottinger is a feminist literary icon despite herself. Her best-selling book, *Beyond Motherhood*, is "a candid look at my life" in which she chronicles her "remov[al] from the bioreproductive track or trap that nature had created for me" (5). Her worldwide fame brings her to the attention of Kalki, né James Kelly, a Vietnam veteran who, claiming to be the reincarnation of Vishnu, has announced the end of the world or at least this cycle, the Age of Kali. Kalki has offered a magazine editor an exclusive interview so long as Teddy conducts it. Meeting him in Kathmandu, Teddy discovers that Kalki is actually interested not in her journalistic skills but in her ability to fly large aircraft. He hires her as his personal pilot, one of whose jobs is to circle the globe in a 747 dispersing bacteria Kalki has fashioned into a biological weapon that kills all but five people on the planet. The novel is the record of Teddy's experience of the months leading up to doomsday, written from a desk at the White House, where the five survivors—Kalki, his wife Lakshmi (a nuclear physicist), Dr. Lowell (a physician), Lakshmi's best friend Geraldine (a geneticist), and Teddy herself (an engineer as well as pilot)—have holed up since the global die-off.

Kalki revives themes that go far back in Vidal's fiction. *Myra Breckinridge* (1968) gives us a narrator obsessed with Malthusian catastrophism. But whereas that earlier novel is a fantasia, *Kalki* starts off at least as resolutely secular, squarely located in the here and now. It is thus notable that Vidal indexes the present by way of the cult, which the novel treats as ubiquitous, from the "kids with shaved heads" who "chant *Hare Krishna*" (10) on Hollywood Boulevard to the *"est* meeting" Teddy has attended "the year before" (24). "The seventies," Teddy notes, "were a perfect time to start a religion" (71). In presenting the ordinary world through a highly textured realism, Vidal reaches for the verisimilar shorthand of the new religious movements. Hence Teddy's ex-husband and mother-in-law are "perfect 'clears,' to use Scientologist jargon" (18); and Kalki himself is "likened . . . to the Reverend Sun Moon, another messiah at work in the United States" (31). The cult's ubiquity is unsurprising. Yet far from panic-inducing, cults in the novel are at worst a nuisance and at best another avenue for the self-improvement Teddy is after by pursuing her master's in French literature. Indeed, if going to an est seminar leaves Teddy "discouraged" (15), it is because the prevalence and ordinariness of the cult betray the falsity of the high expectations it encourages. Whereas reading Pascal is its own reward, following the cult is no more or less effective than buying a product as seen on TV—a medium that Teddy avoids even though her lover, Arlene Wagstaff, is "the highest paid TV pitchperson, after Barbara Walters" (20). In *Kalki*, the cult has long since sold out.

The Kalki cult, on the other hand, is not in the business of self-improvement. Kalki's "mission is . . . eschatological" (11), and his "message of non-hope" (154) is delivered not to prepare his followers to live their best lives but to foster their faith that they'll be "reborn in the next cycle of the human race" (23). Though Teddy doesn't believe that Kalki is Vishnu, she does share his view that the world needs rebooting. They reach the same conclusion by way of different discourses. Teddy holds that "as entropy increases, energy hemorrhages" (120); Kalki teaches that "with each age since the original Golden Age, all things human have lost energy" (155). Kalki strikes a chord, Teddy reasons, because his doomsday stylings are tuned to the "mood of most of the world," which is keenly aware that "things were running down" (24). Though never conceding Kalki's divinity, Teddy is thus not exactly unhappy with the extinction event he has brought about. It is merely an extreme version of the visionary tradition to which she herself belongs: "Dr. Paul Ehrlich, Dr. Barry Commoner and Teddy Ottinger, Test Pilot, were the chief prophets of that day" (16). As we have observed, ecologists like Ehrlich had a grim view of the human plague in developing nations, a prejudice Teddy shares. "Too many cows plus too many people," she notes on arrival in New Delhi.

"India was a microcosm of what had gone wrong with the human race" (40). "Indira Gandhi" is thus "the greatest woman of our time because of her campaign to sterilize the Indian male" (5).

The cult in *Kalki* is a rather flat affair, then, because it takes no interest in—and makes no promises about—inwardness. Vidal fashions the Kalki cult as a spectacle of pure image, a cult of personality amplified by mass media technologies that position its charismatic leader for the kind of global domination we now associate with Hollywood stars bankable in China or pop acts with sold-out world tours. Teddy calls Kalki's "voice . . . an aphrodisiac" (57), the same "voice with which he spun his curious web around the world" (155). Kalki's "essence of sandalwood and blondness" (142) helps build his brand: the messiah as universal celebrity. Vidal's depiction of the cult plays like a parody of how the anticult movement imagines the cult's allure for the clueless. But Vidal doesn't so much mock as believe the conventional wisdom that the horde of followers—any horde, any followers—is ripe for bedazzlement by a magnetic voice or photogenic face.[92] "TV-viewing" heralds "the end of the age of Kali" (150). In other words, Vidal has no truck with the promises of inwardness or self-examination that Burroughs and Hubbard associate with media. Whereas Burroughs's tape recorder can give him access to his inner life, allowing him to play back his memories at will, in Vidal such devices afford only one-way transmissions beaming from the corporate mothership to the human receiver, a wholly conditioned behaviorist object. Hence Teddy takes "for granted that the huge KALKI on top of the building" of the local ashram "were the call letters of some new FM outfit" (11).

Vidal's send-up of the cult is the pretext for a critique of mass media's inexorable power to manipulate us against our will. He is uninterested in the "libertarian" version of consumerism that Sunstein and Thaler locate in the "good choice architecture" of modern media and design. "Peace" at the end of the world, as Dr. Lowell puts it, means "no more pollution. No more hideous cities, slums, people. No more television" (173). The grouping of these things as like forms of waste is recognizable from radical ecology's entropic turn. In *Kalki*, the indistinctness of matter as such does double duty. The novel hews not just to the ecologist's understanding of the human presence as a toxin but also to the antiutilitarian's defense of individualism. For Kalki's betrayal of the seventies cult ideal is nowhere more apparent than in his rejection of subjectivity on the basis of the most vulgar materialism. "Physically you and I and all of us are the same stuff," Kalki tells his tiny band of fellow survivors, "and so interchangeable" (239). On the other hand, the Kalki cult *epitomizes* the seventies cult's "epistemological individualism," to use Wallis's term, by way of its leader's insistence that "there are no rules, except those that I choose to make" (63).

Kalki takes the cult's withdrawal from the social to a frenzied extreme. Ending the world of course ends all threat of social control.

Near *Kalki*'s conclusion, Doctor Lowell refers to Milton Friedman as "the real hero of our era" (230). In a novel that thrives on facetiousness, the reference is not merely a throwaway joke. While Vidal scarcely favored free-market capitalism, he was himself a devout libertarian. Teddy is not the only one who has been "reading Foucault" (12). Vidal appears to heed that master's lesson that "it is always the body that is at issue—the body and its forces, their utility and their docility, their distribution and their submission."[93] Vidal took frequent aim at "the regulation of our private morals," at laws "controlling what we smoke, eat, put in our veins—not to mention trying to regulate with whom and how we have sex" (*SE*, 451). But Vidal's libertarianism extended into the terrain cultivated by Friedman, Nozick, and other champions of the minimal state. In "The Second American Revolution" (1981), he writes:

> Those who fear that Milton Friedman's cheerful visage will be swiftly hewn from Dakota rock underestimate the passion of the majority not to be unemployed in a country where the gap between rich and poor is, after France, the greatest in the Western world. Since the welfare system is the price that the white majority pays in order to exclude the black minority from the general society, entirely new social arrangements will have to be made if that system is to be significantly altered. (*SE*, 395)

Far from being lionized on Rushmore, according to Vidal, Friedman is a "hero[ic]" everyman with the courage to say what we're all thinking. Racial equality will emerge only after the repeal of the welfare state because that political system stunts the sense of responsibility of a citizenry turned into recipients of government largesse. "The hallmark of the age of Kali," Teddy reminds us, "is not good government" (168). Good government for Vidal no less than Friedman means a rolling back of those paternalistic policies that usurp our agency ostensibly for our own good. The fantasy of the indolent black welfare case is par for the course with Vidal, who was infamous for treating racial stereotypes as if they were uncomfortable truths. In *Kalki*, the "derelict" are "most[ly] black or Hispanic," a "parade of monsters" whom Teddy "watched, beyond horror" (130). The monstrosity is endemic to politics itself, a "parasitic trade" that in turn spawns "people who wanted something from the government" (113). Faced with such a cycle of dependency, Teddy "could not imagine any of these people wanting to go on" (130).

The occasion for "The Second American Revolution" is the passage of California's Proposition 13 (1978), which drastically curtailed that state's ability to levy property taxes. For Vidal, this statute augured the promise of a more participatory democracy that, "by requiring . . . a limitation on the federal government's power to print money" (*SE*, 372), could mitigate the evils of a system engineered by "oligarchs" (*SE*, 395) to part us from our hard-earned dollars. Likening Prop 13's passage to the "Boston Tea Party" (*SE*, 371), Vidal sees it as an opportunity for the nation to "put things right" (*SE*, 372), to return its "honest yeoman" citizen to the road not taken of what, in the 1972 essay "Homage to Daniel Shays," he calls the "Jefferson I" model of governance. The "Jefferson I society" is characterized by a "frugal government" with "no taxes beyond a minimal levy in order to pay for a few judges, a postal service, small executive and legislative bodies." The "Jefferson II" world we inhabit, full-blown by the "Second Inaugural," is characterized by a "Hamiltonian" emphasis on "the uses to which taxes might be put . . . within each State" (*SE*, 323). For Vidal, Prop 13 won because "we do not like paying taxes on our houses, traditionally the only form of capital that the average middle-class American is allowed to accumulate" (*SE*, 372). Vidal echoes the counter-history, imagined in Rothbard and Burroughs and given a robust defense in Nozick, of a polity whose legitimacy rests on the degree to which it affords "self-determination" (*SE*, 323) to its freeholder majority.

In reality, Prop 13 has led not to a reinvigorated civil society but to the drastic decline of California's ability to deliver a public service sector remotely close to its population's needs in the past forty years—which is what Friedman wanted, despite Vidal's quaint insistence that his interest lay in closing "the gap between rich and poor." The lesson of Friedman's 1962 book *Capitalism and Freedom* was that "concentrated power is not rendered harmless by the good intentions of those who create it."[94] That book chronicles the state's failure to bring about progressive outcomes, including integration. Just as Vidal sees welfare reform as the only way to make black Americans full citizens rather than wards of the state, so Friedman claims that "discrimination against groups of particular color or religion is least in those areas where there is the greatest freedom of competition" (109). Whereas its "paternalistic" policies oblige the state to enforce status distinctions ("every individual has to carry an identity card" [149]), "the essence of a competitive market is its impersonal character" (119), which thus "protects men from being discriminated against in their economic activities for reasons that are irrelevant to their productivity—whether these reasons are associated with their views or their color" (21).

In addition to safeguarding the interests of "those minority groups which can most easily become the object of the distrust and enmity of the majority" (21), the market provides Friedman with a rationale for doing away with state-sponsored protections. These rest on a "supposedly general interest" that Friedman (like the antiutilitarians) faults for "forcing people to act against their own interest" and "substitut[ing] the values of outsiders for the values of participants" (200). Precisely what Friedman likes about the market is its ability to transcend ideology as much as status distinctions. "This is why," Friedman claims, "capitalist societies are less materialistic than collectivist societies" (201). By bracketing references to belief, by making one's thoughts "irrelevant" to the market's workings, capitalism "foster[s] diversity" against collectivism's "excess of conformity" (97). "The poverty of our imagination" reinforces "the tyranny of the status quo" when we cede to the state our decisions about what society should look like (158). As Nozick puts it, "People tend to forget the possibilities of acting independently of the state" (14). By contrast, the "fertility of the market" for Friedman allows us to entertain "many alternatives to the present organization" (158). Friedman's market is the condition, then, for the neo-idealist reimagining of social life on grounds other than merely material satisfaction. Its impersonality paradoxically guarantees "the dignity of the individual" (195) and encourages "millions of individuals . . . to live their lives by their own values" (200).

In DeLillo's *The Names*, the most striking feature of the titular cult is its impersonality. In a departure from the seventies depiction of the cult as a haven for togetherness, the murderous sect at the floating center of the novel has no use for the social bonding that drives the new culture of consumption and its "invisible ideology." Unlike "the mass murderers . . . working outward from some private screen, conscious of an audience they might agreeably excite" (169), as DeLillo puts it, the Names cult shuns publicity. Its cells continually relocate as a result of the murders that render them liable to prosecution, and (more to the point) they refuse to submit to what Friedman calls "the values of outsiders." Like the pirate cult in Burroughs, DeLillo's cult strives for a purely autonomous community. Unlike *Cities of the Red Night* and *The Place of Dead Roads*, which are narrated from within the cult mind, DeLillo's novel takes the outsider's view. Yet the outsider in question, the novel's narrator James Axton, is not exactly the viewer at home transfixed by nightly broadcasts of the cult epidemic. For one thing, he is (like the cult that rivets him) effectively homeless, a nomad based in Athens who belongs to a "subculture" of "business people in transit, growing old in planes and airports" (4). "I traveled between places," he tells us, "never in them" (141). James's job involves monitoring threats to precariously balanced nation-states in regions of "political instability" (174) on behalf of global capital.

To describe the novel as an "outsider's view" of the cult is thus a bit misleading, since James is scarcely an outsider. On "discovering the secret" of the cult's mission, he feels a jealous desire to withhold it from those who haven't "earned" such knowledge, as if "it conferred a cult-hood all its own" (245). The secret in question is the cult's fetishistic relation to proper names. "Ta Onómata" (186) ("the names" in Greek) chooses victims whose initials match the names of the places into which they happen to wander. As though carrying out a bizarrely literal version of Saul Kripke's argument that names are "always rigid designators" rather than "disguised descriptions" of objects, Ta Onómata's human sacrifices perform what Kripke calls "an initial baptism" that consecrates the proper names of people and places by "fixing [their] reference."[95] When Kripke calls a name "necessary," he means that it is not a contingent way of describing an object but in fact a property of the object, "having the same reference in all possible worlds."[96] Names at first appear to have a similar fastening role in DeLillo's novel. Because the "places where we did business were not always as different to us as the names assigned to them," James notes, "we needed the names to tell them apart" (101). But as James's friend Charles remarks of the shifting transnational landscape in which they circulate: "They keep changing the names" (237). Far from "fixing reference" in DeLillo's novel, names are fungible placeholders on an endlessly revisable map.

The cult's naming rituals are designed not merely to pin down names over and against their elusiveness in late-capitalist onomastics, then, but to compete with the fluctuations of a geopolitical terrain that seems to render all meaning precarious. Its members seek a more primal condition reminiscent of the "cynegetic lifestyle" discussed in the last chapter, what Frank Volterra, a filmmaker obsessed with making a movie about Ta Onómata, calls "the situation" of "people in a wilderness . . . the desert, the movie screen, the strip of film . . . here to work out their existence" (196). According to Volterra, film does not exteriorize life by turning everything into surface—the charge leveled against film by older opponents of mass culture or its more recent postmodern celebrants. It is rather "another part of the twentieth-century mind . . . the world seen from inside" (198). Such comments could be absorbed into DeLillo's trademark paranoia about surveillance culture: "The whole world is on film, all the time" (198). Yet Volterra sees film less as an instrument wielded by a panoptic society than as a means of radical reflexivity. Film on this view does not objectify us; it reveals to us our subjectivity. Thus to Volterra a "personal film" is redundant, since all films amount to "personal statements" (244). "Movie-dealing" is "like psychoanalysis" (139). In keeping with this understanding, David, the narrator of DeLillo's first novel, *Americana* (1971), has devoted himself to making a "home movie" in "an attempt to explore parts of my consciousness."[97] The idea that film is a technology of self-realization rather than reification recalls the medium's role in both Burroughs and Scientology, where seizing control of one's awareness means getting one's hands on the culture industry's apparatus, in order (as Burroughs puts it) to "tamper with the prerecordings" or (as Scientology imagines) to look at one's inner self as clearly as possible, as if film and other recording technologies gave us high-resolution images of our own minds at work.

Ta Onómata rejects the technological prostheses favored by Burroughs and Hubbard on the view that the mind is already equipped with everything it needs for its own self-exploration. Film would interfere with the basic program of DeLillo's cult: to observe itself without any mediation (hence their refusal of Volterra's request to film them). "Cults tend to be closed-in," James's friend Owen Brademas observes. "Inwardness is very much the point" (114). The Names cult takes this axiom to an extreme: everything counts as the outside. But its rigorous hermeticism is intended not so much to preserve group coherence as to enforce the sort of perpetual withdrawal that anarchist and libertarian thinkers endorse. "No one *has* to be here," James learns from Andhal, a kind of nonce informant for the cult. People continually drift in and out of the cult's ambit: "We are no longer in a place" (205). The cult's philosophical "purpose" (168) indeed amounts to absenting its members from any specific circumstance. The appeal of that purpose to both James and his creator lies in the novel's unease with what Lefort calls "the great closure." *The Names* presents us not with a postmodern logic that has severed the chain of signification but rather with a world saturated with connectivity, "self-referring, a world in which there is no escape" (295). That last word, however, implies a claustrophobia DeLillo's novel does not endorse. "Modern communications don't shrink the world, they make it bigger," James's friend Lindsay observes. "They give us more, they connect more things. The world isn't shrinking at all" (321). This world is not the "entropy trap" over which radical ecologists brood. Its exhaustions are of a different order. Its "complications" require increasingly strenuous efforts to "keep up" (321) with what amounts to an ever-expanding universe.[98] Traveling "between places" thus necessitates a perpetual logistics, a "systems planning" that a character in *Americana* describes as the "true American artform" ("We excel at maintenance. We understand interrelationships. We make it all work" [265]).[99]

James's position with his company, the Northeast Group, involves just such maintenance. His job is to monitor various "control points" (32), individuals situated in geopolitical hotspots whose actions and experiences are snapshots of the world working its own issues out. The Names cult thus comes into being as a sort of redoubt, an effort to preserve the value of human autocritique, of human reflexivity, against its devaluation by an autoreferential world in which, as DeLillo puts it in *Americana*, "Things become more real in proportion to the unreality of individual lives" (281).[100] The cult attracts James (who calls it "the only thing I seem to connect with" [298]) because it cannot be subsumed under the protocols of control that James evaluates. It is "something you cannot analyze" (206), Andahl tells the risk analyst. James interprets the cult's "denial of our elemental nature" (173) as a refusal to serve as a metric for any larger social reality. "We are inventing a way out" (207), Andahl says. The cultists' sheer unworldliness—"they're secular monks" who "want to vault into eternity" (201)—is a means to transcend "our base reality" (173), which the novel figures as an indistinct collective of people and things. "Masses of people scare me" (22), we hear from the equally cult-obsessed Owen, for whom "the nightmarish force of people in groups . . . suggested worship and delirium" (274). The cult's cells never include more than five people, and even within these tiny collectives members remain isolated from one another, practicing "the tradecraft of a confined life" (289). This is epistemological individualism with a vengeance.

It is a commonplace in studies of *The Names* that Owen and James are subtle antagonists playing out DeLillo's own struggles with linguistic meaning. In this reading, Owen nurses a wish to share in the unity of word and faith that he both envied and feared in the tongues-speaking church members of his Pentecostal childhood. An unbeliever despairing at his lack of faith, Owen is drawn into "complicity with the Names cult," according to Matthew Morris, because it affords "the formal euphoria Owen could not attain through [the] glossolalia" of his Midwestern church. Despite disavowing the fundamentalism of his upbringing, Owen remains a literalist at heart. By virtue of his "overly formal thought" and "interest in alphabets for their own sake," as Morris puts it, Owen is no less what DeLillo calls an "Abecedarian" (208) than the cultists, who also divorce languages from "the people who use them."[101] With James Axton, by contrast, DeLillo recovers what Matthew Mutter calls "a sense of wonder over our ordinary life with language." Like Morris, Mutter finds in the cultists' demands on language "a moral evasion, a refusal to encounter and live in the world as it is given to them."[102] For this claim to be correct, we would have to conclude that DeLillo holds any brief for "the world as it is given." But as I have suggested, *The Names* treats "ordinary life" as a kind of phantasm. "The world is so big and complicated we don't trust ourselves to figure out anything on our own" (321), Lindsay tells James. Whereas Sennett claims that oversized "ideologies" block our access to human-scaled "care," Lindsay's point is ontological. The "external world" (101) itself, like radical ecology's biosphere, has eclipsed our ability to know it even with the help of the most coherent ideologies.

Though James and Owen are not precisely antagonists for DeLillo, neither are they identical in their view of the cult. Owen finds himself "bound to the cult, as an object to a neutron star, pulled toward its collapsed mass" (284). As a globe-trotting contract worker, James is finally invested in the cult because it seems to confer on the historical contingency of his own precarious life a certain gravitas. James appears to entertain the view of really deep ecologists like Paul Shepard that we were always meant to be nomads. As the last chapter showed, those thinkers take nomadism as a solution to the ills befalling *Homo sapiens* on the assumption that the agency evolved in us by natural selection has been denatured by settlement. Really deep ecology is committed to the idealist's assumption that we have the power to recategorize the world even if we suffer from the delusion that some categories—agricultural civilization, urbanization, mass society—are perdurable. Indeed, Shepard's hunters, Nozick's utopians, and Burroughs's pirates all imagine mobility as a weapon against the idées fixes of statism.

The problem in *The Names*, though, is not that categories are fixed but that they are virtually nonexistent. The novel withholds the possibility—not to say the consolation—of a paranoiac prime mover, an "unknown authority . . . behind the categories" (252) manipulating human action from a central location. *The Names*, in fact, proves something of an exception to the rule that DeLillo is a master of the paranoid style. The novel does not so much enact as critique his characteristic paranoid plot. This might strike some readers as implausible, given that one of the late revelations in the book is that, from his sinecure in the Athens office of the Northeast Group, James has been unwittingly running "a back-channel dialogue" (313) for the Central Intelligence Agency. Yet suspicious readers might hesitate before plucking such low-hanging allegorical fruit, if only because it is dangled so ostentatiously in front of us. "The CIA is America's myth," James observes. "All the themes are there, in . . . whole bureaucracies of silence, in conspiracies and doublings and brilliant betrayals" (315).

The CIA is the objective correlative of the paranoid style, "giv[ing] a classical tone to our commonly felt emotions" (315). But try as he might, James cannot make its "bureaucracies of silence" speak to him. Like the shifting terrain of the global system that renders his own footing unstable, the "myth" is too malleable, "embodying whatever we need at a given time to know ourselves or unburden ourselves" (315). We might say that what James takes from the CIA is its policy of *deniability*. In a halfhearted bid to make amends for his inadvertent complicity with the agency, James looks up a Greek executive, Andreas, who himself may or may not be a secret agent for a Greek separatist group. James's plan falls through; the two men never reconnect. Yet even so, his intended confession is really a nonapology for a state of affairs in which James maintains a steadfast sense of noninvolvement. "Any data passed on to the CIA" through his office, he intends to tell Andreas, "was not related in any way to affairs in Greece" (318).

Earlier in the novel, Andreas, who suspects James of being a spy before James does, takes him out to a dinner that doubles as a lecture on the Greek people's history of persecution. "The final enemy is government," Andreas tells James at the end of the meal. "Only government threatens their existence" (235). But if government threatens the Greek dissident's existence, it also ratifies it. The "humiliation" wrought by "foreign interference" and "occupation" is, Andreas says, "the drama that is so essential to our lives" (233). That "drama" is the epic of nationalism, in which neither the anarchist cell nor the small-group cult has much interest. Nor for that matter does the "subculture" to which James and Andreas belong, as the latter points out: "I don't think there's any nationality in companies such as ours" (233). James lacks not only the nationalist cause that gives dramatic tension to the restless Greek activists but *any* antagonist to motivate or test him, against which to assert his "distinctiveness." He is, as he says in response to a query about what he does for the Northeast Group, "a presence" and nothing more: "The higher the post, the vaguer the job." He is merely a vector with no "specific duties" (240).

When Owen tells him of his final days with the cultist Emmerich, James marvels at the latter's virtually tautological self-possession: "His crime, the largeness of it, furnishes endless material for speculation and self-knowledge. Everything he reads and learns is made to serve as a personal philosophy.... The murder has ... become part of the dream pool of his self-analysis" (289). James's envy of Emmerich's self-possession mingles with a horror at his monstrousness. The crime's premeditation is more important to Emmerich than its consequences. Remorse is absent because the victim scarcely counts for Emmerich as a person. Emmerich's self-possession amounts to the narcissistic fantasy of imagining his identity as parallel to—and in competition with—the globe. His assumption that the world "has a self" (289) makes other merely human selves superfluous. Where the Greeks have the government as their enabling antagonist, Emmerich sees the planet as his. The cultist's narcissism mirrors what Fredric Jameson calls the "satisfaction of paranoia," the fantasy of inclusion it induces in its sufferers, whether enemies of the state or of the CIA.[103] For all its drawbacks, the paranoid system affords the consolation that the system is paying attention to you, that you belong in its grasp.

The Names ends with an assassination attempt on his friend David that renews James's struggle with his inability to be paranoid *enough*. The issue, "one more thing to vex me with its elusiveness," is whether the assassin's bullet was intended for James himself. "I want to believe they plotted well" (326), James says, though he cannot escape the fact that he has been mistaken for David in the past by Andreas, whom James suspects of the attempt on David's life. Like Owen's wish for "formal euphoria," to use Morris's term, such belief would mean that "exact correspondence" prevails over the "formlessness of motive and plan and execution" (325), that design supplants accident. It is hardly coincidental that *Underworld* (1997), the pivotal novel for exciting critical interest in DeLillo as a religious writer, as Amy Hungerford has remarked, is also his most explicitly paranoid work. What Hungerford calls that novel's "mystical structures" make the subterranean actions of state and nonstate power look like a divine plan, or at least imbues such power with the "logics of secret and mystery."[104] Yet James's "I want to believe" (the motto of *The X-Files*, mass culture's exemplary paranoid narrative) tells us that he remains unconvinced that fate rather than chance brings him and David to the same park for a run on the morning of the botched assassination. Giving his company records to the investigators in charge of David's case, James decides to "let them muse on the plausibilities." Their "job," not his, "was public order" (326). Embodying the conspiratorial outlook it provokes in its subjects, the system is a fashioner of hidden designs from which James remains locked out.

Wanting to believe in a well-plotted murder, of course, returns us not only to Owen's futile wish to find meaning in system but also to the novel's titular cult, the merits of whose designs James can never quite figure out. James fails to connect the dots when he finds himself nearly on the receiving end of a ritualistic murder similar to those carried out by the Names cult. Political terrorists in Athens have taken to killing Americans who don't know their own place, just as the Names cult kills people whose initials correspond to the name of whatever place they find themselves. And just as the cult never advertises its murders, so no group takes responsibility for the assassination attempt. "No one claims credit for the worst of the terror," James says of his last days in Athens, when "bombings will become commonplace" (328). In a sense, "credit" in the novel's global imaginary has become so abstract, or so costly, that it cannot inhere in persons, the way an earlier epoch made it a synonym for character. Rendered free of any person, credit (like Emmerich's "world") "has a self," or at least behaves like one. We might say that the novel's political murders are designed to expose the violence of a system, dominated by "martial law, black markets, and the International Monetary Fund" (48), in which credit masquerades as humanitarianism. "When you reschedule a debt . . . it amounts to an aid program" (231), James tells David, who is "a credit head at the Mainland Bank" (48).

Yet it would be inaccurate to push such a political account of the novel, just as it doesn't make sense finally to see the cult itself as a political undertaking. In divorcing Ta Onómata's commitment from politics, *The Names* makes a case against the cult in line with neither the period's anticult panic nor the versions of the cult found in the other novelists who take up or deride its cause. Where Vidal's Kalki cult and Burroughs's transmigrant cult also take on a global enemy, their defeat of the world means vanquishing the ills of an officialdom that begets squalor, suffering, stasis. For all relevant purposes in these novels, government is coincident with planet, as if the appendages of bureaucratic power overlay the globe like a secondary ecosystem slowly strangling all its inhabitants. But DeLillo's cult breaks this linkage. Its members have no interest in, much less awareness of, the "political" world. They take the stance of "learners of the alphabet" and absolute "beginners" (208) because they strive to see the world as elemental and innocent of strong institutions. But here too the cult, which prefers the desert's "vast sweep" (68) for its murders, merely ritualizes a pattern in James's habitat, likewise an "empty land" traversed by "lines of data-gathering," "political currents," and "secrecy" (44).

"Deserts are the waking awareness, the simple and clear solution," the cultist Singh tells Owen, "like a mathematical solution applied to the affairs of the planet" (292). But we are far removed from the utopian polis to which Edward Abbey imagines his barren desert community might lead. For while the cultist links neo-idealism to desert life ("My mind works better in the desert" [292]), he also links the desert's unleashing of his reason to the rationality of those cost-benefit analyses the market imposes on the world system. Volterra calls the desert a "frame" (196) for the Names cult. But it is just as apt a framing for the frictionless transnational exchanges of the Northeast Group and the Mainland Bank. The Names cult's commitment to its own hermeticism turns out on the novel's terms to be redundant, since the world as DeLillo depicts it already privileges *privatization* in every sense, not only "impelling us toward a sense of inwardness" (251) but also rejecting any form of regulation as an obstacle to liquidity. For Burroughs and Vidal no less than for Nozick or Hubbard, the adversary is control by externalities not of our choosing. For DeLillo, at least in *The Names*, the adversary is an "obliteration of control" (274) at every scale, from the individual to the planetary system. The novel suggests that our patterns and programs are not overly effective but never effective enough. *The Names* sees no emancipation in the constant headway of Burroughs's pirates or outlaws because the world of the novel never stops moving. Hence the dismal finale of Ta Onómata. "Nearly dead" (289) when Owen comes upon them in the Thar Desert, its members have entirely run down like broken clockwork by the time he leaves, while the world spins on.

CHAPTER 4

Millennial America and the World to Come

Rapture for the Market

In "How to Build a Universe That Doesn't Fall Apart Two Days Later" (1978), Philip Dick recounts a visit in 1974 from a woman who, in addition to bearing a Darvon prescription, "wore a shining gold necklace in the center of which was a . . . gold fish," a "sign worn," she tells him, "by the early Christians."[1] The fish "hypnotized" Dick into a state of "anamnesis," a loss of forgetting, in which he learns that he shares his body with a second-century Christian named Thomas: "The girl was a secret Christian and so was I. We lived in fear of detection by the Romans" (*SR*, 271). This finding leads Dick to compare his apparently prophetic fiction to the Book of Revelation. "It is an eerie experience to write something into a novel," he observes, "and to learn later on . . . it is true" (*SR*, 266). A John of Patmos for the consumer age, Dick imagines himself "stamped from the original mold of Christian revolutionary against the legions of Roman force" (*SR*, 289), whose modern embodiment is the triumvirate of "media," "governments," and "big corporations" (*SR*, 261).

Despite its theological grounding, Dick's origin myth is continuous with Burroughs's effort to locate the "timeless struggle" (*SR*, 289) between freedom and tyranny in a remote historical moment that it is within our agency to recover. What makes the "crisis" of liberty "timeless" indeed is the Escher-like temporality in which these writers couch the persistence either of "hateful

Rome" (*SR*, 271) (for Dick) or of the Enlightenment project that continually swerves from the commitment to wresting freedom from authority (for Burroughs). When time is a loop, reincarnation and prophecy appear equally fruitful measures for liberation. If the empire never ended, as Dick believes, then the only way forward is backward, by welcoming in whichever past persons happen to cohabit our bodies. The Dianetic echo reveals a further commonality between Dick and Burroughs. Yet whereas Burroughs is a mixture of L. Ron Hubbard and Jürgen Habermas, Dick is closer to a blend of Herbert Marcuse and the Gnostics. For just as Burroughs has little interest in the Habermasian task of finishing the Enlightenment project of an authentically *public* freedom (since the public is just another name for social control), so it is tempting to say that Dick, who prized his outsider status even as he coveted acclaim, was more allured by the "secret" than the Christian part of his new—or rather very old—identity.

This tension between sharing and preserving the mysteries—between his hope for common cause and his attraction to ingroup prestige—has a long pedigree in Dick's work, but it takes on a distinctive cast in the last decade of his life, which saw him immersed in what we might dub a *Countercultural Christology*. The 1981 novel *The Divine Invasion*, his curious entry into the burgeoning post-sixties rapture genre, reproduces central aspects of Dick's 1974 encounter. God, a boy named Emmanuel without any memory, seeks to unravel the mystery of Zina, who may be a demon, a rival, or (as is the case) a missing portion of Himself. Emmanuel's own anamnesis—his recovery of Zina as the "female side of God"—allows Him to battle Satan in a world ruled by the Catholic-Islamic Church and the Communist Party, which have combined into the rapture narrative's favorite nemesis: a global superpower.[2] *The Divine Invasion*'s plot is stitched together with extracts from Kabbalah and the Gnostic gospels, as if to demonstrate as ostentatiously as possible the erudition of the book's intellectually insecure maker. The scholastic longueurs that make *The Divine Invasion* a dull read also suggest that, in embracing the mass-cultural rapture movement, Dick cannot help opting for esoterica. Weaving an even more apocryphal plotline into the already noncanonical rapture story keeps Dick on the countercultural bandwagon, its bumper now decaled with an ichthus. Dick embraces the rapture because end-times fundamentalism is both populist and antinomian, and so appears to provide a way out of the impasse between collectivity and privacy in his own ideal vision of the social. In fundamentalism, Dick finds a club he wouldn't mind joining because its believers reject all clubs, in particular those of organized religion.[3] As Nathan Hatch has argued, "Fundamentalist movements have all shared an anti-elitist and anticentralist ideology."[4]

Thus in *The Late Great Planet Earth* (1970), Hal Lindsey treats the real church, members of which need not even meet to enjoy the solidarity of their faith, as antithetical to "the visible church which is characterized by increasing unbelief."[5] If its anti-institutionalism begins to explain *The Late Great Planet Earth*'s ascent from religious right curio to the best-selling nonfiction book of the seventies, its framing of nonconformity in the language of things not seen suggests a certain convergence of evangelicalism and neo-idealism, which also casts a mistrustful eye on the visible world. This chapter considers the rising belief in the end times alongside the emergence of "channeling," the period's other popular mystical movement, in which earthbound mediums become conduits for otherworldly spirits. Looking at neo-idealism in the supposedly antirational precincts of fundamentalist and New Age spirituality, I show that these movements embrace the primacy of subjectivity we are more accustomed to seeing in the Kantian renewal espoused by Rawls and Nagel. Adherents of rapture and channeling profess a stronger reverence for self-authorization and reason than the precepts of their faith might lead us to imagine. Then, too, they predicate that respect on the kinds of social sorting we are used to seeing in various seventies enterprises. Where contemporary post-apocalyptic fictions run toward nihilism, presenting failed worlds in which no one makes it, the next-life narratives I am concerned with divide the human remnant between the many who cannot rise above mere physicality and the few who break through to a paradise of reason in the world to come.

As with other movements we have observed, rapture and channeling reveal the friction between freedom and equality in millennial America. What Christopher Douglas calls the "hunger for apocalypse" seems to draw out of its enthusiasts an unusually strong commitment to the idea that the truly free are also socially superior.[6] Thus in his anthology *Apocalypse Culture*, Adam Parfrey juxtaposes "the hoi polloi" who "have settled into their homely predestined epiphanies" with those "individuals who have the audacity to consider themselves their own best authority, in repudiation or ignorance of the orthodoxy factories of Church, University or State."[7] Like Dick, the essayists in *Apocalypse Culture* (which includes, among other things, an interview with a practicing necrophiliac) imagine that the true survivor belongs to an end-times avant-garde. They pride themselves on a militant unconventionality, a stance they oppose to Christians whose "homely predestined" sensibilities they gleefully *épater*.

Yet in the view of the sociologist of religion Rodney Stark, the invariably square Christian is a myth perpetrated by those who insist, against the evidence, that secularization has triumphed over religiosity. In a 1981 essay, Stark concludes that American Christians are less like Parfrey's "Pod People," "filtering any information that does not impinge on their prefab gestalt," than like the rogues' gallery of fringe radicals in his anthology.[8] The reason for the resemblance is that, according to Stark, resistance to convention is normative for the faithful: "religion is never so robust as when it is an underground church."[9] His point is that in "making faith more costly," as in the former Communist bloc, "repressive states . . . fuel the religious impulse" by making it "more necessary and valuable."[10] Stark is the foremost proponent of the rational choice theory of religion. Once the dominant model in economics, the rational choice approach exemplified by the Chicago economist Gary Becker has lately found a powerful challenger in the behavioral economics pioneered by Daniel Kahneman and Amos Tversky.[11] Yet rational choice has become prominent if not exactly hegemonic elsewhere in the social sciences. Rejecting the intuition that "religion is rooted in the irrational," Stark and his collaborator Roger Finke instead "model religion as the behavior of rational, reasonably well-informed actors who choose to 'consume' religious 'commodities' in the same way that they weigh the costs and benefits of consuming secular commodities."[12]

The coupling of rational choice and religion makes particular sense for the study of contemporary (white) evangelicals, who have widely embraced the free market's virtues as their own.[13] Lindsey derides "the basic promise and goal of Communism" because it proposes "the changing of man's nature by the complete change of his environment" (85). The prophetic populism of the seventies breaks with the dour anticonsumerism of an older Christianity (which persisted in Dick's self-exile from a "society" dominated by "corporations" or, alternatively, in the short-lived Christian socialism of the Jesus freak movement). Opting out of the doomsday rhetoric characteristic of books like Ehrlich's *The Population Bomb*, *The Late Great Planet Earth* is composed in the upbeat, market-savvy prose of a hip street preacher, a style Lindsey honed as a minister for the Campus Crusade for Christ. Lindsey presents himself as a laid-back champion of the disaffected young, and his sympathy with their "search for answers" (8) makes *The Late Great Planet Earth* read at times like a pamphlet from the Esalen Institute. Come the rapture, he predicts, all believers will trade up from "the face or body you now have" to "a glorious new body" in which "you will [still] be recognizable" (141). Like New Age hustlers from Abraham Maslow to Werner Erhard, Lindsey addresses his readership (always directly, with the generic you) by appealing to the inner self.

That appeal is rooted in the fundamentalist refrain that no one can bring unbelievers to belief but themselves. Insisting that only a consultation with one's own mind can lead to a summons from Jesus, Lindsey paradoxically embraces the autonomous will the reborn Christian is supposed to surrender in welcoming Jesus inside. This paradox is more superficial than it appears. As Jennie Chapman notes in *Plotting Apocalypse* (2013), "evangelicals in America have always been individualists."[14] Or as a character puts it in *The Divine Invasion*: "Salvation is on a one by one basis."[15] With their disloyalty to institutions, evangelicals look like what period economists saw as the necessary and sufficient building blocks of a just society. Defining "the country" as "the collection of individuals who compose it, not something over and above them" in *Capitalism and Freedom*, Friedman posited that the citizen "regards government as a means" rather than "a master or god to be blindly worshipped and served."[16] Government's only purpose is to facilitate "the freedom of individuals to pursue activities of their own choice" (142).

What drives people is not the merely "economic motive," F. A. Hayek wrote in *The Road to Serfdom* (1944), a text that has a scriptural centrality for the Chicago School economists not unlike Revelation for Lindsey, but "the widest choice in enjoying the fruits of our efforts."[17] Planned societies are bound to fail, Hayek insists, because they value outcomes that amount to "nobody's conscious choice." According to Hayek, presaging the antiutilitarian views of John Rawls and Bernard Williams, "few want to be relieved through having choice[s] made for them by others."[18] Like Friedman and Hayek, Lindsey identifies the meaningfulness of our choices with their self-authorization. Historically, the choices "determining the course of people" have been out of their hands; "decisions," for example, "have been made because special court seers have read certain signs of omen from the entrails of a chicken!" Jettisoning the "strange customs" (12) of the hieratic past means that any important "decision" must take place "in the quiet of your heart" (150). Thus the "decision concerning your presence during this last seven-year period in history," he says of the Tribulation, "is entirely up to you" (138).

In *When Your Money Fails: The "666 System" Is Here* (1981), Mary Stewart Relfe invokes Friedman on his favorite canard, the inflation triggered by an exuberant monetary policy. "Financing government spending by increasing the quantity of money looks like magic," Relfe writes, "like getting something for nothing."[19] No less vexed than the Chicago School economist by a system that overrides individuals and currencies by fiat, Relfe goes quite a bit afield of Friedman's account. For Relfe, runaway inflation is really a form of *black* "magic" that heralds a "One World Government, destined to control all peoples and nations the last seven years of this age" (x). Yet the alarm bells she sounds are actually eccentric to the rapture discourse to which Lindsey is central. Scarcely exempt from the paranoia that leads Relfe to see UPC codes and pop songs as easing a hapless citizenry into "the irreversible trend toward One World Socialism" (78), Lindsey nonetheless takes the death of the free market in relative stride. While *The Late Great Planet Earth* does not skimp on invective for the overregulated society, the book's attitude toward regulation along with everything else is strikingly nonchalant. On the one hand, Lindsey can breezily note that "of course the world will choose the Antichrist" (184); on the other, he can observe, with the timbre of a fantasy football enthusiast, that "as world events develop, prophecy becomes more and more exciting" (89).

The Tribulation holds little terror for fundamentalists like Lindsey, of course, because they are already saved. Even more to the point, fundamentalists' justification by grace rather than works helps explain their passion for the market. If the rapture is the outcome the believer prefers, then laissez-faire is the means. And since rapture will occur with or without intervention, laissez-faire is thus not merely an ideal to aim for but a destiny that cannot be thwarted. Mainline "religion" encourages "man . . . to achieve goodness . . . by his own efforts," Lindsey writes, and so fundamentally mistakes the "process" by which the world turns (115). Lindsey's is the most widespread version of fundamentalism, dispensationalism, made popular in the early twentieth century by the influential *Scofield Reference Bible* (on which Lindsey's gloss of Revelation is based). For dispensationalists, world history is marked by successive stages (with the current or church age preceding the rapture and end times). Dispensations resemble the cycles of "creative destruction" that Joseph Schumpeter identified as "the essential fact about capitalism," in which the capitalist economy rises phoenix-like from the ashes of its former stage.[20]

The writing is on the wall for the church age, since "joining an institutional church" for the sixties generation is no more appealing than joining a "country club" (183). "Youth today reject impersonal, highly structured organizations" (182), Lindsey observes, just as they scorn the "idealistic view of life" proffered "by various shades of welfarism, socialism, or drugs" (183). For Lindsey, these external fixes do not preserve individuals so much as dissolve them in the "ego-shattering" experience of psychedelics (the rapture itself is "the ultimate trip" [137]) or submerge them in the indistinct herd of collectivism. *The Late Great Planet Earth* confronts us with staggering multitudes—a Red Chinese Army of two hundred million on the field at Armageddon, for example. But its deeper concern, like that of other rapture forecasts, is with the specter of *singularity*, as nations, religions, and economies converge in a unilateral social engineering program. Lindsey puts a theological spin on Friedman's claim that "the concentration of power" is "the great threat to freedom" (2). Yet Lindsey defines collectivism so broadly that it embraces geopolitical formations whose alignment might confound a secular reader. Soviet communism, Arab nationalism, and American Protestantism share a common cause. For Lindsey, all signs point to the inexorable unification of the many (states, belief systems) under the one, a union that paves the way for the "world dictator" (98) at the head of a "one-world government" (117). While 666 may be his number, oneness marks the reign of Antichrist, who "will make the regimes of Hitler, Mao, and Stalin look like Girl Scouts" (110).

Lindsey subordinates the threat to true belief that comes from false prophets and pretender institutions to the even worse threat to *freedom of belief* that comes from the fusion of the manifold, atomized world into a diabolical "super-organization" (182). The "glorious goal of uniting all mankind into a brotherhood of reconciliation and understanding," as he mockingly puts it, looks identical to Hayek's road to serfdom (136). Rapture forecasts habitually identify such bids for unity with tyranny. In the 1970 novel *666*, written by the health food crank Salem Kirban and regarded as the template for the *Left Behind* series, a "spokesman" for the unified "countries of Europe and America" points out that "we must now be as one under one head, under one government."[21] "The False Prophet" who arises when "the various churches begin to amalgamate in one unwieldy body" (131), Lindsey predicts, will serve not just as the head of the world church but as the CEO of the post-Rapture era. "Given control over the economics of the world system . . . he will cause everyone who will not swear allegiance to the Dictator . . . to be in a situation where they cannot buy or sell or hold a job" (112).

The devil's work during the Tribulation is thus most pernicious for Lindsey in the "economic vise" it substitutes for freedom of contract. The dread that "people" might be "controlled economically" (113) originates in Revelation 13:16, where the false prophet "causeth all . . . to receive a mark" without which "no man might buy or sell, save he that had the mark, or the name of the beast, or the number of his name." Rapture narratives take this bit of scripture as prophesying the nightmarish caretaker state envisioned by Friedman, who holds that "welfare rather than freedom became the dominant note in the western democracies" (11) after World War II. Kirban's Antichrist, Brother Bartholomew, "unanimously" elected president by both parties, not only provides for every citizen's needs but accompanies his "good works" (54) with sinister executive orders designed for maximum social control, from forced sterilization to the elimination of private automobiles. Relfe likewise sees ubiquitous harbingers of the extinction of voluntary contracts, from "a drastic decrease in the need for branch banks" to "the one and final [credit] card which will bear each individual's own secret code number" (32).

A society bent on "meeting the social needs of our time" (94), as Kirban puts it on behalf of all rapture adherents, is indistinct from a dictatorship. Providing for "the social welfare of the people" (93) is merely a ruse for turning the citizen into a means to the government's ends. Brother Bartholomew exercises a godlike power over life and death, wiping away whole cities with his Ruby Laser Ring (which he also uses to pulverize the Dome of the Rock). For the evangelical, only God—rather than the godlike state—can exercise such power, and the only way to curb God's secular usurpers is through a proliferation of self-determined choices to accept Jesus. In 666, all the fundamentalist sects have been destroyed by order of the false prophet Bishop Arthur, head of the United World Church. But as we have seen, fundamentalists do not need churches to honor their covenant with God. The faithful in Kirban's book are churchless and lawless; they read the banned Bible in secret. What makes them outlaws also makes them autonomous. The promise of the rapture narrative is that by heeding Jesus's call in defiance of the institutions of welfarism, one might fulfill not merely the distant promise of translation into the clouds but the more immediate desire to bring about an earthly paradise of contract, of individuals unconstrained by idolatry of the state.

As I have noted, some recent sociologists of religion have taken to seeing the market as the model for a robust religious life. For rational choice theorists like Stark and Finke, the late-century sectarian boom refutes the older paradigm of religion in society—the "secularization thesis," which holds that the more a religion loses a monopoly within a culture the fewer faithful practitioners there will be.[22] As a character in Philip Dick and Roger Zelazny's *Deus Irae* (1975) puts it,

> All creeds tend to split into two . . . until . . . there are fewer human beings in any given region, no matter how large, than there are creeds, and further attenuations of the original dogma embodied in the first creed dilute it to a transparent gas too subtle to sustain faith in any human being.[23]

The evidence points to the opposite conclusion: "To the degree that a religious economy is competitive," Stark writes, "overall levels of religious participation will tend to be high."[24] And Finke identifies "deregulation" as key to religious "flourish[ing]."[25] These sociologists hold a view of the one true church as damning as Lindsey's. Yet where Lindsey predicts Armageddon, the sociologists predict apathy. "To the degree that a religious economy is monopolized by one or two state-supported firms," Stark writes, "overall levels of participation will tend to be low."[26]

Sectarianism thus approaches the ideal of "wide diversity" that, in Friedman's view, makes market relations superior to political participation when it comes to valuing individuals. "The characteristic feature of action through political channels is . . . conformity," Friedman writes. But the market's "system of proportional representation" allows "each man" to "vote, as it were, for the color of tie he wants" without having "to see what color the majority wants and then, if he is in the minority, submit" (15). Friedman's neckties may seem far removed from Stark and Finke's sects, but rational choice theorists see such "goods" as less discontinuous than plotted at different points on the commodity spectrum. "Religious commodities," as the economist Lawrence Iannaccone puts it, "are not tangible goods like cars" nor "commercial services like haircuts" but "fall into a third category . . . labeled 'household commodities'— valued goods and services that families and individuals produce for their own consumption."[27] The reflexivity of such commodities suggests that in the pursuit of a religious affiliation understood as a consumable object, one is buying something like belief itself. What Iannaccone calls the "religious marketplace" thus entails a kind of choosing squared.[28] If rational choice posits that decision makers choose what they assume will bring about their preferred end, the end in religious consumption is nothing more than the preference for one's personal beliefs.

It is by virtue of their sanctifying everyone's choices that Stephen Warner, also an advocate of rational choice, sees "American religious institutions" as "constitutively pluralistic" and thus as "vehicles of empowerment for minorities and otherwise subjugated people."[29] As we saw in chapter 3, Friedman promoted the market on just such grounds. Its impersonality made it a paradoxically faithful respecter of persons, a haven of nondiscrimination. Markets, whether religious or secular, can do what the most well-intentioned government policies cannot. Whereas the state is bound to average things out or appeal to the lowest common denominator, a market is under no such constraint. It can thus satisfy the individual's wishes regardless of how many conflicting parties are involved in its transactions. Anyone who finds the cost of a church membership too high can always choose a different church, or—even better—start one.

False Prophets and True Gods

If the free market remains always just beyond our grasp, any criticism of the havoc it plays with human lives can be chalked up to the distortions that have yet to be weeded out of a system that, blighted by human error or original sin, strives but never quite manages to perfect itself. Like the evangelical's heavenly kingdom to come, the free market is never yet free. Yet its fallen state does not prevent the market's apostles from sounding its trumpet in the struggle against the control economy's false prophets. In *The Late Great Planet Earth*, "Satan . . . has been able to work miracles from the beginning" (106).

But the state's ostensible miracle workers are "false messiahs" (79) whose "'social action' gimmicks" are a poor "substitute" for "the authority and power . . . to meet real human needs" (182).

"Christians should not get too excited when they see a miracle" (106), Lindsey notes, striking a chord of hermeneutic suspicion that runs through much fundamentalist exegesis and that in fact links Lindsey's interest in the end times with some of the most influential avant-garde views at the turn of the seventies. In *Learning from Las Vegas*, Robert Venturi, Denise Scott Brown, and Steven Izenour repudiate the International Style by demonizing its practitioners as false prophets whose "messianic" ambitions lead to the autocratic nightmare of "public housing." "Only the very poor . . . are dominated by architects' values," they write. "Developers build for markets rather than for Man and probably do less harm than authoritarian architects."[30] Against the modernist "utopia" that delivers only suffering by "pure architecture" (163), Venturi and his coauthors propose a built environment in which persons can have some say in how they want to live: "people's architecture as the people want it" (161). "Markets" can deliver "people's architecture" because they reject the zealotry of true believers. "Neither fraud nor coercion is within the ethics of the market system," according to Friedman's Chicago colleague George Stigler, because "pure enterprise . . . provides alternatives to every buyer or seller," who thus need never tolerate an unfair, involuntary, or deceitful exchange for long. The market's "competitive" pluralism is the basis for its ethical superiority.[31]

The bid Venturi and his coauthors make for the "ugly and ordinary" (93) over the graven images of modernist "dead ducks" (162) is reminiscent of the iconoclasm that forms a key feature of Lindsey's evangelicalism. "Enormous signs in vast spaces at high speeds," *Learning from Las Vegas* insists, are necessary for "a space of no enclosure and little direction" (13). Vegas is a domain of signs and wonders, and even its vaguely lawless reputation fits into the reborn Christian's embrace of a cutting-edge antinomianism. For Venturi and his coauthors, the most venal place in American culture becomes the site of a negation of materialism, or a certain kind of materialism: the cityscape as a manifestation of institutional power. With its rapid turnover of facades, billboards, and inhabitants, Vegas demands "a changing attitude toward monumentality in our environment" (50); its lack of anchors renders urgent the need, like that of Bunyan's Pilgrim, to choose one's own way. The keynote of both Lindsey's account of the end times and Venturi's account of the here and now is a vernacular pitted against authoritarian coercions to which the market is understood to be immune. With its ironic appeal to "silent-white-majority architecture" (154), *Learning from Las Vegas* inverts the usual avant-garde sorting and relocates the cachet of knowingness from the specialist elite to the vulgar masses. Just as Lindsey's all-purpose countercultural rhetoric implies that everyone can be hip to the second coming, Venturi and his coauthors suggest that residents of Levittown and visitors to Vegas embrace a spontaneity unknown to the killjoy apostles of the International Style.

Hunter S. Thompson's 1971 novel *Fear and Loathing in Las Vegas* does for the drug culture what *Learning from Las Vegas* does for the built environment, although Thompson's antinomianism has a more explicit grounding. Whereas housing is overregulated, drugs are illegal. This fact makes Thompson's narrator Raoul Duke, a reporter consuming prodigious amounts of "extremely dangerous drugs" on assignment in Las Vegas, an outlaw.[32] Like Dick's "secret Christian" keeping the Romans at bay, Raoul continually imagines himself one step ahead of the omnipresent but ineffective police. *Rolling Stone* has commissioned a story that requires him, in his perpetually intoxicated state, "to mingle with a thousand ranking cops from all over America, while they harangued each other about the Drug Problem" (80). "We would be attending the conference under false pretenses and dealing," he observes, "with a crowd that was convened for the stated purpose of putting people like us in jail" (109).

The "we" here includes Raoul's lawyer and traveling companion, Gonzo, whose purpose, apart from supplying him with drugs, is to provide a kind of spur-of-the-moment contractualism unmediated by the judiciary state. "I was tempted," Raoul tells us of a hitchhiker they have picked up in their rented Corvette, "to have my attorney arrange some kind of simple, common-law contract whereby we could just give the car to this unfortunate bastard" (17). While not surrendering to this temptation, Raoul yields to many others. Yet these too are modeled on the principle of unfettered contract. Both "pure gonzo journalism" and the copious intake of drugs are forms of "Free Enterprise" (11), a means to "give the public what it needs" (101). Staking Raoul's autonomy on his being an outlaw, Thompson justifies this equation by appealing to his protagonist's study of the New Testament. By "tak[ing God's] gibberish seriously," Raoul has reverted to a time and place before what dispensationalists would call the "church age": "My primitive Christian instincts have made me a criminal" (88). But while the commitment to the truth of God's word rather than man's makes him "a fugitive in the eyes of the law" (85), Raoul—who turns out to be something of a biblical literalist—is guiltless in the kingdom of Heaven. Since "*institutional* debts" are not "binding," he concludes in a direct address to "the Lord," "the incredible truth is that I am not guilty" (88).

Like much of his writing, *Fear and Loathing* by Thompson's own admission takes its inspiration from the Book of Revelation. "I have stolen more quotes and thoughts and purely elegant little starbursts of writing from the Book of Revelation than from anything else in the English Language," Thompson writes in the introduction to his 1988 collection *Generation of Swine*.[33] Thompson maintained that his interest in Revelation amounted to "love . . . for the sharp and terrible power of the language"—unlike Ronald Reagan, for example, who "really *believes* it" (*GS,* 296). Yet the distinction between appreciation and literal belief belies Thompson's fondness for parsing current affairs through the lens of Biblical prophesy. However ironic such gestures appear (like "the ominous imprint of what appeared to be the Mark of the Beast" on Gorbachev's "forehead" [*GS,* 35]), taking Revelation as a model might account for *Fear and Loathing*'s view of Las Vegas as "a closed society where everybody's guilty" (71), for Thompson's conviction that as "a multiple felon" he will come out a winner with "the Great Scorer" (73), and for the "fantastic universal sense" he had at the height of his LSD use "that whatever we were doing was *right*, that we were winning . . . that sense of victory over the forces of Old and Evil" (68). These echoes of the jeremiad in Revelation—"back then," he notes, "*everybody* was guilty" (*GS,* 296)—speak to Thompson's staging of Las Vegas as an American Sodom whose laws it would be evil to heed and righteous to flout.

Despite its frenetic hilarity, *Fear and Loathing* is finally an elegiac book. It mourns the "central illusion" of the "whole life-style" of the "Acid Culture" (179). As Thompson presents it, LSD promised to enable "the long jump from chemical frenzy to preternatural consciousness" (64). What he calls the "grim meat-hook realities" (187) of the Acid Culture concern the fact that few really had the courage to defy "the desperate assumption that somebody—or at least some force—is tending that Light at the end of the tunnel" (179). His requiem for psychedelics recalls Lindsey's caution that sixties youth should be leery of the "idealistic view of life" found no less in drugs than in the welfare state. Yet whereas drugs for Lindsey exemplify conformity to hollow ideals, drugs for Thompson amount to the limit case of autonomy under duress from the monoculture. In keeping with his book's sacralization of contract, drugs for Thompson don't so much involve as obviate consent: you cannot refuse consent to yourself. In *The Late Great Planet Earth*, drugs epitomize externalism, an incursion on the soul; in *Fear and Loathing*, they embody internalism, since their effects are *only* in us, a sanctuary that ought to be inaccessible by the state. The tragedy of the "Drug Explosion" (66) is that, abandoning this sanctuary, its users could not surmount "blind faith in some higher and wiser 'authority'" (179).

Despite what we would expect to be a radical departure from Lindsey's view of drugs, then, Thompson comes to a similar conclusion about their failed promise. In doing so, he puts an intriguing spin on the next-life narrative's delineation of in- and out-groups. Those who signed up for "'Consciousness Expansion'" (201) have turned into casualties, "permanent cripples, failed seekers" (179). The voyager to distant, otherworldly realms has become the subsistent hanger-on. "In this doomstruck era of Nixon," he writes, "we are all wired into a *survival* trip now" (178). And yet notwithstanding his inclusion in this first-person plural, Thompson himself is finally spared such debasement by virtue of believing neither the promises of LSD nor the prophesies of Revelation. Instead he occupies a grace-saving distance from the very things—drugs, scripture—to which he endlessly returns. In hotels he confesses to "looking for a Gideon Bible" with "a King James Version" of the "Book of Revelation" (*GS*, 10), to "ripping drawers out of the nightstands and bed-boxes" (*GS*, 10) ostensibly in the service of leisure reading, an idle pursuit no more informed by a sense of mission than LSD trips are to the "drug dilettantes" (202) that Raoul and his lawyer have become.

It is thus unsurprising to Thompson that Revelation's most powerful modern adherent, Ronald Reagan, also believes that drug users can never be "dilettantes." Reagan's war on drugs "is taking on all the trappings of a holy war" (*GS*, 154) because faith and drugs represent powers vying for the nation's soul in a rehearsal of the Last Judgment. From the vantage of *Fear and Loathing*, Reagan need not have worried about drugs as a rival mode of ecstatic experience. While Thompson's novel revels in a particular form of libertarian abjection, the victimization of people whose benign choices run afoul of the state, it wrings comic value from the irony that the police are convening over a crisis that lacks any culprits. The ostensibly ungovernable members of the "Drug Culture" are as law-abiding as one would hope. Whereas "acid is widely known—to everybody but cops—to be the Studebaker of the drug market" (201), the drug of choice, "today, is whatever . . . short-circuits your brain and grounds it out for the longest possible time" (202). Consciousness-raising has ceded to consciousness-lowering because LSD users could not kick the habit of obedience to authority, and so remain unfree in their choices.

In Philip Dick's *VALIS* (1981), by contrast, there are no unauthorized or unfree choices. More accurately, all choices—from committing suicide to undertaking a DIY "cosmogony"—originate in self-authorization.[34] As much an elegy for the sixties as *Fear and Loathing*, *VALIS* handles the problem of external authority rather differently from Thompson's novel, which cannot escape the Lindsey-style suspicion that a substance as minimal as "a grey lump of sugar" (65) laced with LSD undermines—rather than inaugurates—the agent's bid for transformative self-possession. Dick's protagonist, Horselover Fat, experiences a "theophany" (the appearance of God) unmediated by drugs and so made to appear a purer psychic episode than what Raoul experiences. And while Fat may or may not be schizophrenic, the novel treats this possibility as incidental to his discovery that the creator god most people worship is as fraudulent as Lindsey's Antichrist, an insane usurper who has arranged the universe such that sentient creatures have forgotten the "true God" (65), the "*deus absconditus*, the hidden . . . or unknown god" (38).

Dick recycles his earlier self-reported "anamnesis" (96) as fodder for *VALIS*.[35] Fat, a science fiction writer in Orange County, California (where Dick made his home), claims to share his body with the very Thomas introduced in Dick's 1978 essay. Fat sees his occupation by Thomas not as reincarnation but as a takeover of which he has, like a Scientologist enduring the rigors of clearing, become painfully aware. The analogy to Hubbard's system is not trivial. We are told that "when Thomas found himself dying, he would engram himself on the Christian fish sign" (111), to await reactivation two thousand years later by Fat's encounter with the assistant pharmacist wearing the ichthus symbol around her neck. That callback is but one of the self-borrowings that inundate *VALIS*, which also includes generous boldfaced helpings of Dick's visionary "Exegesis" in the guise of Fat's "*Tractate: Cryptica Scriptura*" or "hidden discourse" (91). With its "disreputable aura of high weirdness," as Jonathan Lethem puts it, this 7,700-page handwritten document, on which Dick worked for nearly a decade, was his effort to encompass the visionary event of 2-3-74, the date on which Dick was visited by God, who revealed to him that the universe was composed of information.[36] This is only to say that Horselover Fat is just barely an alter ego for Dick himself ("'Philip' means 'Horselover' in Greek," and "'Fat' is the German translation of 'Dick'" [168]). To complicate matters, Dick surfaces in the book in his own voice to proclaim his desire to render his experience in the third person: "I am Horselover Fat, and I am writing this in the third person to gain much-needed objectivity" (28). Such an effort cannot help faltering the moment it is announced. Toggling between third- and first-person perspective, Dick's goal of self-observation demonstrates what Thomas Nagel calls "the ineliminable subjectivity of some aspects of our own experience."[37]

This might sound implausible. From its start, as surely every critic can agree, Dick's career charted the instability of the self under the sway of technological, mystical, or extraterrestrial forces. The Dick protagonist is not unlike the evangelical for whom rebirth in Christ means yielding to powers unknown. But it would be more precise to see Dick's notion of selfhood as confirming rather than abandoning subjectivity. The fish symbol that "disinhibits" the "meta-circuits in Fat's brain" (108) functions the way Revelation works for Thompson: a form of inspiration in its etymological sense, an absorption into oneself of the world outside that reveals the self's core reality. And this turns out to be the case for fundamentalists as well. Thus the historian Charles Strozier concludes that the divine summons not only signals accession to a transcendent force—the reborn Christian becomes "a passive agent in divine hands"—but also serves as an "inner text" by virtue of which the fundamentalist approaches life "without apparent reference to the world."[38] Their relative indifference to "context" means that "most fundamentalists do little actual work converting people."[39]

In this respect, evangelicalism marks perhaps the most dramatic (because widespread) instance of the turn toward inwardness and subjectivity in the neo-idealist seventies. And while *VALIS* has a curious relationship to evangelical Christianity (insofar as it can be discerned, *VALIS*'s theology is gnostic), the book is unambiguous in its judgment that mental events are determinate, that "the phenomenal world . . . is a hypostasis of the information processed by the Mind," and that we are all "stations in a single Mind" (110). Dick defines "Mind" as "the essence of the rational human being" (120), a commitment that finds *VALIS* embracing an idealization with which critics often charge rational choice theorists: that we exercise absolute control over our decisions even in uncertain circumstances. In the novel's understanding, the world might be riven with mixed motives, but "in the center of an irrational universe governed by an irrational Mind stands rational man" (121). The goal of Fat's *Tractate* is to recover the memory of the true world withheld by the "insane" creator god and thereby "to free the initiate from . . . fate" (121). Anamnesis for Dick entails an omniscience—an eidetic recall of past desires and a clairvoyance regarding future wants—in which no actual rational choice theorist believes.

Such a fantasy of transparency leads *VALIS* not only to defend the rationality of ostensibly irrational acts but also to take a dubious stand on things that do not by most canons of ethical decency count as choices. Fat worries that his suicidal friend Gloria "was not even committing her irrational act rationally" (10), only to conclude that "Gloria's mind had total control over her body," that she was "rationally insane" when she jumps out of a window in "the Synanon Building in Oakland" (11). Fat "could find no error" in "her account" of her wish to die. "It was rationality . . . at the service of nonbeing" (13). It is worth noting that suicide is one of Gary Becker's examples of how rational choice theory "calls into question" our intuitions about determinism and free will. "According to the economic approach," Becker writes, *"most* (if not all!) deaths are to some extent 'suicides' in the sense that they could have been postponed if more resources had been invested in prolonging life." The "common distinction between suicides and 'natural' deaths" disappears once we recognize that death, too, is a marketplace.[40]

Meanwhile Fat's friend Sherri, in remission from a terminal lymphoma, may have "got it on purpose," since "cancer represents a deliberate failure of the immune system of the body; the person turns it off" (84). For *VALIS*'s author, suicide attempts or lymphoma relapses are merely unfortunate choices. And while Dick appears to be parodying "a view floating around in advanced psychological circles" (28) that blames the patient for her disease, *VALIS* in fact presents us with a character, the musician Brent Mini, who willingly contracts "multiple myeloma" (182) in order to receive as much "exposure" as possible from the "VALIS . . . construct" (185), an interstellar device that "emanated from a planet in the star-system Sirius" (239) but was really sent by "the true God" (65), says Mini, "to fire rational instructions at us" (185). The upside of VALIS shooting laser beams of insight into your third eye is that "we act rationally . . . under its jurisdiction." The downside is that "too much . . . is a poison" (185). Mini's choices are transparent and maximizing. He "wanted to know VALIS as much as possible" and considers his impending death "worth it, to experience VALIS again" (186).

Horselover Fat and his friends come to learn of VALIS after seeing a movie that confirms all the events that have befallen Fat/Dick. In the film, VALIS is a high-earth satellite that transmits information to the minds of various characters, weaponizing their reason in order to overthrow the presidency of Ferris F. Fremount, a stand-in not only for Richard Nixon but also for Antichrist (since "'F' is the sixth letter of the English alphabet," Dick writes, "FFF, Ferris F. Fremount's initials, are in numerical terms 666" [155]). Eric and Linda Lanton, the film's creators, have made it to advertise "subliminally" (145) the return of the savior, a two-year-old girl named Sophia. In some versions of gnosticism, Sophia or "Wisdom" is the creator of the Old Testament God (the "demiurge").[41] In *VALIS*, she is "an artificial intelligence in a human body" (193) who "shall sit down on the judgment seat" (199). As the first to crack the movie's code, Fat is allowed to meet Sophia. She not only "reincorporate[s] him" into Dick, "reversing the original process of projection" (194), but shares with him the "kerygma" (198) or lesson she wants him to preach: "there is only one god and that god is man himself" (199).

We find in *VALIS* a sacralization of rationality even more vivid than that admitted by rational choice theorists of religion. "Man as he really is," according to Mini, "his true state," is "enlightened" (187). Or as Dick puts it in Fat's *Tractate*, which appears as an appendix to the novel: "We ourselves are information-rich; information enters us, is processed and is then projected outward once more" (233). Dick produces as human essence the equation of rationality and information that shapes Becker's "economic approach to human behavior." "The assumption that information is often seriously incomplete because it is costly to acquire is used in the economic approach," Becker writes, "to explain the same kind of behavior that is explained by irrational . . . behavior in other discussions." But where Becker demurs from the view that people—"decision units"—"are necessarily conscious of their efforts to maximize or can verbalize or otherwise describe in an informative way reasons for the systematic patterns in their behavior," Dick thinks that they can.[42] Or rather, he thinks they *should*. Dick considers our "entelechy" (88) to be the moral imperative of becoming as information-rich as possible, since "it is really information and information-processing which we substantialize" (234).[43] Dick's attraction to gnosticism combines the dream of perfect understanding with a revolt against an officialdom spanning two millennia of ignorance and slavery.

Channeling Choice

To be sure, it is not easy to reconcile Dick's worship of rationality in *VALIS* with the truly deranged "Exegesis" in which he unfolds his faith. *VALIS* holds out the promise that "information will save us" (235). But what Dick counts as valuable knowledge might give us pause. "We appear to be memory coils (DNA carriers capable of experience)," he writes, echoing the cosmogonies of Burroughs and Hubbard, "in a computer-like thinking system" containing "thousands of years of experiential information" (238). Dick's eschatology of information foretells what the philosopher Luciano Floridi has recently dubbed the "infosphere," the "environment constituted by all informational entities, their properties, interactions, processes, and mutual relations."[44] Drawing on cybernetics and digital culture to herald the informational singularity, Floridi adapts a phrase of Hegel's ("what is real is rational and what is rational is real") to conclude that "what is real is informational and what is informational is real."[45] Like Dick, Floridi closes the gap between the computer theory of mind and neo-idealism. The world spirit now moves through "information and communication technologies," which we continually mistake for "tools for interacting with the world" rather than "deep . . . forces" of progress, "shaping our understanding of ourselves as informational entities."[46] In *The Divine Invasion*, "information" is both "sentient" and "keeps us human."[47]

Dick was a legendary autodidact, and his understanding of consciousness relies on (among others) Heraclites, the Nag Hammadi library, and Norbert Wiener ("entropy," he writes in *VALIS*, is "derangement of the brain" [234]). Dick forges a view of mind that seems consistent with his externalist model of consciousness in such high-sixties masterpieces as *Androids* and *Ubik*. *VALIS*, which stands for "Vast Active Living Intelligence System" (8), posits an alien rationality that "overrides" (151) our own. As Mini puts it, *"Something outside had to enter"* his brain in order to reopen "the eye of discernment" (188). In earlier novels, such alien minds overpower Dick's characters, bringing them under the sway of a domineering consciousness. *Ubik*'s Jory, whose "cephalic activity is particularly good," "preys on" the weaker minds trapped with him in purgatorial "half-life," shaping their reality according to his whims.[48] "It's as if," Joe Chip muses, "some malicious force is playing with us, letting us scamper and twitter like debrained mice."[49] Yet though mind control is no less prevalent in *VALIS* than in his earlier novels—"VALIS overruled me, held control of my mind" (207)—the alien mind is not threatening but affirming. Dick writes that "to be 'born again' . . . means to become healed; which is to say . . . restored to sanity" (235). Control shifts to recovery, and the external agent or "Macrobrain" is a "physician" (234) rather than tyrant. Likewise only by overruling his mind can VALIS impart the "medical knowledge" that "saved" the "life" of Dick's son Christopher, who suffers from an undiagnosed birth defect. The alien mind is less an invader commandeering Dick's psyche than a life coach staging an intervention. Its "gnosis . . . consists of disinhibiting instructions, with the core content actually intrinsic to us" (239).

Dick's 2-3-74 event—named for the date he discovered that he shared his body with a second-century Christian—took place at a moment of widespread enthusiasm for otherworldly visitations. Influential channeling texts like Jane Roberts's *The Seth Material* (1970) and Helen Shucman's *A Course in Miracles* (1976) share *VALIS*'s view that the alien is just an estranged aspect of the channel's own mind. "What I am is also what you are," Seth, the "energy personality essence" who takes up residence in Jane Roberts's head, tells her: "individualized consciousness."[50] Roberts considers her spirit guide less an uninvited guest than an intimate companion with whom she has reunited: "Seth made absolutely no attempt to 'invade'" her (44).[51] In channeling discourse, possession is all but synonymous with self-possession (which is why Dick calls such possession "anamnesis"). Seventies channeling texts join mysticism to an autocritique grounded in modern rationalism, as if subjectivity were best experienced as a pedagogy. *A Course in Miracles* is not only the transcription of Shucman's "inner dictation" of a "Voice" that she identifies as Jesus of Nazareth but also a self-guided tutorial. Almost half of the 1,300-page volume is a "Workbook for Students," with hundreds of exercises whose "purpose is to provide a way in which some people will be able to find their own Internal Teacher."[52] Roberts aspires to make her investigations of Seth "academically legitimate" (55). Her "'scientifically responsible'" (55) examination entails a sharp turn inward, a rigorous plan "to study my own psychological behavior" (44). Roberts likens channeling Seth to being "a professor at a small seminar"

(40). It is a rather advanced course, since Seth tells Roberts that his kind "must wait until personalities on your plane have progressed sufficiently for lessons to begin" (43).

The channel's precociousness is a fixture of the literature. According to Robert Anton Wilson, the author of *Cosmic Trigger* (1977), we have always been receiving messages from the extraterrestrial universe, but until now our frameworks were too limited to hear them clearly. "Interstellar ESP may have been going on for all our history," Wilson concludes, "but we just haven't understood."[53] "Our nervous systems translated their message into terms we *could* understand," retooling extraterrestrials as "angels" or "messengers from God" (118). Alien contact has been misperceived as what Dick calls "theophany," rather than as evidence of what Wilson describes as a galactic mind transmitting our future to us. "However incredible to the ordinary reader," Wilson asserts, "there is nothing" about contact from outer space "which cannot be accounted for within the possibilities of the growing edge of quantum theory" (196). *Cosmic Trigger* is a chronicle of a year in which its author "was receiving telepathic messages from entities residing on a planet of the double star Sirius" (9). In *VALIS*, Horselover Fat tells Mini that he has "read *The Cosmic Trigger*" (185); in the preface to *Cosmic Trigger*, Wilson records the resemblance between his own and Dick's visitations (which also emanate from Sirius). Wilson is most famous for coauthoring the *Illuminatus!* trilogy, a satire of "all conspiracy theories of Left and Right" (64). Yet he is not exactly an unbeliever. A full-throated "Libertarian" (55), he insists on "remaining Utopian, without a visible Utopia to believe in" (56). The Utopia he *does* believe in is not perceivable by our crude "mammalian" senses (146). Luckily, the "Higher Intelligences from Outer Space" have found a workaround, devising "methods of interstellar telepathy between Earth and the Sirius system" (10) to direct the "most intelligent, advanced, courageous of your species" (105) to the promised land.

In support of his scientific method, Wilson leans on the work of the physician and futurist John C. Lilly, the basis (as we have noted) for the protagonist of Paddy Chayevsky's *Altered States* (1978). Wilson sees his memoir as charting an "experiment" in "*induced brain change*, which Dr. John Lilly more resoundingly calls 'metaprogramming the human biocomputer'" (iv). Lilly helps Wilson reach the conclusion that "*consciousness is chemical in nature and changes as its chemistry changes*" (21); he ratifies Wilson's view, shared by such materialist thinkers as Daniel Dennett, that mind is by and large a matter of *matter*. But Lilly and Wilson's is a different account of mental programming from Strong AI's computational theory of mind. For Wilson, we are the programmers—or "editors" (iv)—of our own consciousness. Just as Dick sees the VALIS beam as "disinhibiting" what is "intrinsic" in us, so Wilson and his fellow explorers in "inner technology" (209) treat interstellar psychic communiqués as a form of self-actualization. "Seemingly external Superhuman Beings . . . are really masks of the greater selves we are evolving into," Wilson writes. "As we advance toward Higher Intelligence, our brains can increasingly contact other Higher Intelligences" (16).

In addition to inverting the "Pavlovian-Skinnerian robotism" (201) of Dennett-style externalism, Wilson's book describes a future that seems diametrically opposed to the entropic turn. *Cosmic Trigger* devotes many pages to the myriad scientists who predict a world in which people will live forever. "By the turn of the next century," Wilson writes (by which he means the year 2000), "we will be a completely new species in many dimensions: living in space, not on a planet; able to program our nervous systems for any degree of any function we wish; possessing a lifespan in centuries, and well on our way to immortality" (123). Wilson praises Alan Harrington's "brilliant polemic" *The Immortalist* (1969) for proposing a "national commitment to death-elimination" that, on the scale of the Manhattan Project, would "mobilize the scientists . . . and hunt down death like an outlaw" (123). Harrington argues that only "medical engineering" can effectively arm us in what he calls the "final War Against Death."[54] Yet for all its "faith" in biomedical "salvation" (21), *The Immortalist* has little interest in the body's survival. The "permanent . . . ownership of life" (95) entails the realization of the desire of "human consciousness . . . to perpetuate itself" (11). In the same vein, Wilson holds that *"consciousness probably precedes the biological unit"* (205), a theory proved by the frequency of "out-of-body experiences" over "thousands of years" (205).

As though confirming John Searle's and Hubert Dreyfus's charge that the computational theory of mind is a barely disguised form of dualism, *Cosmic Trigger* models immortality as a triumph of consciousness over extant physical laws. Like Wilson, who sees our intelligence evolving to free itself of the mortal coil, Jane Roberts is a Cartesian extremist. "What you are," Seth tells his listeners, "is not dependent upon physical matter" (2). "The body appears to be largely self-motivated and independent," Shucman writes, "yet it actually responds only to the intentions of the mind" (xii). The channel's goal is to rediscover what we have always intuited but misrecognized: the omnipresence of our will through time and space. Rational choice theory's "decision unit" is an idealization, a means of modeling predictive deductions. Channeling texts by contrast imagine the chooser as a real person who reaches her ideal in a life where nothing is contingent. "We cannot blame God, society, or our parents for misfortunes," Seth teaches Jane Roberts, "since before this physical life we chose the circumstances into which we would be born and the challenges that could best bring about our development" (4). In his memoir *The*

Scientist, Lilly likewise imagines himself as a being of pure choice whose decisions led to his current identity even before he was born: "The Form it chose was that of a human. . . . It chose to be male. . . . It chose the genetic code that would regulate its Form as it grew in the future."[55] Radicalizing Dick's fantasy of third-personal observation, Lilly consistently describes his autobiographical self with the neuter pronoun.

These rhetorical and grammatical gestures sustain the idea that searching for subjectivity is no less rigorous a pursuit than accelerating particles or splicing genes. Wilson, Lilly, and Dick treat the experience of their own minds as a matter of *discovery*. Revelation is central to channeling because the point of knowledge in channeled subjectivity is less to acquire something outside oneself than to be shown what was always present within.[56] Whereas Dick discovers a second-century apostle living inside him, Wilson concludes that "the Higher Intelligence behind" the Sirian bulletins he receives "is, then, *literally* ourselves-in-the-future*" (228). "You have lived before and will live again, and when you are done with physical existence," Seth explains, "you will still live" (2). Like Scientology, channeling imagines consciousness as a place outside "physical existence" where no mental event is lost. Our world-making powers of mind entail that all our thoughts, perceptions, and memories—however trivial or evanescent—are on tap. "Your identity as you know it," Jane Roberts insists, "is always retained" (227).

James Merrill's Subjective Economy

Dick's channeling narrative is infused with the hectic and centrifugal energies that continue to make his work a hard sell on the "literariness" market. James Merrill, by contrast, the author of by far the most distinguished literary take on channeling in the period, was everything Dick was not: rich, exquisitely cultured, *establishment*. Yet Merrill's epic trilogy, *The Changing Light at Sandover* (1982), is instructive for what it shares with the déclassé likes of *The Seth Materials*, not to say *VALIS*. It is notable, for example, that the last stanza of Merrill's "Lost in Translation" begins: "But nothing's lost."[57] That lyric appeared in *Divine Comedies* (1976), whose final poem, the ninety-page "Book of Ephraim," would become the first book of *Sandover*. Large swaths of Merrill's epic are direct transmissions from what he calls "the galactic radio," each of whose "lesson[s]," in the spirit of Dick's or Wilson's Sirian communiqués, "leads us to a plane of greater / Power and light."[58]

For channels like Wilson, immortality represents the triumph of mind over loss. Wilson sets great store by the immortality that lies just around the corner, awaiting a population primed for that gift. In *Sandover*, a scientist of Merrill's acquaintance, George Cotzias, is pulled out of the world before finishing his experiments on "THE PROLONGATION OF . . . LIFE" (141) because the powers that be have determined that we are not ready for immortality. But in an important sense, Cotzias's experiments are unnecessary. Merrill's poem demonstrates that death is not a matter of losing *anything*. The Ouija board that serves as the interface between Merrill and the afterlife grants the poet access to a variety of dead friends whose voluble presence in his 560-page poem suggests that they cannot really be said to have gone missing. As one of the poem's ghostly speakers (W. H. Auden, in fact) puts it: "NOTHING IS EVER EVER LOST" (117).

It is difficult, I argue, to separate Merrill's account of the next life from his own rather lucky one. Put differently, questions of loss mean something different to someone with so much wealth that material want becomes virtually inconceivable. "It prevailed even as the truth of truths that the girl couldn't get away from her wealth," Henry James (an idol of Merrill's) writes of *The Wings of the Dove*'s Milly Theale in a description that could easily fit Merrill himself. "She couldn't have lost it if she had tried—that was what it was to be really rich." In respect of wealth as *"the* thing you were," channeling's value for the well-born Merrill will of necessity be different from its compensations for a proletarian writer like Dick, to say nothing of the lumpen followers of New Age charlatans.[59] But that difference itself will prove illuminating.

While the otherworldly visitor is a stranger (or a friend you haven't met) in most seventies iterations of channeling, in *Sandover* the visitors from the afterlife are a mix of the familiar and the foreign. JM and DJ, the poem's versions of Merrill and his lover David Jackson, consult a homemade Ouija board that over twenty years (with significant hiatuses) allows them to channel three primary entities or groups of entities apart from dead loved ones like Auden and Maria Mitsotaki, a friend from their Athens life. The first is Ephraim, a "household slave" (47) who, like Dick's Thomas, lived in the early days of Christianity (in Ephraim's case, the first century CE). The second is a creature they name Mirabell, a member of a race of bat-like creatures, "BRAINS WITH WINGS" (118) who "SPEAK FROM WITHIN THE ATOM" (113) and who may be "THE BAD ANGELS" (119) of Christian doctrine. The third is the quartet of archangels (Michael, Gabriel, Raphael, and Emmanuel), custodians of God's "GREENHOUSE" (119). Over the course of the volume's three books, JM and DJ, helped by the shades of Auden and Maria along with assorted kibitzers, puzzle through the cosmology elaborated to them by these otherworldly interlocutors. What emerges is a history of the universe in which human beings, conceived after two false starts in sentient life, will themselves eventually be replaced by even higher beings fabricated in a heavenly *"Research Lab"* (140), or "R/Lab" (145), whose employees—Mirabell and his kind—spend eternity perfecting species for God's approval.

The channeling in *Sandover* is progressive. Each contact prepares JM and DJ for a higher encounter, culminating in a brief exchange with the Creator God, Biology ("God B" [122]). *Sandover* makes explicit the parallel between being channeled (or summoned) and being the best one can be. The poem owes its version of excellence to the hierarchical schedule of the school, the meritocracy's most sacred vertical. Sandover is the name of the would-be campus on which JM and DJ finally arrive in the third book of the trilogy, the ultraexclusive, manorial "CLASSROOM" (407) in which the archangels deliver to them their twenty-five lessons. The poem is preoccupied with leveling up. Ephraim describes nine stages of afterlife that Mirabell later identifies as a "GREAT DULL / BUREAUCRACY OF PATRONS" (149) where spirits like Ephraim guide "run-of-the-mill souls" (139) in their reincarnations. But as with Roberts and Shucman, schooling is the privileged system. JM and DJ's Ouija work "feel[s] like . . . a graduate seminar" in which DJ feels like a "freshman" (324). His perplexity is a feint. The spirit world's authorities frequently award both JM and DJ the schoolroom's superlative honor, an "A PLUS" (199) for each insight they develop.

Some scholars like to claim that *Sandover* plays fast and loose with conventional ideas of consciousness. Critics have aligned Merrill with both the postmodern critique of the subject and the materialist (and externalist) philosophy of mind. Claudia Ingram argues that the poem "dramatizes the opening of the authorial self to relations, systems, discourses, and forces that exceed it" and "the progressive destabilization and revision of identities."[60] Concluding that he "understood subjective experience to be a sum of diverse processes shaped by biological underpinnings," Nikki Skillman makes Merrill out to be the versifying cousin of Daniel Dennett.[61] Such views run counter to Merrill's insistence on the primacy of subjectivity in the poem. "It had to be done in the first person," he told C.A. Buckley in a 1992 interview.[62] In *Sandover*'s opening, Merrill ventriloquizes *Moby-Dick*'s famous narrator: "I alone was left / To tell my story" (4). The "HUMAN SELF" (315) prevails even in the world of the cloned souls that come out of God B's "Research Lab." However extravagant the poem's speculations on what selfhood might consist of (animal and plant "DENSITIES" [182], atomic reactions, reincarnated essence), JM insists that his "own / Imagination working in the world" (260) is the irreducible basis of the poem's various projections. The dignity of Merrill's mind is among the poem's favorite topics. Hence the frequent praise for JM and DJ's progress and prowess. Channeling, we might say, is the paranoid style sunny side up. In a universe in which "THERE IS / NO ACCIDENT" (179), the designer's designs on us are strictly benign: "These secular guardian angels fume and fuss / For what must seem eternity over us" (9). Like the healing Sirian broadcasts in Dick, like Roberts's benevolent Seth, the higher powers imbue JM and DJ with "the glow of being needed" (55).[63]

Merrill's poem reignites the paradox we observed in chapter 1, wherein the specialness of meritocratic subjectivity is frequently attested by one's objective score on a standardized test. Merrill's poem registers some discomfort with such quantification by railing against the cold tyranny of numbers. "'PSYCHE,'" as DJ and JM's friend Robert puts it, "FALLS INTO NO EASY NUMBER SYSTEM" (377). Yet notwithstanding DJ's protest that "we're all for equal rights" (188), it would be a mistake to see the poem as uneasy with distinctiveness as such. For central to *Sandover*'s ostensible ethical project, understood as its environmental conscience, is an extinction fantasy reminiscent of the one endorsed by both rapture enthusiasts and certain radical ecologists, as we saw in chapter 2. For *Sandover*, "POP EXPLO" (145) is the ecological problem for which "THE RULE OF NUMBER" (247) is the solution. The poem's vision of the planetary future is eliminative. People will vanish except for a few "QUALITY" (145) souls. The "elite" comprises "At most two million relatively fleet / Achievers" (140) out of "the three or four billion . . . USELESS LIVES" (196) who won't move forward, "Whom nothing quickens, whom no powers indwell" (139). "WE WANT THE STUFF OF MAN PURE," Mirabell tells the mediums, "TOO MANY / FRACTIONAL HUMANS ON EARTH" (117). With visions of "AN INTELLIGENT RACE ONE 100TH THE SIZE OF EARTH'S POPULATION" (118), *Sandover* returns us to the vicinity of the paleo-republic. "I think it's more important to save the environment than it is to save large sections of the population," Merrill told Buckley. "The earth is sacred; the elements are the sacred things, not their namers and exploiters" (421).

Whereas writers like Ophuls or Shepard take Malthusian overload to be the result of the welfare state's runaway largesse, Merrill worries about the diminishing aesthetic returns from a literary culture taxed beyond its carrying capacity by creative types. In a cutting letter about the Iowa Writers Workshop, which he visited in 1984, Merrill concludes that "youngsters, under the direction of a half-dozen 'names,' mass-produce poetry around the clock" and "will grow up to publish books and attract imitators, and our poets will accordingly prosper like the rabbits of Australia."[64] Where poetry is concerned, Merrill folds the economic malaise of overproduction into the environmental crisis of overpopulation. Mirabell offers up a possible solution to both crises:

THIN OUT THE JOSTLERS FOR SELFREALIZATION
THE FALSE PARADISE ONLY SPARE THE
GREENHOUSE ITS PRECIOUS
NUCLEUS OF MINDS. (119)

Merrill appears to understand "self-realization" as a scarce commodity that—in defiance of economic laws—is devalued precisely in proportion to its demand by the masses. For Merrill, or at least for his "BAD ANGELS," mere "JOSTLERS" are not equipped to bring a viable product to market. Alternatively, as the sort of "household commodity" that individuals reflexively produce for their own consumption, as Lawrence Iannaccone observes, self-realization appears to diminish in value as a result of oversupply. In the early poem "A Tenancy" (1961), Merrill's speaker sits amused in his furnished rental while his landlord rattles off the

> *idées recues*
> Of oak, velour, crochet, also the mantel's
> Baby figures, value told me
> In some detail at the outset. (*CP*, 168)

The landlord's imputing "value" to the room's kitsch ("innocent . . . of annual depreciation") leaves everything to be desired, not least any originality of mind.

By contrast, Merrill is able to transmute the base materials of family money into the gold not only of things worth having but also of "SELFREALIZATION." Founded by Merrill in the fifties and dissolved in 1996 a year after his death, the Ingram Merrill Foundation "was a considered, conscientious way for him to put his wealth to use" (292), according to Merrill's biographer, Langdon Hammer; "at the height of its giving" it awarded stipends that "totaled about $300,000 per year" (291). Focused on rising talents, the foundation proved a shrewd forecaster in artist futures. And while Merrill wanted it to have the look of a merit-driven committee, there was never any doubt that its "list of beneficiaries," as Hammer notes, "reflected his preferences" (292). Armed with a rare combination of cultural and economic capital, Merrill not only put his wealth to work but also made sure that its purchases expressed his taste as clearly as possible. "Our lives led *to* this. It's the price we pay," Merrill writes of the "stripping process" (218), the removal from daily rounds, JM and DJ experience at the Ouija board. They don't see friends; they "can't even watch TV" (217). Yet if the dalliance with the afterlife might have given him pause, it cannot be said to buck the pattern of his existence. For "the cost of being set apart" (218) from the ordinary world was the *point* of Merrill's expensive life.

At the start of "The Book of Ephraim," JM tells us that he had originally planned the chronicle of the Ouija sessions as a novel—the unfinished manuscript of which, we learn in "The Will" (also in *Divine Comedies*), Merrill left in a cab in Atlanta, never to be recovered. Yet *Sandover* implies that the loss seems not to have been painful. This is because, as the genre of "baldest . . . reportage," a prosaic interface with "the public" (3), the novel turns out not to suit the poet's theme. Like Henry David Thoreau, JM is a self-professed exile from what *Walden* calls "universal noveldom," whose chief business is the delivering of "news."⁶⁵ He also shares with Thoreau a vision of himself as a breed apart from the "little crowd of mortals—My readers," whom he surveys from his perch in "the angelic secretariat" (4). Like Thoreau, Merrill imagines himself somewhat out of sync with (or immune to) the trends of his own time. "It never seemed to me," he told Buckley, "that I wanted to adopt fashions in thought or subject matter of the different decades I've gone through" (421). Or to quote "The Broken Home" (1966): "I rarely buy a newspaper, or vote" (*CP*, 199).

Yet unlike Thoreau, whose aloof idealism matched an equally stringent antimaterialism, JM has little interest in self-denial. While he feigns impatience with "possessions / Worldly or otherwise" (99), the pose is short-lived and, in any event, unserious. Reduced to its essence, *Sandover* is a poem that alternates between séances and shopping sprees. These pastimes converge at the end of the poem, when we learn that Maria Mitsotaki is actually Plato, one of the five "immortal souls" who continually return to earth to fulfill God B's plan. Maria characterizes herself as "WHAT U MIGHT CALL A PROFESSIONAL SHOPPER" (467), traipsing through history as if it were a department store stocked with attractive and value-added souls. Maria first lays eyes on JM and DJ in the mirror of a Hermès "COSMETIC CASE," and the compact she forges with the archangel Michael for their cultivation is inseparable from the self-enhancing touch-ups that the luxury "COMPACT" (554) enables.

To attend to *Sandover*'s consumerist aesthetics is by no means to diminish its interest, if for no other reason than that Merrill himself, no less than Maria / Plato, was an extraordinary shopper. Indeed, given his purchasing habits, it is somewhat peculiar to find Merrill's best readers insisting on the poet's sheer *ordinariness*. It is an article of faith among Merrill scholars that, notwithstanding the poem's references to the inevitability (if not desirability) of winnowing the human droves to an elect few in the world to come, *Sandover*'s wellborn "SCRIBE" (143), prone to an exotic and rococo formalism, is a poet of demotic humility. Siobhan Philips includes Merrill in the line of modern poets whose work thrives on an "affirming form of dailiness." "Merrill's quotidian existence," Phillips writes, "is an essential structure as well as subject" for his poetry.⁶⁶ Helen Vendler maintains that Merrill's poetry "locates value in the human and everyday rather than in the transcendent."⁶⁷ The modifier "everyday" here does a lot of heavy lifting, yet it raises more questions than answers. To speak of *Sandover*'s relatability would necessitate an unusually broad definition of the mundane, one that includes establishing your own arts foundation, or driving your carpet to Boston to commission a bespoke wallpaper to match it (an outing recounted at the beginning of *Mirabell*).

This is a catty way of pointing out that, as virtually every poem of his attests, Merrill's "everyday" was meticulously rarefied. Merrill is paradigmatic of a camp taste that pits high (opera, Proust in French, transatlantic residences) and low (Ouija, rough trade) against an extremely vast middle. He offers a very different account of consumption from that found in another brilliant proponent of camp, Andy Warhol. Whereas Warhol celebrates the fact that "no amount of money can get" Liz Taylor, say, "a better Coke than the one the bum on the corner is drinking," Merrill steers deliberately clear of such mass-produced fare.[68] His poems abound not in Pop commodities but in inherited, collectible, or custom-made things (apartments in Manhattan; "Fabergé's royal Easter eggs" in "Transfigured Bird" [*CP*, 34]; suits tailored every year in Venice); *objets trouvés* (the "immense / Victorian mirror" that DJ salvages from "the grandest house" in Stonington [98]); and, perhaps most distinctively, *objets outrés* ("great muffs of albino porcupine" in "The Doodler" [*CP*, 98]). The object world in Merrill is as inaccessible to ordinary mortals as the spirit world.[69] The critical insistence on the everyday flattens the complexity of Merrill's poetry because it inexactly grasps an experience that more resembles the Gilded Age Lebenswelt novelized by Wharton and James than that of almost all Merrill's readers.

Just as they have misrecognized the material culture that informs his poetry, so Merrill's best critics have frequently arrived at a tendentious view of his account of self-identity. It is a truism that *Sandover* critiques what Devin Johnston calls "lyric subjectivity."[70] Johnston argues that, in contrast to the "evasions" of the self-help New Ageism to which it is adjacent, Merrill's project serves "to deconstruct essentialist notions of selfhood" (113). "To read *Changing Light at Sandover* is not so much to experience the ethos of an individual," Johnston remarks, "but rather to experience the flickering dispersal of subjectivity" (93). But if subjectivity is dispersed in the poem, it is hardly in a rout. JM finds himself *everywhere*—in the dead, in the superhuman, in the very elements and atoms composing the universe. This I take to be the force of JM's question, "How can a person not personify?" (172), which *Sandover* treats as rhetorical. For Merrill, anthropomorphizing is as reflexive as breathing. Far from a surrender of agency to automatic writing or dictation, the Ouija sessions enable subjectivity to become automated, to spread out, to blanket the known (and unknown) world.

While it may not be exactly rhetorical, another question late in the trilogy—"Is the cast / Much smaller than we'd thought?" (405)—can be answered only in the affirmative. The poem has played a relentless game of doubles with identity: the first-century Greek Jew Ephraim turns out to be the archangel "Lord Michael" (550); the late friend Maria Mitsotaki is the latest incarnation of the immortal Plato. Yet the "cast" is "smaller" in an even more basic sense than these eleventh-hour unveilings suggest. "I used to / Ask how on earth one got sufficiently / Imbued with otherness," JM remarks at one point. The solution he can "now see" entails taking himself as the default for such alterity (89). In *Sandover*, personal identity does not yield to difference but absorbs it. The "mirror" that JM and DJ "prop in the facing chair" during séances affords a window for the spirits to see through to this side of death. But more obviously, it is a means of reflecting JM and DJ back to themselves: "We saw each other in it" (6). And even more obviously, the mirror figures the logic underwriting the manifestations roaming through Merrill's poem, projections the poet frequently comes close to disclosing as *reflections*. "You see yourselves, then, in the mirror only / Of a live mind?" (105), JM asks the spirits in the interrogative mood typical of the poem's habit of finessing assumptions it all but concedes.

We lose sight of the weirdness of Merrill's achievement in *Sandover*, then, if we insist on its being a testament to "everydayness" or an equally anodyne deconstruction of selfhood. These normalizing moves bypass what is radical about the poem, a feature that it shares with much of the channeling discourse from whose embarrassments Merrill's defenders have sought to distance him. Johnston goes so far as to retrieve *Sandover* from the degraded trappings of New Age thinking by placing it in the separate category of occult literature stretching from Blake through Yeats. This move is itself debatable, given that high-literary mysticism seems no easier to defend from charges of fraud or lunacy than anything in New Age cosmology. But if *Sandover* has more in common with *Cosmic Trigger* or *VALIS* than with Blake's *Milton* or Yeats's *A Vision*, this is because New Age channeling is more provocative in its concept of mind and identity than the critical view suggests. Merrill's account of mind is scarcely distinct from those found among channels throughout the decade in which his poem appeared. Take his belief that DNA, "that sinuous molecule," is a minded entity—"THE NUCLEUS OF MINDS," as Mirabell calls it (119). In channeling discourse, DNA is not merely a repository of what *VALIS* calls the "gene-pool memory" (145) carried by living things but a bearer of consciousness in its own right. "Consciousness congregates just as atoms and molecules do," Roberts avers. "There are clumps of consciousness just as there are clumps of matter" (292). And Wilson calls DNA "the local brain guiding planetary evolution" (206).

There is at least one important sense in which Merrill's project differs from that of channels like Roberts and Shucman. Whereas those figures find their spiritual guides leading them out of the slough of materialist despond, offering alternatives to the banal consumerism of late capitalist life, Merrill's poem celebrates the object world that money can buy.[71] Some of the most beautiful passages in *Sandover* draw on the luxe and ornamental surroundings Merrill inhabited, interiors the poet renders with the detail Henry James lavished on his Gilded Age set pieces. The *"scene"* of the archangels' lessons is the titular *"Sandover, that noble manor,"* with its *"comfy air of things once used and used,"* where

> *dormer windows overlook the moat*
> *The maze, the gardens, paddock where a lonely*
> *Quadruped is grazing.* (320)

It is worth noting that only for Merrill can "manor" connote "comfy." Merrill's model for the "schoolroom" (319) at Sandover, where the archangelic revelations transpire, is the "ballroom of the Broken Home" (557), a reference to Merrill's poem about his parents' divorce in which the Orchard, the Southampton estate of his childhood, figures prominently.

According to Stephen Yenser, coexecutor of Merrill's literary estate, *Sandover* finally rejects its abstractions in favor of the "marriage of mind and nature," by which Yenser means consciousness and material reality.[72] But the materialism that matters in *Sandover* is less the subatomic universe or the biosphere than something on the scale of the commodity, a piece of property (even a house) that Merrill also brings to life, makes signify, makes over into a story. What Merrill's protégé Alfred Corn calls his "ability to make the material world allegorical" (cited in Hammer, *James Merrill*, 549) derived not merely from the rarity or specialness of the things Merrill was capable of buying (Tanagra vases, stone ibises) but from his putting them to work in a flourishing gift economy in which he was the prime mover. This is not simply a case of calling out Merrill's privilege or commodity fetishism. The commodity fetish is guilty of two transgressions, after all, neither of which we find in Merrill. It is a standard object passing itself off as a singleton (unlike the preferred object in Merrill, which really is unique); and it means to replace human relations (rather than serve as a token or promise of relations, as in Merrill).

In "The Will," Merrill writes of a "stone ibis" that he planned to give to Yenser as a wedding present (and which he lost, along with his manuscript, in the fateful Atlanta taxi). He had envisioned the ibis as an object that, "passing into a young, happy pair's / Keeping could stand for the giver" (*CP*, 394). The poem recounts the origins of this "burden" ("I bought it with / A check my father wrote before his death" [*CP*, 394]) and introduces Merrill's first afterlife guide, Ephraim, who consoles the poet for losing the gift by telling him that the ibis is cursed. The lyric's major chord is Merrill's awareness of his talent for turning (paternal) money into meaning. "The dimensions of a man / Of means," at least in his case, are isomorphic with "a man / . . . Of meanings" (*CP*, 395). "The Will" has been read as a turning point in Merrill's career, a poem that finds him surrendering the fey charms of his mannerist style for the cosmic teachings of *Sandover*. "GIVE UP EVERYTHING EXCEPT THE GHOST," Ephraim tells him (*CP*, 396). Yet the poem expresses a defiant retention of the objects the poet has gathered. "I took to heart its funerary chic," the speaker says of the ibis, which resurfaces in a tomb of the mind, a "chamber" where "lost was found," including all the "bric-a-brac" of Merrill's life (*CP*, 397).

The will as testament is the initial conceit of the poem, figured in the tableau of "two men and a woman, dressed in black," who "enter with a will" (*CP*, 392). This conceit overlaps with the will as volition, yet the overlap cannot but produce friction. "A will of mine?" (*CP*, 392) Merrill's speaker asks this Dickensian crew of solicitors, a question that coyly evokes Merrill's well-practiced self-image as a financial naïf. The question, of course, is slightly disingenuous. Merrill knows these are his lawyers, just as he prizes his own volition as a valuable piece of personal property, and any disclaimer for these different forms of self-possession is easily retracted. Yet in its denial of the speaker's material and mental force, "The Will" bears on questions *Sandover* raises about individual choice as a mode of effecting one's agency in the world. "The Will" first appeared in *Poetry* in 1974, the year Nozick's *Anarchy, State, and Utopia* was published. And while it is highly unlikely that Merrill noticed Nozick's book, his poem might as well be a case study for Nozick's claim that society's overwhelming preference for "theories of recipient justice . . . completely ignore any right a person might have to give something to someone."[73] For "The Will" is a poem about a giver reflecting on the merits not just of his gift but of its recipients.

Merrill might find it a campy joke to present a memento mori to a couple starting out on life's journey, after all, yet he cannot be certain that his meaning will be shareable. Losing the item against his will saves him the trouble of misunderstanding, and recovering it in the "chamber" of his mind keeps its meanings if not its substance intact. Merrill's mental storehouse preserves the meanings any such object has for him against the possible misfiring occasioned by its conveyance to another person. It is as if the ibis has been so infused with Merrill's own personality—his morbid humor, his memories of his wealthy father, his Wildean classicism—that he cannot quite make it shareable with a straight married couple on their wedding day. "HARDLY THE BIBELOT TO GIVE A BRIDE" (*CP*, 395), Ephraim remarks. Merrill arrives at this point through his command of great material resources and an equally rich imagination. And from this vantage, the worry that the lost item might send the wrong message becomes hard to untangle from the suspicion that its intended recipient is not equipped to receive the plurality of opposing meanings (love, death, paternity) that Merrill combines in the object. Corn tells Hammer that his mentor "could make anything say more than it said" (549), but there is no guarantee that such surplus inferential value conveys to a less richly endowed receiver.

In his 1993 memoir *A Different Person*, Merrill indeed gives us an indication of how economic status might limit or deform a person's understanding. "The best intentioned people," he writes, "knowing whose son I was and powerless against their own snobbery, could set me writhing under attentions I had done nothing to merit."[74] "Attentions" override intentions, as if the gravity well of Merrill's fortune cannot but exert a distortionary pull on the meaning-making ability of otherwise rational individuals. "What's tiresome is when people exclusively insist on the forms they've imagined," Merrill told J. D. McClatchy in a 1982 *Paris Review* interview in response to McClatchy's gentle prodding about whether Merrill really believed *Sandover*'s cosmology. "Those powers don't need churches in order to be sacred. What they do need are fresh ways of being seen."[75] Ephraim, the tutelary spirit of the early séances, exemplifies such "fresh ways," if only because he allows Merrill to externalize his thoughts ("a will of mine?") so that they return to him in the form of oracles. This externalization has an even deeper resonance with the postmodern religiosity from which some critics have been keen to separate Merrill's ideas. As I have observed, the older antinomian claim that sacredness thrives in the absence of "churches" resurfaces in the rise of contemporary evangelicalism (in fact it never departed). According to Robert Bellah, "today religion in America is as private and diverse as New England colonial religion was public and unified." Exhibit A for this claim in Bellah's *Habits of the Heart* (1985) is a nurse, Sheila, who "has actually named her religion . . . after herself." Requiring no church attendance, "Sheilaism" is "'just my own little voice'" telling the faith's founder and sole adherent "to love yourself and be gentle with yourself."[76]

There is an obvious difference between the (private and humble) faith of Sheilaism and the (public and grandiose) vision of *Sandover*. Yet the qualitative contrasts are hardly incidental to the quantitative resources Merrill had at his disposal. Merrill's biography overflows with efforts to make things happen in "fresh ways" through sheer buying power, often at the expense of the good sense that he could afford to spare. ("We'd felt him warming up for a green bride," Merrill's speaker notes of the oft-married paterfamilias in "The Broken Home." "He could afford it" [*CP*, 197].) Merrill bankrolled businesses for lovers both casual and serious (a "vast + luxurious Tae Kwon Do Academy" [cited in Hammer, *James Merrill*, 608] for Manos Karastefanís, an occasional bedmate in Athens; an orchard in New Hampshire for his infrequent companion Peter Tourville). Yet more to the point, Merrill's cosmogony is as instrumental as Sheilaism in bringing the poet closer to *himself*. "The one thing that holds [*Sandover*] together," Merrill told an interviewer, "is that it all truly happened to us" (cited in Hammer, *James Merrill*, 547). In this respect, the "little voice" that tells Sheila to love herself is not (or not only) a symptom of what Bellah and his coauthors call "therapeutic ideology."[77] Or if it is, we would be hard pressed to separate Merrill from such allegedly false consciousness. While Bellah's Sheila has the one "little voice," Merrill's poem revels in excess, proliferating almost too many voices to count. Even so, this chorus speaks with one voice, delivers one overarching message: *you are special*.

Merrill's source material for what the numbered bats call his "POMES OF SCIENCE" (113) includes *The Origin of Consciousness in the Breakdown of the Bicameral Mind* (1976) by the psychologist Julian Jaynes. The book's thesis is that, prior to 1,000 BCE, *Homo sapiens* was not a "conscious" species. To prove this curious claim, Jaynes cites Homer's *Iliad*, in which "the words . . . that in a later age come to mean mental things have different meanings, all of them concrete," and in which "there is no subjective consciousness, no mind, no soul, or will."[78] "Iliadic men," Jaynes concludes, were "noble automatons who knew not what they did." Jaynes asserts that before the spread of writing, humans had "no internal mind-space to introspect upon," a fact borne out by Homer's divinities (75). The "gods were organizations of the central nervous system" (74), "mere voices" (75) whispering commands in the skulls of primitives. "At one time human nature was split in two, an executive part called a god, and a follower part called a man," Jaynes argues. "Neither part was conscious" (84).

The "subjective conscious mind" (55) arose through what Jaynes sees as a relocation of the human sensorium from a primarily acoustic to a largely visual medium, a shift effected by writing. "The wide use of visual writing for communication," he concludes, "resulted in a change in the very structure of the mind itself" (201). Jaynes's theory of mind fits science to speculation much in the way of Robert Anton Wilson's "turned-on physicists" (206) or Alan Harrington's immortalists. But where *The Immortalist* sees science as paving the way for the "race to get rid of the intimidating gods in its own head" (21) and for "the creation of our own divinity" (13), *The Origin of Consciousness* aims to demonstrate how we have learned to "become our own gods" (79) via the "seen speech" of writing (68), to imagine a "metaphorical mind-space" (60) whose contours emerge for us through the spatial analogy of symbols on a surface.

If seeing is the essence of mind for the functionalist Jaynes, mind is in essence a metaphor, "the invention on the basis of language of an analog space with an analog 'I'" (204). In *Sandover*, the mediums never hear the voices from the *au-delà*, who communicate exclusively through the graphemes of the Ouija board. While it is thus a misnomer to say (as Merrill did) that he took dictation from the board (the dead don't have vocal cords), Merrill's description of his process roughly mimics the emergence of subjectivity in Jaynes. Just as Merrill took down words that he then read back to himself in producing the poem, so for Jaynes we create consciousness through reading about ourselves, reabsorbing thoughts we have first put out of our heads into the world. Only by inventing a location for the voices that speak to us can we turn the hallucinations we mistake for gods into the fiction we believe as subjectivity. "Consciousness," Jaynes writes, in a question-begging definition, "has no location whatever except as we imagine it has" (46).[79]

Despite his disdain for treating it as "imaginative literature" rather than "history . . . to be examined by psychohistorical scientists" (76), Jaynes's understanding of the *Iliad* fits into a recognizable literary history of poetry, a millennia-long progression from the oral and public, "unsubjective times" (83) of epic to the written and solitary world of lyric. Whereas "bicameral man had no internal space in which to be private" (205), his modern counterpart is afflicted with the opposite problem. The alleged impossibility of epic in modern civilization is due not merely to the severing of primordial links between poetry and the common culture but to the triumph of Johnston's "lyric subjectivity," a triumph nowhere so obvious as in Merrill's effort to scale the heights of epic in a poem that reads like a succession of virtuoso formal exercises.[80] The *Iliad* entreats Calliope to jump-start the poet's song. *Sandover* amounts to an emphatically Whitmanian summoning of the heroic first-person. The poem's hermetic cosmology, not to say its in-universe attitude toward JM and DJ's late intimates—a set of relationships from whose intricacies the reader is locked out—secures the unassailability of its maker's point of view.

In *Sandover*'s Coda, "The Higher Keys," JM and DJ note that they have "outgrown" their spirit world interlocutors and are "more and more alone" with their thoughts (540). Whereas Merrill implies that the rise of consciousness is a maturation, Jaynes sees it as a fall from grace. Jaynes concludes that we miss submitting to our gods because we fear having to make our own choices. Consciousness replaces access to "something palpable, something direct, something immediate" with a "hesitant subjective groping about for signs of certainty" (320).[81] Hence the appeal to a supernatural order furnishes "assurance that we are not alone, that the gods are just silent, not dead" (320). In *Sandover*, by contrast, the poet's goal is not merely to engage with the voices in his head but finally to assert his dominance over them. This aim is inseparable from Merrill's interest in treating freedom of choice as the essence of selfhood. "The chosen people," JM observes at one point, "Certainly had the knack of how to choose" (133). The joke's context is the mediums' discovery that Jewish souls were the primal matter in the R/Lab's human experiment, the "SEED" from which "CAME ALL RACES" (138). Merrill's poem posits its first-person hero as omega to the Jew's alpha. Equipped with the "knack of how to choose," he ends the poem with an assertion of his preferences over the spirit world's meddling.

When Ephraim reveals himself as Michael at the end of the poem, he tells the mediums that he pities them for their "IMPOVERISHMENT," by which he means the "YEARS" of "DEVOTION" they have invested in their "V WORK." His revelation amounts to a token of his appreciation, "SOMETHING THEY MAY / KEEP (OR NOT AS THEY CHOOSE)," in the sort of gift economy that Merrill knows well. And sure enough, the poet chooses to share Michael's secret, "THIS GOLD THAT BACKS YOUR CURRENCY," a bestowal that Michael attributes to JM's own "GODLY" nature (551). The gold-backed currency references secular rather than "GODLY" concerns, the concerns of the market. But JM's going public with Ephraim's "true" identity refers even more precisely to the *free* market, in the pure version of which total deregulation is the ideal, a state of transparency undistorted by the noise of nonmarket forces. The difference between JM and the technocratic flunkies of the afterlife could not be more stark. Unlike Mirabell, who "RESISTS GOING TO THE HIGHER INFORMATION BANKS" (554) out of fear of reprisal, Merrill's paradise on earth champions the bankability of maximum information.

In sharing the secret, Merrill departs from the example of Dick (who seeks to preserve arcana) and follows that of Hayek, who sees "decentralization" as the answer to the basic "problem" of economic activity: "how to extend the span of our utilization of resources beyond the span of . . . any one mind."[82] In "The Use of Knowledge in Society" (1945), Hayek argues that knowledge can be economically rational only when removed from the bureaucratic stranglehold of central planners like Mirabell. The market looks like a "single mind possessing all the information" when it really amounts to "limited individual fields of vision sufficiently overlap[ping] so that through many intermediaries the relevant information is communicated to all" (526). Hayek's point is that while the market can be a revelatory entity, a sort of VALIS device optimized to transmit "the most essential information" (527) through the "price system" (525), no actual individual can presume to know what the market is thinking, since such knowledge would be akin to telepathic omniscience, an unlimited access to every mind.

In Merrill's poem, supernatural entities do in fact have unlimited access to everyone's thoughts. Compressing consciousness and high-bourgeois consumption into one of the poem's most gorgeous metonymies, Michael describes himself as a "Persian rug tester" "forever feeling the texture" of JM and DJ's "minds" (555). Yet in rebuking the central planning committee of the R/Lab by giving out the archangel's secret, JM stages an important role reversal at *Sandover*'s conclusion. The scene is a gathering for the poet's recital in Sandover's ballroom, now revealed as a replica of a room in Merrill's childhood home. The essence of Michael's secret is his admission that JM has spent his lifetime "being chosen" by the higher powers. Shifting from "chosen" to chooser, from object to subject, JM becomes a host among guests in a crucial twist on the author-audience relation. It matters to our understanding of the poem's final stanzas that the voices of the dead (twenty-six luminaries assembled as JM's fan club) are all but muted, that the jarring small capital letters have all but fallen away, that JM is at last *in his element*, at home not only as "scribe" but as scion. In his proper capacity as heir not just to Homer but to Charles Merrill, JM's "fear—that, written for the dead, / This poem leave a living reader cold"—yields to the more mundane fretting of the micromanaging host, mindful of his audience's wandering looks

> Toward the buffet where steaming silver urn,
> Cucumber sandwiches, rum punch, fudge laced
> With hashish cater to whatever taste. (559)

If the dead turn out to be as fickle in their preferences as any live reader the poet can imagine, the poet has taken care to cover all bases and satisfy everyone's choices. Or rather, by laying out the "buffet," he has *designed* them. JM's "godly" nature assumes the form not merely of choosing (the Edenic account of humanity's godliness) or even of being first among an array of "decision units," to use Gary Becker's term, but finally of determining what others choose. In effect, he becomes the market, identifying the range of possible choices anyone in his orbit can make. *Sandover* comes full circle; its first word ("Admittedly") is its last (3; 560). But what JM calls the "absolute / Discretion of our circle" (559), the sacred space of the Ouija board, might also be read as implying that Merrill circles back to his roots by exercising absolute discretion. In Merrill's case, the power to exercise one's will as if it were supreme derives not only from the appanage but also from the business model generated by the Wall Street brokerage his father started in 1914. Recounting an audience with the pope in 1950, Merrill describes Pius XII and Charles Merrill as "two men who had 'reached the top' in their respective fields of godliness and finance."[83] The parallelism that makes its founder a "godly" figure is slightly ironic, given that Merrill Lynch came to dominate the market precisely by *democratizing* it—having brought "Wall Street to Main Street," to cite the title of Edwin Perkins's biography of Charles Merrill.

This paradoxical formulation affords a lucid figure for the style of egalitarianism that Friedman and his allies sought to champion in market relations. Merrill's father is credited with having transformed securities investment from the exclusive preserve of the old rich to a middle-class pursuit. The firm advanced a policy of transparency that, as Perkins puts it, would "buck the tradition" of "public ignorance about . . . financial markets." Turning investment into a retail enterprise, Merrill "provided accurate, up-to-date information."[84] Merrill's father marketed the market by exposing its jealously guarded secrets. If the market casts a long shadow in Merrill's life, its inescapability is attested by the fact that his efforts to turn his back on the family business, to keep the market's workings otherworldly, nonetheless found his own unearthly artistic pursuits foregrounding the freedom of choice and information that Merrill Lynch used as its chief selling point in making everyman into a sophisticated investor. Merrill Lynch, after all, was in the business of purveying that flattering if unrealistic image no less than trading stocks.

In the agonistic tradition made salient by Harold Bloom, strong poets seek to overthrow their antecedents and dominate their form.[85] To the degree that Merrill fits this tradition (by Bloom's account no less), *Sandover*'s next-life fantasy places its speaker in the role of the father, the transcendental decision maker to whom other persons become so many objects, so many vectors of the potentate's choices. Notwithstanding Merrill's studious self-distancing from the family firm, the poem's framing of eternal life seems framed in its turn by the father's patrimony. Like the king's two bodies of an earlier epoch, the Merrill Lynch brand persists in a virtual immortality long after Charles Merrill's death in 1956. If *Sandover*'s strongest wish is the possibility that mind persist after physical death, the poem's most jarring insight is its admission that not everyone moves on because some persons, like some preferences, count more than others. The poem treats such inequity as ontological, a built-in feature of a universe that sanctifies a tiny elect while discarding the vast horde. The poem leaves us with the question of whether any subjectivity can survive the presence of another, superior subjectivity. The evidence of *Sandover* by and large answers the question in the negative. But even as it sees first-person ontology as a zero-sum game, it exposes those social structures—markets and meritocracies, in this world or the next—in which asymmetries masquerade as justice.

Afterword
The Marketization of Everything

To some readers, my analysis of Merrill must seem vulgar and dismissive, or at least overzealous in its demystification of his mystifying poem. While I draw on the facts of his well-heeled life to illuminate the ways in which he could not quite rise above them, it would be a mistake to claim that I count this as a strike against his accomplishment. My point is that few readers have taken the full measure of the estrangement effects of his poetry out of what I suspect is reluctance to face the gap between Merrill's life and the contexts (everydayness, say) to which his work is often yoked. I have tried to close that gap by situating his poetics in a context he clearly took to heart: the end times of postmodern capitalism. There is nothing to suggest that Merrill read Jane Roberts or even Philip Dick. But his poetry has a deep affinity with the accounts of choice and subjectivity found in their work, including a dedication to the persistence of mind absent any real-world anchor.

Hence we learn that George Cotzias's "PURE INTELLIGENCE" is busily "AT WORK" (526) in the afterlife, unmodified from its earthly form. Far from "THE CALLUS OF THE SOUL" sloughed off after death, the "self" has a habit of "recomposing stroke by stroke" its "PERSONALITY" by virtue of its lodgment in "A THINKING MIND" (527) that outlives the mortal body. Belief in such survival indexes the centrality of transcendence in the various and conflicting fields of belief to emerge after the sixties, from secular ethics to ecology to new religious movements (including cults and evangelical sects). And that centrality in turn pays tribute to the triumph over a social world understood not only to shape our thoughts (the standard environmentalist view) but to rob us of them, to appropriate them as if exercising eminent domain over our private property. The latter view arises from the intellectual formation I have called neo-idealism.

Merrill is the right place to end this book because his dual inheritance of the modernist poetic legacy and the fruits of modern finance capitalism presents itself as a conflict in his work that closer examination reveals as virtually no conflict at all. Merrill embraces the project of "lyric subjectivity" to the degree that he seeks to disavow his patrimony. I have suggested that these categories are more compatible than we might assume. "Neoliberalism has meant, in short," David Harvey writes, "the financialization of everything."[1] The increasing abstraction of the money system into ever more arcane instruments for conducting ever more opaque transactions has meant the redistribution of money upward from the bulk of the population to the investor class. The massification of consciousness-raising in post-sixties culture has involved a separate but implicated form of abstraction that gives rise to a view of persons as possessed of a subjectivity that cannot—and in its ethical dimension should not—be bound by the externalities of social structure. Like the twenty-first-century money system, the twenty-first-century self is a transcendent being. Moreover, as Merrill's antisocial epic shows, the transcendent agent in neo-idealism is the atomized and indivisible unit. What accounts for the preponderance of beams and rays in New Age discourse, of souls able to be picked out of the interstellar slipstream by sensitive channels, is the assumption that such particles are vectors for illimitably unitary subjectivities that earthly institutions—above all the state—everywhere aim to merge into the nebulous mass of a world construed as no more than a statistical, demographic, material reality, what *Sandover* calls "THE RULE OF NUMBER."

I have held off from reducing the various social configurations this book studies to *the market*, as if the market were the allegorical key to everything from critiques of artificial intelligence to rapture prophesies. I have instead moved in and out of this allegory by scrutinizing a number of categories through which the antistatist seventies sought to announce alternatives to what Ronald Reagan incessantly called "big government" (his favorite slur). None of these categories—meritocracy, communitarianism, anarchism, and of course individualism—readily reduce to a defense of the free market even as they have features compatible with such a defense. As the book progresses, as the seventies yield to the eighties, the market becomes the megastructure for a wide array of antistatist impulses, so that—and at the risk of a spurious periodization—when we reach DeLillo's *The Names* or the final pages of *Sandover*, we find ourselves in the territory of "full-dress and full-blown" marketization, to use Fredric Jameson's adjectives.[2] But even once there we must feel ourselves unsettled, since the market, as we never cease to be reminded, is not a place or a thing but simply the name we give to the incalculable relations of freely choosing individuals. "The Market is the sum of all *voluntary* human action," the libertarian Samuel Konkin concludes. "If one acts non-coercively, one is part of the Market."[3]

There is no comparable account of the bureaucratic state, no apologia that would take the state as composed of individuals whose interactions render the personification of the state untenable or at least suspect. The state always acts in concert with itself and (according to its detractors) against the interests of those it governs. Why should this be? What is it about the state, in the tradition of political theory stretching back to Plato, that equates government in its strong sense with a singleton dominating the masses under its sway by absorbing them into itself?[4] This question aims not to deny that statism tends toward authoritarianism, I hasten to add, nor to feign ignorance of the obvious answer in social theory (the state monopolizes the legitimate use of force), but to pay attention to the kind of person that critics of statism imagine the state to be. In political commentary across history, the state is personified as a formally coherent body with a "constitution" whose telos is as much self-maintenance as self-inflation. The book we call Plato's *Republic* was, after all, originally called "Constitution," and the idea that a state must proceed from a self-organized body has held fast since fifth-century Athens.[5] For Socrates, "cohesion," the chief aim of a state, is a "result of the common feelings of pleasure and pain which you get when all members of a society are glad or sorry at the same successes and failures"; the ideal "state most nearly resembles an individual" whose personhood amounts to the synchronization of every person inhabiting it.[6] For Hobbes, absolutism is the only viable form of the state because it alone allows power to be undivided. Any government that falls short of such guarantees for sovereign authority (democracy and aristocracy are Hobbes's examples) does not really deserve the name "commonwealth," "for powers divided mutually destroy each other."[7]

The figure of Leviathan contrasts vividly with the informal or provisional or unorganized person of the market, whose seeming uniformity is never more than an illusion. Whereas the state is a monolith "constituting a single organism under a ruling principle," the market is an elusive set of actions that it would be foolhardy to try to pin down.[8] According to neoclassical economists, careful attention will reveal that whatever uniformity the market appears to have will consist in the autonomous acts of its independent constituents. What is significant about the market's always being referable to—or dissoluble in—individuals is that this view holds even as economics has shifted from a model of rationality (the market's appearance of reason arises from the rational acts of its users) to a model that accounts for nonrationality (the market's appearance of reason derives just as much from the irrational acts of its users). While the discipline has made room for a more capacious view of economic behavior, in other words, the commitment to the primacy of individual actions over the institution's agency remains. "While behaviorists . . . have poked a lot of holes in the edifice of rational market finance," Justin Fox writes in *The Myth of the Rational Market* (2009), "they haven't been willing to abandon that edifice."[9] The behavioral redescription of the market confirms rather than denies the ideal that Chicago School theorists envisioned in promoting the market as an alternative to the control economy. According to the economist Brian Arthur, models drawn from experimental psychology and chaos theory have enabled the discipline to "shift from assuming there's an objective world out there to saying that the world is created subjectively."[10]

Experimental economics also does away with the neoclassical paradigm's fixation on *fixity*, "its near-exclusive focus on equilibrium." "The system never settles into calm," as Fox puts it. "It oscillates."[11] The recent appreciation among economists for market anomalies and unpredictable behavior finds a resonant echo, ironically enough, in the work of academics explicitly opposed to the neoliberalism for which the discipline of economics provides the rationale. These thinkers may spurn the free market ideal, I suggest, but find common cause with the economists in their shared commitment to *neo-idealism*, to the view that "the world is created subjectively." In *Seeing Like a State* (1998), the political theorist James Scott argues that the state reduces "networks of mutuality" and "adaptability" to "monotonic schemes of centralized rationality."[12] The state insists on "sedentarization" (1) because it needs to contain its subjects after the same pattern by which it seeks to contain itself. Governments are at perpetual war with the human drive to "oscillate," to use Fox's term. With its "formal schemes of order" (7), the state's absorptive morphology bespeaks a rigid and static Leviathan whose chief goal is "imperialism" (6). The equation of formalism and control makes Scott's argument postmodernist in a precise sense. *Seeing Like a State* is a critique of a "high-modernist ideology" (4) against whose damages Scott advocates a reclamation of "historical vernaculars" (323) of the sort favored by Venturi and his coauthors in *Learning from Las Vegas*.

That resemblance makes Scott's frequent disclaimers about "market-driven standardization" (8) feel like special pleading, since *Learning from Las Vegas* is not just a manifesto of architectural postmodernism but, as we have seen, a brief for the demotic pluralism markets are imagined to foster. Scott skips over the fact that neoclassical economists share his disdain for the homogeneity that inevitably arises in an interventionist economy. For thinkers like Friedman, "market-driven standardization" is a contradiction in terms. "The 'market' that came into vogue in the seventies," Daniel Rodgers writes, "is a perpetual plebiscite of desires."[13] Just as notable as his rejection of the market is Scott's demurral from the view that his "argument is an anarchistic critique against the state" (7), a protest all but canceled out by his more recent *Two Cheers for Anarchism* (2012). The publication of that manifesto suggests how far the argument for anarchism has come. Though it could still induce a vague embarrassment in Scott at the turn of the twenty-first century, anarchism has achieved near-respectability in academic circles a decade or so later.[14] The decided turn toward anarchistic critiques of the overgoverned society of late extends into the present a viewpoint embraced by seventies libertarians, anarchists, and communitarians: the suspicion of rules made by others for you to follow. We might even say that pop Kantianism's legacy is that it has reinvigorated the value of autonomy—what Scott calls "individuals' capacity for self-governance" (349)—while severing the accord that Kant imagined between self-rule and the exemplary rule of the state.

Like seventies antistatists, Scott understands the state at its most insidious when it is most detached from the autochthonous communities that underwrite much of radical ecology's communitarianism.[15] For Scott no less than William Ophuls, the model society is Jeffersonian: "The yeomanry was, in short, an ideal training ground for democratic citizenship" (309). In fact, Scott's preferred polis, like Ophuls's, merges Jeffersonian democracy with the wisdom of the ancients. Hence "formulaic simplifications imposed through the agency of state power" (309) are disastrous for "common sense, experience, a knack, or *mētis*" (311), the Greek word for "the knowledge that can come only from practical experience" (6). *Mētis* "represents a wide array of practical skills and acquired intelligence in responding to a constantly changing natural and human environment" (313). Its "best practitioner" was "Odysseus" (314), with his "cunning . . . ability to adapt successfully to a constantly shifting situation" (313). In a sweeping indictment, Scott argues that governments throughout history have "regarded themselves as far smarter and farseeing than they really were and, at the same time, regarded their subjects as far more stupid and incompetent than they really were" (343). Scott's problem with how the state sees, then, concerns its by now familiar paternalistic indifference to the practical flourishing of persons. The state thwarts our inner Odysseus.

Compare Scott's vaunting of *mētis* to the "continuing task" of the contemporary survivalists whom the sociologist Richard Mitchell has profiled in

Dancing at Armageddon (2002).¹⁶ Mitchell argues that survivalists understand themselves "constructing 'what if' scenarios in which survival preparations" are "amenable to individual solutions" and "practical means" (13). The survivalist's preferred scenarios, Mitchell writes, are "a celebration of imagination, an encompassing compelling game of make-believe" (28) that has the virtue of restoring to its players a sense of pride in their cunning and know-how. "The purpose of survivalism is not predominance, supremacy, or triumph," then, "but the achievement of a hypothetical balance between the imagined hazards and hardships ahead and the resources, skills, and knowledge at hand or within reach" (37). What Mitchell calls "survivalist entrepreneurship" (40) is "permeated" with "finding, fixing, and selling, trading and bartering, scrounging, collecting, gathering, recycling, repackaging, and swapping," the kind of informal and on-the-ground "economic activity" (41) alleged by Scott to fall out of the abstract systems of high-modernist culture but recapturable by a *mētis*-friendly world. "For most of Eurasian history, ordinary people used informal credit arrangements," the anthropologist David Graeber writes in *The Utopia of Rules* (2015). "Physical money, gold, silver, bronze, and the kind of impersonal markets they made possible remained mainly an adjunct to the mobilization of legions, sacking of cities, extraction of tribute, and disposing of loot."¹⁷ Leery of being perceived "as potential consumers" to be "exploited," Mitchell's survivalists approach financial civilization and its "marketeers" from the vantage of Graeber-like "informal arrangements" and with a Scott-like *mētis*, thus revitalizing not only their own economic agency but the market itself: "Markets interest survivalists as signs of the times and sites for invention and craft" (26).

As it happens, seventies literature gives us a rather precise adumbration of Mitchell's survivalists in one of its unsung masterpieces. In James Dickey's *Deliverance* (1970), Lewis Medlock thrives on "atomic-survival stuff" to wake him from "the sleep of mild people."¹⁸ He practices a series of "mystiques" (3) or disciplines—"weight lifting, diet, exercise, self-help manuals from taxidermy to modern art"—partly in pursuit of "his own laborious immortality" (7), yet mostly in quest of self-definition. "He was not only self-determined," Ed Gentry (the novel's narrator) observes, "but determined" (3). Lewis's investment in "the business of survival" (36) accords with Mitchell's view that survivalists understand their project as a "game of make-believe"; in other words, he shares with Mitchell's survivalists the constructivism central to neo-idealism. If "all anybody has got," as Lewis tells Ed, "is a fantasy life," then what matters is "how strong your fantasy is, and whether you really—really—in your own mind, fit into your own fantasy, whether you measure up to what you've fantasized" (42). Lewis is the pure pop Kantian in Dickey's novel: "I am what I choose to be, and I am *it*" (43). Moreover, the novel bears out the pop Kantian insistence on opposing self-rule and state authority. The four suburban men on the disastrous canoe trip in the Georgia upcountry, after all, finally take Lewis's advice and hide the body of the predatory man he has killed because they cannot expect fairness—of the sort attached to "justifiable homicide" (104)—from "a jury made up of his cousins and brothers, maybe his mother and father too" (106).

If Mitchell's survivalist believes that "readiness will neutralize institutional and systemic failures" in the "disrupted future" (30), Dickey's survivalist understands that such failure is already upon us. The system that cannot be trusted can only be neutralized. "We're the law" (111), Lewis argues in response to the suggestion that they go to the police. And while Ed mocks his friend's hubris throughout the early part of the novel, by its finish he comes to embrace the idea that self-determination consists in imagining an ideal—an "*it*"—for oneself and then living into it. "I was light green, a tall forest man, an explorer, guerrilla, hunter. I liked the idea and the image," he observes on his first morning along the river. "Even if this was just a game, a charade, I had let myself in for it" (60). But the real test of his capacity for compelling make-believe occurs after he has (with bow and arrow) murdered the man who may or may not have been the accomplice of Lewis's victim. Ed fabricates a story that withstands "the enormous, unfathomable apparatus of crime detection, from which no one is entirely free" (219). "My version of things," he says, "was strong; I had made it and tried it out against the world, and it had held" (234). In *Deliverance*, the apocalyptic fantasy of surviving in a future world that will defeat weaker men gives way to the neo-idealist fantasy of outwitting and so liberating oneself from the power of the present-day state.

Returned to his wife and son by the novel's end, Ed emerges as a wily Odysseus of the late-capitalist suburb whose aim is as true as his lies are convincing. If he starts out with "no wish to surpass our limitations" (11), Ed finishes by fulfilling Lewis's desire to "hold on to his body and mind" and "to rise above time" (7). It is crucial to the novel's understanding of the trial it sets its narrator that Ed's triumph chiefly involves a test of mental strength. A small-time advertising executive, Ed makes his living designing "'what if' scenarios," as Mitchell would say. In the climactic ambush of his victim, Ed brings that skill to bear by imagining how his target will act in order to shoot him at the right moment: "The minds would have to merge" (159). Yet if it seems a little peculiar to see Ed's consciousness raised, this is because we associate that idea with a collective endeavor, a group transformation, broadly in the service of a constructive politics. Ed's *mētis* merely gets him and his friends out of legal trouble and back to "the long, declining routine of our lives" (148). More to the point is its ephemerality. "His brain and mine unlocked and fell apart," he tells us after the murder. "I never had thought with another man's mind on matters of life and death, and would never think that way again" (172).

My argument has been focused on the degree to which the collective consciousness that formed a staple of the New Social Movements—perhaps its key catalyst—gives way in seventies culture to a profound displacement onto subjectivity. But it would be a mistake to see this as a perversion of sixties thinking. The appeal to subjectivity was always the latent grounding of social change among important movements of that earlier decade; hence the coming to dominance of identity politics in the generation after the sixties. It is no surprise that the effort to reclaim consciousness's underappreciated power in sixties discourses should give rise to celebrations of unfettered power in seventies thinking. If Ed practices a "mystique," it would be the antisocial impulse that animates the various movements I have examined in the foregoing pages. "Most people and places are nothing," he concludes upon his survey of the river community at the start of their journey. "Nobody worth a damn could ever come from such a place" (47). His murder of the unknown redneck merely vindicates this judgment. Survivalism expresses the desire to imagine oneself entirely apart, free of all social ties. That desire is imbued in turn with what Disch calls "the intoxication . . . of power" (34) in *The Genocides* (1965), another prescient document of the antisocial impulse that would arise in seventies culture. "Like everyone else, Orville pretended to hate the invasion," Disch writes of a character in that novel, which chronicles the travails of the human remnant after an alien monoculture wipes out all Earthly flora and fauna. "But secretly he relished it, he gloried in it, he wanted nothing else. . . . The world might die about him. No matter: *he was alive.*"[19]

Novels like *Deliverance* and *The Genocides* describe the power to be gained by some individuals in a world emptied of obligation. And while they eschew the more nihilistic byways of seventies novelists, recent scholars of an anarchistic bent have also extolled the benefits of undoing at least that class of obligations that arise from our always compromising relation to the state. Graeber, for instance, rightly points out that the free market is grounded historically not in laissez-faire but in an elaborate and rigidly maintained series of regulations.[20] Far from being the "opposites" that the neoclassical economist likes to imagine, "states created markets" and "markets require states," Graeber concludes in his 2011 best seller *Debt: The First Five Thousand Years*. "Neither could continue without the other."[21] Yet the fundamental takeaway of Graeber's book is that this symbiotic relation between public and private systems has evolved as the principal means for societies to place subjects in their *debt*. For Graeber, the state across time serves as nothing other than a mechanism for turning persons into economic dependents.

The paternalistic state of modernity is merely the latest iteration of government's immemorial role as an omnipotent creditor, reducing the governed to "institutionalized debt peonage" (D, 351) and enforcing the usurious terms of a loan that the governed can never discharge. If the state originates as "the administrator of an existential debt that all of us have to the society that created us" (D, 70), institutions throughout history should be seen "as so many different fraudulent ways . . . to claim the authority to tell us how some aspect of that unlimited debt ought to be repaid" (D, 69). Like Paul Shepard, Graeber looks dimly on what Scott calls "sedentary" (338) civilizations: "For most of human history—at least, the history of states and empires—most human beings have been told that they are debtors" (D, 8).[22] And just as Shepard urges a return to the nomadic hunting life as the best way to overcome the "stoic numbness" and "lack of imagination" of "peasants,"[23] so Graeber is interested in reversing the "collapse of our collective imaginations" (D, 392) to which the state's exactions have led.

We have had occasion to observe that the positioning of "imagination" as central to "human freedom" is a tenet of the neo-idealism that emerges, for example, in Rawls's influential revival of Kantian constructivism. The difference between Rawls and late entrants to neo-idealist thought like Graeber and Scott is that Rawls understood the state as a product of the imagination, albeit a deeply faulty or flawed one, whereas Graeber and Scott see the state as antithetical to it. Hence the desire to recover freedom of imagination outside the time of the state. Graeber goes farther along this line than Scott, who presents its lack of imagination merely as a function of the state's overweening rationality. Graeber sees the state not as an ever-diligent surveillance system composed of keen-eyed experts always on alert (the Foucauldian paradigm) but as the structural embodiment of a pervasive mindlessness. The state's "ultimate purpose is to extract wealth in the form of profits" (UR, 17), a task it accomplishes by "organizing stupidity" (UR, 81) through "bureaucratic procedures" (UR, 57). Bureaucracy's elaborate maze of compulsory paperwork is designed "to make even the smartest people act like idiots" (UR, 95), to second-guess the evidence of their own intuitions (or *mētis*). Even when people are good at their jobs, the state introduces obstacles (like credentials) designed to remind them of their own inadequacy: "One could repeat the story in field after field, from nurses to art teachers, physical therapists to foreign policy consultants" (UR, 23).

"Bureaucracy" is Graeber's version of Scott's "high-modernist ideology," an abstract and generally arbitrary system that thwarts our native endowments: "Bureaucratic procedure invariably means ignoring all the subtleties of real social existence" (UR, 75). The state is a fiendishly perfect machine of structural violence because it secures the status quo of unequal life chances by deadening anyone's ability to imagine an alternative to this state of affairs. Just as Nozick claims that "people tend to forget the possibilities of acting independently of the state" (14), so Graeber concludes that bureaucracy's "war against the human imagination" (UR, 82) has stifled our ability to "realize we're being threatened, since we cannot imagine what it would be like not to be" (UR, 42). Even worse than its "legal extortion" of its subjects' money, then, is the state's depriving its subjects of their consciousness.

This is only to observe that Graeber alights on the neo-idealist claim that even the most generous of "welfare states," by virtue of their externalist indifference to valuing what goes on inside us, will inevitably subject the citizens under their aegis to a "soul-destroying conformity" (UR, 5). Thus though "the European social welfare state . . . can justly be considered . . . one of the greatest achievements of human civilization," according to Graeber,

> at the same time, in taking forms of willful blindness typical of the powerful and giving them the prestige of science—for instance, by adopting a whole series of assumptions about the meaning of work, family, neighborhood, knowledge, health, happiness, or success that had almost nothing to do with the way poor or working-class people actually lived their lives, let alone what they found meaningful in them—it set itself up for a fall. (UR, 82)

Drawing conclusions reminiscent of the antiutilitarian arguments canvased in chapter 1, Graeber traces the decline of the welfare state not to Thatcherism and Reaganomics—union-busting, tax breaks, and the privatization of public resources in the service of human greed—but to its unwillingness to take seriously the subjectivity of its explicit beneficiaries. As Rawls says of the utilitarian approach to social justice, welfarism "does not take seriously the distinction between persons."

Calling back to Milton Friedman's populism, Graeber's argument even reproduces one of the chief grievances aired in that economist's work: the proliferation of a credential culture whose effect is to generate jobs for bureaucrats at the expense of ordinary people's practical knowledge and the human benefits that follow from it. "Whether they be dentists, lawyers, cosmetologists, airline pilots, plumbers, or morticians," the Friedmans write in *Free to Choose*, "there is no occupation so remote that an attempt has not been made to restrict its practice by licensure."²⁴ As in Graeber and Scott, so in Friedman the authority of mindless rule-following takes priority over whatever aspirations to *mētis* average people might harbor. For all these writers, the state is an agentless agent, forever spinning itself away from and occluding the ground of its own possibility in "the many ordinary people's lives" (*UR*, 14) to which it pretends to be accountable. This overlap is not lost on Graeber, who freely admits admiration for a "libertarian Right" that "at least *has* a critique of bureaucracy" (*UR*, 6).

It might be unfair to overstate Graeber's sympathies with libertarians here. Fortunately, the point holds just as well when we look to seventies writers whose politics are as forward-thinking and anarchistic as his own. In the 2016 preface to her classic utopian novel *Woman on the Edge of Time* (1975), Marge Piercy describes her book as "profoundly anarchist and aimed at integrating people back into the natural world and eliminating power relationships."²⁵ But it is a striking feature of this novel that, notwithstanding its manifest class politics, Piercy's protagonist, Consuelo "Connie" Ramos, is continually besieged less by the predations of corporate capitalism or the free market run amok than by the machinery of the welfare state, "those experts lined up against her in a jury dressed in medical white and judicial black—social workers, caseworkers, child guidance counselors, psychiatrists, doctors, nurses, clinical psychologists, probation officers" (60). *Woman on the Edge of Time* is a novel of channeling if not precisely a next-life narrative. Connie is a "receptive" (41) contacted by Luciente, a woman from 150 years in the future who shows Connie the advances in the "Mattapoisett" (52) of 2137—a paleo-republic where everything is scarce except "space of your own" in which to "meditate, think, compose songs, sleep, study" (73). In keeping with the ratio in Paul Shepard's cynegetic society, Mattapoisett's low-density population enjoys a correspondingly high quality of individual life; its scarcity economics prepares the ground for an abundance of "inknowing resources" (56). If "your vocabulary is remarkably weak in words for mental states, mental abilities, and mental acts" (40), as Luciente tells Connie, it is because the welfare-state technologies that have "caught her and bound her in their nets" (60) have also worked chiefly to bring about the cessation of her consciousness. Involuntarily committed to a state psychiatric hospital, Connie is "injected" with drugs "right in the brain" to "turn you into a zombie" (208), then forced into an experimental surgery designed to control her very thoughts, to subdue her mind into permanent docility.

Connie learns that the future Luciente inhabits is but one possible path for which Connie's own time, the mid-seventies, is the inflection point in the "race between technology, in the service of those who control, and insurgency—those who want to change the society in our direction." At war with forces who use "brain control" and "birth-to-death surveillance" (242) to effect a universal incarceration, Luciente's people enjoy an equally absolute freedom that includes the power to manipulate their own mental states. Luciente teaches Connie how to "to go into delta in a few lessons" (243), a state "every six-year old could zip in and out of" (248) with ease in the future Luciente inhabits. Indeed among the wide array of "discipline[s]," to use Dickey's word, in the stateless Mattapoisett—where people are "often part-time hunters or gatherers, part-time shamans, part-time scientists" (297)—conditioning one's mind is by far the most impressive form of *mētis*. Mattapoisett's villagers can commune with the recently dead, meld minds with one another, and place their bodies into various states of being and feeling on command. Whereas "welfare . . . had been bitter to swallow, bitter as vomit," because it has reduced Connie's mental life to a "meager" (277) shadow of its former possibility, her time in Mattapoisett gives her a vision of the "better habits of minding" (301) that might thrive when consciousness is unleashed from the stupefactions of the state.

Both Graeber's and Piercy's antipathies to the state should put us in mind of the caveat I made in chapter 3 about forcing a clear divide between libertarians and anarchists. Graeber's critique of the state's monopoly on both taxation and imagination is virtually identical to Nozick's critique of the view that society should prevail over individuals, an ordering that both Graeber and Nozick treat as a form of indenture. "The fact that we partially are 'social products' in that we benefit from current patterns and forms created by the multitudinous actions of a long string of long-forgotten people," Nozick argues, "does not create in us a general floating debt which the current society can collect and use as it will" (95). Graeber seeks to overturn "the notion that there is this thing called society, that we have a debt to it, that governments can speak for it, that it can be imagined as a sort of secular god" (D, 69). The new anarchists share the antiutilitarian aim of locating the problem with statism in its impermissible bid for transcendence. "There is no social entity with a good that undergoes some sacrifice for its own good," Nozick concludes. "There are only individual people, different individual people, with their own individual lives" (32).

No one can have the omniscient vantage the state pretends to have. High-modernist ideology is self-defeating, according to Scott, because it insists on viewing everything—whether the city or the farm or the industrial division of labor—"from above" (2), a penchant made clear in the modernist urban planner's mania for "scale models upon which patron and planner gaze down"

(57), pretending to "a perspective that no or very few human observers will ever replicate" (58). Contrary to Henry Sidgwick, the universe doesn't have a point of view that it would be possible—or even desirable—for any individual to assume. What makes the state's transcendence illegitimate is finally its usurping the potential for individuals to achieve their own transcendence by binding the multiplicity of persons to the ultimate person of the state. It is instructive to compare the state as a "secular god" to a relevant personification in seventies thought, James Lovelock's Gaia. Like the state, Gaia possesses a self-maintaining body; unlike the state, it has the virtue of *indifference* to human subjects. Rather than absorb them, Gaia appears intent on expelling persons from its ambit, as radical ecology has shown us.

To speak of transcendence as a live concern in seventies culture is to run aground on the most influential account of late-capitalist culture of the last generation: Fredric Jameson's *Postmodernism, or, The Cultural Logic of Late Capitalism* (1991). Jameson characterizes postmodernism as a "denial of the transcendent" (185), a "flight from transcendence" (250), and, relatedly and more famously, as a regime in which "Utopian transformation" is no longer "expected or desired" (42). The "Utopian transcendence" that matters to Jameson requires escape velocity from "the market" (95). From the vantage I have pursued here, utopianism is not nearly so moribund as Jameson suggests. But the contemporary variant of Utopianism is not particularly amenable to the dialectic of social reimagining that Jameson's argument encourages. It might be more accurate to say that our time presents us with an inverted utopianism, in which imagining alternative worlds means imagining the *absence* of the world and the thrill of being its only survivor rather than imagining how to overcome any given social limits. Jameson acknowledges this point in a later, now notorious adage about contemporary narratives of apocalypse like those of Dick or Le Guin: "Someone once said it is easier to imagine the end of the world than to imagine the end of capitalism."[26] Implicit in this claim is the idea that utopias count for Jameson only when they pose alternatives to capitalism; anything short of such portrayal can be discarded as ideology.

Jameson's glib aperçu takes for granted that we can understand the vicissitudes of late capitalism merely by invoking "capitalism" itself as what constrains imagination. The claim is at best tautological; and like many tautologies, it fairly hollows itself out. It tells us little about the structural conditions Jameson vaunts as explanations. My approach has been to fill in such hollowness by restoring to the seventies, that pivotal postmodern decade, something like its "inner life," a task aptly suited to the study of the decade by virtue of its fulsome embrace of subjectivity and consciousness. Famously for Jameson, "the windless present of the postmodern" fosters a correspondingly static and flattened subjectivity incapable of "breaking . . . back into real historical time, and a history made by human beings."[27] Like the stultifying bureaucracy in Graeber, postmodern "reification" at its most menacing for Jameson tends to "occupy our minds" so completely that it convinces us of our "inability to control our own destiny" (318). This complaint resonates with the calls for agency not just from Graeber or Scott but also from, say, the economist and Republican presidential adviser Allen Wallis, who writes in his 1976 polemic *An Overgoverned Society*: "Our economy must provide conditions that develop the mind and the spirit. . . . It must provide expanding opportunities for every individual to realize his own potentialities to the utmost."[28]

Jameson might object that the fixation on individuals gives the game away, since "social classes" (53) are the locus of agency and any consequent bids for "Utopian transcendence." And though from the Marxist angle he would be right to emphasize the promise of the "achieved collective" (342), his own examples of the "Utopian gesture" (7) derive overwhelmingly from singular artists. Where utopia is concerned, collectivity and individuality are in persistent tension in *Postmodernism*. (Van Gogh's *Shoes* as read through Heidegger is the book's most poignant example of this tension.) The modernist fetishization of individualism via the cult of genius furnished the ground for a "universalizing and utopian spirit" (58), a condition lost after the defeat of modernism's ideology of aesthetic and personal autonomy. The "extinction of the 'great moderns'" (306) follows from a more general extermination: "the disappearance of the individual subject, along with its formal consequence" (16).

To the extent that my book has insisted on the individual subject's rebirth in post-sixties culture, I cannot help finding Jameson's view inadequate. On his theory of postmodernism, the market triumphs because it breaks the subject down into a more or less automated unit, a creature of "schizophrenic flux" (175), a "fragmented . . . self" (345) unhampered by the Kantian imperative to collect itself in a coherent whole. The postmodern subject is the flashpoint for affects, appetites, and intensities made irresistible by the "immense dilation" (x) of the forces of consumerism and the "conditioning mechanisms of bureaucratic society" (88). Jamesonian postmodernism presents as a "post-individualistic age" (306) where externalism reigns supreme, where behaviorism was never put to rout, where a Skinnerian "nonessentialism without the last shred of essence in it" (xii) has altogether displaced essentialist versions of "innate" (306) or "deep subjectivity" (311). The cultural logic of late capitalism deletes first-person ontology.

The story I have been telling is different. In the account this book lays out, markets triumph because they prize the very subjectivity retrieved from the mechanistic and deterministic and utilitarian world, the high-modernist world, of the twentieth-century welfare state. The "centered subject" (339), as Jameson puts it, hasn't succumbed to the marketization of the lifeworld. If anything, the market has brought back to life a subject whose rumored death has been greatly exaggerated. To observe this point, however, is to circle back to the question of what, exactly, it means in twenty-first-century US culture to be a subject. Proof of massive upwellings of fair and reciprocal interpersonal relations or the flourishing of individual dignity is not easy to find. Indeed, we have no more reason to imagine we've eliminated statist overreaching in our society than to think of it as a full-fledged meritocracy.[29] In the age of what we might term *big nongovernment*, concerted efforts from the right, housed in think tanks bankrolled by billionaires and sustained by a vast network of media propagandists, fundamentalist churches, and astroturfing outlets, has actually generated a shadow state dedicated less to winding down government than to reallocating its use of force to the regulation of private lives while freeing markets up to regulate themselves.

We need not pine for the heyday of corporate liberalism to feel a certain ruefulness at the discovery that the autonomy promised by neo-idealism has been realized above all in the person of the corporation on a scale far beyond what literal persons can expect. Yet given this turnabout, we might also be forgiven for asking why some academics on the left have been quite happy to see corporate liberalism undone. To be clear, the phrase alone affords its own answer, since it compounds terms against which the left academy has long defined itself. If corporate liberalism once seemed the last redoubt of a capitalism willing to undertake any means to preserve its own necessity, to convince us that liberalism and corporatism had brought us to the end of history, it is conceivable that some left academics take consolation in that system's collapse and inevitable replacement by socialist revolution. Few of us entertain this improbable vision, of course, despite the fact that corporate liberalism is all but defunct. In the interest of clearing a path to this book's finish line and also clearing up a question that has occurred to some early audiences for this work, I suggest that the rejection of corporate liberalism has become our name for what I have been calling antiutilitarianism. That critique suffers from a distortion that carries over into the antistatism, and in particular the antiliberalism, found throughout the contemporary "cultural disciplines." It is past time to admit that utilitarianism has never been hegemonic in the way that some otherwise careful philosophers liked to present it. Along with the meretricious meritocracy and the selective deregulation of the paternalistic state, this is a mid-century myth worth scrutinizing.

Some early responders to this book have been curious about what my own politics might be, whether in particular my analysis of antiutilitarianism arises from a prior commitment to utilitarian theory. The query is both understandable and regrettable. We like to know where others stand in relation to their own arguments. But that preference often makes us overlook the fact that political or moral positions are divorcible in theory from critical analysis. While so self-evident as to need no articulation in many areas outside the cultural disciplines, this norm has been off the map of the literary academy for a while. To the extent that utilitarianism is attractive to me as practice, at any rate, I would happily out myself as an adherent. But such a profession is fairly meaningless, I would also urge, since what utilitarianism looks like in practice has never been pursued in the way that its harshest critics have imagined, to say nothing of how its strongest defenders would like to see it executed. (This is likely true of all ethical theories.) Bernard Williams archly notes that utilitarianism can never be put into practice because to be a utilitarian obliges one to deny its central precepts. No one in her right mind would abide the theory's willingness to trade up individuals for an imagined greater good, much less its stipulation that individuals should be only too willing to sacrifice themselves in that cause. What he calls the "capacity of utilitarianism . . . to annihilate itself" follows from the fact that a "reflective utilitarian must finally settle on . . . a world in which . . . enough people enough of the time are deeply disposed against thinking in a utilitarian fashion." "If utilitarianism is true," Williams concludes, "then it is better that people should not believe in utilitarianism."[30]

Peter Singer, the most famous utilitarian philosopher alive, has popularized various efforts to get people to "believe in utilitarianism." His advocacy work, whether in animal liberation or effective altruism, has found receptive if not exactly mainstream audiences. But among his many critics we find a consistent group of them who take Singer to task for a perceived excess of rigor that makes utilitarian morality impossible to live with. For the philosopher Susan Wolf, Singer-style utilitarianism is what Larissa MacFarquar calls an "extreme morality," akin to an extreme sport or energy drink: superficially invigorating and even tempting but ultimately bad for your health.[31] "Moral perfection," writes Wolf, "does not constitute a model of personal well-being toward which it would be particularly rational or good or desirable for a human being to strive," since "there seems to be a limit to how much morality we can stand."[32] Such judgments recall the charge among seventies antiutilitarians that the theory is boundaryless, indeed so unrestricted in its scope as to be self-defeating from the vantage of what Wolf calls "the recognition of our own dignified rationality" (432).[33] Utilitarians will ransom their beliefs if it means bringing the theory to fruition (Williams's view) or surrender their identities if it means serving as altruistic vessels through which the milk of human kindness passes

(Wolf's view).³⁴ And underlying *this* assumption is the notion that the utilitarian is a pure instrumentalist eager to seize on any means to bring about best outcomes, even (or especially) if these include the full force of the state.

Beneath the masks of moral saints we find officious bureaucrats whose commitment to government largesse proves their indifference to persons. Such at least is the inference of Tyler Cowen, a libertarian economist who criticizes Singer for "suggest[ing] that government should take a lead role in directing [wealth] redistribution" by levying "much higher levels of taxation and government spending."³⁵ For Cowen, this "misplaced" (302) preference for "coercive taxation" (301) is in line with the unsavory demandingness of utilitarian theory, since both impose undue burdens on ordinary individuals. In Cowen's view, "major benefits" flow to people the world over through "economic growth" (313), which he considers "a better means of helping the poor than is redistribution" (317). In painting Singer as a cheerleader for the "welfare state" despite "the risk of personal enslavement or massive redistribution" (317) it entails, Cowen rehearses the drama, recognizable from antiutilitarian discourse, in which utilitarian theory is the enemy of a human worth that only the free market can uphold.

The problem with Cowen's portrayal of Singer in particular and utilitarianism in general is that it's false. In a reply to Cowen's essay, Singer begins: "Tyler Cowen spends much of his time arguing against positions I have never held."³⁶ Even casual readers of Singer's work might recall that his "emphasis has always been on voluntary giving to non-government organizations," which he sees as "more effective than government aid" (320). And Singer is not so "hostile to markets" as Cowen takes him to be. "I am not willing to endorse a capitalist market economy," Singer writes, "as a *sufficient* means of poverty alleviation" (324). Singer's utilitarianism looks rather different from the seventies version. Whereas antiutilitarians saw the theory as a kind of statist apologetics, Singer manifests little patience for state power to effect change. As he puts it in *How Are We To Live?* (1993), "it is not in the interests of politicians to challenge the fundamental assumptions of the society they have been elected to lead."³⁷ And by the same token, he seems if anything *too* convinced of the agency of individuals when it comes to doing the right thing (giving to the poor, holding their governments accountable, using their reason).

One reason states have such low prestige in his work is that Singer understands ethics as a "realistic and viable alternative to the present," with real-world effects that need to be distinguished from the political as such (278). Ethics is Singer's name for the sort of action—or even activism—designed to assert the power of responsible human beings over and above any state structure: "If 10 percent of the population were to take a consciously ethical outlook on life and act accordingly, the resulting change would be more significant than any change of government" (278). I am less interested in passing judgment on the wisdom of this claim, which surely raises urgent questions about what counts as "an ethical outlook" and who gets to decide *that*, than in observing how close it comes to the values of what I have called neo-idealism. The keyword is "consciously," of course—the central desideratum of the neo-idealist "outlook." As if responding to the charge that the utilitarian submerges herself in what Wolf calls "the general happiness" at the cost of any "aspects of life unique to *herself*" (429), Singer appears to retrieve self-identity as one of the ends of utilitarian practice. If you embrace "a consciously ethical outlook," "you will find plenty of worthwhile things to do," "you will not be bored, or lack fulfilment in your life" (280). This address to the generic second-person, the singular reader, rubs up in the same paragraph of *How Are We to Live?* against the "impartial" and "impersonal" nonsubjectivity that has long menaced utilitarian theory: "Anyone can become part of the critical mass that offers us a chance of improving the world" (279).

Singer suspends his ethics between the critical mass and the individual who finds "fulfilment" in ethical practice. In his view, neither can do without the other. But what both can surely do without, it might surprise us to learn, is the superstate that relentlessly dogs our subjectivity, an intrusion that utilitarianism has mistakenly been understood to encourage. Perhaps it is time to reckon with this misunderstanding. But doing so may require us to take up the subject of ethics even if we decline Singer's own "ethical outlook." Philosophical ethics affords an assist to the cultural disciplines that they have largely ignored. I'm speaking not of the "ethical turn," which proceeds as if canonical texts from William Shakespeare to Henry James provide models for how to live, but of the discipline's value in combating neoliberalism's advances on the terrain of morality. Neoliberalism has found in neo-idealism a way to present "capitalism," to quote Singer, as "an *ethically sanctioned* way of life" (66). At this juncture, we could do a lot worse than revisit utilitarian theory and its supposedly dubious principle of the greater good, if only as a counterpoint to an ethics founded on the suspicion that programs designed to benefit the disadvantaged somehow rob them of both freedom and dignity.

Notes

Introduction

1. One reason not to align this book with the ethical turn in literary studies is that few if any critics can say precisely what that turn is, much less whether any contemporary critic is actually engaged in it. Elaine Scarry is perhaps the most eligible candidate for "ethical critic" in the contemporary academy; but it seems to me that a book like *On Beauty and Being Just* (Princeton, NJ: Princeton University Press, 1999) is a defense of aesthetic value as a liberating or progressive force rather than a brief for ethics—in other words that it indexes less the ethical than the aesthetic turn. In the introduction to *The Turn to Ethics*, edited by Marjorie Garber, Beatrice Hanssen, and Rebecca Walkowitz (New York: Routledge, 2000), the editors describe "ethics" as "not only a praxis, but also a principle," as well as "a process of formulation and self-questioning that continually rearticulates boundaries, norms, selves, and 'others'" (viii). Such descriptions might bewilder any reader of moral philosophy (if not simply any reader). They lead this particular reader to the conclusion that the "ethical" in the anthology's title is just a rebranding of "poststructuralist." The scare quotes around "others" are of course a giveaway, as is the claim that "the decentering of the subject has brought about a recentering of the ethical" (ix). Meanwhile, the last generation has seen an interesting development among some moral philosophers whose goal is to promote the edifying work of literary texts. The definitive critique of such arguments, with representative examples from Colin McGinn, Robert Pippin, and Martha Nussbaum, is Candace Vogler, "The Moral of the Story," *Critical Inquiry* 34, no. 1 (2007): 5–35. Vogler sees the philosophical turn to literary moralism as mired in category mistakes. If "the usual ambition in this sort of work is to gain insight into moral psychology" (6), its procedure typically entails a "slide from fictional figure to literary character to imaginary person to person, and back again, with scarcely a bump or a wobble" (8).

2. John Rawls, *A Theory of Justice* (Cambridge, MA: Harvard University Press, 1971), 53. Hereafter cited in text.

3. Raël, *Geniocracy: Government of the People, for the People, by the Geniuses* (1977; Edison, NJ: Nova Distribution, 2008), 9.

4. Raël, *Geniocracy*, 11.

5. While hundreds of mindfulness apps are now available online, the industry is a virtual duopoly controlled by Headspace and Calm, which are "locked," according to a 2018 *Wall Street Journal* article, "in a head-to-head fight to dominate the booming $1.2 billion meditation market." Hilary Potkewitz, "Headspace vs. Calm: The Meditation

Battle That's Anything but Zen," *Wall Street Journal*, December 15, 2018, 3. On the takeover of the corporate boardroom by the mindfulness industry, see David Gelles, *Mindful Work: How Meditation Is Changing Business from the Inside Out* (New York: Eamon Dolan, 2015).

6. On survivalism among the one-percenters, see Evan Osnos, "Doomsday Prep for the Super-Rich," *New Yorker*, January 30, 2017; on the capital investment in immortality, see Tad Friend, "Silicon Valley's Quest to Live Forever," *New Yorker*, April 3, 2017; on the revival of social Darwinism in a "paleo" guise, see Marlene Zuk, *Paleo-Fantasy: What Evolution Really Tells Us About Sex, Diet, and How We Live* (New York: Norton, 2013). Tech culture is notable for combining bleeding-edge innovation with what are taken to be facts of life that evolved eons ago. Consider the mission statement of Bulletproof® Diet, founded by Dave Asprey, "a Silicon Valley investor and technology entrepreneur who spent two decades and over $1 Million to hack his own biology": "Our mission is to help people perform better, think faster, and live better using a proven blend of ancient knowledge and brand new technologies." See "Welcome to Bulletproof," accessed July 7, 2019, https://www.bulletproof.com/about-us.

7. But here, too, seventies observers point the way to the union of high and low against an "establishment" middle, their common enemy. "On the whole," Joan Didion writes in a 1977 essay on the Getty Museum, "'the critics' distrust great wealth, but 'the public' does not." J. Paul Getty's lavish marble pile rising above the Pacific Coast Highway thus stands "as one of those odd monuments, a palpable contract between the very rich and the people who distrust them least." *The White Album* (New York: Simon and Schuster, 1979), 78.

8. I mean less the refutation of Marxist thought (an important though ancillary matter) than the widely shared assumption that society was broken in ways that did not admit of repair. These connotations, antisocial and anti-Marxist, frequently overlap. Consider Robin Morgan's legendary feminist manifesto "Goodbye to All That" (1970), whose very title gestures toward a repudiation of the world as found, including the "bullshit" ideas of "socialist revolution" and "socialist equality" that "all our good socialist brothers want us to believe." See "'Goodbye to All That,' by Robin Morgan (1970)," September 29, 2007, http://blog.fair-use.org/2007/09/29/goodbye-to-all-that-by-robin-morgan-1970/.

9. Cited in Peter N. Carroll, *It Seemed Like Nothing Happened: America in the 1970s* (1982; New Brunswick, NJ: Rutgers University Press, 2000), 339.

10. Albert O. Hirschman, *Exit, Voice, and Loyalty: Responses to Decline in Firms, Organizations, and States* (Cambridge, MA: Harvard University Press, 1970). Hereafter cited in text.

11. Hirschman attributes some of the asymmetry between exit and voice to the fact that exit is a strategy of the privileged, who will respond faster to the deterioration of a good than to its rising price by willingly opting into alternatives—like private schools—whose costs they can bear. "The presence of the exit alternative can therefore tend to *atrophy the development of the art of voice*" (43), Hirschman concludes, on the view that high-prestige social actors will defect rather than seek remediation from an imperfect or unsatisfactory system.

12. A rather drastic contemporary effort to apply "exit" strategies to the political order is the Seasteading Institute, founded by Patri Friedman, Milton's grandson, and funded by the billionaire Peter Thiel. "Because there are no truly free places left in

our world," Thiel writes, "I suspect that the mode for escape must involve some sort of new and hitherto untried process that leads us to some undiscovered country." See "The Education of a Libertarian," April 13, 2009, https://www.cato-unbound.org/2009/04/13/peter-thiel/education-libertarian. Hence Thiel's partnering with the Seasteading Institute, which plans to build ocean platforms two hundred nautical miles from any sovereign state, "where those who wish to experiment with building new societies can go to test out their ideas." See "About," accessed July 7, 2019, https://www.seasteading.org/about/.

13. For an example of this moralism, see Edwin Schur's *The Awareness Trap: Self-Absorption Instead of Social Change* (New York: Quadrangle, 1976). Schur is committed to the view that (to use his title) "social change" stops where the project of "self-absorption" begins. The "ideology of awareness," according to Schur, is "socially harmful" (2). Rejecting this zero-sum game, neo-idealism's advocates argue for the continuity between personal consciousness and political experience, with implications for politics that the current book spells out.

14. Carroll, *It Seemed Like Nothing Happened*, 349.

15. Theodore Roszak, *Unfinished Animal: The Aquarian Frontier and the Evolution of Consciousness* (New York: Harper & Row, 1975), 10. Hereafter cited in text.

16. Theodore Roszak, *The Making of a Counter Culture: Reflections on the Technocratic Society and Its Youthful Opposition* (1969; Berkeley: University of California Press, 1995), 62.

17. Other observers had a less enthusiastic view of consciousness-raising. "Forecast for the next five years: Consciousness will be the country's quickest-flourishing growth industry" (5), the sixties stalwart Michael Rossman wrote in a 1972 essay for *Creem* reprinted in *New Age Blues: On The Politics of Consciousness* (New York: Dutton, 1979). Lamenting that "too many people will take to the easy lotus, giving up the task of integrating what we have begun" (5), Rossman predicts a steep decline in "the investment of our energies in political change" as "devotional ideologies" take center stage (20).

18. Tom Wolfe, *The Purple Decades: A Reader* (New York: Farrar Straus Giroux, 1982), 269, 290. Hereafter cited in text.

19. Christopher Lasch, *The Culture of Narcissism: American Life in an Age of Diminishing Expectations* (1979; New York: Norton, 1991), xv.

20. Alvin Toffler, *Future Shock* (New York: Bantam, 1971), 2. Hereafter cited in text.

21. George W.S. Trow, *Within the Context of No Context* (New York: Atlantic, 1997), 43. Hereafter cited in text.

22. Robert Ornstein, *The Psychology of Consciousness* (New York: Harcourt Brace Jovanovich, 1977), 10.

23. It is arguable that the scholarly aversion to libertarianism as a literary genre marks something of a limit to the aspiration to "open the canon" in the contemporary humanities, which have been very welcoming of subcultures and genres from romance to science fiction to heavy metal. One name for that limit might be *patience*. To the extent that libertarian novels are more instructive than delighting, they attract true believers rather than skeptics, the ego ideal of the literary critic. Here we might think of the entire corpus of Ayn Rand's fiction along with many of the novels of Robert Heinlein and those of such self-styled libertarian science fiction writers as L. Neil Smith. These are texts whose messaging is so explicit and absolute that it allows *almost* no

room for rhetorical interpretation, the critic's stock in trade. To be sure, this is not the only site of hermeneutic interest in any text, which one might fairly argue is always open to interpretation. But libertarian fiction is a particularly inhospitable venue for criticism of any sophistication because its blunt-force messaging is also affixed to a style that willfully negates aesthetic complexity. Libertarian novels are in the business of inculcation rather than plurisignificance. It may be more accurate to say that libertarian fiction denies any *formal* interest of the sort that even the most context-driven critic requires of a text to make it worthy of a "reading." (This is not quite the same thing as simply judging such fiction bad.) Dialogue in libertarian novels features characters who talk like this: "A free, unregulated laissez-faire market should, and can, take care of everything government *claims* to do, only better, cheaper, and without wrecking individual lives in the process." L. Neil Smith, *The Probability Broach* (1979; New York: Orb, 2001), 27. Or this: "In writing your constitution let me invite attention to the wonderful virtues of the negative! Accentuate the negative! Let your document be studded with things the government is forever forbidden to do. No conscript armies . . . no interference however slight with freedom of press, or speech, or travel, or assembly, or of religion, or of instruction, or communication, or occupation . . . no involuntary taxation." Robert A. Heinlein, *The Moon Is a Harsh Mistress* (1965; New York: Orb, 1994), 302.

24. John Searle, *Mind: A Brief Introduction* (New York: Oxford University Press, 2004), 4; Thomas Nagel, *The View from Nowhere* (New York: Oxford University Press, 1986), 153.

25. John Searle, *The Rediscovery of the Mind* (Cambridge, MA: MIT Press, 1992), xii.

26. Daniel T. Rodgers, *Age of Fracture* (Cambridge, MA: Harvard University Press, 2011), 3.

27. Rodgers, *Age of Fracture*, 2.

28. Rodgers, *Age of Fracture*, 3.

29. Searle, *Rediscovery*, xiv.

30. Jacques Derrida, *Of Grammatology*, trans. Gayatri Spivak (Baltimore: Johns Hopkins University Press, 1997), 158.

31. Richard Rorty, *Contingency, Irony, and Solidarity* (New York: Cambridge University Press, 1989), 5.

32. Nelson Goodman, *Ways of World-Making* (Indianapolis: Hackett, 1978), 20.

33. Paul Feyerabend, *Against Method* (1975; London: New Left Books, 1993), 11. Hereafter cited in text.

34. Both these earlier movements specifically define idealism against materialism first and foremost. "The materialist insists on facts, on history, on the force of circumstances," Emerson writes in "The Transcendentalist" (1842); "the idealist on the power of Thought and of Will." For the idealist, "Mind is the only reality, of which men and all other natures are better or worse reflectors." Joel Porte, ed., *Ralph Waldo Emerson: Essays & Lectures* (New York: Library of America, 1983), 193, 195. "Pragmatism . . . has no such materialistic bias as ordinary empiricism labors under," James writes. It is "interested in no conclusions but those which our minds and our experiences work out together." More method than doctrine, pragmatism for James "unstiffens our theories," with which "we move forward, and, on occasion, make nature over again by their aid." "What Pragmatism Means," in *William James: Writings 1902–1910*, ed. Bruce Kuklik (New York: Library of America, 1987), 518, 510. As Richard Hofstadter long ago pointed out, James—while clearly taking aim at what he calls the "barrenness of

transcendental idealism" (483) in "What Pragmatism Means"—construed pragmatism as a weapon against Herbert Spencer's materialism, much vaunted on both sides of the English-speaking Atlantic. "The Spencerians had attributed social changes to geography, environment, external circumstances," Hofstadter writes, "in brief to everything but human control." Hence "James's objection to Spencer arose partly because James was in search of a philosophy that would acknowledge active human effort in the bettering of life." *Social Darwinism in American Thought* (1944; Boston: Beacon Press, 1992), 132, 129.

35. Immanuel Kant, *Critique of Pure Reason*, trans. and ed. Paul Geyer and Allen Wood (New York: Cambridge University Press, 1998), 419.

36. Nagel, *The View from Nowhere*, 7.

37. Kant claims in the *Critique of Pure Reason* that, as a noumenon (derived from the Greek for "mind"), consciousness or understanding cannot itself be submitted to analysis, even though its close proximity to us—we all have it, after all—renders almost irresistible the temptation to make of it a knowable substance. "Since . . . intellectual intuition," he writes, "lies absolutely outside our faculty of cognition, the use of the categories can by no means reach beyond the boundaries of the objects of experience" (361). The price we pay for the mind's freedom from the determinism of nature is an inability to grasp whatever laws govern it.

38. Colin McGinn advances the view that consciousness is an "absolutely insoluble" mystery in *The Problem of Consciousness: Essays Toward a Resolution* (Cambridge, MA: Blackwell, 1991), 16. Owen Flanagan dubbed McGinn and Nagel "mysterians" in *The Science of Mind* (Cambridge, MA: MIT Press, 1991), 313.

39. John C. Lilly, *Center of the Cyclone: An Autobiography of Inner Space* (1972; Portland, OR: Coincident Control, 2017), 34.

40. John C. Lilly, *The Scientist: A Metaphysical Autobiography* (1978; Berkeley, CA: Ronin, 1997), 3. Hereafter cited in text.

41. "Around 1970," according to Kurt Anderson, "*consensus reality* became a permanent interdisciplinary term of art in academia." It was popularized by the psychologist Charles Tart, who earned tenure at the University of California, Davis partly on the strength of an experiment in which a "'young woman who frequently had spontaneous out-of-body experiences' . . . spent four nights sleeping in his lab," where she managed to "send her mind or soul out of her body while she was asleep." *Fantasyland: How America Went Haywire: A 500-Year History* (New York: Random House, 2017), 195, 196.

42. Amartya Sen, *Collective Choice and Social Welfare* (Cambridge, MA: Harvard University Press, 2017), 341.

43. Stuart Hampshire, "Morality and Pessimism," in *Public and Private Morality*, ed. Stuart Hampshire (Cambridge, UK: Cambridge University Press, 1978), 12, 13.

44. Robert Boguslaw, *The New Utopians: A Study of System Design and Social Change* (Englewood Cliffs, NJ: Prentice-Hall, 1965), 1, 29. Hereafter cited in text.

45. Michael Sandel, "Political Liberalism," *Harvard Law Review* 107, no. 7 (1994): 1765.

46. The fallibility of Rawls's judgment can be inferred from the conclusion of Henry Sidgwick's *The Methods of Ethics* (London: Macmillan, 1907), modern utilitarianism's canonical text: "The distinction between any one individual and another is real, and fundamental" (498).

47. Lincoln Allison, "Utilitarianism: What Is It and Why Should It Respond?" in *The Utilitarian Reply*, ed. Allison (London: Sage, 1990), 5–6.

48. Thomas Nagel, *The Possibility of Altruism* (Oxford: Clarendon, 1970), 138. Not all of Rawls's students agree that utilitarianism fails to account for human distinctiveness. In the 1982 essay "Contractualism and Utilitarianism," T. M. Scanlon defines utilitarianism as "the thesis that the only fundamental moral facts are facts about individual well-being" (131). In contrast to the "contractualism" he supports, utilitarianism for Scanlon is finally too abstract to be a plausible "account of moral motivation" (150). See *The Difficulty of Tolerance: Essays in Political Philosophy* (Cambridge, UK: Cambridge University Press, 2003).

49. Nagel, *Possibility*, 138.

50. G. E. M. Anscombe, "Modern Moral Philosophy," *Philosophy* 33, no.124 (1958): 12, 13.

51. Lyons, *The Forms and Limits of Utilitarianism* (Oxford: Clarendon Press, 1965), xi, 189.

52. Bernard Williams, *Morality: An Introduction to Ethics* (Cambridge, UK: Cambridge University Press, 1993), 94.

53. Lasch, *Culture*, xiii.

54. William Appleman Williams, "Introduction: A Profile of the Corporate Elite," *A New History of Leviathan*, ed. Murray Rothbard and Ronald Radosh (New York: Dutton, 1972), 1.

55. Williams, "Introduction," 4, 6.

56. Rothbard and Radosh, "Preface," *A New History of Leviathan*, viii.

57. Williams, *Morality*, 89.

58. Robert Paul Wolff, *Understanding Rawls: A Reconstruction and Critique of A Theory of Justice* (Princeton, NJ: Princeton University Press, 1977), 14. Hereafter cited in text.

59. Robert Nozick, *Anarchy, State, and Utopia* (New York: Basic, 1974), 168, 320.

60. For an antiutilitarian like David Gauthier, the alternative to utilitarianism is explicitly the free market. "Those who had been converted to the utilitarian gospel abandoned the free market for the welfare state," Gauthier writes, "little realizing that . . . they had also abandoned the framework of value and reason." "On the Refutation of Utilitarianism," in *The Limits of Utilitarianism*, ed. Harlan Miller and William H. Williams (Minneapolis, MN: 1982), 162. Gauthier's Hobbesian contractualism is eccentric to antiutilitarian thought to the degree that it refuses to mask its stark ideological commitment to laissez-faire. Rawls's Kantian contract theory is the preferred mode in which liberal political philosophy represents what economic relations look like in a just society.

61. In the preface to the revised edition of *A Theory of Justice* (Cambridge, MA: Belknap, 1999), Rawls explicitly contrasts the "welfare state" with what he calls a "property-owning democracy." For the purpose of affording the best framework for a well-ordered society, according to Rawls, the former loses from the comparison. Whereas the welfare state merely doles out assistance to society's unfortunates in a way that "may allow large and inheritable inequities of wealth incompatible with the fair value of the political liberties," a property-owning democracy strives "to put all citizens in a position to manage their own affairs and to take part in social cooperation on a footing of mutual respect under appropriately equal conditions." It thus provides the right context for "reciprocity, or mutuality, for society seen as a fair

system of cooperation among free and equal citizens from one generation to the next" (xv).

62. R. M. Hare, "Rawls's Theory of Justice, Part I," *Philosophical Quarterly* 23, no. 91 (1973): 145.

63. John Rawls, "Kantian Constructivism in Moral Theory," *Journal of Philosophy* 77, no. 9 (1980): 519.

64. In *Postmodernism, or, The Cultural Logic of Late Capitalism* (Durham, NC: Duke University Press, 1991), Fredric Jameson notes the "strategic regression to Kant" in seventies "post Marxism," which pursued a "rolling back of Marx and Hegel by way of the conceptual discrediting of contradiction and the dialectical opposition" (344).

65. Rawls, "Kantian Constructivism," 519.

66. Christine M. Korsgaard, *Self-Constitution: Agency, Identity, and Integrity* (New York: Oxford University Press, 2009), 19. Another pop Kantian parallel: Compare Korsgaard's claim that "a human being is an animal who needs a practical conception of her own identity" (*Sources*, 123) to Roszak's claim that "Alone among the creatures, we can fail to become what we were born to become" (85). Korsgaard argues that "personhood is quite literally a form of life, and being a person . . . is being engaged in an activity of self-constitution" (19); Roszak writes: "As we discover ourselves in the world at any stage of life, we are incomplete—and so we remain until, by an act of reflection and decision, we resolve to achieve our being" (85).

67. Christine M. Korsgaard, *The Sources of Normativity* (New York: Cambridge University Press, 1996), 248.

68. "There is no self that is prior to the convergence" of "discursive conjunctions," Butler writes, "or who maintains 'integrity' prior to its entrance into this conflicted cultural field." Nor is there "a transcendental subject who enables action in the midst of such a convergence." *Gender Trouble: Feminism and the Subversion of Identity* (New York: Routledge, 1990), 185. What Butler disagrees with in the Kantian account, of course, is the status of first-person ontology. When she writes that "'I' deploy the grammar that governs the genre of the philosophical conclusion, but note that it is the grammar itself that deploys and enables this 'I'" (185–186), her implication is that "grammar itself" is one of those "discursive conjunctions" that performatively bring about a construct we mistake for essence. It is worth noting, in advance of the argument in chapter 1, that Butler's view of "grammar" is essentially Skinnerian. More specifically, it appears to hew to the Sapir-Whorf hypothesis, a theory of linguistic determinism whereby a language controls the mode of thought of the language's user. The Chomskyan paradigm that long ago defeated behavioral linguistics insists on the innateness of both our capacity for language and our subjectivity. The two are inseparable evolutionary facts. Whether Chomsky's universal grammar can withstand the forceful criticisms made against it by evolutionary psychologists is not a concern I take up in these pages, except to note that such critiques often fault the theory of universal grammar for not being evolutionary *enough*.

69. Nozick, *Anarchy*, 214.

70. G. A. Cohen, *If You're an Egalitarian How Come You're So Rich?* (Cambridge, MA: Harvard University Press, 2000), 140, 135.

71. Milton and Rose Friedman, *Free to Choose: A Personal Statement* (New York: Harcourt, 1990), 309. Hereafter cited in text.

72. In *The Great Persuasion: Reinventing Free Markets since the Depression* (Cambridge, MA: Harvard University Press, 2012), Angus Burgin describes Friedman's "unapologetic populism" thus: "He worked to convince his audiences that he shared their most humane ends—the well-being of the poor and the establishment of a broad-based prosperity" (188). Burgin observes that Friedman's attitude was not strictly rhetorical: "He attempted to treat all people equally regardless of their rank or position, and his personal files are filled with multi-page responses to the peculiar questions of obscure individuals" (192).

73. "Neoliberalization," David Harvey observes in *A Brief History of Neoliberalism* (New York: Oxford University Press, 2005), "required both politically and economically the construction of a neoliberal market-based populist culture of differentiated consumerism and individual libertarianism." Harvey takes a cynical view of the defense of "individual freedoms," which he sees as "more than a little compatible with that cultural impulse called 'postmodernism'" (42). But as I have already observed, it would be hard to square a philosopher like Rawls, not to say Searle or Nozick, with "the postmodern turn" (57).

74. In *Free to Choose*, the critique of regulation is aimed not so much at the state that creates red tape as at the industries that use regulation to guard their own interests from "the full rigors of competition" (193). In a series of papers over two decades, Friedman's Chicago colleague George Stigler argued that far from serving the public interest, regulatory agencies become captive to business sectors that lobby the state for policies—from restriction on entry to licensing and price controls—that help them realize monopolies: "Regulation is acquired by [an] industry and is designed and operated primarily for its benefit" (3). See "The Theory of Economic Regulation," *Bell Journal of Economics and Management Science* 2, no. 1 (1971): 3–21.

75. In *A Brief History of Neoliberalism*, Harvey describes how "neoliberal rhetoric" from the seventies on has made it "extremely difficult within the US left, for example, to forge the collective discipline required for political action to achieve social justice without offending the desire of political actors for individual freedom and for full recognition and expression of particular identities." In a crucial respect, the current book is an attempt to lay out the means by which neoliberalism availed itself of what Harvey calls the "cause," which it "did not create . . . but could easily exploit," of "those seeking individual freedoms and social justice" (41).

76. Daniel Dennett, *From Bacteria to Bach and Back: The Evolution of Minds* (New York: Norton, 2018), 61, 62.

77. "Autonomy and strong responsibility seem to me empirically false" (37), Jane Bennett writes in *Vibrant Matter: A Political Ecology of Things* (Durham, NC: Duke University Press, 2010), and to persist in these delusions is to ignore "the active role of *nonhuman* materials in public life" (2). "In the posthuman view," Katherine Hayles writes in *How We Became Posthuman: Virtual Bodies in Cybernetics, Literature, and Informatics* (Chicago: University of Chicago Press, 1999), "conscious agency has never been 'in control'" (288). In "Context Stinks!" *New Literary History* 42, no. 4 (2011), Rita Felski concludes: "Non-human actors are participants in chains of events; they help shape outcomes and influence actions. To acknowledge the input of such actors is . . . to place people, animals, texts, and things on the same ontological footing" (583). In *When Species Meet* (Minneapolis: University of Minnesota Press, 2008), Donna Haraway faults the Kantian investment in rationality on the view that "the claim to have Sufficient

Reasons is a dangerous fantasy" (89). "Unless they are delusional," she writes, "what people (and other organisms) do not have (except in a very special sense in mathematical and logical proof) is transcendent sufficient reasons" (244).

78. Haraway, *When Species Meet*, 292.

79. The refutation of Dennett's position proceeds by observing that consciousness *just is* the name for the way things seem to their experiencer, and no further fact about its causation—say, its amounting to the firing of neurons—could possibly eliminate this appearance without running into incoherence or emptiness. With regard to consciousness, appearance is reality.

80. Consider Wendy Brown's *Undoing the Demos: Neoliberalism's Stealth Revolution* (New York: Zone, 2015), which argues that neoliberalism "takes shape as a governing rationality extending a specific formulation of economic values, practices, and metrics to every dimension of human life" (30) and "configures human beings exhaustively as market actors always, only, and everywhere as *homo oeconomicus*" (31). Both the reflexive contempt for what economics encompasses and the breathtaking one-dimensionality of Brown's claims reflect the standard view of neoliberalism among progressive academics. Perhaps the greatest peculiarity in Brown's book is her tracing of neoliberal subjectivity to utilitarian precepts espoused by Jeremy Bentham (whom she puzzlingly describes as having written "one hundred years ago" [32]). "Bentham's utilitarian subject," Brown maintains, is "an early prototype of the neoliberal subject" (96). As chapter 1 will make clear, the values that we now call neoliberal began to take hold through a set of post-sixties arguments that explicitly and staunchly *opposed* utilitarian theory, Benthamite or otherwise.

81. Ron Suskind, "Faith, Certainty and the Presidency of George W. Bush," *New York Times Magazine*, October 7, 2004, 17.

82. Paddy Chayefsky, *Altered States* (New York: Harper and Row, 1978), 2. Hereafter cited in text.

83. For this and other details of the novel and its translation to the screen, see Shaun Considine, *Mad as Hell: The Life and Work of Paddy Chayefsky* (New York: Random House, 1994). Considine quotes one studio executive who says that Chayefsky "got close to one million dollars" for the script as well as "unprecedented" control over the film's production, including a "time-completion guarantee" (355).

84. Considine notes that "on September 21, 1979, [studio] lawyers were informed that the name of Paddy Chayefsky had to be removed from the script of *Altered States*" (379).

85. According to Considine, Chayefsky "consider[ed] writing novels déclassé," but Dan Melnick at Columbia Pictures convinced him that a "book would be a wonderful weapon in selling the picture" (355).

86. The term "relaxation tanks" was a stab at rebranding isolation tanks as household goods. See "Relaxation Tanks: A Market Develops," *New York Times*, November 21, 1981. The article notes that "about 500 . . . units have been sold this year by . . . three companies" (35).

87. For a provocative defense of "literature's uniqueness" against those who see "denial" of the same as "an important, or at least a promising, instrument of institutional and political change" (2), see Steven Knapp, *Literary Interest: The Limits of Anti-Formalism* (Cambridge, MA: Harvard University Press, 1995). For a more up-to-date critique of anti-formalism, which rejects the New Historicism's model of "text-as-object and

context-as-container" (156), see Rita Felski, *The Limits of Critique* (Chicago: University of Chicago, 2015).

88. Frances Ferguson, "Now It's Personal: D. A. Miller and Too-Close Reading," *Critical Inquiry* 41, no. 3 (2015): 521–540.

89. D. A. Miller, *Jane Austen, or The Secret of Style* (Princeton, NJ: Princeton University Press, 2005) 57.

90. Walter Benn Michaels, *The Beauty of a Social Problem: Photography, Autonomy, Economy* (Chicago: University of Chicago Press, 2015), xii.

91. On some of the disciplinary implications of "the new formalism," see Jonathan Kramnick and Anahid Nersessian, "Are We Being Interdisciplinary Yet?" *Critical Inquiry* 43, no. 2 (2017): 650–679.

92. Samuel Konkin, *New Libertarian Manifesto* (Huntington Beach, CA: KoPubCo, 2006), 18.

93. Vladimir Nabokov, *Pale Fire* (New York: Vintage, 1989), 46.

94. Nozick, *Anarchy*, 313.

95. Knapp, *Literary Interest*, 139, 103.

96. This assumption has entered literary criticism of the last two decades in a forceful way, as attested by the current boom in cognitive-scientific approaches to literature. Such work entirely dispenses with an earlier generation's suspicion of psychological criticism, although it must be said that the disciplines of mind on which most cognitive approaches draw, from neuroscience to evolutionary biology, are rather different from midcentury ego psychology.

97. Nozick calls such teleological principles "end state" or "patterned conceptions" (172) and disclaims justice as fairness on the view that Rawls smuggles teleology into his theory when he avows that "individuals in the original position would choose a principle that focuses upon groups, rather than individuals" (190). On Nozick's view, that is, Rawls is a closet collectivist.

1. Artificial Intelligence and the Rise of the Meritocracy

1. Robert Nozick, *Anarchy, State, and Utopia* (New York: Basic Books, 1974), 42, 34. Hereafter cited in text.

2. We might say that the ancestor of Nozick's "experience machine" is E. M. Forster's "The Machine Stops" (1909), in which all human experience from sleeping and eating to reading poetry and viewing nature is simulated by a "Machine" whose substitutions its subjects embrace with "the delirium of acquiescence": "'Something good enough' had long since been accepted by our race." *Selected Stories* (New York: Penguin, 2001), 96, 93.

3. Bernard Williams, "The Self and the Future," *Philosophical Review* 79, no. 2 (1970): 170. Nothing if not consistent, the utilitarian philosopher Peter Singer admits in a 1975 review of Nozick's book that he *would* use the experience machine: "Maybe it would seem a pointless world, and plugging into the machine a pointless kind of existence, but that is because we are used to having the possibility of improving experiences, our own or those of another, to give point to our normal existence. . . . Maybe life as a whole doesn't have any point beyond experience itself." "The Right to Be Rich or Poor," *New York Review of Books*, March 6, 1975, 17. In *Reasons and Persons* (New York: Oxford University Press, 1984), Derek Parfit argues that the utilitarian focus on experiences at

the expense of distinct persons becomes defensible on his "Reductionist View," which denies that "we are separately existing entities, distinct from our brains and bodies, and our experiences." Objecting to the claim that our "continued existence" as persons "must be a deep, further fact, distinct from physical and psychological continuity" (445), Parfit concludes: "It is more plausible to focus, not on persons, but on experiences, and to claim that what matters morally is the nature of these experiences. On the impersonal Utilitarian Principle, the question *who* has an experience is as irrelevant as the question *when* the experience is had" (446). Embracing the externalism that Nozick implicitly derides in the utilitarian account of personhood, Alva Noë writes: "We are brains in vats on life support. Our skulls are the vats and our bodies the life-support systems that keep us going." *Out of Our Heads: Why You Are Not Your Brain, and Other Lessons from the Biology of Consciousness* (New York: Farrar, Straus and Giroux, 2009), 4.

4. Ursula K. Le Guin, *The Lathe of Heaven* (New York: Scribner, 2008), 17, 164, 1. Hereafter cited in text.

5. Ursula K. Le Guin, *The Dispossessed: An Ambiguous Utopia* (New York: Harper Collins, 1991), 178. Hereafter cited in text.

6. Actually there is nothing contrarian about joining Le Guin and Nozick. Nozick, after all, tried his hand at science fiction; "Philosophical Fictions," part IV of his *Socratic Puzzles* (Cambridge, MA: Harvard University Press, 1999), is a series of sci-fi stories. And *The Dispossessed* was chosen in 1993 as the Prometheus Hall of Fame Award Winner, "designed to honor classic libertarian fiction," according to the prize's grantor, the Libertarian Futurist Society. The prize itself "is a gold coin, representing free trade and free minds, mounted on an engraved plaque." Ayn Rand's novels have entered the hall of fame twice; Robert Heinlein's novels and stories, six times. See Libertarian Futurist Society, "Prometheus Awards," accessed January 20, 2020, http://lfs.org/awards.shtml.

7. John Rawls, *A Theory of Justice* (Cambridge, MA: Harvard University Press, 1971), xviii. Hereafter cited in text. Rawls brought out a revised version of *Theory* in 1999, in which he clarifies some of his positions in response to twenty-five years of criticism. Since my concern is less with the rightness or wrongness of Rawls's views than with their historical interest, I have chosen (with the exception of one note in the introduction) to consult the original edition of *A Theory of Justice*.

8. The landmark 1966 Coleman Report, commissioned by the Department of Education following the Civil Rights Act of 1964, was the opening salvo in the defeat of environmental explanations of the race gap in schooling. Finding that "whites . . . are less affected one way or the other by the quality of their schools than are minority pupils" (22), the report prefigured the account of *dependency* that foes of the welfare state curried: "minority pupils . . . have far less conviction than whites that they can affect their own environments and futures" (23). See James S. Coleman et al., *Equality of Educational Opportunity* (Washington, DC: US Department of Health Education and Welfare, 1966).

9. Richard Herrnstein, *IQ in the Meritocracy* (Boston: Little, Brown, 1973), 8, 5. Hereafter cited in text.

10. Take Skinner's infamous plea, in *Beyond Freedom and Dignity* (1971; Indianapolis: Hackett, 2002), for "abolish[ing] autonomous man" (200) from discussions of social welfare.

11. Arthur Jensen, "How Much Can We Boost IQ and Scholastic Achievement?" *Harvard Educational Review* 39, no. 1 (1969): 6.

12. Jensen, "How Much Can We Boost IQ," 46.

13. Noam Chomsky, "A Review of B. F. Skinner's *Verbal Behavior*," *Language* 35, no. 1 (1959): 49. Chomsky saw behaviorism as "just a kind of play-acting at science" (57).

14. John R. Searle, *Mind, Language, Society* (New York: Basic Books, 1998), 43. A likeness between philosophy and cognitive nativism was sometimes encouraged, as when Rawls ties Chomsky's universal grammar, "known to require theoretical constructions that far outrun the ad hoc precepts of our explicit grammatical knowledge," to the "similar situation . . . in moral theory." "Moral capacities" for Rawls are as "native" as linguistic ones (47). But it would be a mistake to see the period's philosophers and psychologists reaching any deeper agreement than their shared intolerance of behaviorism. Indeed, a prominent philosophical critique of psychology in the seventies takes as given that the discipline's physicalism—along with its problems—has merely been transferred from behaviorism to cognitivism. In "The Nature and Plausibility of Cognitivism" (1978), John Haugeland sees cognitive psychology as "a natural development from behaviorism" and saddled with some of the latter's flaws: "Like their predecessors, cognitivists have made undeniably important and lasting discoveries. But also as before, these discoveries are conspicuously narrow, even small, compared to the depth and scope of psychology's pretheoretic purview. The brilliance of what has been done can blind us to the darkness that surrounds it, and it is worth recalling how many shadows cognitivism has not (yet) illuminated." *Having Thought: Essays in the Metaphysics of Mind* (Cambridge, MA: Harvard University Press, 1998), 43.

15. Thus in "Mental Events" (1970), which is reprinted in *Essays on Actions and Events* (New York: Oxford, 2001), Donald Davidson concludes that the "holism of the mental realm" (216) cannot be captured in behaviorist or physicalist reduction because "we know too much about thought and behavior to trust exact and universal statements linking them" (217). Taking "essentially the Kantian line" (209), Davidson specifies "the anomalism of the mental" as "a necessary condition for viewing action as autonomous" (225), which is to say that mental life gives personhood an autonomy not subject to physical reduction.

16. Charles Taylor, "Peaceful Coexistence in Psychology," *Social Research* 40, no. 1 (1973): 81. Taylor's 1964 book *The Explanation of Behavior* inaugurated his ongoing critique of psychological reductionism.

17. Charles Taylor, *Sources of the Self: The Making of Modern Identity* (Cambridge, MA: Harvard University Press, 1992), 15, 23, 5, 21. Hereafter cited in text.

18. Antiutilitarian writing abounds in efforts to connect utilitarian thinking to gross violations of human rights and values. Amartya Sen argues that welfare utilitarians who accept a society with redistributive tax over a society without such a tax because it generates a higher amount of utility must also be committed to a society in which people who take pleasure in torturing others are allowed to torture if it too contains more utility than one without such an allowance. "Welfarism would insist," he writes, "that the state of affairs with redistributive taxation . . . is better than that without taxation . . . if and only if the state of affairs with the torture . . . is better than that without torture" (474). One is tempted to say that the most important thing about Sen's example is its treatment of taxation and torture as equivalent states of affairs. See "Utilitarianism and Welfarism," *Journal of Philosophy* 76, no. 9 (1979): 463–489.

19. John R. Searle, "Minds, Brains, and Programs," *Behavioral and Brain Sciences* 3 (1980): 417. Hereafter cited in text as "MBP." While my chief interest in Strong AI is historical, it would be a mistake to equate such periodization with the dimming of Turing's flame. Jerry Fodor notes that computational theory's contemporary defenders retain a "commitment to Turing's *syntactic* account of mental processes" (6) in "the attempt to ground psychology in the idea that mental processes are computations" (12). See *The Mind Doesn't Work That Way: The Scope and Limits of Computational Psychology* (Cambridge, MA: MIT Press, 2000).

20. Alan Turing, "Computing Machinery and Intelligence," in *The Essential Turing: Seminal Writings in Computing, Logic, Philosophy, Artificial Intelligence, and Artificial Life*, ed. B. Jack Copeland (Oxford: Clarendon, 2004), 441. Hereafter cited in text as *ET*.

21. John R. Searle, *Mind: A Brief Introduction* (New York: Oxford University Press, 2004), 100.

22. Edward Banfield, *The Unheavenly City Revisited* (Boston: Little, Brown, 1974), 161, 160.

23. Hubert Dreyfus, *What Computers Can't Do: A Critique of Artificial Reason* (New York: Harper & Row, 1972), xxxiii, 6. Hereafter cited in text.

24. Hence the "AI winter," so named to denote the period in the seventies when government and foundation funding for AI research all but disappeared in both the US and England. Artificial intelligence research follows a boom and bust cycle; now, at the end of the 2010s, we appear to be at the peak of an inflationary moment of AI exuberance and due for contraction.

25. Daniel C. Dennett, *Brainstorms: Philosophical Essays on Mind and Psychology* (Cambridge, MA: MIT Press, 1981), 320. Hereafter cited in text as *B*.

26. Daniel C. Dennett, *Content and Consciousness* (New York: Routledge, 2010), 43. Hereafter cited in text as *CC*.

27. Daniel C. Dennett, *Consciousness Explained* (Boston: Little, Brown, 1991), 274. Hereafter cited in text as *CE*.

28. David M. Armstrong, *A Materialist Theory of the Mind* (London: Routledge, 1993), 273.

29. Daniel C. Dennett, *Kinds of Minds: Toward an Understanding of Consciousness* (New York: Basic, 1997), 56. Dennett's account owes something to the pioneer AI researcher Marvin Minsky, who models the mind as a "society" made up of "many little parts, each mindless by itself." *The Society of Mind* (New York: Simon & Schuster, 1985), 17. Minsky's "society of mind" makes explicit what is problematic about the systems reply on the view of Searle and other opponents of Strong AI: its understanding of consciousness on the pattern of (a caricatured) collectivism. While the decomposition of mental life into what Minsky calls nonpsychological "agents" (23) is the reductionist goal, the notion of a society made up of mindless agents looks like the nightmare polis invoked by antiutilitarians like Nozick.

30. Samuel Delany, *Babel-17/Empire Star* (New York: Vintage, 2002), 140. Hereafter cited in text.

31. Searle's belief that "intentionality is some marvelous fluid secreted by the brain," according to Dennett, makes him the "victim" of "superannuated myths." "Searle does not see how any mere computer chopping away at a formal program could harbor . . . consciousness," Dennett writes, "because he is looking too deep. It is just as mysterious if we peer into the synapse-filled jungles of the brain and wonder where

consciousness is hiding." "The Milk of Human Intentionality," *Behavioral and Brain Sciences* 3 (1980): 430.

32. Daniel Dennett, *The Intentional Stance* (Cambridge, MA: MIT Press, 1987), 214.

33. Steven Pinker, *The Stuff of Thought: Language as a Window into Human Nature* (New York: Viking, 2007), 124.

34. Robert Chodat argues that the "Heideggerian" (694) critique of Strong AI found in Dreyfus, Taylor, and Haugeland implies "objections that might broadly be termed ethical" (686). While Chodat does not reference the critique of utilitarianism, the ethical objections he describes are those largely shared by advocates of subjectivity and self-authorship like Williams and Rawls, who nonetheless reject the phenomenological approach of the philosophers in Chodat's analysis. See "Naturalism and Narrative, or, What Computers and Human Beings Can't Do," *New Literary History* 37, no. 4 (2006): 685–706.

35. Stuart Hampshire, "Morality and Pessimism," in *Public and Private Morality*, ed. Stuart Hampshire (Cambridge, UK: Cambridge University Press, 1978), 3, 4.

36. Hampshire, "Morality and Pessimism," 1.

37. Thomas Schwartz, "What Human Welfare Is Not," in *The Limits of Utilitarianism*, ed. Harlan Miller and William Williams (Minneapolis: University of Minnesota Press, 1982), 205.

38. Schwartz, "What Human Welfare Is Not," 202.

39. Bernard Williams, *Moral Luck: Philosophical Papers 1973–1980* (Cambridge, UK: Cambridge University Press, 1981), 5, 4.

40. Williams, *Moral Luck*, 101, 102.

41. J. J. C. Smart and Bernard Williams, *Utilitarianism: For and Against* (Cambridge, UK: Cambridge University Press, 1973), 83, 95. Hereafter cited in text.

42. In *Ethics and The Limits of Philosophy* (1985; New York: Routledge, 2006), Williams concludes that utilitarianism cannot help giving rise to "two classes of people" (108) because its value system is so "shocking" (109) to the norms by which most people abide. Utilitarianism is thus always "Government House Utilitarianism"; befitting its roots in Britain's "colonialist" heyday, it is "indifferent to the values of social transparency" (109).

43. John Elster, "Sour Grapes: Utilitarianism and the Genesis of Wants," in *Utilitarianism and Beyond*, ed. Amartya Sen and Bernard Williams (Cambridge, UK: Cambridge University Press, 1982), 223.

44. J. J. C. Smart, "Reports of Immediate Experiences," *Synthese* 22 (1971): 353.

45. Herbert A. Simon and Allen Newell, "Human Problem Solving: The State of the Theory in 1970," *American Psychologist* 26, no. 2 (1971): 147, 149.

46. David Lyons, *The Forms and Limits of Utilitarianism* (Oxford: Clarendon Press, 1965), 197.

47. David Lyons, "Utility as a Ground of Rights," *Noûs* 14.1 (1980): 25.

48. Thomas Nagel, "What Is It Like to Be a Bat?" in *Mortal Questions* (Cambridge, UK: Cambridge University Press, 1979), 178. Hereafter cited in text as *MQ*.

49. Thomas Nagel, *Equality and Partiality* (New York: Oxford University Press, 1991), 15.

50. As we have seen, Searle also sees the Turing test as "behavioristic." This is not a unanimous view. Donald Davidson "conclude[s] that Turing's Test is not behavior-

istic in a way that limits its interest." *Problems of Rationality* (New York: Oxford University Press, 2004), 80.

51. Andrew Hodges, *Alan Turing: The Enigma* (Princeton, NJ: Princeton University Press, 2012), 362.

52. Joseph Buchanan, *Manual of Psychometry: Dawn of a New Civilization* (Boston: Frank Hodges, 1893), 5.

53. Nicholas Lemann outlines the history of ETS in *The Big Test: The Secret History of the American Meritocracy* (New York: Farrar, Straus and Giroux, 2000). The most successful feature of its rebranding would have to be ETS's makeover of the SAT, its flagship product, as a neutral identifier of aptitude rather than the test for IQ it largely is.

54. Richard Herrnstein and Charles Murray, *The Bell Curve: Intelligence and Class Structure in American Life* (New York: Free Press, 1994), 109. Earlier in *IQ in the Meritocracy*, Herrnstein spelled out the social-Darwinist logic at work behind this critique of Great Society policies: "If parents no longer can pass social and economic advantages on to their children—let us say, because of taxes and welfare and public housing and uniformly excellent public schools—they will instead contribute to their children's success and failure only by their genetic legacy" (10).

55. Michael Young, *The Rise of the Meritocracy* (New Brunswick, NJ: Transaction, 1994), 66.

56. "A machine will quite critically need to acquire the order of a hundred thousand elements of knowledge," Marvin Minsky writes, "in order to behave with reasonable sensibility in ordinary situations. A million, if properly organized, should be enough for a very great intelligence. If my argument does not convince you, multiply the figures by ten." Minskey, ed., *Semantic Information Processing* (Cambridge, MA: MIT Press, 1968), 26.

57. Hilary Putnam, "Robots: Machines or Artificially Created Life?" *Journal of Philosophy* 61, no. 21 (1964): 678, 691.

58. Putnam, 678, 680. Multiple realizability, the view that similar mental states are functionally expressible by different physical kinds, was Putnam's answer to identity theory in the sixties.

59. Young, *Rise*, 5.

60. Philip K. Dick, *Ubik* (New York: Mariner, 2012), 49.

61. N. Katherine Hayles, *How We Became Posthuman: Virtual Bodies in Cybernetics, Literature, and Informatics* (Chicago: University of Chicago Press, 1999), 288.

62. Philip K. Dick, *Do Androids Dream of Electric Sheep?* (New York: Del Rey, 1996), 30. Hereafter cited in text.

63. Philip K. Dick, *The Shifting Realities of Philip K. Dick: Selected Literary and Philosophical Writings*, ed. Lawrence Sutin (New York: Vintage, 1996), 263. Hereafter cited in text as *SR*.

64. Philip K. Dick, *The Simulacra* (New York: Mariner, 2011), 16.

65. Philip K. Dick, *We Can Build You* (New York: Mariner, 2012), 29. Hereafter cited in text.

66. Thomas M. Disch, *334* (New York: Vintage, 1999), 12. Hereafter cited in text.

67. Thomas M. Disch, *The Prisoner* (New York: Penguin, 2009), 55, 119. Hereafter cited in text.

68. Charles Taylor, "The Diversity of Goods," in Sen and Williams, *Utilitarianism and Beyond*, 140.

69. Bernard Williams, *Morality: An Introduction to Ethics* (Cambridge, UK: Cambridge University Press, 1993), 89, 87.

70. Thomas M. Disch, *Camp Concentration* (New York: Vintage, 1999), 84. Hereafter cited in text.

71. Eichmann's "taped police examination," according to Arendt, "constitutes a veritable gold mine for a psychologist—provided he is wise enough to understand that the horrible can be not only ludicrous but outright funny." *Eichmann in Jerusalem: A Report on the Banality of Evil* (New York: Penguin, 2006), 48.

72. Joseph Francavilla, "Disching It Out: An Interview with Thomas Disch," *Science Fiction Studies* 12, no. 3 (1985): 247.

73. Henry Sidgwick, *The Methods of Ethics* (London: Macmillan, 1907), 420.

74. According to Howard Brick, McNamara "brought systems analysis . . . to the Kennedy administration," where he "hoped . . . to achieve rational control . . . over Vietnam." Brick notes that "even before the horrors" of that conflict, McNamara's fondness for cybernetics "was attacked for bearing antihumanist implications." *The Age of Contradiction: American Thought and Culture in the 1960s* (Ithaca, NY: Cornell University Press, 2000), 126.

75. Hampshire, "Morality," 4. John Searle describes a concrete instance of utilitarian reasoning for questionable ends in *Rationality in Action* (Cambridge, MA: MIT Press, 2001), where he recalls a "visit to a friend . . . who was a high official of the Defense Department" and whom Searle tried to argue "out of the war policy the United States was following, particularly the policy of bombing North Vietnam." This friend "went to the blackboard and drew the curves of traditional microeconomic analysis; and then said, 'Where these two curves intersect, the marginal utility of resisting is equal to the marginal disutility of being bombed. At that point, they have to give up'" (6).

76. The prisoners' esoteric pursuit may be an homage to Dreyfus's 1965 RAND paper "Alchemy and Artificial Intelligence," of which *What Computers Can't Do* is essentially an expansion.

77. Armstrong, *A Materialist Theory*, 19.

78. John R. Searle, *Philosophy in a New Century: Selected Essays* (Cambridge, UK: Cambridge University Press, 2008), 83. Elsewhere Searle writes against the epiphenomenalism found among some evolutionists, who hold that "because consciousness is non-physical, it could not have physical effects[:] the question 'what is the evolutionary advantage of consciousness?' is asked in a tone which reveals that we are making the Cartesian mistake." "How to Study Consciousness Scientifically," *Philosophical Transactions: Biological Sciences* 353 (1998): 1939. Searle's own account of mental causation treats "consciousness" as a "causally emergent property of the behavior of neurons" in *The Rediscovery of the Mind* (Cambridge, MA: MIT Press, 1992), 116. David Chalmers considers Searle a property dualist in *The Conscious Mind: In Search of a Fundamental Theory* (New York: Oxford University Press, 1996), 130.

79. John R. Searle, *Seeing Things as They Are: A Theory of Perception* (New York: Oxford University Press, 2015), 15.

80. John R. Searle, *The Campus War: A Sympathetic Look at the University in Agony* (New York: World, 1971), 190. Hereafter cited in text as *CW*.

81. Bentham's "dictum" is cited in John Stuart Mill, *Utilitarianism*, in Jeremy Bentham and Mill, *Utilitarianism and Other Essays*, ed. Alan Ryan (Harmondsworth, UK: Penguin, 2004), 336.

82. John Rawls, "Social Unity and Primary Goods," in Sen and Williams, *Utilitarianism and Beyond*, 181.

83. Frances Ferguson, *Pornography, the Theory: What Utilitarianism Did to Action* (Chicago: University of Chicago Press, 2004), xvi.

84. Ferguson, *Pornography, the Theory*, 24, 54.

85. Ferguson, *Pornography, the Theory*, 110.

86. His infrequent forays into moral philosophy reveal Searle's position as essentially Kantian. In a 1964 essay, he enlists Kant's "distinction between regulative and constitutive rules" (55) to overturn what he calls the "naturalistic fallacy fallacy [*sic*]" (48). Searle argues that "factual premises can entail evaluative conclusions" (58) by showing that a description of promising (the moral paradigm in Kant) entails that one should keep one's promises on the view that "institutionalized forms of obligation" (56) lose their descriptive force if not accorded their normative force. See "How to Derive 'Ought' from 'Is,'" *Philosophical Review* 73 (1964): 43–58.

87. Arjun Appuradai, *Fear of Small Numbers: An Essay on the Geography of Anger* (Durham, NC: Duke University Press, 2006), 59.

88. Banfield, *Unheavenly City*, 232.

89. Peter Singer, *Practical Ethics* (Princeton, NJ: Princeton University Press, 2011), 27, 28. Hereafter cited in text. Needless to say, Singer's definition of "important" has occasioned a great deal of controversy among moral philosophers.

90. Stephen Jay Gould, *The Mismeasure of Man* (New York: Norton, 1996), 60.

91. Rawls's claim that the "outcome of the natural lottery . . . is arbitrary from a moral perspective" (64) has seemed to critics both inconsistent with his defense of individual liberty and intent on an impermissible demarcation of the boundary between accident and essence.

92. Peter Singer, "The Right to Be Rich or Poor" (note 2), 18.

93. Singer, "The Right to Be Rich or Poor," 19.

94. Williams, *Moral Luck*, 3.

95. Williams, *Ethics*, 77.

96. Given the perennial appeal of IQ fundamentalism to racists, it is worth mentioning the work of James Flynn. "The Flynn effect" (307), so named by Murray and Herrnstein in *The Bell Curve*, refers to the dramatic gains in raw IQ scores Flynn has documented across all racial groups (but especially minorities) in each generation since the early twentieth century. Given that "the Blacks of 1995 . . . matched the mean IQs of the Whites of 1945," Flynn concludes, "an environmental explanation of the racial IQ gap need only posit this: that the average environment for Blacks in 1995 matches the average environment for Whites in 1945" (15). See "Searching for Justice: The Discovery of IQ Gains Over Time," *American Psychologist* 53, no. 1 (1999): 5–20. The case against environment's effect on IQ is effectively demolished by the longitudinal evidence Flynn has pieced together.

97. The "best" brains, according to Herrnstein and Murray's *The Bell Curve*, are Asian ones: "East Asians (e.g., Chinese, Japanese), whether in America or in Asia, typically earn higher scores on intelligence and achievement than white Americans" (269).

98. Walter Benn Michaels, *Our America: Nativism, Modernism, and Pluralism* (Durham, NC: Duke University Press, 1995), 118, 119.

99. Nella Larsen, *Quicksand and Passing*, ed. Deborah McDowell (New Brunswick, NJ: Rutgers University Press, 1986), 192.

100. Michaels, *Our America*, 119.

101. Thomas M. Disch, *The Dreams Our Stuff Is Made of: How Science Fiction Conquered the World* (New York: Touchstone, 2000), 15.

102. Disch, *Dreams*, 15.

103. Thomas M. Disch, *The Word of God: Or, Holy Writ Rewritten* (San Francisco: Tachyon, 2008), 69.

104. Disch, *Word*, 5.

105. Daniel Keyes, *Flowers for Algernon* (New York: Mariner, 2005), 68. Hereafter cited in text.

106. Erving Goffman, *Asylums: Essays on the Social Situation of Mental Patients and Other Inmates* (New York: Doubleday, 1961), 4.

107. Singer asserts thus that "to bring into existence a child, most of whose preferences we will be unable to satisfy, is to create a debit that we cannot cancel and is therefore wrong." Parents err when they "unnecessarily bring into existence a child who is likely to have a larger negative balance in the moral ledger than a child they could have brought into existence." Singer's example is a severely disabled child "who, because of a genetic defect, will lead a thoroughly miserable existence for a year or two and then die" (114). Given the centrality of future planning to Singer's sense of what it means to have viable preferences, preferences worth defending, it is hard not to see how the principle could be extended to less disabled persons. Then too, the notion that all potential parents are mathletes and certified public accountants when it comes to future planning, much less family planning, is as problematic as the idea that we can determine with any certainty—or even a passable sense of probability—what the "balance" of a life will be.

108. Peter Singer, *Rethinking Life and Death: The Collapse of Our Traditional Ethics* (New York: St. Martin's Press, 1994), 213. For forceful rejoinders to Singer's position, see Michael Bérubé and Jennifer Ruth's *The Humanities, Higher Education, and Academic Freedom: Three Necessary Arguments* (New York: Palgrave, 2015), in which Bérubé indicts Singer for requiring a "performance criterion for being fully human" (42); and Eva Feder Kittay, "Relationality, Personhood, and Peter Singer on the Fate of Severely Impaired Infants," *APA Newsletter on Philosophy and Medicine* (Spring 2000), which "disput[es] that the concept of personhood is given by a denumerable set of attributes, especially ones that privilege cognitive capacities" (254). Though Singer's own claim that "important human interests . . . are not affected by differences in intelligence" would seem to conflict with his views on intellectual disabilities, Singer appears to mean differences in the so-called normal range. As Rachel Adams points out in her memoir of parenting a child with Down syndrome, "the full integration of people with disabilities challenges our ideas about what counts as normal." *Raising Henry: A Memoir of Motherhood, Disability, and Discovery* (New Haven, CT: Yale University Press, 2013), 85.

109. Keyes shared the 1967 Nebula award with Delany, who won for *Babel-17*, a novel that, as we have seen, takes a different view of the moral compass of personhood. Whereas Keyes derives a normative ideal from the fact of first-person subjectivity, Dela-

ny's politics argue for eliminating first-person subjectivity as a fiction that mars the project of what in the ensuing decades would come to be multiculturalism.

110. Notwithstanding its lack of headway as a research program, Strong AI has had remarkable staying power as an ideal, reincarnating itself with striking frequency in our collective consciousness. There is a vast literature dedicated to fostering both academic and popular belief in the imminence of intelligent if not outright sentient computers. A sampling by decade gives the flavor of this mission. "Artificial intelligence will change our view of ourselves," Pamela McCorduck writes in her 1979 book *Machines Who Think: A Personal Inquiry into the History and Prospects of Artificial Intelligence* (Natick, MA: A. K. Peters, 2004). "The change will be gradual: we'll continue to think of ourselves as the intellectual center of the universe at the same time we acknowledge a new species is on the horizon" (397). "Within the next century," the roboticist Hans Moravec claims in *Mind Children: The Future of Robot and Human Intelligence* (Cambridge, MA: Harvard University Press, 1988), machines "will mature into entities as complex as ourselves" (1). Indeed "within fifty years," he predicts, "I believe that robots with human intelligence will be common" (6). In *The Age of Spiritual Machines: When Computers Exceed Human Intelligence* (New York: Penguin, 1999), the computer scientist Ray Kurzweil speculates that "intelligent machines [will] surpass us in intelligence . . . in the twenty-first century" (15), by the end of which "there won't be a clear difference between humans and robots" (148). More recently, Nick Bostrom claims in *Superintelligence: Paths, Strategies, Dangers* (New York: Oxford University Press, 2014): "A big breakthrough in artificial intelligence . . . seems somewhat likely . . . in this century" (v). While more leery of prognostications than Moravec or Kurzweil, Bostrom remains convinced of "the possibility of greater-than-human AI" (5); as its title indicates, that is the alarm his book exists to sound.

111. Richard Powers, *Galatea 2.2* (New York: Farrar, Straus and Giroux, 1995), 57, 4. Hereafter cited in text.

112. Powers's protagonist seems to embody the behavior that John McCarthy (who coined the term "artificial intelligence") calls "ascribing mental qualities to machines" in a 1979 paper of that title. Such ascription resembles Dennett's "intentional stance," his view that consciousness is more or less a function of the human willingness to attribute it as the best explanation of some forms of behavior in persons. Dennett considers such attribution akin to religious and other superstitions—a powerful working fiction. In a 2008 interview, Powers told Stephen T. Burn that he "sees" not just "strong affinities" but "equivalences" between Dennett's "theory of consciousness" and his own. He calls *The Echo-Maker* (2006) "a narrative working-out of [Dennett's] ideas." Stephen T. Burn, "An Interview with Richard Powers," *Contemporary Literature* 49, no. 2 (2008): 174.

113. Silvan Tomkins, *Affect, Imagery, Consciousness, Volume II: The Negative Affects* (New York: Springer, 1963), 133.

114. "As he is training her," Hayles points out in *How We Became Post-Human*, "the experience of working with her is also training him" (264). But the crucial point is that Rick is imagined as *trainable* to begin with.

115. The "Hebbian rule" is named after the neuroscientist Daniel Hebb, who posited in 1949 that the repeated firing of neurons in the brain brings about the synaptic assemblies that cause awareness and learning: "When an axon of cell *A* is near enough

to excite a cell *B* and repeatedly or persistently takes part in firing it, some growth process or metabolic change takes place in one or both cells such that *A*'s efficiency, as one of the cells firing *B*, is increased." *The Organization of Behavior: A Neuropsychological Theory* (New York: Wiley, 1949), 62.

116. Chodat notes that Rick's sense of "homelessness has led him to a feeling of disorientation" (698) in "Naturalism and Narrative."

2. Radical Ecology's Mindfulness

1. Arne Naess, "The Shallow and the Deep, Long-Range Ecology Movement," in *The Deep Ecology Movement: An Introductory Anthology*, ed. Alan Drengson and Yuichi Inoue (Berkeley, CA: North Atlantic, 1995), 4. Hereafter cited in text.

2. The reason for this usage is that all deep ecologists are radical ecologists but not all radical ecologists embrace deep ecology. When I use the latter term, it denotes figures (like Naess) who identify as deep ecologists. While thinkers as diverse as the anarchist Murray Bookchin and the technocrats behind the Club of Rome are radical ecologists (seeing dramatic social change as the only answer to environmental peril), they do not subscribe to "the idea," as Warwick Fox puts it, "that we can make no firm ontological divide in reality between the human and the nonhuman realms." "Deep Ecology: A New Philosophy of Our Time?" *Ecologist* 14, nos. 5–6 (1984): 196.

3. George Sessions and Bill Devall, *Deep Ecology: Living as if Nature Mattered* (Layton, UT: Gibbs Smith, 1985), 10.

4. Sessions and Devall, *Deep Ecology*, 7, 8, 18.

5. Bernard Williams, *Ethics and the Limits of Philosophy* (1985; New York: Routledge, 2006), 51.

6. Arne Naess and George Sessions, "Platform Principles of the Deep Ecology Movement," in Drengson and Yuichi, *The Deep Ecology Movement*, 49.

7. Edward Abbey, *Desert Solitaire* (New York: Simon and Schuster, 1990), 135. Hereafter cited in text as *DS*.

8. In *Steps to an Ecology of Mind: Collected Essays in Anthropology, Psychiatry, Evolution, and Epistemology* (1972; Chicago: University of Chicago Press, 2000), the anthropologist Gregory Bateson describes "the cybernetic explanation" of ecology as a "hierarchy of contexts within contexts." In cybernetics, Bateson observes, "*context*" determines "content" (408).

9. James Lovelock, *Gaia: A New Look at Life on Earth* (New York: Oxford University Press, 2000), viii.

10. Hence Sessions and Devall in *Deep Ecology* write that "all things in the biosphere have an equal right to live and blossom and to reach their own individual forms of unfolding and self-realization within the larger Self-realization" (67). Peter Singer takes a different view: "The fact that . . . the biosphere can respond to events in ways that resemble a self-maintaining system does not in itself show that the biosphere consciously desires to maintain itself." *Practical Ethics* (Princeton, NJ: Princeton University Press, 2011), 253.

11. J. Baird Callicott, "Animal Liberation: A Triangular Affair," *Environmental Ethics* 2 (Winter 1980): 332. Hereafter cited in text. Mark Sagoff likewise opposes ecological ethics to Singer's "humane utilitarianism": "An ecological community has a beauty and an authenticity that demands [sic] respect, but plainly not on humanitarian grounds."

"Animal Liberation and Environmental Ethics: Bad Marriage, Quick Divorce," in *Environmental Philosophy: From Animal Rights to Radical Ecology*, ed. Michael Zimmerman (Upper Saddle River, NJ: Prentice-Hall, 2001), 91.

12. Alan Drengson, "Shifting Paradigms: From Technocrat to Planetary Person," in Drengson and Inoue, *The Deep Ecology Movement*, 76. Hereafter cited in text.

13. Bill Devall, "The Ecological Self," in Drengson and Inoue, *The Deep Ecology Movement*, 120.

14. Ayn Rand, with Nathaniel Branden, *The Virtue of Selfishness* (New York: Signet, 1964), 16. The comment is actually Rand quoting herself, or rather "Galt's speech" (16), in *Atlas Shrugged*. In "On the Randian Argument" (1971), Robert Nozick dismantles Objectivism as a "moral foundation" for laissez-faire on the grounds that its arguments, including the central premise that life is value, are incoherent if not hopelessly opaque: "it is not clear (to me) what the argument is." *Socratic Puzzles* (Cambridge, MA: Harvard University Press, 1997), 249.

15. Consider George Sessions's claim that "massive funding and implementation" of programs for "dramatically reducing birthrates" is "needed immediately throughout the world" (251) in order for "humanity" to avoid "an era of what some ecologists are calling *biological meltdown!*" (250; emphasis in original). See "Ecocentrism, Wilderness, and Global Protection," reprinted in Zimmerman, *Environmental Philosophy*.

16. Paul Ehrlich, *The Population Bomb* (Cutchogue, NY: Buccaneer Books, 1995), xii.

17. Garrett Hardin, "The Tragedy of the Commons," *Science* 162 (December 13, 1968): 1248.

18. Garrett Hardin, "The Economics of Wilderness," *Natural History* 78 (1969): 176.

19. On radical ecology's flirtation with fascism, see Michael Zimmerman, "Ecofascism: A Threat to American Environmentalism?" in *The Ecological Community*, ed. Roger Gottlieb (New York: Routledge, 1997), 229–254. Observing the "proximity" of Callicott's views and those of National Socialists on the subject of a "healthy" environment, Zimmerman writes: "There can be no doubt that the messy, pragmatic, time-consuming, and unsatisfying processes of democratic politics pale in comparison with the ecstatic promises of fascist leaders who appeal to those who are repelled by the social disintegration and ecological destruction associated with modernity, and who yearn for an ethnically unified, prosperous, and beautiful society living in harmony with the 'laws' of nature" (248–249).

20. In *The Population Bomb*, Ehrlich writes in support of William and Paul Paddock, authors of *Famine 1975!*, who propose a system of triage that would deny aid, as Ehrlich puts it, to "those countries that are so far behind in the population-food game that there is no hope that our food aid will see them through to self-sufficiency" (147). One of radical ecology's greatest embarrassments—not to say lasting sins—is its insistence that famines are natural as opposed to political disasters, a view that fits the discourse's derivation of political problems from natural causes. "No substantial famine has ever occurred in a democratic country—no matter how poor," Amartya Sen famously concludes, "because famines are extremely easy to prevent if the government tries to prevent them, and a government in a multiparty democracy . . . has strong incentives to undertake famine prevention." *Development as Freedom* (New York: Random House, 1999), 52.

21. "During the first part of the 20th century, immigration to the United States was biased to favor those who were most like the people who created this legal entity—

the northern Europeans," Hardin writes in a 1991 essay. "Then popular anthropology came along with its dogma that all cultures are equally good and valuable. To say otherwise was to be narrow-minded and prejudiced, to be guilty of the sin of ethnocentrism. . . . That which was foreign and strange, particularly if persecuted, became the ideal. Black became beautiful, and prolonged bilingual education replaced naturalization." "Conspicuous Benevolence and the Population Bomb," *Chronicles* (October 1991): 20. Hardin's view of anthropology as relativist "dogma" recalls the IQ innatists' critique of behaviorism as politically motivated constructionism.

22. Rand, *Virtue*, 36.

23. As Ursula Heise observes of "the neo-Malthusian literary texts of the period," the "intense anxiety" spurred by "overpopulation" is "described as consisting principally of human bodies" saturating what would otherwise be the open spaces of an ecologically balanced system, "as if physical crowding were the most immediate or most significant consequence of excessive population growth." *Sense of Place and Sense of Planet: The Environmental Imagination of the Global* (New York: Oxford University Press, 2008), 74. Less high-profile than in the heyday of population explosion's moral panic, Malthusian unease has not really subsided in the twenty-first century. James Howard Kunstler voices the idea that the biosphere can be saved only by curing itself of its human plague: "The earth itself seems to be sending forth new and much more lethal diseases, as though it had a kind of protective immune system with antibody-like agents aimed with remarkable precision at the source of the problem: *Homo sapiens*." *The Long Emergency: Surviving the End of Oil, Climate Change, and Other Converging Catastrophes of the Twenty-First Century* (New York: Grove Press, 2005), 10.

24. Flushing the human contaminant for the good of the biosphere looms large as a theme in seventies popular culture. In the 1976 film *Logan's Run*, the human remnant of a postatomic earth enjoys a hedonistic existence under a geodesic dome administered by a computer program; the society maintains resource equilibrium by killing off citizens when they turn 30. Based on data from a "world-simulation program" (23) he devises along the lines of the Club of Rome's World3 model, a character in John Brunner's *The Sheep Look Up* (New York: Harper and Row, 1972) concludes: "We can just about restore the balance of the ecology, the biosphere, and so on . . . if we exterminate the two hundred million most extravagant and wasteful of our species" (473).

25. Nicholas Georgescu-Roegen, *The Entropy Law and Economic Process* (Cambridge, MA: Harvard University Press, 1971), 142. Hereafter cited in text.

26. "The great debate over the future of Western technological society has been captured by the entropists," Alvin Weinberg wrote in a 1982 issue of *Bulletin of the Atomic Scientists*, "the Neo-Malthusian disciples of the economist Nicholas Georgescu-Roegen." "Avoiding the Entropy Trap," *Bulletin of the Atomic Scientists* 38, no. 8 (October 1982): 22.

27. Jeremy Rifkin with Ted Howard, *Entropy: A New World View* (New York: Viking, 1980, 7). Hereafter cited in text.

28. John Barth, *The Friday Book: Essays and Other Nonfiction* (New York: Putnam, 1984), 64. "The second law of thermodynamics, the principle of entropy," Barth writes in "How to Make a Universe," "informs the whole show with a splendid dying fall" (24).

29. Robert Nisbet, *The Twilight of Authority* (New York: Oxford University Press, 1975), 221. Hereafter cited in text.

30. Barry Commoner, *The Closing Circle* (New York: Knopf, 1971), 89. Hereafter cited in text.

31. Herman Daly, "Introduction to the Steady State Economy," in *Economics, Ecology, Ethics: Essays toward a Steady State Economy*, ed. Herman Daly (San Francisco: W. H. Freeman, 1980), 8.

32. E. J. Mishan, *The Costs of Economic Growth* (Westport, CT: Praeger, 1993), 174.

33. Donella H. Meadows, Dennis L. Meadows, Jorgen Randers, and William W. Behrens III, *The Limits to Growth: A Report for the Club of Rome's Project on the Predicament of Mankind* (New York: Universe Books, 1972), 178, 151. Hereafter cited in text.

34. Kenneth Boulding, *The Meaning of the Twentieth Century: The Great Transition* (New York: Harper and Row, 1964), 138.

35. Lewis Thomas, *The Lives of a Cell: Notes of a Biology Watcher* (New York: Penguin, 1978), 22.

36. Gary Snyder, *The Old Ways* (San Francisco: City Lights, 1977), 65, 61. Hereafter cited in text.

37. Arne Naess, "Self-Realization: An Ecological Approach to Being in the World," in Drengson and Inoue, *The Deep Ecology Movement*, 19. Hereafter cited in text.

38. Bill McKibben, *The End of Nature* (New York: Random House, 2006), 77.

39. Paul Shepard, *The Tender Carnivore and the Sacred Game* (Athens: University of Georgia Press, 1998), 23, 34, 237. Hereafter cited in text.

40. Robert Ardrey, *The Hunting Hypothesis: A Personal Conclusion Concerning the Evolutionary Nature of Man* (New York: Atheneum, 1976), 4.

41. Richard B. Lee and Irvin Devore, "Problems in the Study of Hunters and Gatherers," in *Man the Hunter*, ed. Lee and DeVore (New York: Aldine de Gruyter, 1968), 3. Drawn mainly from a 1966 University of Chicago symposium of the same name (where Sahlins delivered his thesis on the original affluent society), the essays in this volume arguably launched radical ecology's interest in the hunter as a social type on the model of identity politics. Hence Shepard sees the displacement of hunting by agriculture not as an instance of adaptation as usual but as "the great prototype of genocide: the ten thousand years of eradication of hunters by farmers" (30).

42. Marshall Sahlins, *Stone Age Economics* (1972; New York: Routledge, 2017), 1. Hereafter cited in text. "The Original Affluent Society" is of course a play on John Kenneth Galbraith's influential 1958 book *The Affluent Society*, which concluded (perhaps with too much optimism, given the entropic turn) that the task facing a world of "increasing opulence" and its "deepening filth" is "to find a way of obtaining and then maintaining a balance in the great flow of goods and services with which our wealth each year rewards us." *The Affluent Society* (New York: Mariner, 1998), 223.

43. William Ophuls, *Ecology and the Politics of Scarcity: Prologue to a Theory of the Steady State* (San Francisco: W. H. Freeman, 1977), 110. Hereafter cited in text.

44. Gary Snyder, *The Practice of the Wild* (Berkeley, CA: Counterpoint, 2004), 100.

45. Edward Goldsmith and Robert Allan, *A Blueprint for Survival* (Harmondsworth, UK: Penguin, 1972), 107. Hereafter cited in text. The text is actually credited to "the editors of *The Ecologist*," but Goldsmith and Allan identify themselves as the lead authors in the preface.

46. Robert Nisbet, *Community and Power: A Study in the Ethics of Order and Freedom* (formerly *The Quest for Community*) (1953; New York: Oxford University Press, 1962), x.

47. Robert Nisbet, "The Nemesis of Authority," *Encounter* 39, no. 2 (1972): 11, 12.

48. Aldo Leopold, *A Sand County Almanac: And Sketches Here and There* (New York: Oxford University Press, 1968), 204.

49. Kirkpatrick Sale, *Human Scale* (New York: Coward, McCann & Geoghegan, 1980), 179. Hereafter cited in text.

50. On this score, Sale cites the primatologist Robin Dunbar, who has demonstrated that "in primates, species-typical brain size correlates rather closely to the species' group size" (122). This citation appears in Sale's *Human Scale Revisited: A New Look at the Classic Case for a Decentralist Future* (White River Junction, VT: Chelsea Green, 2017), which reproduces most of the 1980 volume along with new information drawn largely from the life sciences.

51. "We are not equipped, like termites, to become willing members of a vast community," writes the zoologist Desmond Morris in *The Human Zoo* (1969; London: Vintage, 1994), "and probably always will be, at base, tribal animals" (26).

52. E. F. Schumacher, *Small Is Beautiful: A Study of Economics as if People Mattered* (London: Blond & Briggs, 1973), 139. Hereafter cited in text.

53. The "magic Numbers '25' [for a band] and '500' [for a tribe]" (245) derive from Joseph Birdsell, "Some Predictions for the Pleistocene Based on Equilibrium Systems among Recent Hunter-Gatherers," in Lee and DeVore, *Man the Hunter*, 245.

54. In *The Imperial Animal* (Toronto: McLelland, 1971), the anthropologists Robin Fox and Lionel Tiger likewise attribute "the pathological events" of civilization to "the incarceration of our hunting selves" (22). Along with Shepard and other advocates of Pleistocene social models, Fox and Tiger consider "bands of 50 or so" (21) the natural size of human populations and argue that with "the advent of agriculture . . . ten thousand years ago we cut adrift from nature with a vengeance" (226).

55. John Livingston, *One Cosmic Instant: Man's Fleeting Supremacy* (Boston: Houghton Mifflin, 1973), 132. Hereafter cited in text.

56. R. Buckminster Fuller, *Operating Manual for Spaceship Earth* (Zurich: Lars Muller, 2008), 143, 40.

57. Jean Auel, *Clan of the Cave Bear* (New York: Bantam, 2002), 13. Hereafter cited in text.

58. "There is no evidence anywhere in the Mousterian [that is, European Neanderthal] culture of personal adornment or the rudest experiments with art" (112), Ardrey observes in *The Hunting Hypothesis*.

59. On Auel's book as a "feminist parable" (808) that dooms the Neanderthal species because of its rigid gender dimorphism, see Heather Schell, "The Sexist Gene: Science Fiction and the Germ Theory of History," *American Literary History* 14, no. 4 (2002): 805–827.

60. On a related theme, Cora Diamond rejects the utilitarian animal ethics of Peter Singer because "the abstract appeal to the prevention of suffering as a principle of action" (478) denies any "response to animals as our fellows in mortality, in life on this earth" (474). "I am not concerned here to ask whether we should or should not do these things to animals," Diamond thus argues, "but rather to bring out what is meant by doing something *to an animal*" (476). See "Eating Meat and Eating People," *Philosophy* 53, no. 206 (1978): 465–479.

61. Murray Bookchin, *The Ecology of Freedom: The Emergence and Dissolution of Hierarchy* (Palo Alto, CA: Cheshire, 1982), 44. Hereafter cited in text.

62. In part this is a function of the Neanderthals' (implausible) failure to connect sex and reproduction; despite their huge brains, "any relationship between sexual activity and childbirth was beyond conception" (134).

63. Jean Auel, *The Valley of Horses* (New York: Bantam, 2011), 8.

64. In the recent novel *The Overstory* (New York: Norton, 2018), Richard Powers comes close to offering a perspective that displaces exclusively human interest by chronicling the lives of various characters who are interconnected not just by their involvement with trees but because those trees have been communicating with one another using a chemical language transmitted through root systems. The world's forests weave the lives of Powers's characters together across space and through time. But given that "people will only read stories about people," as Barbara Kingsolver points out in a review of the novel, Powers's book amounts to a "breathtaking hoodwink" wherein he channels his talking trees through the "character development" that is no less normative for the ecological novel than the novel as such. See "The Heroes of This Novel Are Centuries Old and 300 Feet Tall," *New York Times Book Review*, April 9, 2018, 4. Note also Claire Miye Stanford's review in *The Los Angeles Review of Books*: "Even if humans form the understory, they are still necessary for the novel to work." See "Speaking for the Trees: Richard Powers's 'The Overstory,'" May 10, 2018, https://lareviewofbooks.org/article/speaking-for-the-trees-richard-powerss-the-overstory/.

65. In a survey of efforts to adapt the legal concept of personhood to the biota of rivers and forests, Gwendolyn Gordon writes: "What we are seeing now is . . . the destruction of the hegemony of the liberal understanding of individual personhood." "Environmental Personhood," *Columbia Journal of Environmental Law* 43, no. 1 (2018): 88. But of course the extension of personhood to natural objects, now construed as subjects with interests and rights, including property rights, would more accurately be described as the *triumph* of "the liberal understanding of individual personhood."

66. Edward Abbey, *The Monkey Wrench Gang* (New York: Avon, 1975), 43. Hereafter cited in text. The most visible such activism is the work of Earth First!, a group founded in 1980 by environmentalist Dave Foreman, who began his career as a policy wonk and professes to have been radicalized by Abbey's novel. In *Confessions of an Eco-Warrior* (New York: Crown, 1991), Foreman lists as one of the "purposes for environmental radicalism": "To inspire others to carry out activities straight from the pages of *The Monkey Wrench Gang*" (18). Like Abbey's characters, who have turned to industrial sabotage after trying "everything else—'lawsuits, big fucking propaganda campaigns, politics'" (169)—Foreman and his fellow Earth Firsters construe direct action as the only moral response to a system designed to wear down anyone who tries to work for change from within.

67. Robert Venturi, Denise Scott Brown, and Steven Izenour, *Learning from Las Vegas* (Cambridge, MA: MIT Press, 1977), 155. Hereafter cited in text.

68. For Abbey, the billboard is but a symptom of the underlying disease: the paved road itself. "Highways are the problem, not highway beautification" (16), write Sam Love and David Obst in the introduction to *Ecotage!* (1972), an anthology born of a contest sponsored by the group Environmental Action, which invited correspondents to devise the most effective "tactics for harassing polluters" (13). Abbey's attack on the billboard is no eccentricity. Given the number of contest entries for halting their spread, it is striking how many of the period's environmentally minded people, both lay and expert, understood billboards as a moral and ecological blight, second only to

overpopulation in occasioning what Love and Obst call "ecological indignation" (15). See Sam Love and David Obst, eds., *Ecotage!* (New York: Pocket Books, 1972). On the long and embattled history of billboards, see Catherine Gudis, *Buyways: Billboards, Automobiles, and the American Landscape* (New York: Routledge, 2004).

69. Robert Smithson, *The Collected Writings*, ed. Jack Flam (Berkeley: University of California Press, 1996), 151, 303. Hereafter cited in text.

70. Of a series of power lines Hayduke has taken down along a railway: "They fell inward, upon the tracks, pulled by the weight of the cantilevered power line. An instant before the crash Hayduke saw a blue spark 50,000 volts strong leap the gap from cable to rail" (231).

71. In "The New Atomic Wilderness: Ed Abbey's Post-Apocalyptic Southwest," *Southwestern American Literature* 34, no. 1 (2008): 41–53, Alex Hunt takes a dimmer view of Abbey's treatment of Indians, seeing him as not merely unsentimental toward but "disparaging, denying, and finally supplanting indigenous identity." Whereas Hunt concludes that Abbey installs "eco-warriors" as "the new breed of 'Native American'" (48), I argue that Abbey's gang members appeal to a very old—a precolonial, if not prehistoric—ideal of Indian experience. Identity has little to do with this commitment.

3. That Seventies Cult

1. Brainwashing remains the central tenet of what Scott Selisker in *Human Programming: Brainwashing, Automatons, and American Unfreedom* (Minneapolis: University of Minnesota Press, 2016) calls the "*topos* of the cult." Selisker presents an accurate picture of the moral panic around seventies cults, an anxiety heightened by the cults' intense insider-outsider divide. The *topos* he describes is largely the outsider's view, "a set of narrative conventions and a shape or *form* of social organization, one whose continuities with the closure and control of totalitarian society have been continually emphasized by experts, reporters, literary and popular fiction writers, and ordinary citizens alike" (127). I focus on taking the cults at their word. An examination of their self-descriptions, I argue, yields a different account of seventies cults from Selisker's. He is interested in the cult as a postmodern iteration of "mental unfreedom" (127). I am interested in the cult as a template for seventies libertarianism, or mental freedom.

2. Flo Conway and Jim Siegelman, *Snapping: America's Epidemic of Sudden Personality Change* (1978; New York: Stillpoint, 2011), 288.

3. Conway and Siegelman, *Snapping*, 330, 135.

4. Roy Wallis, *The Road to Total Freedom: A Sociological Analysis of Scientology* (New York: Columbia University Press, 1977), 14.

5. Murray Rothbard, *For a New Liberty: A Libertarian Manifesto* (1973; Auburn, AL: Ludwig von Mises Institute, 2006), 10. Hereafter cited in text.

6. Osho [Shree Rajneesh], *Come, Come, Yet Again Come* (1980; New Delhi: New Age Books, 2003), 35.

7. "There's only one act of free will . . . , a decision which determines everything else: to think or not to think," observes a character in L. Neil Smith's *The Probability Broach* (1979; New York: Orb, 2001), a novel about an alternate reality in which America has become the libertarian utopia it was meant to be. "If you decide upon the latter, then it's back to good old heredity and environment again, by default. They'll call the tune if you don't call it yourself" (303). Smith seems to be referencing a view of

Morris and Linda Tannehill, who write in their 1970 anarcho-capitalist manifesto *The Market for Liberty* (Auburn, AL: Ludwig von Mises Institute, 2007): "The choice to think or not to think is his, and it is a choice that every man must make" (7).

8. John Hospers, *Libertarianism: A Political Philosophy for Tomorrow* (1971; Los Angeles: Nash, 2013), 25. In *The Market for Liberty*, the Tannehills write: "In order to survive, *man must think*. . . . The more fully and clearly he uses his mind, the better he will be able to live" (7).

9. Murray N. Rothbard, *Man, Economy, and State* (1962; Auburn, AL: Ludwig von Mises Institute, 2009), 341, 319, 2.

10. F. A. Hayek, *The Collected Works, Volume 4: The Fortunes of Liberalism*, ed. Peter Klein (Chicago: University of Chicago Press, 1992), 161.

11. F. A. Hayek, *The Counterrevolution of Science* (1952; New York: Free Press, 1964), 15, 31.

12. James Buchanan, *Cost and Choice: An Inquiry in Economic Theory* (1969; Chicago: University of Chicago Press, 1979), 9.

13. Rothbard, *Man, Economy, and State*, 324.

14. Murray N. Rothbard, *Anatomy of the State* (1974; Auburn, AL: Ludwig von Mises Institute, 2009), 13.

15. Marvin Harris, *America Now* (New York: Simon & Schuster, 1981), 147, 146.

16. John Lofland, *Doomsday Cult: A Study of Conversion, Proselytization, and Maintenance of Faith* (Englewood Cliffs, NJ: Prentice-Hall, 1966), 28.

17. Cited in Tim Reiterman, *Raven: The Untold Story of the Rev. Jim Jones and His People* (1982; New York: Penguin, 2008), 214.

18. Rawls, *A Theory of Justice* (Cambridge, MA: Harvard University Press, 1971), 11. Hereafter cited in text.

19. The libertarian society in Smith's *The Probability Broach* has flourished because Jefferson adds the word "unanimous" to "consent of the governed" in the Declaration of Independence (303). Recall too that Milton and Rose Friedman praise "the marketplace" over the "ballot box" because market relations afford "unanimity without conformity." *Free to Choose: A Personal Statement* (1980; New York: Harcourt, 1990), 66.

20. "The language of the totalistic environment is characterized by the thought-terminating cliché" (429), Robert Jay Lifton writes in the 1961 book *Thought Reform and the Psychology of Totalism: A Study of "Brainwashing" in China* (Chapel Hill: University of North Carolina Press, 1989). Somewhat to his chagrin, Lifton's analysis of mind control in the fifties spawned many decades of debate on brainwashing as a diagnosis. As evidenced by the title of the book, he preferred the phrase "thought reform" to "brainwashing" (xi), and lamented that the word in scare quotes became the adopted nomenclature. Few would deny that mass media's most prized speech act, the sound bite, effects the kind of brain freeze that cults and other "totalistic environment[s]" (Lifton's examples are authoritarian dictatorships) are understood to induce. Lifton himself refrained from linking mind control practices in Communist China, however, to the small group manipulations of sectarian movements in the rich democracies.

21. Richard Thaler and Cass Sunstein, *Nudge: Improving Decisions about Health, Wealth, and Happiness* (New Haven, CT: Yale University Press, 2008), 13, 99. Hereafter cited in text.

22. Derek Parfit justifies "paternalistic intervention" on the view that "we have a general right to prevent people from acting *wrongly*." "Since we ought to believe that

great imprudence is seriously wrong," he concludes, "we ought to believe that we should prevent such imprudence, even if this involves coercion." *Reasons and Persons* (New York: Oxford University Press, 1984), 446.

23. Cass Sunstein, "Nudges: Good and Bad," *New York Review of Books* 61, no. 16 (2014): 7.

24. L. Ron Hubbard, *The Way to Happiness: A Common Sense Guide to Better Living* (Los Angeles: Bridge Publications, 2007), 48.

25. L. Ron Hubbard, *Dianetics: The Modern Science of Mental Health* (1950; Los Angeles: Bridge Publications, 2007), 160, 135, 51. Hereafter cited in text.

26. Daniel Kahneman's *Thinking, Fast and Slow* (New York: Farrar, Straus and Giroux, 2011) describes the segue from automatism to reflection in the post-behaviorist era. Where the classic behaviorist sees consciousness as secondary if not illusory, Kahneman concludes that our consciousness works *too* well for our own good in many instances, setting up "simplifying shortcuts" ("heuristics") in our "intuitive thinking" (8) that make "our minds . . . susceptible to systematic error" (10). The system in question is crucial. For Kahneman (and Amos Tversky, his longtime collaborator), "mental life" is divided into "two agents, System 1 and System 2, which respectively control fast and slow thinking." The goal is to show that "the automatic operations of System 1" dominate our thoughts in ways we don't expect in order to get System 2, with its "controlled operations" and "deliberative thought" (13), more in view. Kahneman aims to help us reflect on our impulsive minds and "improve the ability to identify and understand errors of judgment and choice, in others and eventually in ourselves, by providing a richer and more precise language to discuss them" (4).

27. "Space opera" is Hubbard's term, and while the Church's official position is to deny the Xenu story (called "Incident II" in Scientology), its existence has long been known outside the Church. Hubbard conceived the plot in 1969, making it available only to Scientology's Operating Thetan (OT) III members. Robert Kaufman, who defected from the Church after reaching—but failing—the OT III course, leaked the plot in his exposé *Inside Scientology: How I Joined Scientology and Became Superhuman* (London: Olympia Press, 1972).

28. During the shooting of BBC 1's *Scientology and Me* (2007), for example, "a Scientology film crew showed up to document the making of the BBC documentary," according to Lawrence Wright. "Cameras were pointed at cameras." *Going Clear: Scientology, Hollywood, and the Prison of Belief* (New York: Knopf, 2013), 339.

29. "Tech" is a keyword in Scientology jargon, one of the three branches of the Church teachings (the others are "Ethics" and "Admin"); it is shorthand for the totality of "scientific" techniques and technologies gathered in the Church's canonical "Tech Volumes" (the "Red Volumes"). These consist chiefly of the Hubbard Communications Office Bulletins in which Hubbard worked and reworked the theoretical and methodological requirements for Scientology.

30. Wright, *Going Clear*, 141.

31. Richard Rorty, *Philosophy and the Mirror of Nature* (Princeton, NJ: Princeton University Press, 1979), 166.

32. Margaret Thaler Singer, with Janja Lalich, *Cults in Our Midst: The Hidden Menace in Our Everyday Lives* (New York: Wiley, 1995), 114. The sexual recruitment practiced by Children of God—women seducing potential male converts—was called "flirty fishing" (13).

33. Claude Lefort, "Outline of a Genesis of Ideology in Modern Society," in *The Political Forms of Modern Society: Bureaucracy, Democracy, Totalitarianism* (Cambridge, MA: MIT Press, 1986), 229.

34. Louis Althusser, *On Ideology* (London: Verso, 2008), 34.

35. Althusser, *On Ideology*, 55.

36. Lefort, "Outline," 229, 227.

37. Lefort, "Outline," 235, 236.

38. Although it was not his framework, the American context was certainly ripe for Lefort's argument. The outset of the sixties saw the publication of Daniel Bell's *The End of Ideology* (1960), a collection of essays that did not so much diagnose as symptomatize the titular fantasy for Cold War consensus culture. For Bell, "ideology" really meant "radicalism," which really meant "communism." The "strong response to radical appeals," Bell concludes, arises mainly in situations where "popular expectations" outstrip the reality of, say, "economic expansion." *The End of Ideology: On the Exhaustion of Political Ideas in the Fifties* (Cambridge, MA: Harvard University Press, 2000), 32. Ideology for Bell was a substantive doctrine, something one adopted to fill the gap between expectation and reality, not (as for the French Marxists) a formal structure of domination. We might frame this contrast by saying that for the line of conservative-ish intellectuals from Bell to Francis Fukuyama, the belief that ideology is a set of ideas one could embrace or reject after careful reflection was among the most ideological facets of US society in the view of Lefort. The essence of this determination was the taking for granted of rationality on the part of subjects faced with substantive choices.

39. Peter Sloterdjik describes an analogous structure in what he calls "enlightened false consciousness" (5), and attributes its prevalence to "an intellectual state of affairs in which all thinking has become strategy" (xxix), the model of cognition that dominates Strong AI and behaviorist research. See *Critique of Cynical Reason*, trans. Michael Eldred (Minneapolis: University of Minnesota Press, 1987).

40. Claude Lefort, *Democracy and Political Theory*, trans. David Macey (Cambridge, UK: Polity, 1988), 215. Hereafter cited in text as "OP."

41. Wallis, *Road*, 14.

42. Paul Goodman, *Little Prayers and Finite Experience* (New York: Harper & Row, 1972), 35.

43. Carol and Jo Anne Parke, *All God's Children: The Cult Experience—Salvation or Slavery?* (1977; New York: Penguin, 1979), 92.

44. Parke, *All God's Children*, 85.

45. Richard Sennett, *The Uses of Disorder: Personal Identity and City Life* (1970; New York: Norton, 1992), 120. Hereafter cited in text.

46. Cited in Reiterman, *Raven*, 147.

47. Luke Rhinehart, *The Book of est* (New York: Holt, Rinehart and Winston, 1976), 16, 95, xiii. Hereafter cited in text.

48. Murray Bookchin, *Post-Scarcity Anarchism* (1971; Montreal: Black Rose Books, 1986), 67. Hereafter cited in text.

49. The traditional distinction between anarchism and libertarianism concerns each theory's view of private property. For libertarians, it is more or less sacrosanct; for anarchists, it is often excluded. But many anarchists are also "propertarians," holders of the view that individuals must be allowed to contract freely with one another without

any state intermediation. The hostility that anarchism maintains toward private property is often defended on historical grounds. The origins of modern anarchism with Pierre-Joseph Proudhon took the rejection of capitalism as central to its platform. As "anarcho-capitalists" like Rothbard and the Tannehills demonstrate, anarchism is not logically opposed to propertarianism and appears on a plausible reading to entail a commitment to it. The same Proudhon who declared that "Property is theft" (in an 1840 book of that title), after all, wrote: *"Commutative justice,* the *reign of contract,* the *industrial or economic system,* such are the different synonyms for the idea which by its accession must do away with the old systems of *distributive justice,* the *reign of law,* or in more concrete terms, *feudal, governmental,* or *military* rule." *General Idea of Revolution in the Nineteenth Century* (New York: Cosimo, 2007), 112. One might object that my argument is really concerned with the subset of anarcho-capitalists (like Rothbard) whom real anarchists disown as libertarians in anarchist clothing. But my intent is to resist the view that anarcho-capitalists are less real than other anarchists. As my discussion of Bookchin in this chapter makes clear, the anxiety over what counts as real anarchism is a driving force of anarchism in general, which on its own terms professes an amorphousness that makes gatekeeping both impossible and interminable. "I am an anarchist," the Libertarian Party member Karl Hess wrote in the 1980 essay "Anarchism Without Hyphens." "There is only one kind of anarchist. Not two. Just one. An anarchist, the only kind, as defined by the long tradition and literature of the position itself, is a person in opposition to authority imposed through the hierarchical power of the state." The essay can be found at https://www.panarchy.org/hess/anarchism.html.

50. Bookchin, *Post-Scarcity Anarchism,* 45.

51. William Reichert, "Anarchism, Freedom, and Power," *Ethics* 79, no. 2 (1969): 147.

52. Nicolas Walter, *About Anarchism* (1969; London: Freedom Press, 2002), 81.

53. Kurt Zube, *An Anarchist Manifesto: The Manifesto of Peace and Freedom* (Freiburg, GDR: Mackay, 1977), 8.

54. Maharishi Mahesh Yogi, *The Science of Being and the Art of Living* (New York: Signet, 1963), 46.

55. Reichert, "Anarchism," 144, 146.

56. Ted Patrick, *Let Our Children Go!* (New York: Ballantine, 1976), 43, 47.

57. In *If God Meant to Interfere: American Literature and the Rise of the Christian Right* (Ithaca, NY: Cornell University Press, 2016), Christopher Douglas points out that "conservative Christians reshaped the political and moral landscape of the nation in recent decades by making universal claims within the culture wars" (6). Such Christians "emerged" alongside the "context of a developing "multiculturalism" (18) whose pluralistic tenets they heartily rejected: "their universalism entailed the belief that people who believed in evolution or who had abortions or engaged in homosexual sex were not just culturally different, but were in error" (6).

58. Philip Jenkins, *Mystics and Messiahs: Cults and New Religions in American History* (New York: Oxford University Press, 2001), 186.

59. The fate of the "Cult Awareness Network" (CAN) is instructive. Formed in 1979 in the aftermath of Jonestown, CAN came under fire during its brief life span for its members' persecutory methods and *cult-like* devotion to their cause before being bought in a hostile takeover by the Church of Scientology.

60. The perennial fascination with Scientology might be seen as the exception that proves this point. Scientology would scarcely incite interest were it not for those celebrities who account for its mass appeal. The church's celebrity centers speak to the obvious centrality of the star to its mission. To the degree that we are all gawkers at the lifestyles of the rich and famous, we are more ripe for conversion to the Church of Scientology than Pentecostalism. But we are also well inoculated against conversion, since it is a fact about our engagement with celebrity culture that in vital respects we do not treat it seriously—or more exactly, that even our most passionate identifications with it are partial and fleeting. The true zealots of fandom—the army of Beliebers, say—are never more than temporarily captive; in other words, they turn thirteen. And it is worth noting the obvious point that even Scientology's own stars have flamed out. Tom Cruise, John Travolta, and Kirstie Alley are far less likely to be adored than mocked in 2020. Such ridicule garners its own kind of fame, of course. There is a vast star system composed of one-time red giants who escape the black hole of obscurity through their canny willingness to be in on the joke they make of themselves (Travolta in *Pulp Fiction*; Alley in *Fat Actress*). The dismal failure—not to say sheer awfulness—of Paul Thomas Anderson's *The Master* (2012) has much to do with its mistaking public interest in Scientology for a transfixing unease with its sinister mind games, which *The Master* treats as ominous because flawed (illegitimate, coercive) avenues to some desired meaning or depth. The whole mood of the film, with its vintage cinematography, hectic improvisations, mumblecore dialogue, and a backstory out of Steinbeck at his most maudlin, gets Scientology wrong. Travolta's legendary box office disaster, *Battlefield Earth*, precisely by virtue of its supreme camp value, gets Scientology right.

61. Wallis, *Road to Total Freedom*, 16.

62. Robert Nozick, *Anarchy, State, and Utopia* (New York: Basic, 1974), 312. Hereafter cited in text.

63. Mack Reynolds's *Commune 2000 A.D.* (1974; Cabin John, MD: Wildside Press, 2017), released the same year as *Anarchy, State, and Utopia*, envisions a futuristic welfare state where "ultramation" and "Universal Guaranteed Income" have resulted in "one-hundred-percent leisure." This dystopic world has also spawned a rebellion made up of countless people rejecting that fate by setting up equally countless utopias. Just as Nozick juxtaposes the experience machine with "utopias" of "many different and divergent communities" that "will wax and wane" (312), Reynolds's novel pits the computer against the commune and sees mobility as the latter's chief virtue. Whereas "the political state" uses its "National Data Banks" for the "regimentation" (164) of the citizenry by putting "everything, no matter how trivial," in the computers, which thus become the inescapable interface for accessing "human knowledge" (32), communes "came and went at such a pace that no record could be kept. . . . A communard might be in a local commune in New England one day and travel down to one on the Florida peninsula the next. Or, for that matter, the whole commune might make such a move" (33).

64. Robert Paul Wolff, *In Defense of Anarchism* (1970; Berkeley: University of California Press, 1998), 80.

65. Wolff, *In Defense of Anarchism*, 81.

66. Walter, *About Anarchism*, 29.

67. Murray Bookchin, *Social Anarchism or Lifestyle Anarchism: The Unbridgeable Chasm* (San Francisco: AK Press, 1995), 54. Hereafter cited in text.

68. Rothbard's breakaway anarcho-capitalism applies this schismatic pattern to contemporary libertarianism, which descends from what he calls (in keeping with this chapter's theme) "the Rand Cult." A Rand apostate, Rothbard chronicles the decline of the Objectivist circle thus: immediately after "the organized cult came into being," it led to "excommunications and purges," which in turn precipitated an "irrevocable split" and the cult's "self-destruction." See "The Sociology of the Rand Cult," 1972, accessed January 20, 2020, https://www.lewrockwell.com/1970/01/murray-n-rothbard/understanding-ayn-randianism/.

69. See Murray Bookchin, "Libertarian Municipalism: An Overview," originally published 1991, posted April 28, 2009, https://theanarchistlibrary.org/library/murray-bookchin-libertarian-municipalism-an-overview.

70. Samuel Konkin, *New Libertarian Manifesto* (Huntington Beach, CA: KoPubCo, 2006), 19, 22.

71. Konkin, *New Libertarian Manifesto*, 25.

72. John Bucci, "The Search for Anarchism," *Journal of Education* 154, no. 2 (1971): 61.

73. William S. Burroughs, *Cities of the Red Night* (New York: Holt, Rinehart and Winston, 1981), xii, 265. Hereafter cited in text.

74. This origin myth also finds its way into John Hospers's 1971 manifesto *Libertarianism: A Political Philosophy for Tomorrow* (note 8): "The nearest approach to a libertarian government was the government of the United States at the time of its inception" (15).

75. William S. Burroughs, *Junky* (New York: Grove, 2003), 127.

76. William S. Burroughs, *Ali's Smile / Naked Scientology* (Bonn: Expanded Media, 1973), 87, 72, 75. Hereafter cited in text.

77. William S. Burroughs, *The Place of Dead Roads* (New York: Picador, 2001), 105. Hereafter cited in text.

78. Lee Konstantinou suggests that Burroughs did not include references in his novels to Xenu's invasion of earth and overthrow by the Galactic confederacy because he did not rise high enough in the Church's levels to become privy to such secrets, available only to the most advanced OTs. But having reviewed Robert Kaufman's *Inside Scientology* for *Rolling Stone* in 1972, Burroughs was well aware of the space-opera doctrines of the Church even if he did not reach the stage where that story was revealed to him. See "William S. Burroughs's Wild Ride with Scientology," May 11, 2011, https://io9.gizmodo.com/5800673/william-s-burroughss-wild-ride-with-scientology.

79. William S. Burroughs, *Last Words: The Final Journals of William S. Burroughs* (New York: Grove, 2001), 140. Hereafter cited in text.

80. My sense that Burroughs views self-control as a zero-sum game resonates with Michael Clune's insight that "Burroughs sees in the intersubjective relation the elemental principle of control, oppression, domination" (99). "Intersubjectivity" for Burroughs "is a veil thrown over the true nature of the mind" (102). See *American Literature and the Free Market, 1945–2000* (New York: Cambridge University Press, 2010).

81. On the Deleuzian approach to Burroughs, see Nathan Moore, "Nova Law: William S. Burroughs and the Logic of Control," *Law and Literature* 19, no. 3 (2007): 435–470; Mario Vrbančić, "Burroughs's Phantasmic Maps," *New Literary History* 36, no. 2 (2005): 313–326; Brent Wood, "William S. Burroughs and the Language of Cyberpunk," *Science Fiction Studies* 23, no. 1 (1996): 11–26.

82. Kathryn Hume, "William S. Burroughs's Phantasmic Geography," *Contemporary Literature* 40, no. 1 (1999): 132. Hereafter cited in text.

83. Daniel Oder and William S. Burroughs, *The Job: Interviews with William S. Burroughs* (New York: Penguin, 1989), 202.

84. Hence in *Scientologist! William S. Burroughs and the "Weird Cult"* (London: Beatdom, 2013), David Wills refers Burroughs's embrace of Scientology to his personal anguish: "Burroughs was a perfect target for people like the Scientologists. He was broken and hurt, confused and seeking something to fix himself. In Scientology he found hope" (158). Hume also argues that "as Burroughs alters the symbolism in later books, we see shifts in his outlook that spell a lessening of his psychic malaise" (131).

85. In an unfavorable review of *Cities of the Red Night*, Thomas Disch notes that "the 22 intervening years" between *Naked Lunch* and *Cities* "have impinged little on Mr. Burroughs's consciousness" by virtue of the fact that no traumatic historical events, including "the Manson murders or the Jonesville [sic] massacre," could possibly "divert his imagination from its own perfected self-absorption." "Pleasures of Hanging," *New York Times*, March 15, 1981, 24. Despite his low opinion of the novel, Disch pays Burroughs the backhanded compliment of recognizing that his self-absorption was an impeccably manicured career-spanning project.

86. Kim Carsons thus "was under no pressure to maintain the perimeters of a defensive ego and this left him free to *think*" (113).

87. Ted Morgan, *Literary Outlaw: The Life and Times of William S. Burroughs* (New York: Henry Holt, 1988), 252.

88. These quotes are from an interview Burroughs gave to *The International Times*, an underground newspaper, in 1969. The interview is cited in Wills, *Scientologist!*, 149. Claiming that Scientology ceased to be a cult when it abandoned epistemological individualism "as a result of the general tightening of control and the authoritarian imposition of Org practices" (185), Roy Wallis lends credence to Burroughs's view that Scientology betrayed its own origins.

89. John Irving, *The World According to Garp* (New York: Dutton, 1978), 340. Hereafter cited in text.

90. Don DeLillo, *The Names* (New York: Vintage, 1989), 206. Hereafter cited in text.

91. Gore Vidal, *Kalki* (New York: Random House, 1978), 5, 12. Hereafter cited in text.

92. "The oligarchs think the people are . . . stupid," Vidal wrote in the 1981 essay "The Second American Revolution." *The Selected Essays of Gore Vidal* (New York: Doubleday, 2008), 395. Hereafter cited in text as *SE*. It is far from clear that Vidal doesn't share this belief. Strong evidence for his holding it can be found in his writing itself, which is always most lively when throwing shade on human foolishness. "American literature," he concluded in an essay on Edmund Wilson, "is where stupidity . . . is deeply revered, and easily achieved" (*SE*, 154). We might argue that Vidal at his best, which is to say his campiest, needs a prevailing stupidity to bring out his sharpest voice. I have argued this about camp in general in "What School Culture Teaches Us about Queer Theory," *American Literary History* 25, no. 1 (2013): "Though it may be overstating things to say that camp preys on people's stupidity . . . it usually *requires* such stupidity as an enabling and unchanging condition" (12).

93. Michel Foucault, *Discipline and Punish: The Birth of the Prison*, trans. Alan Sheridan (1975; New York: Vintage, 1995), 25. It would be impossible in this space to

adjudicate the matter of Foucault's politics, but I am sympathetic to the case made for their being essentially anarchistic. Yet Foucault's anarchism appears oriented toward (and even to embrace) a fundamentally behaviorist or externalist view of subjectivity, whereas sixties anarchists, as I have argued, tend to model theirs on the neo-idealist understanding of subjectivity. *Discipline and Punish* has no patience for the "delusions" of the liberal humanist tradition: "The man . . . whom we are invited to free is already in himself the effect of a subjection much more profound than himself" (30). For Foucault, "psyche, subjectivity, personality, consciousness, etc." are mere "effects" of a "reality-reference" generated by the operations of power/knowledge (29).

94. Milton Friedman, *Capitalism and Freedom: Fortieth Anniversary Edition* (Chicago: University of Chicago Press, 2002), 201. Hereafter cited in text.

95. Saul Kripke, *Naming and Necessity* (Cambridge, MA: Harvard University Press, 1980), 58, 27, 97, 59.

96. Kripke, 38.

97. Don DeLillo, *Americana* (New York: Penguin, 1989), 288, 263. Hereafter cited in text.

98. In "'A Presence Almost Everywhere': Responsibility at Risk in Don DeLillo's *The Names*," *Contemporary Literature* 51, no. 1 (2010), Heather Houser uses this passage to mount an important corrective to the paranoid reading of DeLillo. Examining *The Names* through the lens of Ulrich Beck's theory of risk, Houser argues that the novel explores how "the process of modernization has 'become its own theme,'" "has become a problem for itself" (128). Risk is both antithetical to and twinned with paranoia. It requires us to entertain the thought that the world is rife with accidents and unanticipated events at the same time that it forces us to see that the world is designed to go wrong, even to the point of undoing our place in it.

99. Another way of coping with the need to "keep up" is offered by *White Noise* (1985; New York: Penguin, 1999), which makes great fun of the countless new pedagogies summoned by the complexified world. "There is a teacher for every person," Jack Gladney notes at one point (55). His wife, Babette, "is teaching" her mainly elderly students "how to stand, sit and walk" (27), as if the rules for how to orient oneself to the ground itself have become radically esoteric.

100. Emily Apter describes a version of this phenomenon in "On Oneworldedness: Or Paranoia as a World System," *American Literary History* 18, no. 2 (2006), which sees DeLillo's *Mao II* as exemplary of its title concept: "As the world expands to include everybody, it paradoxically shrinks into a claustrophobic all-inclusiveness" (370). Below I argue against reading *The Names* as a specifically paranoid novel.

101. Matthew J. Morris, "Murdering Words: Language in Action in Don DeLillo's *The Names*," *Contemporary Literature* 30, no. 1 (1989): 117, 120.

102. Matthew Mutter, "'Things That Happen and What We Say about Them': Speaking the Ordinary in Delillo's *The Names*," *Twentieth-Century Literature* 53, no. 4 (2007): 510, 496.

103. Fredric Jameson, *Postmodernism, or, The Cultural Logic of Late Capitalism* (Durham, NC: Duke University Press, 1991), 309.

104. Amy Hungerford, *Postmodern Belief* (Princeton, NJ: Princeton University Press, 2010), 74.

4. Millennial America and the World to Come

1. Philip Dick, *The Shifting Realities of Philip K. Dick*, ed. Lawrence Sutin (New York: Vintage, 1996), 271. Hereafter cited in text as *SR*.

2. Philip Dick, *The Divine Invasion* (1981; New York: Mariner, 2011), 215.

3. John Nelson Darby, the nineteenth-century British preacher who almost singlehandedly shaped the modern eschatology of rapture, "lived with his vision of the end so intensely that he would not establish institutions meant to last," according to Garry Wills. "His followers gathered in various types of 'assemblies' and 'brotherhoods' . . . too aware of this world's transience to build church structures." *Under God: Religion and American Politics* (New York: Simon & Schuster, 1990), 145.

4. Nathan Hatch, *The Democratization of American Christianity* (New Haven, CT: Yale University Press, 1989), 212.

5. Hal Lindsey, *The Late Great Planet Earth* (Grand Rapids, MI: Zondervan, 1970), 127. Hereafter cited in text.

6. Christopher Douglas, *If God Meant to Interfere* (Ithaca, NY: Cornell University Press, 2016), 147.

7. Adam Parfrey, "Preface," in *Apocalypse Culture*, ed. Adam Parfrey (Townsend, WA: Feral House, 1990), 7.

8. Adam Parfrey, "GG Allin: Portrait of the Enemy," in Parfrey, *Apocalypse Culture*, 45.

9. Rodney Stark, "Must All Religions Be Supernatural?," in *The Social Impact of New Religious Movements*, ed. Bryan Wilson (New York: Rose of Sharon Press, 1981), 175.

10. Stark, "Must All Religions Be Supernatural?," 175.

11. In a project spanning three decades, Tversky and Kahneman opposed their own "prospect theory," which accounts for the "psychophysical factors" (2) of decision making, to the expected utility theory regnant in economics. See Amos Tversky and Daniel Kahneman, eds., *Choices, Values, and Frames* (New York: Cambridge University Press, 2000). As I noted in the previous chapter, behavioral economics is a slightly misleading term for Kahneman and Tversky's project to the extent that it bears little resemblance to Skinner's version of behaviorism.

12. Rodney Stark and Roger Finke, *Acts of Faith: Explaining the Human Side of Religion* (Berkeley: University of California Press, 2000), 44, 43.

13. On the (by now well-attested) alignment of "fundamentalist religion" and "the fundamentalism of the market," see Linda Kintz, *Between Jesus and the Market: The Emotions that Matter in Right-Wing America* (Durham, NC: Duke University Press, 1997), 2. For a zealous defense of the natural fit of Christianity with what he calls "the praxis of democratic capitalism," see Michael Novak's *Toward a Theology of the Market* (1981; rev. ed., Washington, DC: American Enterprise Institute, 1990): "Morally serious young Christians will better save their souls and serve the cause of the Kingdom of God all around the world by restoring the liberty and power of the private sector than by working for the state" (34).

14. Jennie Chapman, *Plotting Apocalypse: Reading, Agency, and Identity in the Left Behind Series* (Jackson: University of Mississippi Press, 2013), 13.

15. Dick, *Divine Invasion*, 253.

16. Milton Friedman, *Capitalism and Freedom* (Chicago: University of Chicago Press, 2002), 1–2. Hereafter cited in text.

17. F. A. Hayek, *The Road to Serfdom*, ed. Bruce Caldwell (1944; Chicago: University of Chicago Press, 2007), 125. According to Justin Fox, "both Friedman and [George] Stigler," each a "crusader" for the free market at Chicago in the postwar era, "said that the crucial turning point in their thinking came when they read Friedrich Hayek's *The Road to Serfdom.*" *The Myth of the Rational Market: A History of Risk, Reward, and Delusion on Wall Street* (New York: Harper Collins, 2009), 88.

18. Hayek, *Road*, 130.

19. Mary Stewart Relfe, *When Your Money Fails: The "666 System" Is Here* (Montgomery, AL: League of Prayer, 1981), 89. Hereafter cited in text.

20. Joseph Schumpeter, *Capitalism, Socialism, and Democracy* (New York: Harper Perennial, 2008), 83.

21. Salem Kirban, *666* (Wheaton, IL: Tyndale House, 1970), 137. Hereafter cited in text.

22. The secularization thesis was popularized in Peter Berger's *The Sacred Canopy* (1967), although Berger later disavowed it (in books like *The Desecularization of the World* [1999]).

23. Philip Dick and Roger Zelazny, *Deus Irae* (New York: Mariner, 2013), 193.

24. Rodney Stark, "Bringing Theory Back In," in *Rational Choice Theory and Religion: A Summary and Assessment*, ed. Lawrence Young (New York: Routledge, 1997), 18.

25. Roger Finke, "The Consequences of Religious Competition: Supply Side Explanations for Religious Change," in Young, *Rational Choice Theory and Religion*, 48.

26. Stark, "Bringing Theory Back In," 18.

27. Lawrence Iannaccone, "Rational Choice: Framework for the Scientific Study of Religion," in Young, *Rational Choice Theory and Religion*, 29.

28. Iannaccone, "Rational Choice," 26.

29. R. Stephen Warner, "Convergence Toward the New Paradigm," in Young, *Rational Choice Theory and Religion*, 88.

30. Robert Venturi, Denise Scott Brown, and Steven Izenour, *Learning from Las Vegas* (Cambridge, MA: MIT Press, 1972), 149, 154. Hereafter cited in text.

31. George Stigler, "The Intellectual and the Marketplace," *Kansas Journal of Sociology* 1, no. 2 (1965): 70.

32. Hunter S. Thompson, *Fear and Loathing in Las Vegas* (1971; New York: Vintage, 1998), 4. Hereafter cited in text.

33. Hunter S. Thompson, *Generation of Swine: Tales of Shame and Degradation in the Eighties* (New York: Summit, 1988), 9. Hereafter cited in text as *GS*.

34. Philip Dick, *VALIS* (New York: Mariner, 2011), 91. Hereafter cited in text.

35. According to Emmanuel Carrère, "Valis" was the "code name" Dick "secretly" used for the "entity that had first made direct contact with him" during the 2-3-74 event. See *I Am Alive and You Are Dead: A Journey into the Mind of Philip K. Dick*, trans. Timothy Bent (1993; New York: Metropolitan, 2004), 247.

36. Jonathan Lethem, "Introduction," in *The Exegesis of Philip K. Dick*, ed. Pamela Jackson and Jonathan Lethem (Boston: Houghton Mifflin, 2011), xvi. The "Exegesis" seeks to invent wholesale the sort of "cosmogony," as Dick puts it in *VALIS*, that typically arises as a "group production" (91). Whereas exegeses like Lindsey's invite the believer to read along with the hermeneutic expositor, Dick's exegesis tends to shut the reader out, to withhold the cypher. It takes the form of an annotation without disclosing to the reader what precise referent is being annotated. It is as if, even in the

explicit role of postmodern visionary or high priest, Dick cannot resist the urge to occlude himself, to refuse revelation, to announce that the secret of the universe is, finally and tautologically, a secret. Erik Davis captures "the indeterminacy" of his philosophical musings by observing that Dick "constantly liquefied his own revelations." *TechGnosis: Myth, Magic, and Mysticism in the Age of Information* (1998; Berkeley, CA: North Atlantic, 2015), 298.

37. Thomas Nagel, "The Limits of Objectivity," in Sterling McMurrin, ed., *The Tanner Lectures on Human Values* (Cambridge, UK: Cambridge University Press, 1980), 91.

38. Charles B. Strozier, *Apocalypse: The Psychology of Fundamentalism in America* (Eugene, OR: Wipf and Stock, 1994), 21, 29.

39. Strozier, *Apocalypse*, 29, 19.

40. Gary Becker, *The Economic Approach to Human Behavior* (Chicago: University of Chicago Press, 1976), 10.

41. See Elaine Pagels's gloss on the gnostic theologian Valentinus: "To shape and manage her creation, Wisdom brought forth the demiurge, the creator-God of Israel, as her agent." *The Gnostic Gospels* (1979; New York: Vintage, 1989), 52.

42. Becker, *The Economic Approach*, 7.

43. Davis has written perceptively about the mesh of materialist and idealist assumptions in Dick's home-brewed mythology: "Spiritualizing the notion of an information virus," Dick "redeems the world through the very materiality of its infectious code" (298).

44. Luciano Floridi, *The 4th Revolution: How the Infosphere Is Reshaping Human Reality* (New York: Oxford University Press, 2014), 41.

45. Floridi, *The 4th Revolution*, 41.

46. Floridi, *The 4th Revolution*, vi, 65.

47. Dick, *Divine Invasion*, 17, 15.

48. Philip K. Dick, *Ubik* (New York: Mariner, 2012), 16, 218.

49. Dick, *Ubik*, 75.

50. Jane Roberts, *The Seth Material* (Cutchogue, NY: Buccaneer Books, 1970), 2, 4. Hereafter cited in text.

51. In *I Am Alive*, Carrère observes of Dick and Thomas that "once several reforms had been instituted, their cohabitation proved rather pleasant. It was like one of those cars that driving schools use, with two steering wheels" (251).

52. Dr. Helen Shucman, *A Course in Miracles: Combined Volume* (Mill Valley, CA: Foundation for Inner Peace, 2007), 8.

53. Robert Anton Wilson, *Cosmic Trigger, Volume I: Final Secret of the Illuminati* (1977; Tempe, AZ: New Falcon Press, 1986), 89. Hereafter cited in text.

54. Alan Harrington, *The Immortalist* (1969; Millbrae, CA: Celestial Arts, 1977), 21, 231. Hereafter cited in text.

55. John C. Lilly, *The Scientist: A Metaphysical Autobiography* (1978; Berkeley, CA: Ronin, 1997), 19–20.

56. In Toni Cade Bambara's celebrated 1980 novel *The Salt Eaters* (New York: Vintage, 1992), Minnie Ransom—who works medical wonders by "clearing the channels" (47) under the tutelage of a "spirit guide" (43) named Old Wife—instructs the suicidal Velma Henry to "choose your cure" (220), a lesson that finds Velma "waiting for a word from within" (170) and having "a telepathic visit with her former self" (18). The healing session that structures the novel's plot is designed to make Velma "the center of her own life," to

help her "set things up" so that she "could opt for a purely personal solution" (240). As Minnie tells Velma, "the source of health is never outside" (220). Like Dick, Bambara imagines that channeling heals by allowing the wounded Velma to remember who she really is through an act of anamnesis: "the divinely healthy whole Velma waited to be called out of its chamber, embraced and directed down the hall to claim her life from the split imposter" (148). Its insistence on Velma's "hunt for self" (267) seems to confirm some readers' view of the novel as a withdrawal from—if not an elegy for—the political promise of the New Social Movements. But *The Salt-Eaters* shares with Dick's late gnostic works a belief in the compatibility of political action and spiritual awakening: "One would tap the brain for any knowledge of initiation rites lying dormant there, recognizing that life depended on it, that initiation was the beginning of transformation and that the ecology of the self, the tribe, the species, the earth depended on just that" (247).

57. James Merrill, *Collected Poems*, ed. J. D. McClatchy and Stephen Yenser (New York: Knopf, 2001), 367. Hereafter cited in text as *CP*.

58. James Merrill, *The Changing Light at Sandover* (New York: Knopf, 2011), 360, 355. Hereafter cited in text.

59. Henry James, *The Wings of the Dove* (New York: Scribner's, 1902), 135, 136.

60. Claudia Ingram, "'Fission and Fusion Both Liberate Energy': James Merrill, Jorie Graham, and the Metaphoric Imagination," *Twentieth Century Literature* 51, no. 2 (2005): 143, 149.

61. Nikki Skillman, "James Merrill's Embodied Memory," *Twentieth Century Literature* 59, no. 4 (2013): 543.

62. C.A. Buckley, "Exploring *The Changing Light at Sandover*: An Interview with James Merrill," *Twentieth Century Literature* 38, no. 4 (1992): 419. Hereafter cited in text.

63. Jason Schneiderman infers from the dead's "VIP treatment of the Jackson-Merrill household" what he takes to be the chief lesson of *Sandover*: "Merrill isn't just universally loved. He's loved by the universe." "Notes on Not Writing: Revisiting *The Changing Light at Sandover*," *American Poetry Review* 38, no. 5 (2009): 15.

64. Cited in Langdon Hammer, *James Merrill: Life and Art* (New York: Knopf, 2015), 675. Hereafter cited in text.

65. Henry David Thoreau, *The Portable Thoreau*, ed. Jeffrey Cramer (New York: Penguin, 2012), 283, 284. It is on the basis of its hostility to "family news" that Henry Abelove characterizes *Walden* as an "antinovel." *Deep Gossip* (Minneapolis: University of Minnesota Press, 2003), 37. There are other parallels between Merrill and Thoreau one might draw out along Abelove's lines, not least of which is the distance their queerness encourages them to put between themselves and the ordinary run of heterosexual domestic interests.

66. Siobhan Philips, *The Poetics of the Everyday* (New York: Columbia University Press, 2010), 182, 156.

67. Helen Vendler, "*Divine Comedies*," in *A Reader's Guide to James Merrill's The Changing Light at Sandover*, ed. Robert Polito (Ann Arbor: University of Michigan Press, 1994), 140.

68. Andy Warhol, *The Philosophy of Andy Warhol (From A to B and Back Again)* (New York: Harcourt, 1975), 101.

69. Judith Moffett notes that "small, artificial products of highly developed cultures" are characteristic of Merrill's poetry, which strives to be an "attractive artifact" along

the lines of the "Van Eyck angel, etched tumblers, Willowware cup, little glass horse, bells from Isfahan," and other assorted *bijoux* that litter his mature verse (11). See *James Merrill: An Introduction to the Poetry* (New York: Columbia University Press, 1984). In the late poem "Self-Portrait in Tyvek™ Windbreaker" (1992), Merrill sees the "vaguely imbecile / Emporia" where the titular garment was purchased as "catering to the collective unconscious / Of our time" (*CP*, 669). While the unavoidable but degraded trappings of an all-pervading consumerism betoken a universal inanition, the privileged things in Merrill—singular, artisanal, radiant with person-to-person contact—seem to restore intent and consciousness to the material world. The "empty, open hand" that the "best" friend brings as a housewarming gift in "A Tenancy" might stand in for the centrality of handedness and of the handmade, signed, or marked item to meaningful connection throughout Merrill's poetry (*CP*, 170) In *Sandover*, after all, DJ—the essential partner in the seances—is the "HAND" (159) to JM's "SCRIBE."

70. Devin Johnston, "Resistance to the Message," *Contemporary Literature* 41, no. 1 (2000): 95. Hereafter cited in text.

71. The sociologist Michael Brown, the rare academic to take channeling seriously, describes a video in which the celebrity channel J. Z. Knight recalls being "transformed" by an entity she calls "Ramtha," who removed her from "a world of suburban alienation in which nothing mattered more than dinner parties" and "hybrid roses." *The Channeling Zone: American Spirituality in an Anxious Age* (Cambridge, MA: Harvard University Press, 1997), 1.

72. Yenser, *The Consuming Myth: The Work of James Merrill* (Cambridge, MA: Harvard University Press, 1987), 272.

73. Nozick, *Anarchy, State, and Utopia* (New York: Basic, 1974), 168.

74. James Merrill, *A Different Person: A Memoir* (New York: Knopf, 1993), 5.

75. James Merrill with J. D. McClatchy, "The Art of Poetry, No. 31," *Paris Review* 84 (1982): 75.

76. Robert Bellah et al., *Habits of the Heart: Individualism and Commitment in American Life* (Berkeley: University of California Press, 1985), 220, 221.

77. Bellah, *Habits*, 98.

78. Julian Jaynes, *The Origin of Consciousness in the Breakdown of the Bicameral Mind* (1976; New York: Mariner, 2000), 69, 71. Hereafter cited in text.

79. It might seem that insisting on Merrill's poem as an epic of subjectivity runs aground on an obvious fact about the work—namely, the presence at the Ouija board of two mediums (Merrill and David Jackson). Yet as Stephen Yenser points out in a corrective to Edward Mendelson's review of Hammer's Merrill biography, to say that Jackson had a "prominent voice" in the poem's composition is inaccurate. "Everything in *Sandover* went through a process of revision by Merrill alone, starting with the transcription itself," Yenser observes. "Some of the published passages are surprisingly nearly verbatim versions of transcripts, but most of the otherworldly dictation has been edited and recast—corrected, clarified, amplified, retouched, extended." Yenser's point is that however instrumental Jackson was to the experience of the séances, the resulting poem was itself a solo enterprise. See Stephen Yenser, "New Light on Sandover," *New York Review of Books*, January 19, 2017.

80. As Stephen Spender points out in his review of *Mirabell*, "the poem frequently breaks into lyric passages in various forms—terza rima, sonnets, and

seventeenth-century Metaphysical poem stanzas—of great beauty." "Heaven Can't Wait," *New York Review of Books*, December 21, 1978, 36.

81. In imputing to the bicameral mind the backhanded virtue of a more direct relation to the lifeworld, Jaynes is describing what Christine Korsgaard, glossing Kant's notion of "misology (hatred of reason)," calls the nostalgia "for the guidance of mere natural instinct." Such nostalgia arises, says Korsgaard, because of "our banishment from a world that is teleologically ordered by our instincts and presented as such by our incentives," that is, "a world in which we nearly always already know what to do." *Self-Constitution: Agency, Identity, and Integrity* (New York: Oxford University Press, 2009), 118. In the misologue's tragic account of modern subjectivity, we cede the freedom to realize our passions to the degree that we are forced to reflect on them.

82. F. A. Hayek, "The Use of Knowledge in Society," *American Economic Review* 35, no. 4 (1945): 524, 530. Hereafter cited in text.

83. Merrill, *A Different Person*, 38.

84. Edwin J. Perkins, *Wall Street to Main Street: Charles Merrill and Middle-Class Investors* (New York: Cambridge University Press, 1999), 57.

85. "American poets," Bloom writes, "labor . . . to 'complete' their fathers" and "tend to see [them] as not having dared enough." *The Anxiety of Influence: A Theory of Poetry* (1973; New York: Oxford University Press, 1997), 68.

Afterword

1. David Harvey, *A Short History of Neoliberalism* (New York: Oxford University Press, 2005), 33.

2. Fredric Jameson, *Postmodernism; or, the Cultural Logic of Late Capitalism* (Durham, NC: Duke University Press, 1991), 215. Hereafter cited in text.

3. Samuel Konkin, *New Libertarian Manifesto* (Huntington Beach, CA: KoPubCo, 2006), 17.

4. It is because Plato insists that "the state must be self-sufficient" (84), as Karl Popper puts it in *The Open Society and Its Enemies* (1945; Princeton, NJ: Princeton University Press, 2013), that Popper and Hayek, two of the most influential figures for post-sixties neoliberalism, understood Plato as not just an apologist for but an architect of totalitarianism. Plato ranks first among the "enemies" of the "open society" of Popper's title. In *The Road to Serfdom*, ed. Bruce Caldwell (Chicago: University of Chicago Press, 2007), Hayek concludes that Plato sets the "doctrine" for "the strengthening of the organized unity of the state." For a West in the grip of collectivism, Hayek writes, "the nation will grow into a 'closed unity' and will become, in fact, what Plato declared it should be—'*der Mensch im Grossen*' [the human in general]" (195). Needless to say, there is a robust debate over the totalitarian Plato that I leave to its combatants in political philosophy. My point is merely to reference the figuration of the state as an organic unity that overrides the integrity of individuals.

5. Popper writes in *The Open Society*: "The traditional translation 'The Republic' has undoubtedly contributed to the general conviction that Plato could not have been a reactionary," although a "proper English translation" of his book "would be . . . 'The State'" (85).

6. Plato, *The Republic* (New York: Penguin, 2003), 176, 177.

7. Thomas Hobbes, *Leviathan*, ed. Edwin Curley (Indianapolis: Hackett, 2004), 214. "Such government is not government," Hobbes writes, when there is "division of the commonwealth into . . . factions" (216).

8. Plato, *The Republic*, 177.

9. Justin Fox, *The Myth of the Rational Market: A History of Risk, Reward, and Delusion on Wall Street* (New York: Harper Collins, 2009), 299.

10. Cited in Fox, *The Myth of the Rational Market*, 302.

11. Fox, *The Myth of the Rational Market*, 303, 302.

12. James Scott, *Seeing Like a State: How Certain Schemes to Improve the Human Condition Have Failed* (New Haven, CT: Yale University Press, 1998), 354, 348. Hereafter cited in text.

13. Daniel T. Rodgers, *Age of Fracture* (Cambridge, MA: Harvard University Press, 2011), 42.

14. It is worth reminding ourselves that *Anarchy, State, and Utopia* earned its acclaim partly by undercutting the first and most provocative term in its title, as when Nozick sets aside "the moral objections of the individualist anarchist to the minimal state" by showing how a *"de facto* monopoly grows by an invisible-hand process and by morally permissible means, without anyone's rights being violated." *Anarchy, State, and Utopia* (New York: Basic, 1974), 115. Hereafter cited in text.

15. "The big question," Scott writes in language reminiscent of Nisbet or Ophuls, "is whether the existence, power, and reach of the state over the past several centuries have sapped the independent, self-organizing power of individuals and small communities. So many functions that were once accomplished by mutuality among equals and informal coordination are now state organized or state supervised." *Two Cheers for Anarchism: Six Easy Pieces on Autonomy, Dignity, and Meaningful Work and Play* (Princeton, NJ: Princeton University Press, 2012), xii.

16. Richard G. Mitchell, *Dancing at Armageddon: Survivalism and Chaos in Modern Times* (Chicago: University of Chicago Press, 2002), 13. Hereafter cited in text.

17. David Graeber, *The Utopia of Rules: On Technology, Stupidity, and the Secret Joys of Bureaucracy* (Brooklyn: Melville House, 2015), 8. Hereafter cited in text as *UR*.

18. James Dickey, *Deliverance* (New York: Delta, 1970), 9, 30. Hereafter cited in text.

19. Thomas Disch, *The Genocides* New York: Vintage, 2000), 33.

20. This is the claim of Ronald Radosh and Murray N. Rothbard, eds., *A New History of Leviathan: Essays on the Rise of the American Corporate State* (New York: Dutton, 1972), an anthology of essays that "show how a sophisticated group of large corporate reformers managed to replace a freely competitive economy and make a new governing class, through the use of reform mechanisms to mold the government into a mighty instrument of monopolization and cartelization" (5). The volume's most "unusual aspect" (vii) is its editorial partnership. Rothbard and Radosh, at the time ideological opponents, found common cause in the "critique of liberal ideology and concepts," which allowed each "in his own work to transcend the ideological myths that enable the large corporations to mask their hegemony over American society" (viii).

21. David Graeber, *Debt: The First Five Thousand Years* (Brooklyn: Melville House, 2011), 72. Hereafter cited in text as *D*. "The free market," Graeber writes in *The Utopia of Rules*, "required a thousand times more paperwork than a Louis XIV-style absolutist monarchy" (*UR*, 9).

22. In *Two Cheers for Anarchism*, Scott likewise takes the long view to contrast statism with alternative modes of social organization: "Of the roughly five-thousand-year history of states only in the last two centuries or so has even the *possibility* arisen that states might occasionally enlarge the realm of human freedom" (x).

23. Paul Shepard, *The Tender Carnivore* (Athens: University of Georgia Press, 1998), 18.

24. Milton and Rose Friedman, *Free to Choose* (New York: Harcourt, 1990), 239.

25. Marge Piercy, *Woman on the Edge of Time* (1976; New York: Ballantine, 2016), ix. Hereafter cited in text.

26. Fredric Jameson, "Future City," *New Left Review* 21 (May–June 2003): 76.

27. Jameson, "Future City," 76.

28. W. Allen Wallis, *An Overgoverned Society* (New York: Free Press, 1976), 69.

29. Indeed rather than a meritocracy based on objective value, there is good reason to believe that what our extant social arrangements actually reward is luck. "In general," the social policy theorist Christopher Jencks and his coauthors concluded in their 1972 book *Inequality*, "we think luck has far more influence on income than successful people admit." *Inequality: A Reassessment of the Effect of Family and Schooling in America* (New York: Basic, 1972), 227. For Jencks, "merit" (226) is an ex post facto defense by the successful of their good fortune, usually but not exclusively of birth, since things like chance meetings and quirks of geography prove equally decisive in matters of success. Jencks held not only that meritocracy is a poor way to run a society (because it is has seemed a convincing way for society to justify its asymmetries) but also that we don't even really live in one. Countering arguments like Herrnstein and Murray's in *The Bell Curve*, Jencks concludes that meritocracy is not so much destiny as ideology.

30. Bernard Williams, *Morality: An Introduction to Ethics* (Cambridge, UK: Cambridge University Press, 1993), 95, 97.

31. MacFarquar uses the term in David V. Johnson, "Lives of the Moral Saints: An Interview with Larissa MacFarquar," *Boston Review*, April 17, 2013, 17. She herself does not take this view; in fact, she disagrees with Susan Wolf about the hazards of extreme morality. McFarquar's interest is in the hostility she frequently encountered from ordinary people toward "do-gooders" in researching her book *Strangers Drowning: Impossible Idealism, Drastic Choices, and the Urge to Help* (New York: Penguin, 2013). The "extremely ethical," she tells Johnson, appear to ordinary people no less than to Susan Wolf as "so weird that . . . they must have some kind of mental illness" (17).

32. Susan Wolf, "Moral Saints," *Journal of Philosophy* 79, no. 8 (1982): 419, 423. Hereafter cited in text.

33. In fairness it should be pointed out that Wolf appears to see moral systems in general, whether consequentialist or deontological, as ripe for abuse by extremists; systems appear to be the enemy of "a healthy, well-rounded, richly developed character" (421). But whereas Kantians recognize that we have other values and interests in developing character that some Kantians might reject on behalf of duty, *all* utilitarians fail to recognize that we have independent, character-specific values and interests, since (as seventies antiutilitarians insisted) the denial of individualism is embedded in utilitarian theory itself.

34. Wolf claims that the moral saint in general "sacrifices his own interests to the interests of others" (420), a position to which utilitarians are especially liable because they don't think much of their own interests to begin with.

35. Tyler Cowen, "Should Peter Singer Favor Massive Redistribution or Economic Growth?" in Jeffrey Schaler, ed., *Peter Singer Under Fire: The Moral Iconoclast Faces His Critics* (Chicago: Open Court Press, 2009), 301. Hereafter cited in text.

36. Peter Singer, "Reply to Tyler Cowen," in Schaler, *Peter Singer Under Fire*, 320. Hereafter cited in text.

37. Peter Singer, *How Are We To Live? Ethics in an Age of Self-Interest* (1993; Amherst, NY: Prometheus, 1995), 278. Hereafter cited in text.

INDEX

Abbey, Edward, 2, 98, 111, 135; *Desert Solitaire*, 68, 87, 94, 97–99; *The Monkey Wrench Gang*, 27, 90–99, 215n66, 215n68
Abelove, Henry, 228n65
Adams, Rachel, 208n108
aliens, 32, 114–15, 152–54, 179
Allan, Robert, 79–82
Allison, Lincoln, 13
Altered States (1978), 23–25, 154
Althusser, Louis, 106
anarchism, 2, 4, 107–12, 173, 176, 179; Burroughs and, 116–17; Irving and, 119–22; property and, 219n49
Anderson, Kurt, 195n41
Anderson, Paul Thomas, 221n60
Anscombe, Elizabeth, 13
anthropocentrism, 34, 37, 42, 67, 70–72, 78, 90, 92, 95
antirealism, 10, 51
antisocialism, 3–5, 74–75, 179
antistatism, 29–30, 98, 109, 138, 173–74, 183. *See also* statism
antiutilitarianism, 12–22, 29–30, 32–42; corporate liberalism and, 186; reciprocity and, 70; value and, 68; welfarism and, 46, 181 (*see also* welfare state). *See also* Rawls, John; utilitarianism
apocalypse, 4, 11, 71, 75, 138, 178, 184. *See also* extinction; rapture
Appuradai, Arjun, 54
Apter, Emily, 224n100
Ardrey, Robert, 76
Arendt, Hannah, 49, 206n71
Armstrong, D. M., 37, 51
Arthur, Brian, 175
artificial intelligence, 3, 209n112; replaceability and, research funding, 203n24; systems theory and, 67; systems thinking and, 12; threat posed by, 44–45, 58. *See also* Strong AI

Auel, Jean: *The Clan of the Cave Bear*, 27, 84–90; *The Valley of Horses*, 89
Austrian School, 101
authoritarianism, 49–54, 81, 174. *See also* state power
authority, 18; autonomy and, 68, 81, 112–13; disobedience to, 107, 178
autonomy, 2, 146, 176, 185–86; anarchism and, 111; authority and, 68, 81, 112–13; formal, 26; Kant and, 15, 18; local, 97

Bambara, Toni Cade, 227n56
Banfield, Edward, 36, 55, 71
Barth, John, 73, 212n28
Bateson, Gregory, 210n8
Beck, Ulrich, 224n98
Becker, Gary, 139, 150–52, 170
behavioral economics, 104, 139, 225n11
behaviorism: criticism of, 1; dualism and, 51; mental testing and, 33–34, 36; neo-idealism and, 21; testing and, 57; utilitarianism and, 32, 39–40, 44
Bell, Daniel, 219n38
Bellah, Robert, 166–67
The Bell Curve (Murray and Herrnstein), 34, 41–42, 57, 71, 207nn96–97, 232n29
Bennett, Jane, 198n77
Bentham, Jeremy, 32, 48, 53, 199n80
Berger, Peter, 226n22
Bérubé, Michael, 208n108
Bloom, Harold, 171
Blueprint for Survival (Allan and Goldsmith), 79–82
Boguslaw, Robert, 12
Bookchin, Murray, 2, 88, 108, 111–12, 117, 210n2, 220n49
Bostrom, Nick, 209n110
Boulding, Kenneth, 73
brainwashing, 47, 100–101, 103, 121, 216n1, 217n20. *See also* mind control
Brick, Howard, 206n74

235

Brown, Denise Scott. See *Learning from Las Vegas*
Brown, Michael, 229n71
Brown, Wendy, 199n80
Bucci, John, 112
Buchanan, James, 102
Buchanan, Joseph, 41, 43
Buckley, C. A., 158–59
bureaucracy, 4, 40, 73, 78, 116, 132, 135, 169, 174, 180–82, 185, 188. *See also* statism; welfare state
Burgin, Angus, 198n72
Burroughs, William S., 2, 125, 127, 129–30, 132, 135–37, 152, 222n78, 222n80, 223n84, 223n88; *Ali's Smile/Naked Scientology*, 113; *Cities of the Red Night*, 28, 112–14, 116, 119, 122, 128, 223n85; "The Electronic Revolution," 117; *Junky*, 113; *The Place of Dead Roads*, 114–19, 122, 128
Butler, Judith, 18, 197n68

Callenbach, Ernest, 27, 77–78, 87, 98
Callicott, Baird, 69–71
camp, 162, 165, 223n92
capitalism, 20, 108; consumerism and, 7, 76, 125, 128, 162, 164; invisible ideology, 106–7, 128; postmodern, 173–76, 184–86
Carrère, Emmanuel, 226n35, 227n51
Carroll, Peter, 5–6
Carter, Jimmy, 4
channeling, 2, 138, 153–71, 182, 227n56, 229n71
Chapman, Jennie, 140
Chayefsky, Paddy, 23–25, 154, 199nn83–85
Chicago School, 5, 140, 145, 175, 198n74
Children of God, 106–7, 109, 218n32
Chodat, Robert, 204n34
choice, 7–9, 152–56; freedom of, 169–71. *See also* good choice architecture; rational choice theory
Chomsky, Noam, 34, 114, 197n68, 202n14
Christian fundamentalism, 8, 11, 104, 109, 131, 137–45, 150, 186, 225n13. *See also* evangelical sects; rapture
Club of Rome, 73, 80–81, 210n2, 212n24
Clune, Michael, 222n80
cognitive science, 1, 61–62, 200n96, 202n14
Cohen, G. A., 19
Coleman Report (1966), 201n8
collectivism, 141, 200n97, 203n29, 230n4
Commoner, Barry, 73, 124
communitarianism, 29, 79–80, 98, 106, 115, 173, 176

community, ecological, 81–83, 89, 110
computational theory of mind, 36–37, 48, 51–52, 61, 104, 152, 154–55, 203n19
consciousness: brain size and, 82–84; neo-idealism and, 8; postmodernism and, 184; primacy of, 23–24, 28; value of, 2. *See also* mind
consciousness-raising, 1–2; criticism of, 6–8, 193n17; massification of, 25, 173; in the sixties, 1, 6, 14, 84, 86, 120
Considine, Shaun, 199nn83–85
constructionism, 18, 28, 86, 177; Kantian constructivism, 18, 20, 35, 180
consumerism. *See* capitalism
contractualism, 1, 14, 30, 55, 146, 196n48, 196n60
Conway, Flo, 101
Corn, Alfred, 164, 166
counterculture, 6, 42, 84, 119, 146–49
Cowen, Tyler, 188
cults, 1, 28, 100–112, 173, 216n1, 220n59; Burroughs and, 112–18, 135; DeLillo and, 123, 128–35; Irving and, 119–22; Vidal and, 123–28, 135. *See also* brainwashing; mind control
cybernetics, 47–48, 206n74, 210n8
cynegetic society, 79, 85, 129, 182

Daly, Herman, 73, 76–77
Darby, John Nelson, 225n3
Davidson, Donald, 202n15, 204n50
Davis, Erik, 227n36, 227n46
decentralization, 5, 77, 79, 98, 114–15, 169
deep ecology, 1, 132; defined, 67, 210n2. *See also* radical ecology
Deep Ecology (Devall and Sessions), 68
Delany, Samuel, 37–38, 208n109
DeLillo, Don: *Americana*, 129–30; *Mao II*, 224n100; *The Names*, 28, 123, 128–35, 174, 224n98; *Underworld*, 134; *White Noise*, 123, 224n99
Dennett, Daniel, 22, 39, 50, 62, 154–55, 158, 199n79, 203n29, 203n31, 209n112; *Consciousness Explained*, 37; *Content and Consciousness*, 37–38; "Where Am I?," 36–37
deregulation, 101, 143, 169, 186. *See also* libertarianism
Derrida, Jacques, 9–10
Devall, Bill, 68, 70, 210n10
Devore, Irven, 76
Diamond, Cora, 214n60

Dick, Philip, 2, 139, 172; "The Android and the Human," 45; "Beyond Lies the Wub," 46; *Deus Irae*, 143, 146; *The Divine Invasion*, 137, 152; *Do Androids Dream of Electric Sheep?*, 27, 43–45, 152; *Exegesis*, 44; "How to Build a Universe That Doesn't Fall Apart Two Days Later," 136–37; "Progeny," 45; "The Short, Happy Life of a Science Fiction Writer," 44; *The Simulacra*, 44; *Ubik*, 43, 152–53; *VALIS*, 148–54, 156, 163, 169, 226nn35–36; *We Can Build You*, 45–46
Dickey, James, 177–79
Didion, Joan, 192n7
difference principle, 15–17
disabled persons, 60, 64–65, 208nn107–8
Disch, Thomas: on Burroughs, 223n85; *Camp Concentration*, 49–54, 58–59, 86; *The Genocides*, 179; *I Am Not a Number!*, 47; *The Prisoner*, 47–48; *334* (novel), 46–47, 58; *The Word of God*, 57
distinctiveness, 133, 159; subjectivity and, 33, 55–56, 61; utilitarianism and, 12–13, 33, 188, 195n46, 196n48, 201n3
Douglas, Christopher, 138, 220n57
Drengson, Alan, 70, 72, 74
Dreyfus, Hubert, 36, 40–41, 44, 155, 204n34
dualism, 25, 51, 53, 155
Dubos, René, 83
Dunbar, Robin, 214n50

ecological fiction, 27, 89–90
ecology. *See* deep ecology; radical ecology; reform ecology
economics, 4–5; equality and, 29; experimental, 175; neoclassical, 1, 174–75. *See also* capitalism; free market system; liberalism; neoliberalism; welfare state
Educational Testing Service (ETS), 41, 205n53
Ehrlich, Paul, 71, 79, 124, 139, 211n20
Elster, John, 39
Emerson, Ralph Waldo, 9, 194n34
Enlightenment, 9, 11, 22, 78, 81, 113, 116, 137
entropy, 2, 7, 99, 123–24, 212n28
environmental activism, 27, 90–93, 215n66, 215n68
environmentalism, 29, 67, 69, 173. *See also* radical ecology
epistemological individualism, 112, 125, 131, 223n88
equality, 12–13, 54, 80, 127, 159, 232n29; economic, 29; individualism and, 111

Erhard, Werner, 102, 108, 139
ESP (Extra-Sensory Perception), 43, 116
est, 102, 108–9, 117, 124
ethical turn (in literary studies), 1, 189, 191n1
ethics, 30, 188–89; Kantian, 38 (*see also* Kant, Immanuel). *See also* land ethic; morality
evangelical sects, 1–3, 8, 11, 136–52, 173. *See also* Christian fundamentalism; rapture
externalism, 8, 11, 18, 60, 68, 185; drugs and, 147; utilitarianism and, 201n3
extinction, 70, 86–87, 89, 124, 126, 159, 185

Felski, Rita, 198n77
Ferguson, Frances, 53–54
Feyerabend, Paul, 9, 17
Finke, Roger, 139, 143–44
first-person ontology, 34, 38–39, 51, 66–68, 171, 185, 197n68
Floridi, Luciano, 152
Flynn, James, 207n96
Fodor, Jerry, 203n19
Foreman, Dave, 215n66
Forster, E. M., 200n2
Foucault, Michel, 48, 111, 126, 223n93
Fox, Justin, 175, 226n17
Fox, Robin, 214n54
Fox, Warwick, 210n2
free market system, 2, 4, 17, 19–21, 126–28, 173–76, 231nn20–21; cults and, 101; evangelicalism and, 140–45; regulation and, 179; subjectivity and, 185–89; utilitarianism and, 196n60. *See also* capitalism; economics
Friedman, Milton and Rose, 5, 7, 17, 126, 171, 176, 198n72, 198n74, 217n19, 226n17; *Capitalism and Freedom*, 21, 127–28, 140–44; *Free to Choose*, 19–21, 181–82
Friedman, Patri, 192n12
Fuller, Buckminster, 84

Gaia, Earth as, 68–70, 184
Galbraith, John Kenneth, 213n42
Garber, Marjorie, 191n1
Gauthier, David, 196n60
Geniocracy (Raël), 3
Georgescu-Roegen, Nicholas, 72–73, 93, 212n26
gnosticism, 44, 137, 150–53, 227n41, 228n56
Goffman, Erving, 60
Goldsmith, Edward, 79–82
good choice architecture, 103–4, 125. *See also* choice

Goodman, Nelson, 9, 122
Goodman, Paul, 107
Gordon, Gwendolyn, 215n65
Gould, Stephen Jay, 55
Graeber, David, 177, 179–83, 231n21

Hammer, Langdon, 160, 166, 229n79
Hampshire, Stuart, 12, 38–39, 50
Hanssen, Beatrice, 191n1
Haraway, Donna, 22, 198n77
Hardin, Garrett, 71, 74, 79, 212n21
Hare, R. M., 18
Hare Krishnas, 107, 109–10, 124
Harrington, Alan, 155, 167
Harris, Marvin, 102
Harvey, David, 173, 198n73, 198n75
Hatch, Nathan, 137
Haugeland, John, 202n14, 204n34
Hayek, F. A., 101–2, 140, 142, 169, 230n4
Hayles, Katherine, 43, 198n77, 209n114
Heaven's Gate, 115
Hebbian rule, 66, 209n115
Hegel, 152, 197n64
Hegelian dialectic, 14, 49, 53
Heinlein, Robert, 193n23, 201n6
Heise, Ursula, 212n23
Herrnstein, Richard, 34, 36, 41–42, 54, 57, 71; *IQ in the Meritocracy*, 33, 52, 205n54. See also *The Bell Curve*
Hess, Karl, 220n49
Hirschman, A. O., 4–5, 192n11
Hobbes, Thomas, 7, 70, 103, 174, 196n60, 231n7
Hodges, Andrew, 41
Hofstadter, Richard, 194n34
Homer, 167–68, 170
Homo sapiens, 71, 83–89, 132, 167
Hospers, John, 101, 222n74
Houser, Heather, 224n98
Hubbard, L. Ron, 104–5, 108, 113–15, 118, 125, 130, 135, 137, 152, 218n27, 218n29
Hume, Kathryn, 117, 223n84
Hungerford, Amy, 134
Hunt, Alex, 216n71
hunter-gatherers, 75–81, 83, 85, 213n41. See also cynegetic society

Iannacone, Lawrence, 144, 160
idealism, 9–10, 14, 105, 132; materialism and, 161, 194n34; solipsism and, 118. See also neo-idealism
identity theory, 37, 39, 205n58

ideology, 219n38; external world and, 131; free market and, 128; invisible, 106–7, 128; society and, 108; utopias and, 184
immortality, 155–57, 161, 171, 177
Indians (Native Americans), 96–97, 216n71
individualism: consciousness and, 6–7 (*see also* consciousness); empowerment and, 103; epistemological, 112, 125, 131, 223n88; equality and, 111; free market and, 173; hierarchy and, 19; nihilistic, 29; politics and, 11, 78–79; primacy of, 3; utilitarianism and, 232n33
Ingram, Claudia, 158
Ingram Merrill Foundation, 160
innatism, 42, 54–55, 57, 66, 71, 75, 212n21
internalism, 18, 29, 54, 68, 72, 107
IQ tests, 41–44, 50, 58–61; as measure of personhood, 3; racial difference and, 57, 61, 207nn96–97; statistical induction in, 56. See also innatism; mental testing; meritocracy
Irving, John, 27, 119–23
isolation tanks, 23–25, 199n86
Izenour, Steven. See *Learning from Las Vegas*

James, Henry, 157, 162, 164, 189
James, William, 9, 105, 194n34
Jameson, Fredric, 174, 184–86, 197n64
Jaynes, Julian, 167–68, 230n81
Jeffersonian democracy, 176, 217n19
Jencks, Christopher, 232n29
Jenkins, Philip, 109–10
Jensen, Arthur, 33–34, 36, 41–42, 47, 54, 71
Johnston, Devin, 162
Jones, Jim, 102, 108
Jonestown massacre, 100, 109, 220n59
Jong, Erica, 86
justice, 29; as fairness, 55–56; principles of, 15–17

Kahneman, Daniel, 139, 218n26, 225n11
Kant, Immanuel, 1, 10–11, 38, 70–71, 138, 185, 197n64, 207n86; autonomy and, 18; categorical imperative, 15; contract theory, 30, 196n60; *Critique of Pure Reason*, 14, 195n37. See also pop Kantianism
Kantian constructivism, 18, 20, 35, 180
Kaufman, Robert, 218n27, 222n78
Keyes, Daniel, 208n109; *Flowers for Algernon*, 58–61
Kirban, Salem, 142–43
Knapp, Steven, 28
Knight, J. Z., 229n71

Konkin, Samuel, 27, 111–12, 174
Konstantinou, Lee, 222n78
Korsgaard, Christine, 18, 197n66, 230n81
Kunstler, James Howard, 212n23
Kurzweil, Ray, 209n110

laissez-faire, 10, 20–21, 46, 122, 141, 179, 194n23, 196n60, 211n14
land ethic, 69–70, 82. *See also* radical ecology
Lanton, Eric and Linda, 151
Larsen, Nella, 57
Lasch, Christopher, 7–8, 13
Learning from Las Vegas (Venturi, Brown, and Izenour), 91, 145–46, 175–76
Lee, Richard, 76
Lefort, Claude, 106–8, 130, 219n38
Le Guin, Ursula, 32–33, 35
Leopold, Aldo, 69–71
Leviathan, 70, 174–75
liberalism, 231n20; classical, 3, 45–46; conflict between equality and freedom, 2; corporate, 186; ethics and, 29
libertarianism, 8, 154, 176; anarchism and, 108; antistatism and, 183; bureaucracy and, 182; cults and, 4, 101 (*see also* cults); drug culture and, 148; economics and, 102; equality and, 126; on human specialness, 71; as literary genre, 193n23; as popular, 2; progress and, 122; property and, 219n49; science fiction and, 27; utilitarianism and, 32; utopian, 216n7; withdrawal and, 130. *See also* Nozick, Robert
libertarian municipalism, 111
Libertarian Party, 101, 112
libertarian paternalism, 103–4
liberty principle, 15–17, 21
Lifton, Robert Jay, 217n20
Lilly, John C., 10–11, 14, 18, 23–25, 51, 154–56
Limits to Growth (1972), 73, 81
Lindsey, Hal, 2, 138–45, 147–48
Livingston, John, 83–84
Locke, John, 9, 41, 78
Lofland, John, 102
Love, Sam, 215n68
Lovelock, James, 68–70, 184
Lyons, David, 13, 40

MacFarquar, Larissa, 187, 232n31
machines, 3, 7, 200n2; destruction of, 93; empathy and, 46; "experience machine," 31–32, 36, 44–45, 61, 200nn2–3, 221n63. *See also* artificial intelligence; Turing test

Maharishi Mahesh Yogi, 109
Malthusianism, 3, 29, 71, 76, 79, 91–92, 95, 116, 124, 159, 212n23, 212n26
Marcuse, Herbert, 14, 137
Marxism, 10, 19, 106, 108, 185, 192n8, 197n64
Maslow, Abraham, 139
mass media, 105, 125
materialism, 10, 125; consumption and, 162; idealism and, 161, 194n34; Kantian ethics and, 38; negation of, 145; philosophy of the mind and, 34, 51, 158; strong, 22–23
McCarthy, John, 209n112
McCorduck, Pamela, 209n110
McGinn, Colin, 195n38
McKibben, Bill, 75
McNamara, Robert, 49–50, 206n74
Mendelson, Edward, 229n79
mental testing, 32–42; social engineering and, 42–48. *See also* IQ tests
meritocracy, 4, 32–33, 42, 159–60, 173, 186, 232n29; exceptionalness and, 59; replaceability and, 58–66; standardized tests and, 41, 44, 46–47, 159 (*see also* IQ tests; mental testing); utilitarianism and, 54–56
Merrill, Charles, 170–71
Merrill, James, 2, 228n65, 228n69, 229nn79–80; "Book of Ephraim," 156–61; *The Changing Light at Sandover*, 28–29, 156–74; *A Different Person*, 166; *Divine Comedies*, 156, 160; "The Doodler," 162; "The Higher Keys," 168–69; "Lost in Translation," 156; "A Tenancy," 160; "Transfigured Bird," 162; "The Will," 160–61, 164–65
Michaels, Walter Benn, 26, 57
Miller, D. A., 26, 29
mind: brain size and, 82–84; persistence of, 172; Stone Age, 24, 81–90; systems-theoretical account of, 53. *See also* computational theory of mind; consciousness; philosophy of mind
mind control, 4, 100–101, 115, 183, 217n20. *See also* brainwashing
Minsky, Marvin, 203n29, 205n56
Mishan, E. J., 73
Mitchell, Richard, 176–77
Moffett, Judith, 228n69
Moonies, 102, 106, 109–10
morality, 187, 232n31, 232nn33–34. *See also* ethics
moral philosophy, 1, 26, 191n1

Moravec, Hans, 209n110
Morgan, Robin, 192n8
Morgan, Ted, 118
Mormonism, 98, 109
Morris, Desmond, 214n51
Morris, Matthew, 131
Murray, Charles. See *The Bell Curve*
Mutter, Matthew, 131

Nabokov, Vladimir, 27
Naess, Arne, 2, 67–68, 70, 74–76, 97, 210n2
Nagel, Thomas, 9–10, 13, 40, 46, 49, 54–55, 60, 72, 102, 138, 149
Neanderthals, 85–90
neo-idealism, 173; autonomy and, 186; behaviorism and, 21; conformity and, 181; cults and, 135; defined, 1–2; development of, 8–11; formal autonomy and, 26; freedom and, 16–17; free market system and, 19, 21, 175; information and, 152; neoliberalism and, 21, 189; radical ecology and, 67–68
neoliberalism, 2, 8, 173, 198n73, 199n80; neo-idealism and, 21, 189; social justice and, 198n75. See also economics
New Age spirituality, 1, 4, 8, 102, 138, 162–63, 173. See also channeling; cults
Newell, Allen, 40
New Historicism, 25–26, 29–30, 199n87
A New History of Leviathan (1972), 14
New Wave science fiction, 3, 35, 47, 58
Nisbet, Robert, 73, 80–82, 95, 98, 106, 231n15
Nixon, Richard, 5, 151
Noë, Alva, 201n3
Novak, Michael, 225n13
Nozick, Robert, 16, 19, 35–36, 44–48, 55–56, 72, 74, 78, 103, 110–12, 122, 126–28, 132, 135, 165, 181, 183, 198n73, 200n97, 201n6, 211n14, 231n14; experience machine, 31–33, 36, 44–45, 61, 200nn2–3, 221n63

Objectivism, 211n14, 222n68
Obst, David, 215n68
Ophuls, William, 76–77, 81, 83–84, 93–95, 116, 159, 176, 231n15
Ornstein, Robert, 8
overpopulation. See population size

Pagels, Elaine, 227n41
paleo-republic, 3–4, 75–81, 111, 159, 182. See also Stone Age mind
paranoid style, 132–34, 158, 224n98

Parfit, Derek, 200n3, 217n22
Parfrey, Adam, 138–39
passing narrative, 57
paternalism, 16, 59, 103–4, 126–27, 180
Patrick, Ted, 109
Peoples Temple, 102, 109
Perkins, Edwin, 171
phenomenology, 106–7, 204n34
Philips, Siobhan, 161
philosophy of mind, 1, 26, 28, 39; artificial intelligence and, 3; materialisms and, 34, 51, 158; systems theory and, 67
physicalism, 34, 51, 86, 202n14
Piercy, Marge, 182–83
Pinker, Steven, 38
Plato, 82, 161, 163, 174, 230nn4–5
Pleistocene era, 11, 78–79, 83, 88, 214n54
pollution, 71, 84, 91
pop Kantianism, 14–15, 21, 26, 176–78, 197n66. See also Kant, Immanuel
Popper, Karl, 230nn4–5
population size, 11, 83, 159, 182, 214n54; entropy and, 123–24; restrictions on, 67, 71, 111, 211n15, 212nn23–24
posthumanism, 22, 198n77
postmodernism, 158, 198n73
Powers, Richard, 209n112; *Galatea 2.2*, 58, 61–66; *The Overstory*, 215n64
privatization, 119, 135
Proposition 13 (1978), 126–27
Proudhon, Pierre-Joseph, 220n49
psychometrics, 41, 43, 46
Putnam, Hilary, 42, 205n58

queer theory, 18, 56

racial difference, 57, 61, 201n8
racism, 117, 126–27, 207n96
radical ecology, 1–2, 11, 27, 29, 131, 184; defined, 67, 210n2; extinction and, 159; famines and, 211n20; fascism and, 211n19; neo-idealism and, 67–68; paleo-republic, 3–4, 75–81, 111, 159, 182. See also deep ecology
Radosh, Ronald, 14, 231n20
Raëlians, 3, 19, 24
Rajneesh, Bhagwan Shree, 101
Rand, Ayn, 70–71, 193n23, 201n6, 211n14, 222n68
rapture, 2–3, 136–44, 159, 225n3. See also apocalypse; Christian fundamentalism; evangelical sects

rational choice theory, 16–19, 26, 103–4; decision unit, 155; free will and, 150–52; religion and, 139–40, 143–44. *See also* choice
Rawls, John, 2, 7, 18, 28–30, 38, 44, 53, 70, 74, 107, 138, 140, 180, 195n46, 196n48, 196nn60–61, 198n73, 200n97, 207n91; *A Theory of Justice*, 12–22, 33, 55–56, 81, 102–3, 196n61, 201n7
Reagan, Ronald, 109, 147–48, 173, 181
recipient justice, 16, 45, 165
reform ecology, 68, 83–84
Reich, Charles, 14–16
Reichert, William, 108–9
Relfe, Mary Stewart, 140, 142
replaceability, 58–66
Revelation, Book of, 136, 140–42, 146–49
Reynolds, Mack, 221n63
Rhinehart, Luke, 108–9
Rifkin, Jeremy, 73, 81, 83–84, 93, 116
rights, 12, 16–17, 20, 38–39, 42, 47, 100, 119
Roberts, Jane, 153–56, 163, 172
Rodgers, Daniel, 9, 176
Rorty, Richard, 9–10, 105
Rossmann, Michael, 193n17
Roszak, Theodore, 6–8, 11, 16, 24, 197n66
Rothbard, Murray, 14, 101–2, 108, 113, 119, 127, 220n49, 222n68, 231n20

Sagoff, Mark, 210n11
Sahlins, Marshall, 24, 76, 78, 89, 97, 213n41
Sale, Kirkpatrick, 82, 89
Sandel, Michael, 12–13
Sapir-Whorf hypothesis, 38, 197n68
SAT, 54, 205n53
Scanlon, T. M., 196n48
Scarry, Elaine, 191n1
Schneiderman, Jason, 228n63
Schumacher, E. F., 82
Schumpeter, Joseph, 93, 141
Schur, Edwin, 193n13
Schwartz, Thomas, 39
science fiction, 23–27, 43, 57; New Wave, 3, 35, 47, 58
Scientology, 2, 101, 104–5, 109, 113–18, 124, 129–30, 149, 156, 218nn27–29, 220n59, 221n60, 222n78, 223n84, 223n88
Scott, James, 175–77, 180–83, 185, 231n15, 232n22
Searle, John, 1, 9, 34, 43, 54–55, 104, 155, 198n73, 203n29, 203n31, 206n75, 206n78, 207n86; *The Campus War*, 51–52; "Minds, Brains, and Programs," 35–37

secularization thesis, 143, 226n22
Selisker, Scott, 216n1
Sellars, Wilfred, 22
Sen, Amartya, 11–12, 202n18, 211n20
Sennett, Richard, 108, 111, 131
Sessions, George, 68, 210n10, 211n15
Shepard, Paul, 94, 111, 132, 159, 180, 182, 213n41, 214n54; *The Tender Carnivore and the Sacred Game*, 75–79, 83–86, 89, 213n41
Shucman, Helen, 153, 155, 163
Sidgwick, Henry, 49, 184, 195n46
Siegelman, Jim, 101
Simon, Herbert, 40
Singer, Peter, 55–56, 60, 187–89, 200n3, 207n89, 208nn107–8, 210n10, 214n60
singularity, 3, 33, 141, 152, 185
Skillman, Nikki, 158
Skinner, B. F., 33, 40–41, 58, 61, 104, 185, 197n68, 201n10
Sloterdijk, Peter, 219n39
Smart, J. J. C., 39
Smith, L. Neil, 193n23, 216n7, 217n19
Smithson, Robert, 92–94, 99
Snyder, Gary, 74–76, 79
Spencer, Herbert, 9, 195n34
Spender, Stephen, 229n80
standardized tests, 159, 205n53; meritocracy and, 41, 44, 46, 159; state power and, 43–45. *See also* IQ tests
Stark, Rodney, 138–39, 143–44
state power, 49–54, 231n15; communities and, 80; standardized tests and, 43–45. *See also* authoritarianism; statism
states' rights, 117, 127
statism, 2, 19, 43, 74, 132, 231n7, 232n22; repudiation of (*see* antistatism). *See also* bureaucracy; welfare state
steady-state society, 73, 77–78, 81
Stigler, George, 145, 198n74, 226n17
Stone Age mind, 24, 81–90. *See also* paleo-republic
Strong AI, 35–42, 48, 51, 61, 65, 154, 203n29, 204n34, 209n110, 219n39. *See also* artificial intelligence; computational theory of mind
Strozier, Charles, 150
subjectivity: dignity of, 21; evangelicalism and, 149–50; individual distinctness and, 33, 55–56, 61; neo-idealism and, 8; postmodernism and, 184; primacy of, 158; revival of, 1; social change and, 179; unifiable, 107
Sunstein, Cass, 103–4, 125

survivalism, 4, 176–79, 192n6. *See also* apocalypse
systems theory: account of mind, 53; radical ecology and, 67

Tannehill, Morris and Linda, 217nn7–8, 220n49
Tart, Charles, 195n41
Taylor, Charles, 34, 48, 204n34
Thaler, Richard, 103–4, 125
Thiel, Peter, 192n12
Thomas, Lewis, 74
Thompson, Hunter S., 146–49
Thoreau, Henry David, 161, 228n65
Tiger, Lionel, 214n54
Toffler, Alvin, 7, 16–17
Tomkins, Silvan, 64
Transcendental Meditation, 109
Travolta, John, 221n60
Trow, George, 7–8
Turing, Alan, 35, 38, 41–42, 48, 53, 203n19
Turing test, 35–37, 41, 43–44, 49, 57, 61–62, 66, 204n50
Tversky, Amos, 139, 225n11

utilitarianism, 12–13, 30–31, 186–88; behaviorism and, 32–33, 39–40, 44; distinctiveness and, 195n46, 196n48, 201n3; externalism and, 201n3; first-person ontology and, 39; free market and, 196n60; individualism and, 11–12, 59, 232n33; libertarianism and, 32 (*see also* libertarianism); meritocracy and, 54–56; in practice, 187–89; social modeling, 44, 46; systems theory and, 67; as theory of limitlessness, 56, 81; Vietnam War and, 49–50
utopianism, 28, 117, 122, 154, 184–85, 221n63

Vendler, Helen, 161
Venturi, Robert. See *Learning from Las Vegas*
Vidal, Gore, 135, 223n92; *Kalki*, 123–28; "The Second American Revolution," 126–27
Vietnam War, 40, 49–50, 90, 120, 123, 206nn74–75
Vogler, Candace, 191n1
Vorilhon, Claude. *See* Raël

Walkowitz, Rebecca, 191n1
Wallis, Allen, 185
Wallis, Roy, 101, 107, 110, 125, 223n88
Walter, Nicolas, 108, 111, 122
Ward, Barbara, 83
Warhol, Andy, 162
Warner, Stephen, 144
Weinberg, Alvin, 212n26
welfare state, 3, 29, 43, 141, 181–82, 205n54; antiutilitarianism and, 46, 188; birthrates and, 71; individualism and, 21, 58, 74; paternalistic, 16, 59, 103–4, 126–27, 180; property-owning democracy and, 196n61; rapture and, 143; redistributive tax and, 202n18; war economy and, 82. *See also* bureaucracy; statism
Williams, Bernard, 13, 32, 39–40, 48–50, 56, 68, 72, 140, 187, 204n42
Williams, William Appleman, 14, 16
Wills, David, 223n84
Wills, Garry, 225n3
Wilson, Robert Anton, 154–56, 163, 167
Wolf, Susan, 187–89, 232n31, 232nn33–34
Wolfe, Tom, 6–7
Wolff, Robert Paul, 16, 19, 110–12
Wright, Lawrence, 105

Yenser, Stephen, 164, 229n79
Young, Michael, 41–42

Zelazny, Roger, 143
Zimmerman, Michael, 211n19
Zube, Kurt, 109

CPSIA information can be obtained
at www.ICGtesting.com
Printed in the USA
LVHW100746260422
717138LV00006B/433